AN INTRODUCTION TO
MATHEMATICAL METHODS IN ECONOMICS

**McGRAW-HILL
BOOK COMPANY (UK) LIMITED**
London
New York
St Louis
San Francisco
Auckland
Bogotá
Guatemala
Hamburg
Johannesburg
Lisbon
Madrid
Mexico
Montreal
New Delhi
Panama
Paris
San Juan
São Paulo
Singapore
Sydney
Tokyo
Toronto

J. Colin Glass
Economics Department
New University of Ulster

AN INTRODUCTION TO MATHEMATICAL METHODS IN ECONOMICS

Published by
McGRAW-HILL Book Company (UK) Limited
MAIDENHEAD · BERKSHIRE · ENGLAND

British Library Cataloguing in Publication Data

Glass, J Colin
   An introduction to mathematical methods
   in economics.
   1. Economics—Mathematical methods
   2. Economics—Statistical methods
   I. Title
   330'.01'84   HB135   79-42707
ISBN 0-07-084116-0
     0-07-084110-1 Pbk

Copyright © 1980 McGraw-Hill Book Company (UK) Limited. All rights
reserved. No part of this publication may be reproduced, stored
in a retrieval system, or transmitted, in any form or by any means,
electronic, mechanical, photocopying, recording, or otherwise,
without the prior written permission of McGraw-Hill Book Company (UK) Limited

1 2 3 4 5 CUP 8 3 2 1 0

PRINTED AND BOUND IN GREAT BRITAIN

To Tommy and Nui

CONTENTS

Preface   xi

Chapter 1 Introduction   1

1-1   The Dread of Mathematics in Economics   1
1-2   The Method of Presentation and the Level of Difficulty   2
1-3   Points to Remember when Learning Mathematical Methods   4
1-4   Alternative Paths of Study through the Book   6

Chapter 2   The Mathematical Representation of Economic Relationships   8

2-1   Economic Models   8
2-2   Sets   10
2-3   Relations and Functions   13
2-4   Representation of Economic Relationships in terms of Functions   20
2-5   Indices   22
2-6   Polynomial Functions   24
2-7   Functions of More than One Independent Variable   27
2-8   Equalities, Inequalities and Absolute Values   28
2-9   Logarithms   31

Chapter 3 Static-Equilibrium Models — 35

- 3-1 The Slope of a Straight Line — 35
- 3-2 Market Demand and Supply — 38
- 3-3 A Linear Partial-Equilibrium Market Model — 41
- 3-4 The Effect of an Excise Tax in a Competitive Market — 45
- 3-5 Equilibrium in a Linear National-Income Model — 49
- 3-6 The Number of Equations and the Number of Unknowns — 53
- 3-7 A Nonlinear Market Model — 55
- 3-8 Additional Problems — 58

Chapter 4 Matrix Algebra — 60

- 4-1 Matrices Defined — 62
- 4-2 The Algebra of Matrices — 65
- 4-3 Identity Matrices and Null Matrices — 72
- 4-4 The Transpose of a Matrix — 73
- 4-5 The Inverse of a Matrix — 74
- 4-6 Determinants — 77
- 4-7 Properties of Determinants — 82
- 4-8 Calculating the Inverse Matrix — 85
- 4-9 Cramer's Rule — 89

Chapter 5 Linear Economic Models in Matrix Form — 93

- 5-1 A Partial-Equilibrium Market Model in Matrix Form — 93
- 5-2 A National-Income Model in Matrix Form — 95
- 5-3 Equilibrium of an Economy with a Goods Market and a Money Market — 97
- 5-4 A Macro-Model of n Trading Countries — 99
- 5-5 Input-Output Analysis — 103
- 5-6 Additional Problems — 107

Chapter 6 Differentiation of a Function of One Variable — 109

- 6-1 The Difference Quotient and the Slope of a Curve — 110
- 6-2 The Derivative — 113
- 6-3 Rules of Differentiation for a Function of One Variable — 116
- 6-4 Second and Higher Derivatives — 127
- 6-5 Derivatives and Curve-Sketching — 130

Chapter 7 Economic Applications of Derivatives — 132

- 7-1 The Derivatives of Demand and Supply Functions — 132
- 7-2 Elasticity — 135
- 7-3 Total Revenue, Marginal Revenue and the Price Elasticity of Demand — 139

7-4	Other Derivatives in Economics	141
7-5	Additional Problems	142

Chapter 8 Maximization and Minimization 144

8-1	Relative and Absolute Extrema	144
8-2	Criteria for Relative Extrema	145
8-3	Points of Inflection	151

Chapter 9 Economic Applications of Maximization and Minimization 157

9-1	Profit Maximization	157
9-2	Revenue Maximization	162
9-3	Revenue from Taxation	164
9-4	The Theory of Production	171
9-5	The Theory of Cost	177
9-6	Demand for a Productive Service	185
9-7	Additional Problems	189

Chapter 10 Partial and Total Differentiation 191

10-1	Partial Differentiation	191
10-2	Techniques of Partial Differentiation	193
10-3	Second-Order Partial Derivatives	196
10-4	Differentials and Total Differentials	197
10-5	Total Derivatives	200
10-6	Derivatives of Implicit Functions	202

Chapter 11 Economic Applications of Partial and Total Differentiation 205

11-1	Comparative-Static Analysis	205
11-2	Partial Elasticities	209
11-3	Differentials and Elasticity	212
11-4	Production Function Analysis	213
11-5	Additional Problems	216

Chapter 12 Unconstrained Extrema 217

12-1	Unconstrained Extrema of a Function of Two Variables: Graphical Analysis	218
12-2	The First-Order Condition for a Relative Extremum: $z = f(x, y)$	218
12-3	Economic Applications of Unconstrained Extrema	222
12-4	Additional Problems	231

Chapter 13 Constrained Extrema   232

- 13-1 Constrained Extrema of a Function of Two Variables: Graphical Analysis   233
- 13-2 Constrained Extrema via the Lagrange-Multiplier Method   236
- 13-3 Economic Applications of Constrained Extrema   244
- 13-4 Additional Problems   254

Chapter 14 Integration and Exponential Functions   255

- 14-1 The Concept of Integration   255
- 14-2 Indefinite Integrals   256
- 14-3 Definite Integrals   261
- 14-4 Economic Applications of Integrals   266
- 14-5 Exponential Functions   270
- 14-6 Economic Applications of the Exponential Function   272
- 14-7 Additional Problems   278

References for Further Reading   278

Answers to Practice Problems   280

Index   295

PREFACE

This book has been specifically written to assist students who are taking an introductory course in mathematical methods and their application to economics. In particular, the book has been deliberately designed so as to meet the needs of the substantial number of students who not only have a very elementary knowledge of mathematics, but who also have only a very elementary ability in mathematical manipulation. Since I feel strongly that such students need special assistance, Chapter 1 has been utilized to provide a fuller explanation of how both the method of presentation and the level of difficulty of this book have been carefully chosen so as to supply this special assistance.

It is a pleasure to express my gratitude to the many people who have helped and encouraged me in the course of writing this book. First, the economics students, past and present, that I have taught introductory mathematical methods in economics, are to be thanked for convincing me that there is a need for this type of book. Also, these students must be thanked for their questions and comments, which have had an important influence on both the method of presentation and the level of difficulty of this book. Second, Professor Norman Gibson, Professor John Spencer, and the rest of my colleagues in the Economics Department of the New University of Ulster, are to be thanked for their advice and encouragement. Third, Professor John Spencer (New University of Ulster), David Dinour (New University of Ulster), Gerry Steele (University of Lancaster), and

Rodney Thom (University College Dublin), must be especially thanked for their kindness in both reading and commenting upon various parts of the manuscript. I am deeply grateful to these four gentlemen for not only correcting errors but also for making constructive comments that have led to a considerable improvement in the manuscript. While I greatly appreciate this help, I must emphasize that any remaining errors or weaknesses are entirely my sole responsibility. Fourth, Cathleen Murphy, Mary Campbell, and Carol Marks are to be thanked for their cheerful typing assistance. Last, but not least, I must express my warmest thanks to my wife Phyllis. Her presence greatly eased the task of writing this book.

J. Colin Glass

CHAPTER
ONE
INTRODUCTION

1-1 THE DREAD OF MATHEMATICS IN ECONOMICS

Many students, who come to a University or a Polytechnic to study economics, are drawn to the study of economics not only by the wide range of employment opportunities for economics graduates, but also by the wide range of interesting issues (such as wages, inflation, balance of payments, resource allocation, economic growth, pollution, etc.) that are studied under the general heading of economics. This motivation to study economics generally arises from the fact that, before coming to a University or a Polytechnic, many students have enjoyed both the study of economics at school and the discussion of economic problems on television and in the newspapers. However, upon commencing the study of economics at a University or a Polytechnic, many students find to their dismay that the study of economics also entails learning some mathematics. In particular, for the many economics students who have a poor mathematics background, this discovery, that some mathematics is necessary for the study of economics, not only creates anxiety but also results in many students beginning to wonder whether or not they have chosen the correct course of study. Typically, the student in such a situation has two burning questions:

1. How much mathematics is necessary for a reasonable understanding of economics?
2. Will I be able to master this amount of mathematics?

Fortunately, for the majority of undergraduate degree courses in economics, the answer to (1) is that only a certain basic level of mathematics is necessary for a reasonable understanding of economics. Also, fortunately, the answer to (2) is yes. Experience has demonstrated that the majority of students with little or no mathematics background are capable of attaining a reasonable working knowledge of mathematics. In fact, this book has been deliberately written not only to demonstrate the validity of the answers to (1) and (2), but also to remove the dread of mathematics in economics.

The following section indicates the way in which both the method of presentation and the level of difficulty of this book have been carefully chosen so as to meet the needs of economics students with little or no mathematics background.

1-2 THE METHOD OF PRESENTATION AND THE LEVEL OF DIFFICULTY

Economics students at universities and polytechnics are increasingly required to undertake at least an introductory course in mathematical methods and their application to economics. *An Introduction to Mathematical Methods in Economics* is specifically written for students taking such courses. In particular, the method of presentation has been designed to allow for the following facts:

1. Most students possess not only a very elementary knowledge of mathematics, but also a very elementary ability in mathematical manipulation.
2. Most students are studying mathematical methods and economics concurrently.

The implication of (1) and (2) is that students are often in the uncomfortable position of applying a shaky grasp of newly-learnt mathematical methods to barely-grasped, newly-learnt, economic analysis. It is for this very reason that the basic approach of *An Introduction to Mathematical Methods in Economics* is to explain both the mathematical methods and the economic applications in a way which truly recognizes most students' elementary knowledge of mathematics and economics. To achieve this, the method of presentation consists of:

(*a*) An exposition of mathematical methods which not only commences at a level which assumes little or no prior knowledge of mathematics, but which also proceeds at a realistic pace for students with such a limited mathematics background.
(*b*) A brief explanation of why each mathematical method is important for handling aspects of economic analysis.

1-2 THE METHOD OF PRESENTATION AND THE LEVEL OF DIFFICULTY

(c) A non-rigorous, yet adequate, exposition of each mathematical method, amply illustrated by fully-worked examples. To enhance understanding, the exposition is presented in a step-by-step manner and illustrated, where possible, by diagrams. In addition, further problems (denoted as Practice Problems) are provided not only to give students practice at solving mathematical problems, but also to develop mathematical manipulation skill. To achieve this aim, the Practice Problems have been carefully designed not only to test the student's understanding, but also to bolster his or her confidence. Consequently, the Practice Problems have been carefully constructed so as to avoid both excessively difficult problems and problems involving excessive algebraic manipulation. Moreover, not only are all the (non-graphical) answers to the Practice Problems given at the back of the book, but in many cases fully-worked answers are also given.

(d) The application of each mathematical method, to various aspects of economic analysis, in a manner which explicitly assumes little prior knowledge of economics. This means that the book is reasonably self-contained in the sense that the economic application of each mathematical method is made in conjunction with both a verbal and (where possible) a diagrammatic explanation of the economic analysis involved. Also, to enhance the integration of this book with the student's concurrent economics courses, the majority of the economic applications relate to topics included in most first-year, undergraduate, courses in microeconomics and macroeconomics. Moreover, as in the exposition of each mathematical method, the exposition of each economic application is not only amply illustrated by fully-worked examples, but is also followed by Practice Problems (with, in many cases, fully-worked answers at the back of the book). Once more the Practice Problems have been carefully designed so as to both test and encourage, rather than frustrate and discourage, the student. Finally, further unworked problems (denoted as Additional Problems) are included at the end of each chapter containing economic applications. The latter problems are suitable for class work.

(e) A restriction of the mathematical methods and the economic applications to those areas which are generally the subject-matter of introductory 'mathematics for economists' courses. In addition, special emphasis has been given to the discussion of optimization problems, since these are by far the predominant problems that are analysed in undergraduate economics courses.

It should be noted that the pedagogical approach, to the exposition of mathematical methods in economics, as outlined above, represents an attempt to avoid the disadvantages of what might be termed the 'purist' and the 'cookbook' approaches to the exposition of mathematical methods in economics. To explain what is meant by this statement, let us firstly note that the purist approach is characterized by, first, a desire to lay a very strong foundation which will be sufficient to support the build-up of mathematical analysis to the highest possible level, and, second, a rigorous, extensive, exposition of each mathematical method, backed up by mathematical proofs of each step and followed by challenging, unworked (and often unanswered), problems that are designed to really make the student think. As such, while the purist approach rightly stresses the vital importance of a good foundation, it has the unfortunate disadvantage of being both too rigorous and too extensive for the student with a poor mathematics background. In contrast, the cookbook approach is characterized by, first, a desire to proceed as quickly as possible to the use of each mathematical method, and, second, a very sketchy explanation of each mathematical method, followed by a recipe of steps of formulas for solving problems. As such, while the cookbook approach has the laudable goal of 'mathematical economics without tears', it has the very serious disadvantage of not only laying an inadequate foundation for the subsequent building up of mathematical ability, but also of giving an unwarranted degree of confidence initially. Unlike both the purist and the cookbook approaches, the approach of this book has the goal of laying a foundation which is neither excessively rigorous nor excessively extensive, but which still represents an adequate foundation for the mathematical methods discussed.

The next section discusses certain points which are important to remember when learning mathematical methods.

1-3 POINTS TO REMEMBER WHEN LEARNING MATHEMATICAL METHODS

The student who is commencing an introductory course of mathematical methods in economics should, first of all, try to take a realistic mental attitude towards such a course. In particular, the student should take comfort in the fact that it is by no means impossible for students with little or no prior knowledge of mathematics to successfully complete such courses—the numerous economics students, who successfully complete such courses year by year, are a sufficient witness to that fact. Just as the student will encounter problems in learning economics and, with perseverance, will eventually overcome these problems, so the student will also encounter and eventually overcome problems in learning mathematical methods in economics. For example, the author can still recall (with satisfaction) how, the first time he lectured on an introductory course of mathematical methods in economics, the lectures commenced with a pretty female student weeping unhappily (because she was utterly convinced that she would never be able to master mathematical methods) and finished with the same young lady passing the course examination with flying colours!

The correct mental attitude to learning mathematical methods is more important than perhaps many students recognize. For example, when a student, studying a chapter in an economics textbook, is faced with a seemingly incomprehensible paragraph, he or she does not despair or immediately begin to think that he or she will never learn economics. Instead, the student reads the paragraph over again a few times and usually the problem disappears. If the problem still remains, the student will not stop reading, but instead will continue to read on through the chapter in the hope that things will eventually fall into place (as they usually do) as he or she proceeds. It is important that the student should have exactly the same mental attitude whenever he or she is faced with a problem in the study of mathematical methods in economics.

It is also important to remember that many things often look complex initially, but in practice turn out to be much less complex. For example, a book on how to drive a car may seem very complicated to the learner-driver, yet the actual operation of driving a car is not nearly so complicated as it appears. Also, the apparent complexity soon diminishes with practice. This is exactly the situation with mathematical methods. In other words, it is essential for the student to have plenty of practice on the actual operation of each mathematical method. Consequently, the student should not only read through each series of mathematical steps, but should also stop and work through the same series of steps on a sheet of paper. This simple procedure will: first, enhance the student's understanding, especially when it is realized that the actual mathematical operation is not as difficult as it looks at first sight; second, let the student see that one's own mathematical work looks much less complicated than someone else's mathematical work; and, third, give the student practice in mathematical manipulation.

The previous point is also important in the sense that it reminds us that, while certain things are not so hard to do in practice, they may be quite difficult to explain. For example, to change the illustration, it is by no means easy to write a simple explanation of how to tie a shoe-lace. No doubt, the person who has never seen a shoe, or a shoe-lace, would not only find the explanation (and the diagrammatic illustrations) extremely hard to follow, but would also find it very difficult to see the usefulness of such an operation. Yet, with practice in the actual operation of tying shoe-laces, most people not only quickly learn how to tie shoe-laces, but also quickly come to appreciate the usefulness of such an operation. The student will do well to remember this point when faced with a seemingly difficult and pointless mathematical method. In such a case, the student who practises writing out the steps of the particular mathematical method will, on proceeding through the chapter, not only find the mathematical method much less difficult, but will also eventually come to appreciate the usefulness of the particular mathematical method. In other words, it is sometimes necessary to accept the 'how' of a mathematical method and proceed some way before understanding the 'why' of that method.

The student with not only a poor mathematics background, but also a poor ability in mathematical manipulation, should recognize that an increased ability in mathematical manipulation will not be achieved overnight. Such an increased ability only comes after a period of regular practice. While this is so, the student should not be discouraged by this fact, especially as both the level of difficulty and the pace of progress of this book have been designed to allow for the development of this ability. Moreover, to aid the development of ability in mathematical manipulation, the student reading this book should:

1. Read each portion of mathematical analysis and then write it out, doing each step for himself or herself.
2. Attempt all the Practice Problems—if you cannot do a particular problem, then re-read the relevant section in the chapter and try the problem again.
3. Check your answers to the Practice Problems against the answers given at the back of the book.
4. Periodically repeat the Practice Problems of chapters already read.
5. The student should also attempt all the (unanswered) Additional Problems.

Finally, the student should take comfort in the fact that even a modest investment in the learning of mathematical methods, such as learning the various mathematical methods included in this book, will produce a surprisingly large return. As the student progresses through *An Introduction to Mathematical Methods in Economics*, he or she will soon discover that the modest range of mathematical methods discussed has a very wide range of important applications in economics. In addition, the student will soon discover that each mathematical method has many applications in economics. The latter fact not only means that, by the repeated application of a particular mathematical method, the student's understanding of that method will be continually reinforced, but also means that his or her mathematical dexterity will be continually improved.

1-4 ALTERNATIVE PATHS OF STUDY THROUGH THE BOOK

As can be seen from the table of contents, the order of presentation in this book essentially consists of the exposition of each mathematical method followed by the application of that method to various aspects of economic

1-4 ALTERNATIVE PATHS OF STUDY THROUGH THE BOOK 7

analysis. Also, as can be seen from the table of contents, the book concentrates heavily on elementary calculus methods and their application to economics. In addition, there are two chapters on matrix algebra. It should be noted, however, that the order of chapters for study need not follow that given in the table of contents. For example, the two chapters on matrix algebra may be either studied in their present position or, alternatively, studied as two consecutive chapters at a later stage in the book. This flexibility of order is made possible by the fact that the use of matrix algebra is essentially restricted to chapters four and five—the only other chapter where matrix methods are employed is chapter thirteen (where the particular matrix method involved is merely listed as an alternative method of solving a linear simultaneous-equation system).

The alternative location of chapters four and five is not, of course, the only example of a different, yet feasible, order of presentation. For example, at the author's university, the contents of this book are integrated into the undergraduate economics degree course in the following way:

1. The contents of eleven chapters (in the order: 2, 3, 6–11, 14, 4, and 5) are taught, to first-year students, as an introductory course of mathematical methods in economics. This introductory course (which is regarded as an essential supplement to the first-year microeconomics and macroeconomics courses) accounts, time-wise, for one-sixth of the first-year economics programme.
2. The contents of chapters twelve and thirteen are taught as part of a second-year course in microeconomics. This example indicates that *An Introduction to Mathematical Methods in Economics* may be used both as a textbook for introductory 'mathematics for economists' courses and as a supplement to various courses in microeconomics and macroeconomics.

CHAPTER
TWO

THE MATHEMATICAL REPRESENTATION OF ECONOMIC RELATIONSHIPS

2-1 ECONOMIC MODELS

A brief perusal, of almost any introductory economics textbook, quickly reveals that economics is very much concerned with the important issues of everyday life such as inflation, wages, unemployment, balance of payments, taxation, pollution, and so on. In other words, it is the interesting and challenging task of economics to study such phenomena with a view to understanding them and providing an explanation of them. However, while such a task is both stimulating and worth while, the vast complexity of the modern industrial economy makes this task rather daunting. For example, it is clearly not possible to try to study all economic phenomena at once, since this would involve attempting to handle an immense number of economic interrelationships simultaneously. This means we must decide upon some simpler method of procedure. In this respect, the most obvious method of procedure is to select or isolate some particular economic phenomenon, such as consumer behaviour, for detailed study on its own.

Once we have decided to study, say consumer behaviour, we cannot just go along to the nearest supermarket and 'observe' consumers—the simple reason being that we cannot just 'observe', we need to know *what* to observe. This implies that, in order to proceed, we must make some hypothesis about consumer behaviour that will guide our observations. For example, we may hypothesize that a consumer's demand (per time period) for a good will be influenced by the market price of that good. In particular, we may hypothesize that the higher the price of the good, the lower the quantity demanded by the consumer. In essence, what we have now got is a simple *theory* of consumer demand behaviour, which predicts that a consumer's demand for a good will decrease if the price of the good increases. This elementary theory may then be tested by factual observations of the quantity demanded of the good at each price, to see whether or not it provides a good explanation of the facts.

As it stands, our theory of consumer demand is a highly simplified abstraction from reality. For example, we have deliberately excluded the influence of the consumer's income, taste, and the prices of other goods, on the demand for the particular good under consideration. The important reason for adopting such a deliberately simplified theory is that it enables us initially to focus our attention solely on the relationship between the quantity demanded of a good and its price. After analysis of this simple theory we can then proceed to the analysis of a more complex theory of consumer demand. It should be noted, however, that the more complex theory will also be an abstraction from reality. Thus, while such a more complex theory may incorporate the influence of the consumer's income, taste, and the prices of other goods, it may exclude both the presence of durable consumption goods and the possibility of the consumer reacting with some delay to price and income changes. In other words, the more complex theory is still a deliberately simplified analytical framework in comparison with the real world. This is only to be expected since, given the complexity of the real world, any theory must necessarily be an abstraction from reality.

The two theories of consumer demand, which we have briefly referred to above, provide theoretical frameworks for the analysis of certain aspects of consumer behaviour. Such an analytical or theoretical framework, which concentrates solely on selected economic relationships (such as the relationship between the quantity demanded and the price of a good), is known as an *economic model*. Note that while we have presented the above two economic models in verbal form, they may also be presented in diagrammatic form (as in almost all economics textbooks) or in algebraic form. Our concern in this book will be to examine the mathematical representation of economic relationships, including both the diagrammatic and the algebraic forms of presentation.

In order to examine the mathematical representation of economic relationships, we must first examine how relationships between entities in general are handled in mathematics. To do this, we need an elementary knowledge of the concepts of *sets*, *relations*, and *functions*.

Before discussing the concepts of sets, relations and functions, the student suffering from trepidation, or unhappy memories of school mathematics, can take comfort in the knowledge that the following discussion of these fundamental concepts is quite straightforward.

2-2 SETS

A *set* is a collection of entities which can be clearly distinguished from each other. For example, we can speak of the set of economics students in a particular university, the set of employees in a particular firm, the set of consumers of a particular good, and so on. The 'entities' in a set are called the *members* or *elements* of that set.

A set can be defined by listing or enumerating all its elements. For example, if we let A represent the set of four positive whole numbers, 1, 2, 3 and 4, then the set A can be written as

$$A = \{1, 2, 3, 4\}$$

where the elements are listed within braces '{ }'. Alternatively, set A may be defined by describing, rather than listing, its elements. Thus we can write set A as

$$A = \{x \mid x \text{ is a positive whole number less than 5}\}$$

which is read as 'the set, A, consists of elements, x, such that x is a positive whole number less than 5'. Note that when a set is defined in this way, a vertical bar (or a colon) is inserted within the braces to separate the symbol (x in this case) for the elements from the description of the elements.

If we wish to denote that, say, the whole number 2 is a member of set A, we simply write $2 \in A$ which is read as '2 is an element of set A'. Similarly we may write $7 \notin A$ which is read as '7 is not an element of set A'. It should be noted that to speak of membership and non-membership of a set implies that it is possible to distinguish members from non-members. It is for this reason that a collection of elements will only be called a set if it is possible to distinguish members from non-members, as well as from each other.

A set with a finite number of elements, such as set A above, is called a *finite set*. Similarly, a set with an infinite number of elements is called an *infinite set*. At the other extreme, from an infinite set, is a set that contains no elements. Such a set is called an *empty set* or *null set*, and is denoted by the special symbol $\emptyset$. It is important to note that there is only one null set. The null set is *unique*. Also, it should be noted that $\emptyset \neq \{0\}$, which reads as '$\emptyset$ is not equal to $\{0\}$', since $\emptyset$ contains no elements whereas $\{0\}$ contains the element zero.

Subsets

If we take two sets

$$A = \{1, 2, 3, 4\} \quad \text{and} \quad B = \{1, 4\}$$

then we can see that B is a *subset* of A because every element of B is also an element of A. Definitionally, a set B is said to be a subset of set A if and only if every element of B is also an element of A. To show that one set is a subset of another we use the symbol $\subset$ (which means 'is contained in' or 'is a subset of') or the symbol $\supset$ (which means 'includes' or 'has as one of its subsets'). Thus we can write

$$B \subset A \quad \text{or} \quad A \supset B$$

which reads 'set B is contained in set A or set A includes set B'. As a mnemonic device note that the open end of the symbol indicates the main set and the closed end of the symbol indicates the subset.

If two sets C_1 and C_2 contain identical elements, as given by

$$C_1 = \{6, 7, 5, 9\} \quad \text{and} \quad C_2 = \{9, 5, 6, 7\}$$

then C_1 and C_2 are said to be *equal* ($C_1 = C_2$). Note that the definition of equality does not require the elements of C_1 and C_2 to be listed in the same order. Also, note that in the case of equal sets, such as C_1 and C_2, either can be a subset of the other. More formally, we can have $C_1 \subset C_2$ and $C_2 \subset C_1$ iff $C_1 = C_2$, where the symbol iff denotes the expression 'if and only if'.

An interesting application of the subset definition is that a set, such as C_1, will be a subset of itself since every element of C_1 is also an element of C_1. Hence C_1 itself is the largest possible subset of C_1. At the other extreme, the smallest possible subset of C_1 is a set that is devoid of elements—in other words, the null set $\emptyset$. To disqualify $\emptyset$ from being a subset of C_1, $\emptyset$ would have to contain at least one element x such that $x \notin C_1$. But since, by definition, $\emptyset$ contains no elements, then $\emptyset$ is a subset of C_1 (that is, $\emptyset \subset C_1$). Note that this implies that $\emptyset$ is a subset of *any* set.

If any two sets D and E have no elements in common, as given by

$$D = \{1, 3, 6, 7\} \quad \text{and} \quad E = \{2, 5, 4\}$$

then D and E are said to be *disjoint*. Two sets, such as C_1 and D, which have some elements common to each and some elements peculiar to each, are neither disjoint nor equal. Also, C_1 and D cannot be subsets of each other.

The Real-Number System

We can illustrate the concepts of sets and subsets by reference to what is known as the *real-number system*. To do this, let us firstly note that positive whole numbers such as $1, 2, 3, \ldots$ (which are called *positive integers*), and negative whole numbers such as $-1, -2, -3, \ldots$ (which are called *negative integers*), and the unique number 0 (zero), which is neither positive nor negative, can all be classified under the single term *integers*. Thus we can refer to them collectively as the *set of all integers*. Consequently, if we let P denote the set of all integers and Q the set of all positive integers, as given by

$$P = \{x | x \text{ is an integer}\} \quad \text{and} \quad Q = \{x | x \text{ is a positive integer}\}$$

then clearly Q is a subset of P or $Q \subset P$.

If we visualize the integers $-3, -2, -1, 0, 1, 2, 3$ on the following one-dimensional graph (or line segment) then *fractions*, which may be

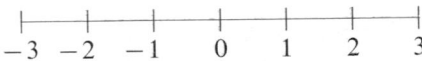

positive (such as $\frac{1}{2}, \frac{5}{3}$ and $\frac{9}{4}$) or negative (such as $-\frac{1}{3}, -\frac{3}{2}$ and $-\frac{7}{3}$) will be located between the integers on the graph. All positive and negative fractions together form the *set of all fractions*.

It should be noted that all fractions have the property that each can be expressed as a ratio of two integers. Integers also possess this property of being *ratio*-nal, since any integer p can be expressed as the ratio $p/1$ (including 0 since $0/1 = 0$). Numbers which are *ratio*-nal are called *rational numbers*. Together, the set of all integers and the set of all fractions make up the *set of all rational numbers*. Thus if we let R denote the set of all rational numbers and S the set of all fractions, then clearly S is a subset of R or $S \subset R$. Likewise $P \subset R$.

There are other numbers, however, which *cannot* be expressed as a ratio of two integers. Such numbers are called *irrational numbers*. Examples of such numbers are $\sqrt{2}, \sqrt{3}, \sqrt{5}$ and π (which represents the ratio of the circumference of any circle to its diameter). When expressed in decimal form, all irrational numbers can be seen to be nonrepeating, nonterminating decimals (e.g., $\sqrt{2} = 1.4142\ldots$; $\sqrt{3} = 1.7321\ldots$; $\pi = 3.1415\ldots$;). In contrast, all rational numbers can be expressed either as a terminating decimal (such as $3139/100 = 31.39$) or as a repeating, nonterminating decimal (such as $685/99 = 6.91919\ldots$).

While an irrational number cannot, by definition, be expressed as a ratio (or fraction), it can still be represented on our one-dimensional graph. For example, the number $\sqrt{2}$ lies between the two rational numbers 1.41421 and 1.41422. This demonstrates that each irrational number can be located between two rational numbers, just as each fraction can be located between two integers, on the one-dimensional graph above. Together, the set of all irrational numbers and the set of all rational numbers make up the *set of all real numbers*. Utilizing this terminology, it can now be seen that our one-dimensional graph represents the set of all real numbers greater than or equal to -3 and less than or equal to 3. Symbolically, this set can be expressed as

$$T = \{x | -3 \leqslant x \leqslant 3\}$$

which reads as 'T is the set of all real numbers x, such that x is greater than or equal to -3 (indicated by $-3 \leqslant x$) and less than or equal to 3 (indicated by $x \leqslant 3$)'.

In this book only *real numbers* will be used. However, it should be noted that there are also *imaginary numbers* (which involve the square root of a negative number) and *complex numbers* (which have a *real* component and an *imaginary* component).

Finally, in relation to the number zero, note that while $a \times 0 = 0$ and $0/a = 0$, the expressions $a/0$ and $0/0$ are undefined (where a is some real number).

2-A PRACTICE PROBLEMS

2-1 State whether each of the following is a set:
(a) all the best economists; (b) all positive even integers less than 10; (c) all the owners of Renault cars; (d) all the rarest paintings.

2-2 Write the following in set notation:
(a) the set of all nonnegative real numbers; (b) the set of all real numbers greater than or equal to -19 but less than or equal to 29.

2-3 Given the sets $A = \{0, 1, -2\}$, $B = \{6, 5, 3\}$, $C = \{-2, 1, 0\}$, and $D = \{1, 0, 2, -2\}$, state whether each of the following statements is true or false:
(a) $-2 \notin A$ (b) $5 \in B$ (c) $A \neq C$ (d) $C \subset D$ (e) $D \supset A$ (f) $B \subset D$ (g) $\emptyset \subset B$
(h) $C \subset A$ (i) $D \supset \emptyset$ (j) B and C are disjoint.

2-4 List all the subsets of the set $B = \{6, 5, 3\}$.

2-3 RELATIONS AND FUNCTIONS

In Sec. 2-1 we noted that in order to examine the mathematical representation of economic relationships, such as the relationship between the quantity demanded and the price of a good, we need to examine how relationships between entities in general are handled in mathematics. As we have seen, the first step in doing this involved defining a (distinct) collection of entities as a set. The next step will consist of an examination of the concept of *ordered pairs*, followed by the final step which involves the concepts of *relations* and *functions*.

Ordered Pairs

In our discussion of equal sets, in Sec. 2-2, we noted that a set $\{a, w\}$ can also be written as $\{w, a\}$, since by definition $\{a, w\} = \{w, a\}$. In such a case, where the ordering of the elements is unimportant, the elements a and w are said to be an *unordered pair*. However, if we let the elements a and w denote a person's age (in years) and weight (in pounds), respectively, then the ordering of a and w will have a particular significance. In the latter case we can write two distinctly different *ordered pairs*, given by (a, w) and (w, a), which have the property that $(a, w) \neq (w, a)$ unless $a = w$. For example,

14 THE MATHEMATICAL REPRESENTATION OF ECONOMIC RELATIONSHIPS

when $a = 21$ and $w = 147$, the ordered pairs $(21, 147)$ and $(147, 21)$ have clearly very different meanings! In general, a set consisting of two elements, with the order of the elements specified, is called an *ordered pair*. Note that it is usual to write an ordered pair in ordinary brackets as we have done here.

If we let the element h denote a person's height (in inches), then we can write the *ordered triple* (a, w, h). In a similar fashion we can obtain ordered quadruples, ordered quintuples, and so on. Note that, in each case, we have simply a set in which the elements have a specific order.

The information provided by an ordered pair, such as $(a, w) = (5, 50)$ can be represented on a two-dimensional graph such as Fig. 2-1a. Note that this graph consists of two scales or axes placed at right angles to each other, with the horizontal scale for the first element in the ordered pair, and the vertical scale for the second. Thus the ordered pair $(5, 50)$ can be represented by the unique point plotted in Fig. 2-1a as shown. In general each ordered pair of numbers will have a unique point on the particular graph corresponding to it and, conversely, each point on the particular graph will also correspond to a unique ordered pair of numbers. More formally, it is said that a *one-to-one correspondence* exists between ordered pairs of numbers and points on a graph.

The above graphical representation of ordered pairs of numbers can be given a more general treatment in terms of the rectangular coordinate plane presented in Fig. 2-1b. Note that, in this case, we have an x axis and a y axis which intersect each other at right angles to divide the plane into four quadrants as shown. This plane (known as the xy plane) is an infinite set of points, with each point representing an ordered pair whose first element is an x value (known as the x coordinate or the *abscissa* of the point) and whose second element is a y value (known as the y coordinate or the *ordinate* of the point). Since any point on the xy plane, such as $(2, 2)$ or $(-2, 3)$, is plotted in Fig. 2-1b by measuring distances parallel to axes which are at right angles to each other, we can see why the xy plane is referred to

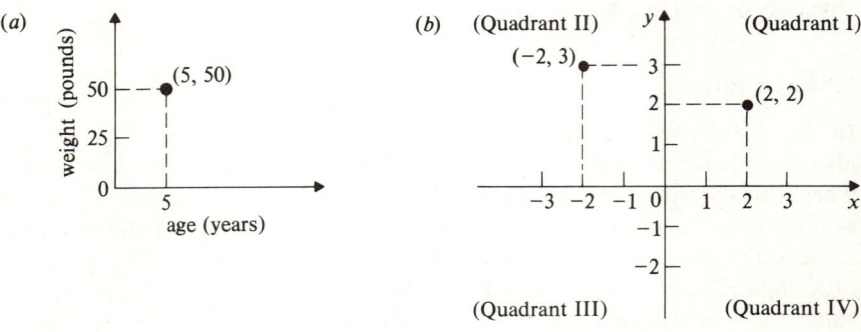

Figure 2-1

as the rectangular coordinate plane. It is also known as the cartesian coordinate plane (being named after Descartes).

Note that the ordered pair $(2, 2)$ was formed by associating a particular y value with a particular x value. If, instead of doing this, we now take a *set* of x values (such as $x = \{-2, 2\}$) and a *set* of y values (such as $y = \{2, 3\}$), how many ordered pairs can then be formed by taking the first element from set x and the second element from set y? The answer is four—the four ordered pairs being $(-2, 2)$, $(-2, 3)$, $(2, 2)$, and $(2, 3)$. This set of four ordered pairs is called the *cartesian product* of the sets x and y, and is denoted symbolically as $x \times y$. Thus the cartesian product can be expressed either as

$$x \times y = \{(-2, 2), (-2, 3), (2, 2), (2, 3)\}$$

or

$$x \times y = \{(a, b) | a \in x \text{ and } b \in y\} \tag{2-1}$$

where the latter expression reads '$x \times y$ is the set of ordered pairs (a, b), such that a is an element of set x and b is an element of set y'. Notice that the *order* of the letters denoting the cartesian product is important: x is written first because the first elements of the ordered pairs are chosen from x. Also, note that while x and y are sets of numbers, $x \times y$ is a set of ordered pairs.

If we now extend the definition of the sets x and y to include all the real numbers, then the new cartesian product, given in (2-2),

$$x \times y = \{(a, b) | a \text{ and } b \text{ are both real numbers}\} \tag{2-2}$$

will represent the set of all ordered pairs whose elements are real numbers. This infinite set of ordered pairs corresponds to the infinite set of points in the cartesian coordinate plane of Fig. 2-1b. More formally, a one-to-one correspondence is said to exist between the set of ordered pairs in the cartesian product (2-2) and the set of points in the cartesian coordinate plane.

In practice it is convenient to refer to the elements of the cartesian product (2-2) generally as (x, y) rather than (a, b). Thus we can conveniently speak of any ordered pair in $x \times y$ as (x, y), remembering that both x and y can take on any real value. Similarly, we can conveniently speak of any (x, y) point, or any (x, y) value, remembering once more that both x and y can take on any real value.

With this foundation we are now ready to proceed to the concepts of *relations* and *functions*.

Relations and Functions

As noted above, the cartesian product (2-2) is an infinite set of ordered pairs of real numbers. This means that a particular collection of ordered pairs of

16 THE MATHEMATICAL REPRESENTATION OF ECONOMIC RELATIONSHIPS

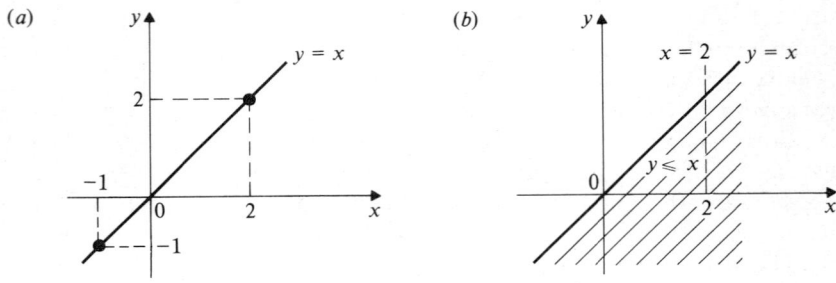

Figure 2-2

real numbers, such as the set of four ordered pairs in (2-1), will therefore be a subset of the cartesian product (2-2). Any such subset of the cartesian product (2-2) is said to constitute a *relation* between y and x.

As an example, let us take the following set

$$\{(x, y) | y = x\}$$

which reads as 'the set of ordered pairs (x, y), such that $y = x$'. If we then take various x and y values we can form a set of ordered pairs, such as $(-1, -1)$, $(0, 0)$, and $(2, 2)$, which satisfies the *equation* $y = x$. This set constitutes a *relation* and is represented graphically in Fig. 2-2a by the set of points lying on the straight line labelled $y = x$. Note, in this relation, that for each different x value there is a different y value. Also, note that the particular rule specifying the relation between y and x is given by the equation $y = x$. In other words, the equation $y = x$ determines the particular y value that is associated with a particular x value in each of the exemplary ordered pairs given above.

A further example of a relation is the set

$$\{(x, y) | y \leqslant x\}$$

which consists of ordered pairs, such as $(2, -1)$, $(2, 0)$, and $(2, 2)$, which satisfy the *inequality* $y \leqslant x$. This set is represented graphically, in Fig. 2-2b, by the set of all points in the shaded area (which includes the straight line $y = x$). The student should not proceed until convinced that all points in the shaded area do fulfil the relation $y \leqslant x$. Also note, in this relation, that a unique x value, such as $x = 2$, may be associated with various y values (in fact, any y value, within the shaded area, which lies on the dotted vertical line labelled $x = 2$). Finally, note that the particular rule specifying the relation between y and x is given by the inequality $y \leqslant x$. This means that each y value that is associated with an x value in an ordered pair must satisfy the inequality $y \leqslant x$.

As a final example, we may have a relation such that for each x value

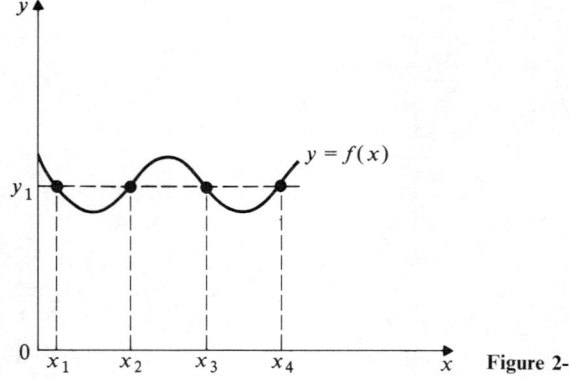

Figure 2-3

there exists only *one* corresponding y value. This type of relation between y and x, consisting of a set of ordered pairs with the property that any x value determines a *unique* y value, is called a *function*. In such a case, y is said to be a function of x, and is expressed symbolically by $y = f(x)$, which is read as 'y equals f of x'. [*Warning*: $f(x)$ does *not* mean f multiplied by x.] Note that the relation represented by the straight line $y = x$, in Fig. 2-2a, qualifies as a function, whereas the relation represented by the shaded area $y \leq x$, in Fig. 2-2b, does not. These two examples show that a function must be a relation, but a relation may not qualify as a function.

An examination of the relation represented by the curve $y = f(x)$, in Fig. 2-3, indicates that it qualifies as a function. This example indicates that while the definition of a function requires a unique y for each x, there may be more than one x value associated with a single y value. Thus, in Fig. 2-3, the function $y = f(x)$ associates the four x values x_1, x_2, x_3, and x_4, with the same y value y_1.

Whenever we write a function as $y = f(x)$, the functional notation f can be regarded as a rule specifying a particular type of relation. Therefore, when we write $y = f(x) = x$, the actual rule is made explicit so that, for example, $x = 2$ is associated with $y = 2$ as in Fig. 2-2a. In this case we say that the x value, $x = 2$, is *mapped* or *transformed* into the y value, $y = 2$. Consequently, the functional notation f can be interpreted as a rule by which a set of x values is mapped or transformed into a set of y values. It is for this reason that a function is also called a *mapping* or *transformation*. This is symbolically expressed by $f: x \to y$, where $\to$ denotes a mapping and f specifies the rule of mapping.

The mapping rule specified by the function $y = f(x) = x$ is illustrated in Fig. 2-4, which shows the mapping of selected x values into y values (known as the *images* of the corresponding x values) as specified by $y = f(x) = x$. Note that the set of values that x can take in a certain context is called the

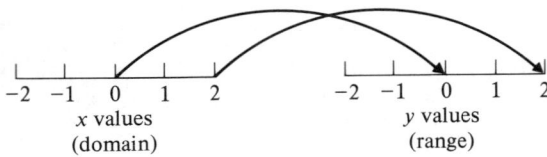

Figure 2-4

domain of the function. For example, in Fig. 2-4, the domain of $y = f(x) = x$ is restricted to the set $\{x|-2 \leq x \leq 2\}$, though in another context it may be extended to the set $\{x|x$ is a real number$\}$. The set of y values, into which the set of x values is mapped, is called the *range* of the function as it consists of the set of all values that y can take in that context. For example, in Fig. 2-4, the range of $y = f(x) = x$ is the set $\{y|-2 \leq y \leq 2\}$. In the more familiar two-dimensional graph, such as Fig. 2-2a, where a set of ordered pairs (exemplified by $(-1, -1)$, $(0,0)$, and $(2,2)$, which are plotted in Fig. 2-2a) specifies the relation between y and x values, the domain is placed on the x axis and the range on the y axis.

It should be noted that whenever the mapping rule is made explicit, as in $y = f(x) = x$, we can use the same functional notation for different functions such as $y = f(x) = 2x$, $y = f(x) = 6 - 3x$, and so on. However, when the mapping rule is not made explicit, different functional notation must be used to denote different functions. For example, we may write $y = f(x)$ and $z = g(x)$, or $y = y(x)$ and $z = z(x)$, for the case where y and z are both functions of x. Also, note that instead of writing, say, $y = f(x) = -3 + 5x$ we may simply write $f(x) = -3 + 5x$.

In the function $y = f(x)$, x is called the *argument* of the function and y is called the *value* of the function. Alternatively, since x and y can assume different values, they can be termed *variables*, with x being referred to as the *independent variable* and y as the *dependent variable*. Thus, given the *specific form* of a function (in contrast to the *general form* $y = f(x)$), such as $y = f(x) = 2x$, the value of the function for a particular x value is obtained by substituting the x value into $f(x) = 2x$. For example,

$$\text{if } f(x) = 2x \quad \text{then} \quad f(2) = 2(2) = 4$$

is the value of the function when $x = 2$. Similarly,

$$\text{if } f(x) = \frac{7x+6}{x} \quad \text{then} \quad f(3) = \frac{7(3)+6}{3} = 9$$

Note that this is the procedure we follow if we wish to graph a function. For example, if we wish to graph the function $y = f(x) = 4 + 2x$, we select a number of x values, such as $-2, -1, 0, 1, 2$, and find the corresponding y values as shown in the following table:

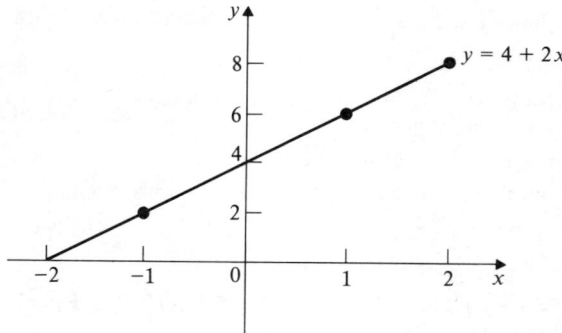

Figure 2-5

x	-2	-1	0	1	2
$y = f(x)$	0	2	4	6	8

Each ordered pair (x, y) can then be plotted as a point on the xy plane in Fig. 2-5, and connected to give the *general* shape of the graph of the function as shown. In the last sentence, the word 'general' should be noted: strictly speaking we need to take every x value in the domain of a function, with its corresponding y value, and plot as points in the coordinate plane to obtain the *exact* shape of the graph of a function.

An examination of the above table, and of Fig. 2-5, indicates that when $x = 0$, the corresponding y value (given by $f(x) = 4 + 2x$) is $y = 4$. This y value is known as the *y intercept* or the *vertical intercept*, because it is at this y value that the vertical axis intersects the graph of the function. Similarly, the value of x, for which the corresponding y value is $y = 0$, is called the *x intercept* or the *horizontal intercept*. For the function $f(x) = 4 + 2x$, this occurs at $x = -2$.

With the above knowledge of the concept of a function, we are now in a position to mathematically represent economic relationships in terms of functions.

2-B PRACTICE PROBLEMS

2-5 Given the sets $A = \{a, b\}$ and $B = \{c, d\}$, find the cartesian products:
(a) $A \times B$ (b) $B \times A$

2-6 In Prob. 2-5, why is $A \times B \neq B \times A$?

2-7 Which of the following relations, consisting of a set of ordered pairs (x, y), is not a function?
(a) $\{(0, -1), (2, 3), (1, 0), (2, -1)\}$
(b) $\{(-2, -10), (-1, -7), (0, -1), (2, 2), (3, 5)\}$
(c) $\{(1, 2), (3, 5), (4, 2), (5, 1), (7, 2)\}$

2-8 If the domain of each of the following functions is $\{x | 0 \leqslant x \leqslant 5\}$, find the range of each function:
(a) $y = -4 + 3x$ (b) $y = 3 - 9x$

2-9 For each of the following functions find $f(-2), f(0),$ and $f(a)$, where a is some number:
(a) $f(p) = 5 - 2p$ (b) $f(t) = (2t - 10)/(3t + 1)$ (c) $f(w) = w(w + 3)$

2-10 Find the y and x intercepts for each of the functions in Prob. 2-8.

2-11 Graph the functions given in Prob. 2-8, taking the domain in each case to be $\{x | 0 \leqslant x \leqslant 5\}$.

2-4 REPRESENTATION OF ECONOMIC RELATIONSHIPS IN TERMS OF FUNCTIONS

In Sec. 2-1 we referred to a highly simplified theory of consumer demand in which the quantity demanded (per time period) of a good was related solely to its price. Also, it was stated that the consumer's behaviour was such that less (more) of the good was demanded as the price of the good rose (fell). We are now in a position to examine the mathematical representation of this economic relationship between the quantity demanded and the price of a good. To do this, let us firstly note that the number of units of the good, and the price per unit of the good, can take on different values. Consequently, quantity demanded and price are *variables* and as such can be represented by Q_d and P, respectively, where Q_d will be in some physical unit (such as pounds weight or number of oranges) and P will be in some money unit (such as pounds sterling or US dollars).

In our simple model of consumer demand, we shall assume that the price of any good under consideration is taken as a *given* datum for the consumer. In other words, the price of each good is determined external to our model. It is for this reason that P is referred to as an *exogenous variable*. On the other hand, we want to construct our consumer demand model so that, given the price of a good, we can determine the quantity of the good demanded. Therefore, since Q_d is determined within our model, Q_d is said to be an *endogenous variable*. As such, Q_d is *dependent*, with its values to be found within the model.

The above model, consisting of the relationship between Q_d and P, can now be represented mathematically by the function

$$Q_d = f(P) \qquad (2\text{-}3)$$

which implies that, for each price of the good under consideration, there will be a corresponding unique quantity of the good demanded. In economics terminology, we read (2-3) as 'demand is a function of price' meaning that the quantity demanded of a good depends upon its price. In this respect, it should be noted that (2-3) is not only a mathematical representation of an economic relationship, but it is also a mathematical representation of consumer *behaviour*. Essentially (2-3) postulates a

2-4 REPRESENTATION OF ECONOMIC RELATIONSHIPS IN TERMS OF FUNCTIONS

relationship between a consumer's demand behaviour and the price of a good.

If we assume a specific form for (2-3), which is known as the consumer's *demand function*, then the specific form of the relationship between Q_d and P can be represented graphically. For example, let us assume that

$$Q_d = f(P) = 10 - 2P \qquad (2-4)$$

which is graphed in Fig. 2-6a, using the values of P and Q_d given in the following table:

P	0	1	2	3	4	5
$Q_d = f(P)$	10	8	6	4	2	0

Note that, to make economic sense, the domain (and the range) of (2-4) has been restricted to include only nonnegative (meaning positive or zero) values. Consequently, (2-4) is drawn only in the first quadrant in Fig. 2-6a. Such restriction of the domain (and of the range) of a function, to make economic sense, is common in economic models. In addition, note that Fig. 2-6a follows the mathematical convention of placing the *dependent* variable on the vertical axis. While this is contrary to the 'demand diagrams' of most economics textbooks, where price appears on the vertical axis, the reader should be convinced that Fig. 2-6a can easily be redrawn with the axes reversed as in Fig. 2-6b.

An examination of Fig. 2-6a provides us with the following detailed information about the consumer's demand behaviour: (i) when the good is free ($P = 0$), 10 units are demanded, (ii) as the good's price rises from $P = 0$ to $P = 5$, the quantity demanded falls, (iii) when $P = 5$, the quantity demanded is zero. This information should make it clear that the function (2-4) embodies definite assumptions with respect to the behaviour pattern of Q_d.

The simple example given above demonstrates the importance of functions as a means of representing economic relationships. Consequently, in economic models in general, functions are frequently used to represent various forms of behaviour. For example, functions may be used to

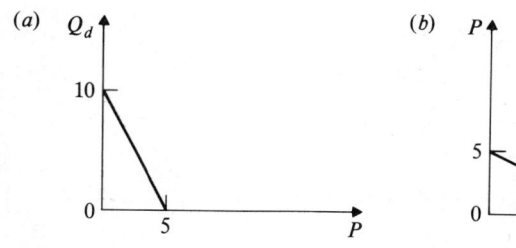
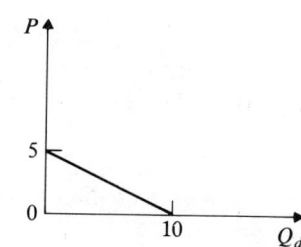

Figure 2-6

represent human behaviour (such as the supply of hours worked at various wage rates) or technical behaviour (such as the relation between the physical output of a good and the labour input used to produce that output). It should be noted that such functions may appear either in *general form* (as in (2-3)) or in *specific form* (as in (2-4)).

In Chapter 3, the economic meaning of the type of simple demand function given in (2-4) will be explored in greater detail. However, before proceeding to Chapter 3, it is important for the student to work through the remaining sections (and problems) of the current chapter, which contain a brief discussion of several essential, preparatory, concepts.

2-C PRACTICE PROBLEMS

2-12 Graph the following demand functions: (a) $Q_d = 100 - 12P$; (b) $Q_d = 285 - 3P$. In each case restrict the domain so as to make economic sense. In addition, to graphing (a) and (b) with Q_d on the vertical axis, graph (a) and (b) with P on the vertical axis.

2-13 Find (i) the quantity demanded in each case when the good is free, and (ii) the set of prices for which the demand for each good is zero.

2-5 INDICES

When a variable (or a number or an expression) is to be multiplied by itself a number of times, we use *index notation* as follows:

$$x^2 = x \times x; \quad 2^3 = 2 \times 2 \times 2; \quad (3x-3)^2 = (3x-3) \times (3x-3)$$

where the notation x^2 is read as 'x to the *power* of 2', and the superscript indicator of the power of x is known as an *index* or *exponent*. Thus, as a general definition, we have

$$x^n = \underbrace{x \times x \times x \times \ldots \times x}_{n \text{ terms}}$$

which gives $x^1 = x$ and $x^4 = x \times x \times x \times x$ when $n = 1$ and $n = 4$, respectively. We can now examine the rules for *indices* or exponents, noting that x in the following discussion is a *nonzero* number.

Rule 1 $x^m \times x^n = x^{m+n}$
For example, $x^2 \times x^3 = x^{2+3} = x^5$ since $x^2 \times x^3 = (x \times x) \times (x \times x \times x) = (x \times x \times x \times x \times x) = x^5$. Also, $x^n \times x = x^n \times x^1 = x^{n+1}$.

Rule 2 $x^m / x^n = x^{m-n}$
For example, if m is greater than n (written as $m > n$), such as when $m = 4$ and $n = 2$, we have:

$$\frac{x^4}{x^2} = x^{4-2} = x^2 \quad \text{since} \quad \frac{x^4}{x^2} = \frac{x \times x \times x \times x}{x \times x} = x \times x = x^2$$

If m is less than n (written as $m < n$), such as when $m = 2$ and $n = 4$, we have:

$$\frac{x^2}{x^4} = x^{2-4} = x^{-2}$$

The meaning of the *negative power* of x can be seen as follows:

$$\frac{x^2}{x^4} = \frac{x \times x}{x \times x \times x \times x} = \frac{1}{x \times x} = \frac{1}{x^2}$$

Hence $x^{-2} = 1/x^2$. As another example, note that

$$\frac{x}{x^4} = x^{1-4} = x^{-3} \quad \text{since} \quad \frac{x}{x^4} = \frac{x}{x \times x \times x \times x} = \frac{1}{x \times x \times x} = \frac{1}{x^3}$$

Hence $x^{-3} = 1/x^3$. Similarly, $x^2/x^3 = x^{-1} = 1/x$. This provides us with Rule 3.

Rule 3 $x^{-n} = 1/x^n$

As another application of Rule 2, we have the case where $m = n$, which gives $x^{m-n} = x^{m-m} = x^0$. The meaning of the zero power can be seen as follows:

$$\frac{x^2}{x^2} = x^{2-2} = x^0 = 1 \quad \text{since} \quad \frac{x^2}{x^2} = \frac{x \times x}{x \times x} = 1$$

This provides us with Rule 4.

Rule 4 $x^0 = 1$

Rule 5 $(x^m)^n = x^{mn}$

For example, $(x^3)^2 = x^6$ since

$$(x^3)^2 = (x \times x \times x) \times (x \times x \times x) = x \times x \times x \times x \times x \times x = x^6.$$

While the above discussion has been restricted to integer values of exponents, it should be noted that exponents can also have fractional values such as $x^{1/2}$ or $x^{1/3}$. To understand the meaning of $x^{1/2}$, note that the application of Rule 1 gives $x^{1/2} \times x^{1/2} = x^1 = x$. Since $x^{1/2}$ multiplied by itself gives x, then $x^{1/2}$ is the *square root* of x (denoted by $\sqrt{x}$). Similarly, since $x^{1/3} x^{1/3} x^{1/3} = x^1$, $x^{1/3}$ is the *cube root* of x (denoted by $\sqrt[3]{x}$). This provides us with Rule 6.

Rule 6 $x^{1/n} = \sqrt[n]{x}$

Note that Rules 3, 5 and 6 can be combined as follows:

$$x^{-1/2} = (x^{1/2})^{-1} = \frac{1}{x^{1/2}} = \frac{1}{\sqrt{x}}$$

similarly, $x^{-1/4} = (x^{1/4})^{-1} = 1/\sqrt[4]{x}$. This provides us with Rule 7.

Rule 7 $x^{-1/n} = 1/\sqrt[n]{x}$

Also, note that Rules 5 and 6 can be combined as follows:

$$x^{3/2} = (x^3)^{1/2} = \sqrt{x^3}$$

Similarly, $x^{2/3} = (x^2)^{1/3} = \sqrt[3]{x^2}$. This provides us with Rule 8.

Rule 8 $x^{m/n} = \sqrt[n]{x^m}$

This rule can, in turn, be combined with Rules 3 and 5 as follows:

$$x^{-3/2} = (x^{3/2})^{-1} = \frac{1}{\sqrt{x^3}}$$

Similarly, $x^{-4/5} = (x^{4/5})^{-1} = 1/\sqrt[5]{x^4}$. This provides us with Rule 9.

Rule 9 $x^{-m/n} = 1/\sqrt[n]{x^m}$

Rule 10 $x^n \times y^n = (xy)^n$
For example, $3^2 \times 4^2 = (3 \times 4)^2 = 144$.

Rule 11 $(x/y)^n = x^n/y^n$
For example,

$$\left(\frac{3}{2}\right)^3 = \frac{3}{2} \times \frac{3}{2} \times \frac{3}{2} = \frac{3^3}{2^3} = \frac{27}{8}.$$

Finally, note that an even power of any real number is always nonnegative. For example, $3^2 = 9$ and $-3^2 = 9$, while $3^3 = 27$ and $-3^3 = -27$. Also, note that while $0^2 = 0$, 0^0 and 0^{-2} are undefined.

2-D PRACTICE PROBLEMS

2-14 Express each of the following in terms of roots (e.g., $x^{2/3} = \sqrt[3]{x^2}$):
(a) $x^{-7/9}$ (b) $(2x+5y)^{2/3}$ (c) $x^{1/3} - y^{1/4}$ (d) $(xy)^{3/5}$
(e) $(y^2 + x^{-2})^{-1/4}$

2-15 Express each of the following in terms of exponents (e.g., $\sqrt[4]{x^5} = x^{5/4}$):
(a) $(2x)/(\sqrt[3]{y})$ (b) $1/(\sqrt[4]{x-16})$ (c) $-10(\sqrt[5]{x^2y^5})$
(d) $(\sqrt[3]{4x})/(\sqrt[3]{2y})$ (e) $\sqrt[9]{9xy^3}$

2-16 Simplify the following (e.g., $(x^{1/4}y^{5/4})^4 = xy^5$):
(a) $x^4/x^{-1/2}$ (b) $(9x^3y^2)(81x^2y^4)^{1/2}$ (c) $x^{2/3}(x^{7/3} + x^{1/3})$
(d) $x^{3/2}(x^{-7/2} \times x^2)$ (e) $(9^{-1}mn^{-2})/(3mn)^{-3}$

2-6 POLYNOMIAL FUNCTIONS

We can now use our knowledge of indices to briefly discuss the class of functions known as *polynomial functions*, where the word polynomial simply means 'many terms'. Before doing this, however, we need to develop some useful notation.

Firstly, let us note that the function $y = f(x) = 4 + 2x$ contains two *constants* (that is, magnitudes which do not change), 4 and 2, with the constant 2, which is joined to the variable x, being referred to as the *coefficient* of the variable x. If we now replace these two constants with symbols, such as a and b, we obtain the formulation $y = f(x) = a + bx$. The latter formulation is more general since, by assigning different values to a and b, it can represent a large number of different functions such as $y = 5 - 2x$ (where $a = 5$ and $b = -2$), $y = -3 + 6x$ (where $a = -3$ and $b = 6$), and so on. Constants, such as a and b which can take on different values are known as *parametric constants* or *parameters*. Also, note that we could have used a_0 and a_1, instead of a and b, so that the function becomes $y = f(x) = a_0 + a_1 x$. With this notation we can now examine polynomial functions.

The simplest form of a polynomial function is given by

$$y = a_0 x^0 = a_0 \qquad (2\text{-}5)$$

which is known as a *constant function*. An example of this type of function is graphed (for $x \geq 0$) as the horizontal straight line in Fig. 2-7a. Note that

(a) Constant $y = 24$

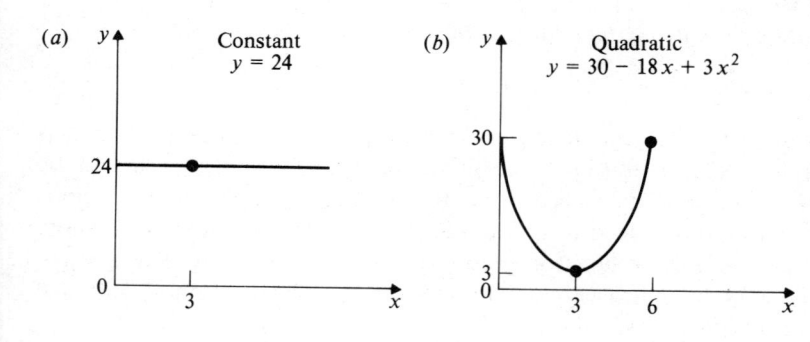

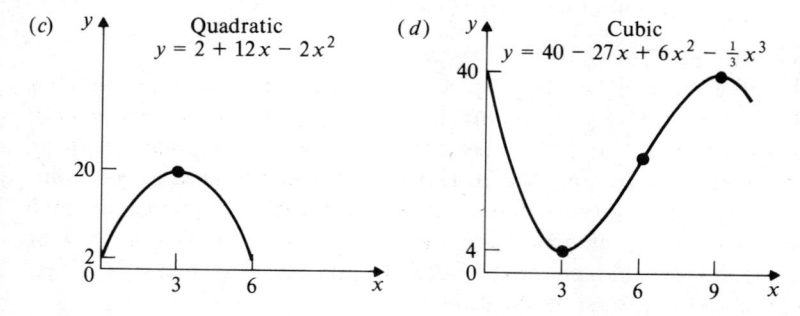

(b) Quadratic $y = 30 - 18x + 3x^2$

(c) Quadratic $y = 2 + 12x - 2x^2$

(d) Cubic $y = 40 - 27x + 6x^2 - \frac{1}{3}x^3$

Figure 2-7

since the function, in Fig. 2-7a, is of the form $y = f(x) = 24$, then $f(x)$ is always equal to 24, regardless of the value of x. For example, $f(0) = 24$, $f(3) = 24$, etc. Also, note that since the highest power of x in (2-5) is zero, (2-5) is known as a *polynomial of degree zero*.

Another form of polynomial function is given by

$$y = a_0 x^0 + a_1 x^1 = a_0 + a_1 x \qquad (2\text{-}6)$$

which is known as a *linear function*. Examples of this type of function were graphed as straight lines in Figs. 2-5 and 2-6. Since the highest power of x in (2-6) is one, (2-6) is known as a *polynomial of degree one*.

Yet another form of polynomial function is given by

$$y = a_0 x^0 + a_1 x^1 + a_2 x^2 = a_0 + a_1 x + a_2 x^2 \qquad (2\text{-}7)$$

which is known as a *quadratic function*. Examples of this type of function are graphed (for $x \geqslant 0$) in Figs. 2-7b and 2-7c, where the procedure for graphing each function is exactly the same as that used to obtain Figs. 2-5 and 2-6. In later chapters we shall encounter techniques which greatly reduce the effort involved in obtaining the graph of a function. For the present, let us note that, in general, a quadratic function graphs as a curve containing either a single 'hill' or a single 'valley'. Since the highest power of x in (2-7) is two, (2-7) is known as a *polynomial of degree two*.

To obtain a *polynomial of degree three* we simply write

$$y = a_0 x^0 + a_1 x^1 + a_2 x^2 + a_3 x^3 = a_0 + a_1 x + a_2 x^2 + a_3 x^3 \qquad (2\text{-}8)$$

which is known as a *cubic function*. An example of this type of function is graphed (for $x \geqslant 0$) in Fig. 2-7d. While the graph in Fig. 2-7d can be obtained by the procedure used in relation to Fig. 2-5, a much less tedious method will be introduced in a later chapter. For the moment, let us note that, in general, a cubic function graphs as a curve containing two 'wiggles' (as in Fig. 2-7d, in contrast to a quadratic function which contains only one 'wiggle' (as in Figs. 2-7b and c)).

Finally, the general form of a polynomial function is given by

$$y = a_0 + a_1 x + a_2 x^2 + a_3 x^3 + \ldots + a_n x^n \qquad (2\text{-}9)$$

which is known as a *polynomial of degree n*.

It should be clear, from the graphs of the various polynomial functions, that different types of polynomial functions represent different relationships between the variables y and x. Consequently, various polynomial functions, especially of degree zero, one, two or three, are frequently used in economic models to represent various economic relationships. Examples of such functions, as a means of expressing various forms of behaviour, will be encountered in later chapters of the book. In addition, we shall meet other types of functions and their application to economics.

2-7 FUNCTIONS OF MORE THAN ONE INDEPENDENT VARIABLE

In the foregoing discussion, all functions were of the form $y = f(x)$ and, as such, were functions of only *one* independent variable, x. However, the concept of a function can be easily extended to deal with the case of more than one independent variable. For example, the function

$$z = z(x, y) \qquad (2\text{-}10)$$

contains the dependent variable z and two independent variables, x and y. Examples of such functions are $z = z(x, y) = 2x + 3y$ and $z = z(x, y) = 3x^2 + 4xy + 7y^2$.

To appreciate the meaning of (2-10), recall that in the function $y = f(x)$, the functional notation f can be interpreted as a rule for mapping a set of x values (the domain) into a set of y values (the range). Similarly, in (2-10), the functional notation z represents a rule mapping a domain into a range. However, in (2-10), the domain now consists of a set of ordered pairs (x, y) rather than a set of x values. It is only when *both* x and y values are given that a z value can be determined. This can be seen clearly in Fig. 2-8a, where ordered pairs, such as (x_1, y_1) and (x_2, y_2) on the two-dimensional graph, are mapped into the unique z values z_1 and z_2 on the (vertical) one-dimensional graph. The same information is presented in the three-dimensional graph of Fig. 2-8b, where the z axis is placed perpendicular to the xy plane so that the association between the three variables is given by points such as (x_1, y_1, z_1) and (x_2, y_2, z_2). These points, on the three-dimensional graph, correspond to ordered *triples* of the three variables. If we join such points, or equivalently find their *locus*, we then obtain the graph of $z = z(x, y)$, which will take the form of a *surface* (which, for example, may look like the surface of an inverted bowl).

Functions of two independent variables are often employed in economic models. For example, we may have a consumer demand model where the quantity demanded (Q_d) depends upon the price of the good (P)

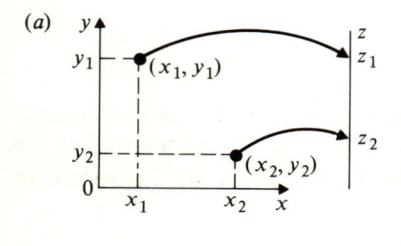

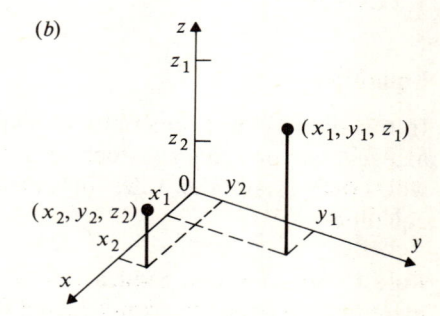

Figure 2-8

and the consumer's income (Y). In this case the demand function is of the form $Q_d = g(P, Y)$. Note that whereas $Q_d = f(P)$ is a set of ordered pairs (P, Q_d), the demand function $Q_d = g(P, Y)$ is a set of ordered triples (P, Y, Q_d).

It should now be intuitively clear that the concept of a function can be extended to any number of independent variables. For example, we could have the demand function

$$Q_{d1} = Q_{d1}(P_1, P_2, Y) \qquad (2\text{-}11)$$

where Q_{d1}, the quantity demanded of good 1, depends upon the prices of goods 1 and 2 (denoted by P_1 and P_2, respectively) and the consumer's income (Y). Since this demand function has three independent variables, it will be a set of ordered quadruples (P_1, P_2, Y, Q_{d1}). These ordered quadruples, in turn, correspond to points in four-dimensional space just as ordered pairs correspond to points in two-dimensional space. This means that we cannot graph (2-11) since we are unable to draw four-dimensional diagrams. However, despite this graphical difficulty, it is conventional to refer to ordered quadruples as 'points' in four-dimensional space. Similarly, in the more general case of a function of $n-1$ independent variables, ordered n-tuples are also referred to as 'points' in n-dimensional space. In each case, the (nongraphable) locus of the respective 'points' is known as a *hypersurface*.

In later chapters we shall encounter interesting economic applications of functions of more than one independent variable. For the moment, let us note that a function of more than one independent variable can, in general, be written as

$$y = f(x_1, x_2, x_3, \ldots, x_n) \qquad (2\text{-}12)$$

where y is the dependent variable and $x_1, x_2, x_3, \ldots, x_n$ are the independent variables.

2-8 EQUALITIES, INEQUALITIES AND ABSOLUTE VALUES

Equalities

In our discussion of functions we expressed the explicit forms of functions as *equations* or *equalities* such as $y = x$ and $y = 2 + 4x$. In this section we will briefly state the rules of operations which apply to equations or equalities.

Rule 1 (Addition and Subtraction): An equality still holds when an equal magnitude is added to or subtracted from each side of it. Thus

$$y = x \Rightarrow y \pm k = x \pm k$$

where $\Rightarrow$ reads 'implies'. For example, if $k = 2x$, then $y = (2+4x) \Rightarrow y \pm 2x = (2+4x) \pm 2x$.

Rule 2 (Multiplication and Division): An equality still holds when both sides of it are multiplied by a nonzero magnitude. Thus

$$y = x \Rightarrow ky = kx$$

For example, if $k = 4$, then $y = (2+4x) \Rightarrow 4y = 4(2+4x)$.

Rule 3 (Powers): An equality still holds when each side of it is raised to some power. Thus

$$y = x \Rightarrow y^n = x^n$$

For example, if $n = 2$, then $y = (2+4x) \Rightarrow y^2 = (2+4x)^2$.

Rule 4 (Transitivity): Equalities are *transitive*, meaning that if $y = x$ and $x = z$, then $y = z$.

Inequalities

An inequality may appear in the form $y > 2+4x$ (meaning that y is greater than $2+4x$) or $y \geqslant 2+4x$ (meaning that y is greater than or equal to $2+4x$). Conversely, an inequality may appear in the form $2+4x < y$ (meaning that $2+4x$ is less than y) or $2+4x \leqslant y$ (meaning that $2+4x$ is less than or equal to y). The following rules of operations for inequalities hold for both strong (or strict) inequalities (denoted by $>$ and $<$) and weak inequalities (denoted by $\geqslant$ and $\leqslant$). [*Warning:* Rules 2 and 3 for inequalities differ somewhat from Rules 2 and 3 for equalities.]

Rule 1 (Addition and Subtraction): An inequality still holds when an equal magnitude is added to or subtracted from each side of it. Thus

$$y > x \Rightarrow y \pm k > x \pm k$$

For example, if $k = -3 + 2x$, then $y > (2+4x) \Rightarrow y - 3 + 2x > (2+4x) - 3 + 2x$.

Rule 2 (Multiplication and Division): (*a*) An inequality still holds when both sides of it are multiplied by a *positive* magnitude. Thus

$$y > x \Rightarrow ky > kx \quad (k > 0)$$

For example, if $k = 6$, then $y > (2+4x) \Rightarrow 6y > 6(2+4x)$.

(b) The direction of an inequality is *reversed* when both sides of it are multiplied by a *negative* magnitude. Thus

$$y > x \Rightarrow ky < kx \quad (k < 0)$$

For example, if $k = -3$, then $y > (2+4x) \Rightarrow -3y < -3(2+4x)$.

Rule 3 (Powers): (a) If both sides of an inequality are *nonnegative*, the inequality still holds when both sides of it are raised to a *positive* power. Thus

$$y > x \Rightarrow y^n > x^n \quad (y, x \geq 0; n > 0)$$

For example, if $n = 2$ and x and y are both nonnegative, then $y > (2+4x) \Rightarrow y^2 > (2+4x)^2$.

(b) If both sides of an inequality are *positive*, the direction of the inequality is *reversed* when both sides of it are raised to a *negative* power. Thus

$$y > x \Rightarrow y^n < x^n \quad (y, x > 0; n < 0)$$

For example, if $n = -3$ and x and y are both positive, then $y > (2+4x) \Rightarrow y^{-3} < (2+4x)^{-3}$. [*Warning*: it is important to note the restrictions imposed upon x, y, and n in Rule 3.]

Rule 4 (Transitivity): Inequalities are *transitive*, meaning that if $y > x$ and $x > z$, then $y > z$.

Absolute Values

The *absolute value* of a real number x is the numerical value of x regardless of its sign, with the absolute value of x being denoted by $|x|$. Definitionally, we have

$$|x| = \begin{cases} x & (\text{if } x > 0) \\ -x & (\text{if } x < 0) \\ 0 & (\text{if } x = 0) \end{cases} \quad (2\text{-}13)$$

For example, if $x = 3$, then $|3| = 3$; but if $x = -3$, then the application of (2-13) for $x < 0$ gives $|-3| = -(-3) = 3$. This means that the expression $|x| = 3$ may imply $x = 3$ or $x = -3$. Hence if we have $|x| < 3$ this may imply that: (a) if $x > 0$, then $|x| = x$ by (2-13). Since $|x| < 3$, then $x < 3$ also; or (b) if $x < 0$, then $|x| = -x$ by (2-13). Since $|x| < 3$, then $-x < 3$ also, or $x > -3$. Therefore, from (a) and (b), $|x| < 3 \Leftrightarrow -3 < x < 3$, where $\Leftrightarrow$ reads 'implies and is implied by'. In general we can state that

$$|x| < a \Leftrightarrow -a < x < a \quad (a > 0) \quad (2\text{-}14)$$

which also holds for the $\leq$ case:

$$|x| \leq a \Leftrightarrow -a \leq x \leq a \quad (a \geq 0) \quad (2\text{-}15)$$

2-E PRACTICE PROBLEMS

2-17 State whether each of the following is true or false:
(a) $y = (x^2+2x)^2 \Rightarrow y-3x^3 = (x^2+2x)^2 - 3x^3$
(b) $y = (x^{2/3}-2)^{1/3} \Rightarrow y^{3/4} = (x^{2/3}-2)^{1/4}$
(c) $y^2 = (x^4+10x)^{-3} \Rightarrow y^{-1} \neq (x^4+10x)^{3/2}$
(d) $y = 2x^3 + 5x \Rightarrow 4^{1/3}y \neq 4^{1/3}(2x^3+5x)$

2-18 State whether each of the following is true or false:
(a) $y < (ax^2+bx)^3 \Rightarrow y-d < (ax^2+bx)^3 - d$ (b) $11 \geq 2 \Rightarrow -143 \leq -26$
(c) $y \leq (5x^3 - 3x)^{-5} \Rightarrow -6y \geq -6(5x^3-3x)^{-5}$ (d) $\frac{a}{b} > \frac{c}{d} \Rightarrow \frac{b}{a} < \frac{d}{c}$
(e) $\frac{2}{3} \geq \frac{1}{9} \Rightarrow (\frac{2}{3})^{1/3} \leq (\frac{1}{9})^{1/3}$ (f) $\frac{1}{2} > \frac{1}{4} \Rightarrow (\frac{1}{2})^{-2} < (\frac{1}{4})^{-2}$

2-19 Use Rules 1 and 2 for inequalities to show that each of the following are valid:
(a) $5x+6 > x-2 \Rightarrow x > -2$ (b) $9x^3 - 4x > 3x^3 + 2x \Rightarrow x^2 > 1$

2-20 State whether each of the following are true or false:
(a) $|-9| = |9| = 9$ (b) $|y| \leq 7 \Leftrightarrow -7 \leq y \leq 7$

2-9 LOGARITHMS

If we have two numbers such as 9 and 3, which are related by the equation $9 = 3^2$, then the *power* 2 can be defined as the *logarithm* (or, log for short) of 9 to the *base* of 3. Thus we can write

$$9 = 3^2 \Leftrightarrow 2 = \log_3 9$$

In other words, a logarithm is simply the power (such as 2) to which a base (such as 3) must be raised to give a particular number (such as 9). Similarly

$$4 = 16^{1/2} \Leftrightarrow \tfrac{1}{2} = \log_{16} 4$$

Or, in general, we can write

$$y = a^x \Leftrightarrow x = \log_a y \quad (a > 0, a \neq 1; \therefore y > 0) \tag{2-16}$$

which states that the log of y to the base a (written as $\log_a y$) is the power to which the base a must be raised to give the value y. It should be noted in (2-16) that a negative number or zero does not possess a logarithm. Also, note that (2-16) can be equivalently written as

$$y = a^x = a^{\log_a y}$$

Common Logarithms

In the logarithm definition (2-16), the base of the logarithm (a) can be any positive number other than one. When the number 10 is taken as the base, the logarithm is known as a *common logarithm*, written as $\log_{10}$. Thus we have

32 THE MATHEMATICAL REPRESENTATION OF ECONOMIC RELATIONSHIPS

$$y = 10^x \Leftrightarrow x = \log_{10} y \qquad (2\text{-}17)$$

Examples of common logarithms, obtained from (2-17), are as follows:

$$100 = 10^2 \Leftrightarrow 2 = \log_{10} 100$$
$$10 = 10^1 \Leftrightarrow 1 = \log_{10} 10$$
$$1 = 10^0 \Leftrightarrow 0 = \log_{10} 1$$
$$0.1 = 10^{-1} \Leftrightarrow -1 = \log_{10} 0.1$$
$$0.01 = 10^{-2} \Leftrightarrow -2 = \log_{10} 0.01$$

Note, in these examples, that $\log_{10} 10 = 1$ and $\log_{10} 1 = 0$. Also, note that the common logarithm of a number between 10 and 100 will be a value between 1 and 2. Similarly, the common logarithm of a number between 1 and 10 will be a value between 0 and 1. While the exact logarithms of such numbers can be readily obtained from common logarithm tables, we shall not be concerned with such tables here.

Natural Logarithms

When the irrational number $e \simeq 2.71828$ (where $\simeq$ reads 'approximately equals') is taken as the base, the logarithm is known as a *natural logarithm*, written as $\log_e$ or ln (meaning natural log). Thus we have

$$y = e^x \Leftrightarrow x = \log_e y = \ln y \qquad (2\text{-}18)$$

At first sight, $e \simeq 2.718$ appears to be a very awkward and unusual base to choose in comparison to the base 10. However, there is good reason for this choice. While common logarithms are very convenient in *computational* work, natural logarithms are much more convenient in *theoretical* work. Unfortunately, however, we must wait until later chapters to appreciate both the mathematical convenience of the base e and to obtain an economic interpretation of e. For the present, let us note the following examples of natural logarithms, obtained from (2-18):

$$y = e^2 \Leftrightarrow 2 = \log_e e^2 = \ln e^2$$
$$y = e^1 \Leftrightarrow 1 = \log_e e^1 = \ln e$$
$$y = e^0 \Leftrightarrow 0 = \log_e e^0 = \ln 1$$
$$y = e^{-1} \Leftrightarrow -1 = \log_e e^{-1} = \ln \frac{1}{e}$$

Note, in these examples, that $\log_e e^1 = \log_e e = 1$ and $\ln 1 = \log_e 1 = 0$. Also, note in general that $\log_e e^n = n$.

Finally, in the following statement of the rules of logarithms, we shall see that it is possible to convert logarithms from one base to another.

Rules of Logarithms

Since, by definition, a logarithm is the exponent to which some base must be raised to give a particular number, we would expect logarithms to obey rules similar to the rules of exponents or indices. This, in fact, is the case. Note that while the following rules are stated in terms of natural logarithms, they also hold for logarithms to any base a ($a > 0, a \neq 1$).

Rule 1: $\ln e = 1$
Similarly, $\log_{10} 10 = \log_a a = 1$.

Rule 2: $\ln 1 = 0$
Similarly, $\log_{10} 1 = \log_a 1 = 0$.

Rule 3 (Log of a Product): $\ln(xy) = \ln x + \ln y$ ($x, y > 0$)
For example, $\ln(e^9 e^{1/2}) = \ln e^9 + \ln e^{1/2} = 9 + \frac{1}{2} = 9\frac{1}{2}$. Similarly, $\ln(ke^{-3}) = \ln k + \ln e^{-3} = \ln k - 3$. Also, for $x, y, z > 0$, $\ln(xyz) = \ln x + \ln y + \ln z$.

Rule 4 (Log of a Quotient): $\ln(x/y) = \ln x - \ln y$ ($x, y > 0$)
For example, $\ln(e^{10}/e^{1/3}) = \ln e^{10} - \ln e^{1/3} = 10 - \frac{1}{3} = 9\frac{2}{3}$. Similarly, $\ln(k/2) = \ln k - \ln 2$. Also, for $x, y, z > 0$, $\ln(xy/z) = \ln xy - \ln z = \ln x + \ln y - \ln z$.

Rule 5 (Log of a Power): $\ln x^n = n \ln x$ ($x > 0$)
For example, $\ln(e^3) = 3 \ln e = 3$. Similarly, $\ln(k^{-1/2}) = -\frac{1}{2} \ln k$.

Note that Rule 5 may be used in combination with Rules 3 and 4. For example, $\ln(xy^2) = \ln x + \ln y^2 = \ln x + 2 \ln y$. Similarly, $\ln(x^2/y^{-3}) = \ln x^2 - \ln y^{-3} = 2 \ln x + 3 \ln y$. [*Warning*: $\ln(x \pm y) \neq \ln x \pm \ln y$.]

Rules 3, 4 and 5 indicate how logarithms can be used to simplify mathematical operations. Thus, in these three rules (which should be compared to Rules 1, 2 and 5 of indices in Sec. 2-5), logarithms convert a multiplicative operation into an additive one, a division operation into an operation involving subtraction, and a power operation into a multiplicative one, respectively. Consequently, logarithms are often used to simplify certain economic relationships. For example, the *Cobb–Douglas production function*, which is of form

$$Q = f(K, L) = AK^\alpha L^\beta \quad (A > 0; 0 < \alpha, \beta < 1)$$

(where Q = output; K, L = inputs of the productive services, capital and labour, respectively; A, α, β = parameters), can be written in simple linear form using logarithms as follows:

$$\ln Q = \ln A + \alpha \ln K + \beta \ln L \tag{2-19}$$

Equation (2-19) is linear in the three variables $\ln Q$, $\ln K$ and $\ln L$. The Cobb–Douglas production function, and this type of linear transformation via logarithms, will be encountered in more detail in later chapters.

Rule 6 (Conversion of Log Base): $\log_a x = (\log_a b)(\log_b x)$ $(x > 0)$
For example, $\log_{10} x = (\log_{10} e)(\log_e x)$. Thus if we know the value of $\log_{10} x$ and $\log_{10} e = \log_{10}(2.71828)$, then the value of $\log_e x$ is simply $(\log_{10} x / \log_{10} e)$ by Rule 6. As a mnemonic device, note that the right-hand side of Rule 6 contains the 'chain'

$$\underset{a}{\diagup}\overset{b}{\diagdown}\underset{b}{\diagup}\overset{x}{\diagdown}$$

Rule 7 (Inversion of Log Base): $\log_a b = 1/\log_b a$
For example, $\log_e 10 = 1/\log_{10} e$. Thus if we know the value of $\log_{10} e$, then the value of $\log_e 10$ is simply the reciprocal of $\log_{10} e$.

Formulae for Conversion between Common and Natural Logarithms

Common logarithm tables indicate that $\log_{10} e = \log_{10}(2.71828) = 0.4343$. Hence, by Rule 7, $\log_e 10 = 1/\log_{10} e = 2.3026$. This permits us, via Rule 6, to write out the conversion formulae between common and natural logarithms as follows:

$$\log_{10} x = (\log_{10} e)(\log_e x) = 0.4343 \log_e x$$
$$\log_e x = (\log_e 10)(\log_{10} x) = 2.3026 \log_{10} x \quad (2\text{-}20)$$

For example, $\log_e(1000) = 2.3026 \log_{10}(1000) = 2.3026(3) = 6.9078$. Using this result, we can see that $\log_{10}(1000) = 0.4343 \log_e(1000) = 0.4343(6.9078) = 3$.

2-F PRACTICE PROBLEMS

2-21 Find the values of the following logarithms:
(a) $\log_{10}(0.001)$ (b) $\log_{10} t^0$ (c) $\log_{10}(1/10^5)$ (d) $\log_{10}(100{,}000)$
(e) $\ln e^7$ (f) $\ln x^0$ (g) $\ln e^{-5}$ (h) $\ln e$ (i) $\log_u u$ (j) $\log_7 49$
(k) $\log_{27} 3$ (l) $\log_2 64$

2-22 Express the following logarithmic expressions in exponential form (e.g., $2 = \log_3 9$ becomes $9 = 3^2$):
(a) $\frac{1}{5} = \log_{32} 2$ (b) $4 = \log_4 256$ (c) $-4 = \log_{1/3} 81$ (d) $1 = \log_t t$
(e) $0 = \ln x^0$

2-23 Use the rules of logarithms to evaluate each of the following:
(a) $\log_{10}(0.0001)^{-17}$ (b) $1/(\log_{125} 5)$ (c) $(\log_2 e)(\log_e 128)$
(d) $\ln 19 e^{1/3}$ (e) $\log_{10}(A/B)$ (f) $\ln xyze^{-9}$ (g) $\ln(e/w)^3$
(h) $2 \log_{10} 100t$

2-24 If $\log_{10} 4 = 0.6021$, evaluate each of the following (without tables):
(a) $\log_{10} 16$ (b) $\log_{10}(1/64)$

2-25 State whether each of the following is true or false:
(a) $\ln r - \ln s + \ln t = \ln(rt/s)$ (b) $\log_{10}(6+3) = \log_{10} 6 + \log_{10} 3$
(c) $\ln \frac{1}{2} + \ln \frac{1}{2} = \ln 1 = 0$ (d) $3 - \ln a - \ln b = \ln(e^3/ab)$

CHAPTER THREE

STATIC-EQUILIBRIUM MODELS

In this chapter we shall extend our knowledge of linear functions and their meaning when applied to economic models. This extension of our knowledge will then permit us to make a mathematical analysis of static-equilibrium models that are familiar to introductory microeconomic and macroeconomic courses. In addition to the analysis of linear static-equilibrium models, we shall also analyse a nonlinear static-equilibrium model.

3-1 THE SLOPE OF A STRAIGHT LINE

In Sec. 2-6 we noted that any linear function can be represented by the general formulation

$$y = f(x) = a + bx \qquad (3\text{-}1)$$

where x, y = variables, and a, b = parameters. If we now assume that a and b are both positive, then we can obtain the graph of (3-1) as follows:

1. Find the y intercept by letting $x = 0$. Thus, when $x = 0$, $y = a$, which permits us to plot the y intercept point $(0, a)$ as shown in Fig. 3-1.
2. Find the x intercept by letting $y = 0$. Thus, when $y = 0$, $x = -a/b$ (i.e., using the rules for equalities we have firstly, $y = a + bx = 0 \Rightarrow a + bx - a = 0 - a$ or $bx = -a$. Secondly, $bx = -a \Rightarrow (1/b)(bx) = (1/b)(-a)$ or $x = -a/b$). This permits us to plot the x intercept point $(-a/b, 0)$ as shown in Fig. 3-1.

36 STATIC-EQUILIBRIUM MODELS

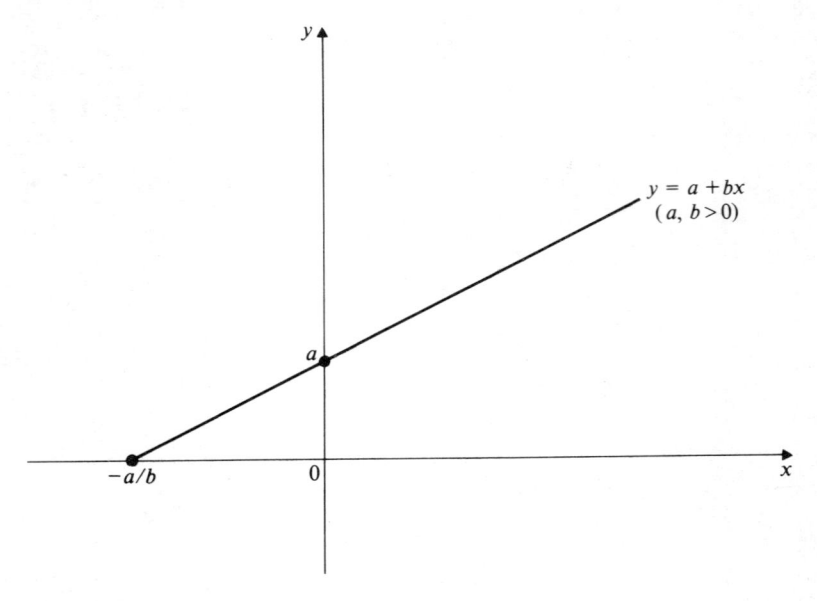

Figure 3-1

3. Since $y = a + bx$ is a linear function, which plots as a straight line, then we simply draw a straight line through $(-a/b, 0)$ and $(0, a)$, as shown in Fig. 3-1, to obtain the graph of $y = a + bx$.

The above procedure, for obtaining the graph of $y = a + bx$, demonstrates that the parameters a and b permit us to locate the intercepts of the line $y = a + bx$. This means that a and b have a particular graphical interpretation in terms of intercepts, with a locating the y intercept and $-a/b$ locating the x intercept. In addition to this, as will be explained below, the parameter b can be given a further graphical interpretation in terms of the *slope* of the line $y = a + bx$.

To obtain the interpretation of b as the slope of the line $y = a + bx$, let us firstly note that the function (3-1) permits us to map certain x values into their corresponding y values. Thus, if we take $x = x_1$, the corresponding y value is

$$y_1 = f(x_1) = a + bx_1 \tag{3-2}$$

Similarly, if we change the value of x from $x = x_1$ to $x = x_2$, the corresponding y value will change from y_1 to

$$y_2 = f(x_2) = a + bx_2 \tag{3-3}$$

If we now subtract Eq. (3-2) from Eq. (3-3) we obtain

3-1 THE SLOPE OF A STRAIGHT LINE

$$y_2 - y_1 = a + bx_2 - a - bx_1$$

or
$$y_2 - y_1 = bx_2 - bx_1 = b(x_2 - x_1) \qquad (3\text{-}4)$$

which states that the change in variable y (measured by the difference $y_2 - y_1$) is equal to b times the change in variable x (measured by the difference $x_2 - x_1$). Or, by introducing the symbol Δ, which reads as 'delta', to denote the change in a variable, we can rewrite (3-4) as

$$\Delta y = b \Delta x \qquad (3\text{-}5)$$

where $\Delta y = y_2 - y_1$ and $\Delta x = x_2 - x_1$. Finally, dividing (3-5) by Δx gives

$$\frac{\Delta y}{\Delta x} = b \qquad (3\text{-}6)$$

which states that b is equal to the ratio $\Delta y / \Delta x$. As will be seen below, this ratio can be given an important graphical interpretation.

The ratio $\Delta y / \Delta x$, which is known as the *difference quotient*, represents the change in y per unit of change in x or, in graphical terms, the *slope* of the line $y = a + bx$. Thus, just as the slope or gradient of a uniformly rising stretch of road is the vertical distance divided by the horizontal distance, the slope or gradient of the line $y = a + bx$ in Fig. 3-2 is simply the vertical change in y (given by Δy) divided by the horizontal change in x (given by Δx). Therefore $\Delta y / \Delta x = b$ is the *slope* of the line $y = a + bx$. Also, note that since $y = a + bx$ in Fig. 3-2 is a straight line, its slope is *constant* as indicated by $\Delta y / \Delta x$ being equal to the constant b.

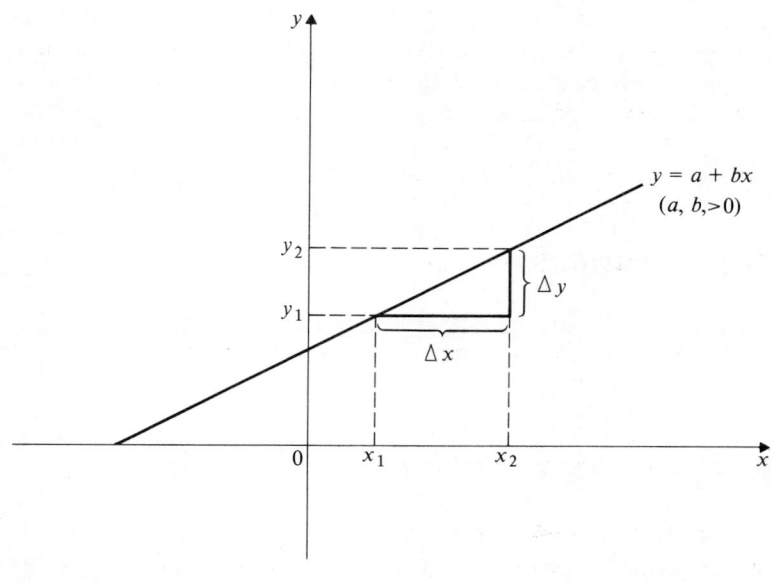

Figure 3-2

(a) Graph: $y = a + bx = 15 - 3x$, y-intercept 15, x-intercept 5.

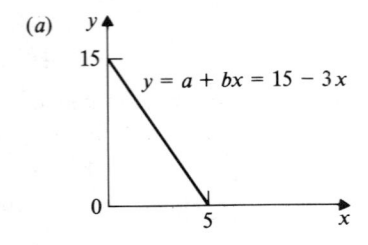

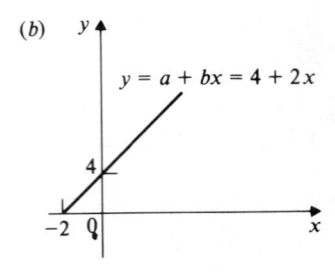

(b) Graph: $y = a + bx = 4 + 2x$, y-intercept 4, x-intercept −2.

Figure 3-3

In Fig. 3-2, the line $y = a + bx$ has been drawn with a *positive* slope since $b > 0$. If $b < 0$, then the line would be drawn with a *negative* slope. For example, in Fig. 3-3a, where $b = -3$, the line $y = 15 - 3x$ has a negative slope. In Fig. 3-3b, where $b = 2$, the line $y = 4 + 2x$ has a positive slope.

The two examples given in Fig. 3-3 help us to appreciate the exact information given by $\Delta y/\Delta x = b$. Thus, in Fig. 3-3a, $\Delta y/\Delta x = b = -3$ indicates that a unit increase (decrease) in x will be associated with a 3 unit decrease (increase) in y. Similarly, in Fig. 3-3b, $\Delta y/\Delta x = b = 2$ indicates that a unit increase (decrease) in x will be associated with a 2 unit increase (decrease) in y. In other words, $\Delta y/\Delta x = b$ provides us with information about (a) the *direction* of change in y in response to a unit change in x (i.e., whether y changes in the same direction as x ($b > 0$) or in the opposite direction to x ($b < 0$)) and (b) the *magnitude* of the change in y in response to a unit change in x (e.g., when $b = -3$ or $b = 2$, a unit change in x results in a 3 unit or 2 unit change in y in the opposite or same direction, respectively). Therefore, given a linear demand function $Q_d = f(P) = a + bP = 20 - 4P$, the ratio $\Delta Q_d/\Delta P = b = -4$ tells us that a unit increase (decrease) in P will result in a 4 unit decrease (increase) in Q_d.

3-A PRACTICE PROBLEMS

3-1 Graph the function $y = a + bx$ for each of the following values of a and b:
(a) $a > 0, b < 0$ (b) $a, b > 0$ (c) $a = 0, b > 0$ (d) $a = 0, b = 1$
(e) $a < 0, b > 0$ (f) $a > 0, b = 0$.

3-2 MARKET DEMAND AND SUPPLY

In Chapter 2 we encountered a simple model of consumer demand, which stated that the quantity demanded of a good (per time period) by an *individual* consumer is a function of the price of the good. In this section we will examine the *market* demand for a good, meaning the aggregate quantity demanded by *all* buyers (or consumers) of a good (per time period) at various prices. Also, we will examine the *market* supply of a good, meaning the aggregate quantities supplied by *all* sellers (or producers) of a good (per time period) at various prices.

Before proceeding to examine market demand and supply, it should be noted that our attention will be confined solely to a *competitive market*. In other words, we will only be dealing with a market where the number of buyers and sellers is so great that no one buyer or seller can individually control or significantly influence the market price of the good in question.

The *market* demand function for a good may be assumed to have the form

$$Q_{d1} = Q_{d1}(P_1, P_2, \ldots, P_n, Y, L, D) \tag{3-7}$$

where Q_{d1}, the quantity demanded of good 1, depends upon the price of good 1 (denoted by P_1), the prices of goods $2, \ldots, n$ (denoted by $P_2, \ldots, P_n$), consumers' income (denoted by Y), the size of the population (denoted by L), and the distribution of income among consumers (denoted by D). Unfortunately, since the demand function given in (3-7) is too complicated for us to handle at this stage of the book, we shall limit our attention solely to the relationship between the market demand for a good and its price. Thus, we shall assume the market demand function to have the following simple form:

$$Q_d = f(P) = a - bP \quad (a, b > 0) \tag{3-8}$$

Equation (3-8) states that the market demand (Q_d) for a good is a linear function of the price (P) of the good, with Q_d and P being regarded as the endogenous and exogenous variables, respectively.

The market demand function (3-8) is graphed (for $P \geq 0$) in Fig. 3-4 as a

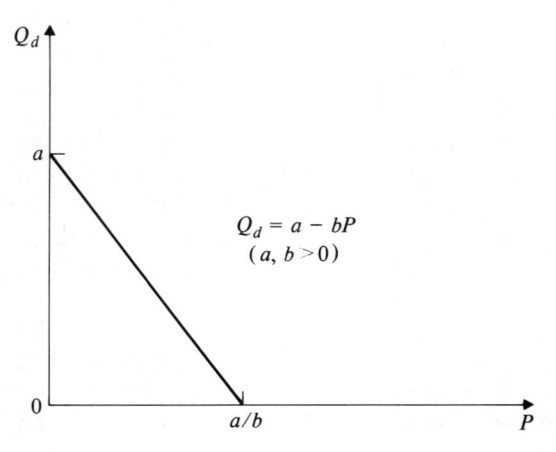

Figure 3-4

negative-sloped straight line with vertical intercept a and slope $-b$. As such, the line $Q_d = a - bP$ in Fig. 3-4 represents a particular relationship between consumers' demand *behaviour* and the price of the good in question. Thus an examination of Fig. 3-4 indicates that (*a*) when $P = 0$, $Q_d = a$, (*b*) when $P = a/b$, $Q_d = 0$, (*c*) a unit increase (decrease) in P results in Q_d decreasing (increasing) by b units. In this respect, it is important to note the role played by the values of the parameters a and b in this representation of consumers' demand behaviour. Clearly, if $a > 0$ and $b < 0$, then instead of the familiar downward-sloping demand curve, as in Fig. 3-4, we would have an upward-sloping demand curve.

The *market* supply function for a good may be assumed to have the form

$$Q_{s1} = Q_{s1}(P_1, P_2, \ldots, P_n, F_1, \ldots, F_m, T) \qquad (3\text{-}9)$$

where Q_{s1}, the quantity supplied of good 1, depends upon the price of good 1 (denoted by P_1), the prices of goods $2,\ldots,n$ (denoted by $P_2,\ldots,P_n$), the prices of factors of production such as capital, labour, etc. (denoted by $F_1,\ldots,F_m$), and the prevailing state of technological progress (denoted by T). Unfortunately, as was the case with (3-7), the market supply function (3-9) is too complex to handle with our present knowledge. Consequently, we shall confine our attention solely to the relationship between the market supply of a good and its price. Thus, we shall assume the market supply function to have the following simple form:

$$Q_s = g(P) = -c + dP \qquad (c, d > 0) \qquad (3\text{-}10)$$

Equation (3-10) states that the market supply (Q_s) of a good is a linear function of the price (P) of the good, with Q_s and P being regarded as the endogenous and exogenous variables, respectively.

The market supply function (3-10) is graphed (for $P \geq 0$) in Fig. 3-5 as a positive-sloped straight line with vertical intercept $-c$ and slope d. As such, the line $Q_s = -c + dP$ in Fig. 3-5 represents a particular relationship between producers' supply *behaviour* and the price of the good in question. Thus an examination of Fig. 3-5 indicates that (*a*) $Q_s \geq 0$ only when $P \geq c/d$, meaning that supply will not be forthcoming unless P is greater than c/d, and (*b*) a unit increase (decrease) in P results in Q_s increasing (decreasing) by d units. Once more, it is important to note the role played by the values of the parameters c and d in this representation of producers' supply behaviour. Clearly, if $c > 0$ and $d < 0$, then instead of the familiar upward-sloping supply curve, as in Fig. 3-5, we would have a downward-sloping supply curve.

It should be noted that Figs. 3-4 and 3-5, in contrast to most economics textbooks, have been drawn with Q_d and Q_s, rather than P, on the vertical axes. The reason for this, as noted in Sec. 2-4, is that Figs. 3-4 and 3-5 follow the mathematical convention of placing the *dependent* variable on

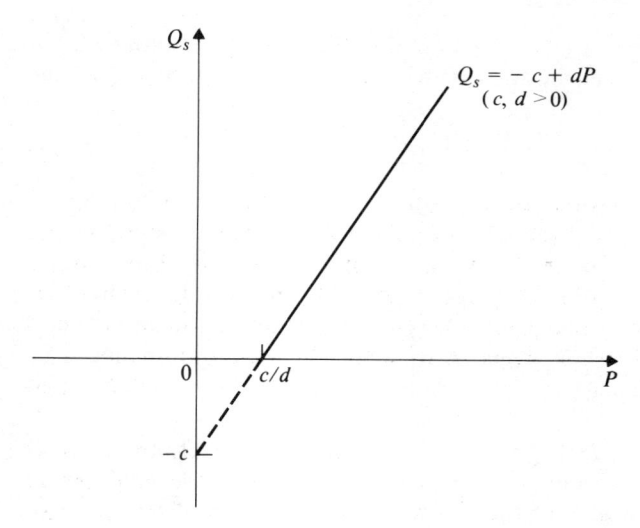

Figure 3-5

A graph showing $Q_s = -c + dP$ $(c, d > 0)$ with vertical axis Q_s and horizontal axis P, intersecting the P-axis at c/d and the Q_s-axis at $-c$.

the vertical axis. The reader should be convinced that Figs. 3-4 and 3-5 can easily be redrawn with the axes reversed. Also, it should be noted that since Eqs. (3-8) and (3-10) represent the behaviour of consumers and producers, they are known as *behavioural equations*.

With the above knowledge of market demand and supply, we are now in a position to proceed to the analysis of a simple linear partial-equilibrium market model.

3-3 A LINEAR PARTIAL-EQUILIBRIUM MARKET MODEL

In this section we shall combine our models of market demand and supply, as given by the equations $Q_d = f(P) = a - bP$ and $Q_s = g(P) = -c + dP$, respectively, into a model of the determination of the market price of a good. To do this we shall assume that the good in question is bought and sold in an isolated market, with changes in this market having negligible effects on other parts of the economy, and vice versa. In other words, our analysis will be a *partial* analysis, not allowing for interactions between the market under consideration and the rest of the economy.

As a first step in our analysis, it is important to remember that the market demand and supply functions represent the *behaviour* of consumers and producers. Thus, these functions represent the intentions or plans of buyers and sellers to purchase or sell certain quantities of the good in response to certain prices. When these intentions coincide, in the sense that the quantity demanded is exactly equal to the quantity supplied, a state of balance or *equilibrium* is said to prevail. Consequently, to ensure such an equilibrium in our market model, it is necessary to specify an *equilibrium condition* of the form

$$Q_d = Q_s \tag{3-11}$$

Equation (3-11) embodies the assumption that equilibrium will be attained in the market if and only if the quantity demanded is exactly equal to the quantity supplied or, if and only if excess demand $(Q_d - Q_s)$ is zero. In other words, equilibrium will obtain if and only if the market is 'cleared'. It should be noted that, in keeping with our assumptions, the equilibrium referred to is a *partial equilibrium*. Also, since this equilibrium has been defined as a state of balance (with no tendency to change), it may be termed a *static equilibrium*.

The introduction of (3-11) means that the market model now consists of the two behavioural equations (3-8) and (3-10), plus the equilibrium condition (3-11). Consequently, the model can be written mathematically as

$$\begin{aligned} Q_d &= Q_s \\ Q_d &= a - bP \quad (a, b > 0) \\ Q_s &= -c + dP \quad (c, d > 0) \end{aligned} \tag{3-12}$$

With the competitive market model constructed as in (3-12), the next step is to solve it. In mathematical terminology, we want to obtain the values of the three variables Q_d, Q_s and P, which satisfy the three equations in (3-12) simultaneously. These solution values, which will be denoted by $\bar{Q}_d$, $\bar{Q}_s$, and $\bar{P}$, are known as the *equilibrium values* of the variables Q_d, Q_s, and P.

Before proceeding to illustrate the solution of (3-12) graphically, it is important to note that *all* the three variables (Q_d, Q_s, and P) in (3-12) are *endogenous* variables, with their equilibrium values to be determined within the partial-equilibrium market model. Note also that, since $\bar{Q}_d = \bar{Q}_s$, we can write $\bar{Q} = \bar{Q}_d = \bar{Q}_s$.

In Fig. 3-6, the solution of (3-12) is presented in graphical form. An examination of Fig. 3-6, which graphs the market demand and supply functions on the one diagram, makes it immediately clear that there is only one price, $\bar{P}$, for which $Q_d = Q_s$. This price is given by the intersection of the demand and supply curves, as shown in Fig. 3-6. Mathematically when $P = \bar{P}$, we have

$$\bar{Q}_d = f(\bar{P}) = g(\bar{P}) = \bar{Q}_s \tag{3-13}$$

The price, $\bar{P}$, which equates Q_d with Q_s is called the *equilibrium price*. Similarly, $\bar{Q} = \bar{Q}_d = \bar{Q}_s$ is called the *equilibrium quantity*. Thus the equilibrium solution of (3-12) is given by the ordered pair $(\bar{P}, \bar{Q})$.

Figure 3-6 indicates how the solution of the market model (3-12) may be determined graphically at the intersection of the demand and supply

3-3 A LINEAR PARTIAL-EQUILIBRIUM MARKET MODEL

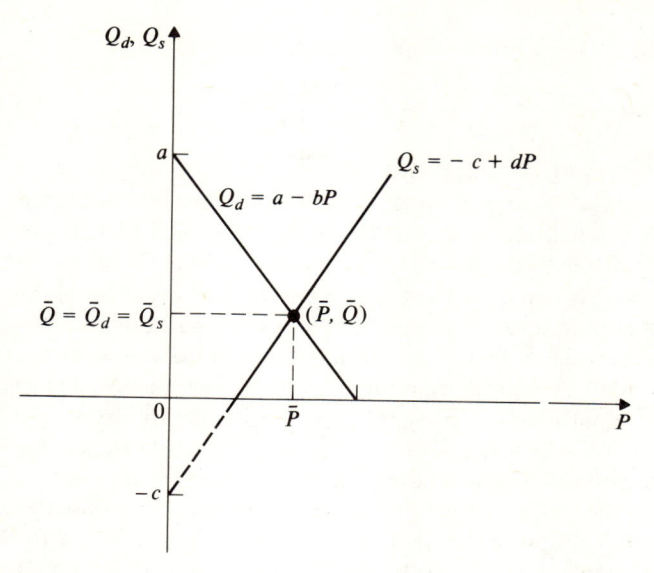

Figure 3-6

curves. Now we can see how this solution may also be obtained by solving the three equations in (3-12) simultaneously. To do this, we simply substitute the last two equations of (3-12) into the first equation of (3-12) as follows:

$$Q_d = Q_s$$
$$\text{or} \quad a - bP = -c + dP \tag{3-14}$$

Note that this step has enabled us to reduce the three-equation three-variable model of (3-12) to the one-equation one-variable model of (3-14). Applying the rules of equalities to (3-14) we obtain

$$a + c = dP + bP \quad \text{or} \quad a + c = (d+b)P$$

which, upon dividing each side by $(d+b)$, gives the solution value of P as

$$\bar{P} = \frac{a+c}{d+b} \tag{3-15}$$

The next step is to find the equilibrium quantity, $\bar{Q} = \bar{Q}_d = \bar{Q}_s$, that corresponds to the equilibrium price, $\bar{P}$. To do this, we substitute (3-15) into *either* of the last two equations of (3-12), and then solve the resulting equation for $\bar{Q}$. For example, substituting (3-15) into the demand function, we obtain

$$\bar{Q} = a - b\bar{P} = a - \frac{b(a+c)}{(d+b)} = \frac{a(d+b) - b(a+c)}{(d+b)} = \frac{ad - bc}{d+b} \tag{3-16}$$

Similarly, substituting (3-15) into the supply function, we obtain

$$\bar{Q} = -c + d\bar{P} = -c + \frac{d(a+c)}{(d+b)} = \frac{-c(d+b)+d(a+c)}{(d+b)} = \frac{ad-bc}{d+b} \quad (3\text{-}17)$$

It should be noted, in (3-15) and (3-16), that $\bar{P}$ and $\bar{Q}$ are expressions in terms of the parameters a, b, c and d. Since these parameters were assumed given, and therefore known, in the construction of the model (3-12), this means that $\bar{P}$ and $\bar{Q}$ are determinate values. However, while $\bar{P}$ and $\bar{Q}$ are determinate values, we also require them to be positive in order to make economic sense. An examination of the expression for $\bar{P}$ indicates that the denominator and numerator of (3-15) are both positive, since $a, b, c, d > 0$. Thus $\bar{P} > 0$ as required. A similar examination of the expression for $\bar{Q}$ shows that the denominator of (3-16) is positive. Consequently, to ensure $\bar{Q} > 0$, the numerator $(ad-bc)$ of (3-16) must be positive also. Hence, for $\bar{Q} > 0$ we require the additional restriction on the parameters of $ad > bc$.

In graphical terms, the above restrictions on the parameters $(a, b, c, d > 0;\ ad > bc)$ simply mean that the intercepts and slopes of the market demand and supply curves must be such to ensure that these curves intersect in the first quadrant to give $\bar{P}, \bar{Q} > 0$ as in Fig. 3-6.

Finally, the generality of the model (3-12), and its solution given in (3-15) and (3-16), should be noted. In other words, since the parameters a, b, c and d can take on any values, subject to the restrictions $a, b, c, d > 0$ and $ad > bc$, then the model (3-12) and its solution in (3-15) and (3-16), represents a whole family of linear partial-equilibrium market models.

Examples of Linear Partial-Equilibrium Models

3-2 For each of the following linear partial-equilibrium market models, find $\bar{P}$ and $\bar{Q}$:

(a) $Q_d = Q_s$
$Q_d = 20 - 7P$
$Q_s = -4 + 5P$

(b) $Q_d = Q_s$
$Q_d = 27 - 4P$
$Q_s = -3 + 2P$

SOLUTION

(a)
$$Q_d = Q_s$$
or $20 - 7P = -4 + 5P$
$\therefore\ 24 = 12P \Rightarrow \bar{P} = 2$

Substituting $\bar{P} = 2$ into Q_d (or Q_s) gives $\bar{Q} = \bar{Q}_d(=\bar{Q}_s) = 20 - 7\bar{P} = 20 - 7(2) = 6$. Thus $(\bar{P}, \bar{Q}) = (2, 6)$.

(b)
$$Q_d = Q_s$$
or $27 - 4P = -3 + 2P$
$\therefore\ 30 = 6P \Rightarrow \bar{P} = 5$

Substituting $\bar{P} = 5$ into Q_s (or Q_d) gives $\bar{Q} = \bar{Q}_s(=\bar{Q}_d) = -3 + 2\bar{P} = -3 + 2(5) = 7$. Thus $(\bar{P}, \bar{Q}) = (5, 7)$.

3-3 For the models given in Example 3-2, find $\bar{P}$ and $\bar{Q}$ using (3-15) and (3-16).

3-4 THE EFFECT OF AN EXCISE TAX IN A COMPETITIVE MARKET

SOLUTION
(a) Since $a = 20$, $b = 7$, $c = 4$ and $d = 5$, then

$$\bar{P} = \frac{a+c}{d+b} = \frac{20+4}{5+7} = 2 \quad \text{and} \quad \bar{Q} = \frac{ad-bc}{d+b} = \frac{20(5)-7(4)}{5+7} = 6$$

(b) Since $a = 27$, $b = 4$, $c = 3$ and $d = 2$, then

$$\bar{P} = \frac{a+c}{d+b} = \frac{27+3}{2+4} = 5 \quad \text{and} \quad \bar{Q} = \frac{ad-bc}{d+b} = \frac{27(2)-4(3)}{2+4} = 7$$

3-4 For the models given in Example 3-2, find $\bar{P}$ and $\bar{Q}$ using graphical methods.

SOLUTION (a)   (b)

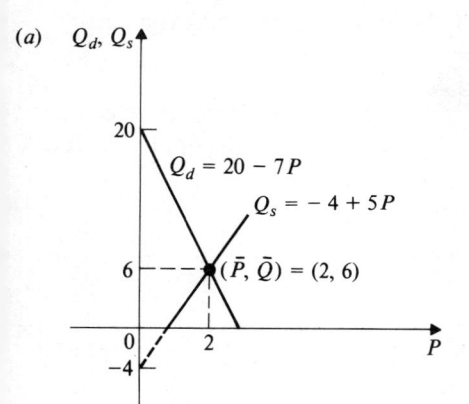

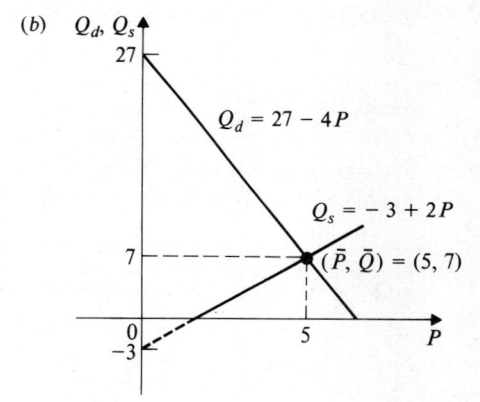

Figure 3-7

3-B PRACTICE PROBLEMS

3-5 For each of the following linear partial-equilibrium market models, find $\bar{P}$ and $\bar{Q}$:

(a) $Q_d = Q_s$
$Q_d = 19.5 - 2P$
$Q_s = -18 + 3P$

(b) $Q_d = Q_s$
$Q_d = \frac{13}{3} - \frac{3}{17}P$
$Q_s = -\frac{41}{3} + 3P$

3-4 THE EFFECT OF AN EXCISE TAX IN A COMPETITIVE MARKET

In this section we shall examine how equilibrium price and quantity, in the competitive market model (3-12), are affected by the imposition of a tax on the good which is bought and sold in this market. In particular, we shall analyse the effect of the imposition of an *excise tax*, meaning a tax which takes the form of a fixed amount of money per unit of the good sold, regardless of the selling price of the good.

To analyse the effect of an excise tax in the competitive market model, let us assume that the excise tax imposed upon suppliers is t per unit, with t being measured in money units (for example, £2 per unit). This means that, for each unit sold, suppliers will no longer receive the whole market price per unit, but instead will only receive the market price per unit (P) minus the tax paid per unit (t). Thus, for suppliers, the relevant supply price per unit is given by

$$P^T = P - t \quad (t \geqslant 0) \qquad (3\text{-}18)$$

where P^T is the price per unit received by suppliers after paying the excise tax of t per unit. Consequently, the supply function will now take the form

$$Q_s = -c + dP^T \quad (c, d > 0) \qquad (3\text{-}19)$$

Since $P^T < P$ when $t > 0$, a comparison of (3-19) with (3-10) indicates that a given price per unit will bring forth a smaller quantity of supply in the excise-tax case than in the non-excise-tax case.

The demand function, as before, is assumed to be

$$Q_d = a - bP \quad (a, b > 0) \qquad (3\text{-}20)$$

and the market equilibrium condition is

$$Q_d = Q_s \qquad (3\text{-}21)$$

The market model, incorporating the excise tax, can now be seen to consist of the system of four equations (3-21), (3-20), (3-19) and (3-18), in the four endogenous variables Q_d, Q_s, P^T and P. Note that t, like a, b, c and d, is a given parameter for the model. Before proceeding to solve this equation system by eliminating variables via substitution, we will obtain its solution by graphical methods, as in Fig. 3-8.

In Fig. 3-8, the demand function is graphed just as it was in Fig. 3-4. The graph of the supply function, however, must now take into account the imposition of the excise tax. Thus, to obtain the adjusted supply function, we substitute (3-18) into (3-19) to get

$$Q_s = -c + dP^T = -c + d(P-t) = -c + dP - dt = -(c+dt) + dP \qquad (3\text{-}22)$$

which is graphed in Fig. 3-8 as shown. It should be noted that, in comparison with the zero tax supply function (given by $Q_s = -c + dP$, which is also graphed in Fig. 3-8 for convenient comparison), the adjusted supply function has the same slope (d) but different vertical intercept ($-(c+dt)$ instead of $-c$). Consequently, the adjusted supply function lies parallel to and vertically beneath the zero tax supply function. [*Note:* the student should redraw Fig. 3-8 with the axes reversed to see what the diagram looks like with P on the vertical axis.]

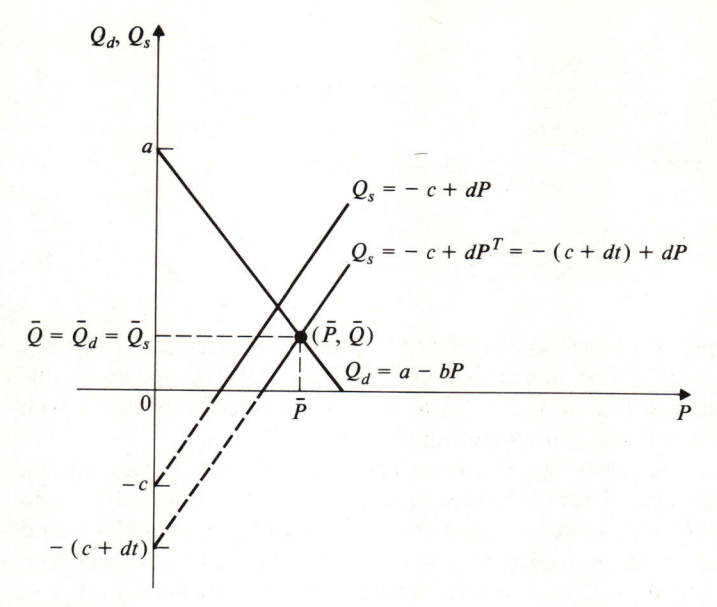

3-4 THE EFFECT OF AN EXCISE TAX IN A COMPETITIVE MARKET

Figure 3-8

The intersection of the demand and supply curves in Fig. 3-8 determines the equilibrium price and quantity, as shown by point $(\bar{P}, \bar{Q})$. It should be noted that this equilibrium point $(\bar{P}, \bar{Q})$ represents a higher price and a lower quantity than the point given by the intersection of $Q_d = a - bP$ and $Q_s = -c + dP$ in the zero tax case.

The above solution can also be obtained by substitution. Thus, by substituting (3-18) into (3-19), we eliminate variable P^T to get

$$Q_s = -c + dP^T = -c + d(P-t) = -c + dP - dt \tag{3-23}$$

Further, by substituting (3-20) and (3-23) into (3-21) we can eliminate Q_d and Q_s. Hence

$$Q_d = Q_s$$
$$\text{or} \quad a - bP = -c + dP - dt \tag{3-24}$$

which is an equation in the one variable P. Rearranging (3-24) gives

$$a + c + dt = dP + bP = (d+b)P$$

which, upon dividing each side by $(d+b)$ gives the solution value of P as

$$\bar{P} = \frac{a+c+dt}{d+b} = \frac{a+c}{d+b} + \frac{d}{d+b}t \tag{3-25}$$

To find the equilibrium quantity, we simply substitute (3-25) into (3-20) as follows:

$$\bar{Q} = a - b\bar{P} = a - \frac{b(a+c+dt)}{d+b} = \frac{a(d+b) - b(a+c+dt)}{d+b}$$

$$= \frac{ad - bc - bdt}{d+b}$$

or
$$\bar{Q} = \frac{ad-bc}{d+b} - \frac{bd}{d+b}t \qquad (3\text{-}26)$$

An examination of the expressions for equilibrium price and quantity, given by (3-25) and (3-26), indicates that $\bar{P}$ and $\bar{Q}$ are expressions in terms of the parameters a, b, c, d and t. Since these parameters represent given data for the model, $\bar{P}$ and $\bar{Q}$ are determinate values.

If we wish to compare the excise tax result, given in (3-25) and (3-26), with the zero tax case of Sec. 3-3, we simply substitute $t = 0$ into (3-25) and (3-26) to obtain $\bar{P} = (a+c)/(d+b)$ and $\bar{Q} = (ad-bc)/(d+b)$ as in (3-15) and (3-16). This substitution indicates that the essential difference between equilibrium in the 'no tax' case and equilibrium in the 'with tax' case lies in the additional two terms

$$\frac{d}{d+b}t \quad \text{and} \quad -\frac{bd}{d+b}t$$

in (3-25) and (3-26), respectively. Consequently, an examination of these two terms permits us to make the following statements about the effect of an excise tax in a competitive market:

1. Since $d/(d+b) > 0$, then the effect of the excise tax on equilibrium price is always positive, with the increase in price due to the excise tax being equal to $d/(d+b)$ times the excise tax per unit (t).
2. Since $d/(d+b) < 1$, then $dt/(d+b) < t$. In other words, the increase in equilibrium price due to the excise tax is less than the amount of the tax.
3. Since $-bd/(d+b) < 0$, then the effect of the excise tax on equilibrium quantity is always negative, with the decrease in quantity due to the excise tax being equal to $bd/(d+b)$ times the excise tax per unit (t).

It should be noted that results (1)–(3) are dependent upon the slope parameters, d and b, only. The intercept parameters, a and c, do not affect these results.

Examples of an Excise Tax in a Competitive Market

3-6 For the market models given in Example 2, find $\bar{P}$ and $\bar{Q}$ after the imposition of an excise tax of amount $t = 2$. Also, using the results of Example 3-2, check whether or not the price increase due to the excise tax is less than the amount of the tax.

SOLUTION

(a) The first step is to replace the supply function $Q_s = -4+5P$ by $Q_s = -4+5P^T = -4+5(P-t) = -4+5(P-2) = -14+5P$. Then we proceed as before:

$$Q_d = Q_s$$
$$\text{or} \quad 20 - 7P = -14 + 5P$$
$$\therefore \quad 34 = 12P \Rightarrow \bar{P} = 17/6$$

Substituting $\bar{P} = 17/6$ into Q_d gives $\bar{Q} = \bar{Q}_d(=\bar{Q}_s) = 20 - 7\bar{P} = 20 - 7(17/6) = 1/6$. Thus $(\bar{P}, \bar{Q}) = (17/6, 1/6)$. Note that the same result is obtained by using (3-25) and (3-26), with $a = 20$, $b = 7$, $c = 4$, $d = 5$ and $t = 2$. Also, note that the effect of the excise tax is to increase $\bar{P}$ from $\bar{P} = 2$ (see Example 3-2) to $\bar{P} = 2\frac{5}{6}$. In other words, the price increase (of 5/6) is less than the amount of the tax (which is 2).

(b) As in (a), we replace $Q_s = -3+2P$ by $Q_s = -3+2P^T = -3+2(P-2) = -7+2P$. Thus

$$Q_d = Q_s$$
$$\text{or} \quad 27 - 4P = -7 + 2P$$
$$\therefore \quad 34 = 6P \Rightarrow \bar{P} = 17/3$$

Substituting $\bar{P} = 17/3$ into Q_d gives $\bar{Q} = \bar{Q}_d(=\bar{Q}_s) = 27 - 4\bar{P} = 27 - 4(17/3) = 13/3$. Thus $(\bar{P}, \bar{Q}) = (17/3, 13/3)$. Note that the same result is obtained by using (3-25) and (3-26), with $a = 27$, $b = 4$, $c = 3$, $d = 2$ and $t = 2$. Also, note that the price increase (of 2/3) due to the excise tax is less than the amount of the tax (which is 2).

3-C PRACTICE PROBLEMS

3-7 For the market models given in Prob. 3-5, find $\bar{P}$ and $\bar{Q}$ after the imposition of an excise tax of amount $t = 1/3$.

3-8 Using the results of Probs. 3-5 and 3-7, check whether or not the price increase due to the excise tax is less than $t = 1/3$.

3-5 EQUILIBRIUM IN A LINEAR NATIONAL-INCOME MODEL

In Sec. 3-3 we examined (partial) equilibrium in a simple microeconomic model of price determination. In this section we shall examine equilibrium in a simple macroeconomic model of income determination. To do this, we shall follow essentially the same procedure that was used in constructing the microeconomic market model. In other words, the macroeconomic income determination model will be constructed in the form of a system of equations, with each equation being either a behavioural equation or an equilibrium condition.

As a first step, to simplify the analysis, we shall assume no government, no foreign trade, constant prices and unemployed resources. Also, we shall define national income to be exactly equal to the total value of all output in the economy, using Y to denote these identical values. The next step

50 STATIC-EQUILIBRIUM MODELS

consists in specifying the single behavioural equation that we will have in this simple income determination model. This behavioural equation is the *consumption function*, which states that current (aggregate) consumption expenditure (C) by households is a function of current national income (Y). Assuming a linear relationship between C and Y, the consumption function can be written as

$$C = C(Y) = \alpha + \beta Y \quad (\alpha > 0; 0 < \beta < 1) \tag{3-27}$$

and graphed as shown in Fig. 3-9. Before proceeding to examine Fig. 3-9, it should be noted that while consumption expenditure may well depend on other variables (such as past consumption, level of wealth and the rate of interest) as well as income, we have deliberately assumed consumption to be a function of income alone in order to simplify the analysis.

Note, in Fig. 3-9, that the vertical intercept of the consumption function is positive, as shown by $\alpha > 0$. In other words, when income is zero, consumption expenditure is still positive. This means that households must either be borrowing money or using up their past savings. Also, note in Fig. 3-9 that the positive slope of the line $C = \alpha + \beta Y$, given by $\Delta C/\Delta Y = \beta$ (which is known as the *marginal propensity to consume*), is less than the unit slope of the 45° line drawn through the origin. This means that a rise in Y of, say, x money units will cause C to rise by an amount greater than zero but less than x money units.

The final step, in the construction of the income determination model, is the specification of an equilibrium condition. Assuming that current

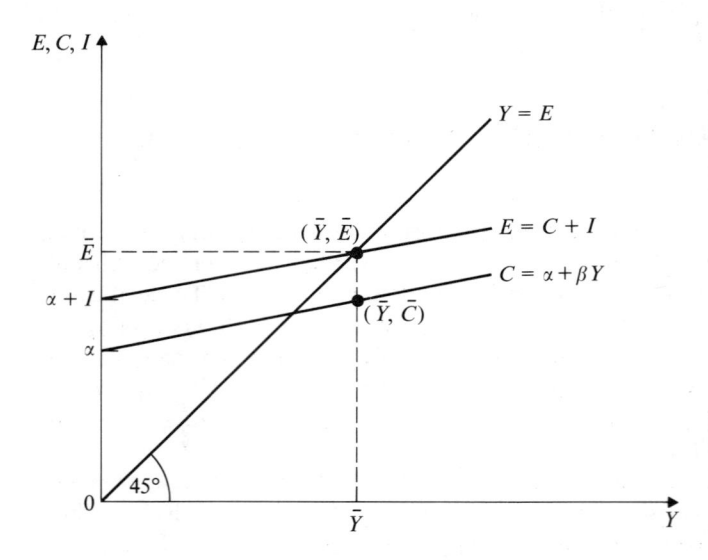

Figure 3-9

3-5 EQUILIBRIUM IN A LINEAR NATIONAL-INCOME MODEL

(aggregate) investment expenditure (I) by business units is exogenously determined, the equilibrium condition can be specified as

$$Y = C + I = E \qquad (3\text{-}28)$$

which states that national income (output) is equal to the sum of consumption and investment expenditures (E). Note that (3-28) embodies the notion of equilibrium in the sense that equilibrium is said to obtain when the value of planned aggregate output (Y) is exactly equal to the value of planned aggregate expenditure ($E = C + I$). In other words, the condition for equilibrium in the level of income (output) is that planned aggregate output (Y) equals planned aggregate demand ($C + I$). It is also essential to note that (3-28) is an *equilibrium condition* describing the prerequisite for the attainment of an income equilibrium. As such it is *not* the same as the national income accounting identity

$$Y \equiv C + I \qquad (3\text{-}29)$$

where $\equiv$ reads 'is identically equal to'. Equation (3-29) is simply a national income accounting *definition* which does not involve the notion of equilibrium.

The national-income model can now be seen to consist of the two Eqs. (3-28) and (3-27), with C and Y being endogenous variables and I an exogenous variable. Thus to find the equilibrium values of Y and C, to be denoted by $\bar{Y}$ and $\bar{C}$, we simply solve (3-28) and (3-27) simultaneously. To do this we substitute (3-27) into (3-28) to get

$$Y = C + I = \alpha + \beta Y + I$$

which, upon rearranging, gives

$$Y - \beta Y = (1 - \beta)Y = \alpha + I$$

Hence the solution (or equilibrium) value of Y is

$$\bar{Y} = \frac{\alpha + I}{1 - \beta} \qquad (3\text{-}30)$$

The equilibrium level of C can then be obtained by substituting (3-30) into (3-27):

$$\bar{C} = \alpha + \beta \bar{Y} = \alpha + \frac{\beta(\alpha + I)}{(1-\beta)} = \frac{\alpha(1-\beta) + \beta(\alpha + I)}{(1-\beta)} = \frac{\alpha + \beta I}{1-\beta} \qquad (3\text{-}31)$$

An examination of (3-30) and (3-31) indicates that both $\bar{Y}$ and $\bar{C}$ are expressed in terms of α, β and I. Since α, β and I represent given (and therefore known) data for the model, then $\bar{Y}$ and $\bar{C}$ are determinate values. Also, since $\alpha > 0$, $0 < \beta < 1$, and assuming $I > 0$, then $\bar{Y}$ and $\bar{C}$ are both positive.

The solution given in (3-30) and (3-31) can also be obtained graphically. Thus, in Fig. 3-9, the aggregate expenditure curve (given by the line $E = C + I = \alpha + \beta Y + I$) intersects the 45° line (which, by construction, is the locus of points for which aggregate output (Y) equals aggregate expenditure (E)) to fulfil the equilibrium condition and to give equilibrium Y and E at point $(\bar{Y}, \bar{E})$. Thus, $\bar{C}$ is given by $\bar{C} = \alpha + \beta \bar{Y}$ as shown.

The above model can now be readily extended to include government expenditure and taxation. For example, an extended model, which consists of an equilibrium condition followed by two behavioural equations, may be written as

$$Y = C + I + G$$
$$C = \alpha + \beta(Y - T) \quad (\alpha > 0; 0 < \beta < 1) \quad (3\text{-}32)$$
$$T = tY \quad (0 < t < 1)$$

where G is current government expenditure, T is the current total income tax paid to the government, and t is the given income tax rate. In this model, variables Y, C and T are endogenous, while variables I and G are exogenous. To solve (3-32) for $\bar{Y}$, $\bar{C}$ and $\bar{T}$, we substitute the second equation of (3-32) into the first equation of (3-32) to obtain

$$Y = \alpha + \beta(Y - T) + I + G \quad (3\text{-}33)$$

Then, substituting $T = tY$ into (3-33) we obtain

$$Y = \alpha + \beta(Y - tY) + I + G$$
$$\text{or} \quad (1 - \beta + \beta t)Y = \alpha + I + G$$

which gives

$$\bar{Y} = \frac{\alpha + I + G}{1 - \beta + \beta t} = \frac{\alpha + I + G}{1 - \beta(1 - t)} \quad (3\text{-}34)$$

Substitution of $\bar{Y}$ into $T = tY$ gives

$$\bar{T} = t\bar{Y} = \frac{t(\alpha + I + G)}{1 - \beta(1 - t)} \quad (3\text{-}35)$$

Finally, substitution of (3-34) and (3-35) into the consumption function yields

$$\bar{C} = \alpha + \beta(\bar{Y} - \bar{T}) = \alpha + \beta(\bar{Y} - t\bar{Y}) = \alpha + \beta(1 - t)\bar{Y}$$
$$= \alpha + \frac{\beta(1 - t)(\alpha + I + G)}{1 - \beta(1 - t)}$$
$$= \frac{\alpha[1 - \beta(1 - t)] + \beta(1 - t)\alpha + \beta(1 - t)(I + G)}{[1 - \beta(1 - t)]}$$

$$\text{or} \quad \bar{C} = \frac{\alpha + \beta(1 - t)(I + G)}{1 - \beta(1 - t)} \quad (3\text{-}36)$$

The student should check that the above restrictions on the parameters α, β and t, plus the assumption that I and G are both positive, ensure that $\bar{Y}$, $\bar{C}$ and $\bar{T}$ are all positive.

Examples of Linear National-Income Models

3-9 Given the following national-income models:
(a) $Y = C + I$
$C = 25 + 0.7Y$
$I = 20$
(b) $Y = C + I + G$
$C = 58 + 0.8(Y - T)$
$T = \frac{1}{3}Y$
$I = 25; \quad G = 15$

Find $\bar{Y}$ and $\bar{C}$ in (a) and $\bar{Y}$, $\bar{C}$ and $\bar{T}$ in (b).

SOLUTION
(a) $\quad Y = C + I$
$Y = 25 + \frac{7}{10}Y + 20$
$\therefore \quad \frac{3}{10}Y = 45 \Rightarrow \bar{Y} = 150$
Substituting $\bar{Y} = 150$ into C gives $\bar{C} = 25 + \frac{7}{10}\bar{Y} = 25 + \frac{7}{10}(150) = 130$
Thus $(\bar{Y}, \bar{C}) = (150, 130)$
(b) $\quad Y = C + I + G$
or $\quad Y = 58 + \frac{8}{10}(Y - T) + 25 + 15 = 98 + \frac{8}{10}(Y - \frac{1}{3}Y) = 98 + \frac{8}{15}Y$
$\therefore \quad \frac{7}{15}Y = 98 \Rightarrow \bar{Y} = 210$
Substituting $\bar{Y} = 210$ into $T = \frac{1}{3}Y$ gives
$\bar{T} = \frac{1}{3}\bar{Y} = \frac{1}{3}(210) = 70$
Finally, substituting $\bar{Y}$ and $\bar{T}$ into C gives
$\bar{C} = 58 + \frac{8}{10}(\bar{Y} - \bar{T}) = 58 + \frac{8}{10}(210 - 70) = 170$
Thus $\bar{Y} = 210; \bar{C} = 170; \bar{T} = 70$.

3-D PRACTICE PROBLEMS

3-10 Given the following national-income models:
(a) $Y = C + I + G$
$C = 10 + 0.75Y$
$I = 40; G = 10$
(b) $Y = C + I + G$
$C = 0.9(Y - T)$
$T = 10 + 0.2Y$
$I = 60; G = 33$

Find $\bar{Y}$ and $\bar{C}$ in (a) and $\bar{Y}$, $\bar{C}$ and $\bar{T}$ in (b).

3-6 THE NUMBER OF EQUATIONS AND THE NUMBER OF UNKNOWNS

In Sec. 3-3 we saw how a linear market model could be expressed in terms of a system of simultaneous equations, such as in (3-12). Also, we saw how this system of three simultaneous equations in the three (unknown) endogenous variables Q_d, Q_s and P, could be solved to yield the *unique* solution values of Q_d, Q_s and P. In a similar fashion, in Sec. 3-5, the

54 STATIC-EQUILIBRIUM MODELS

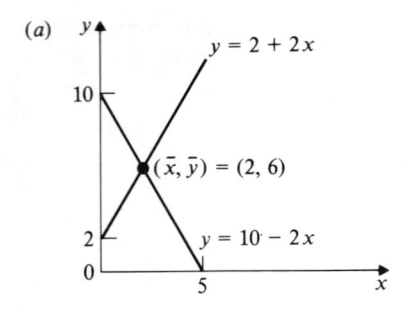

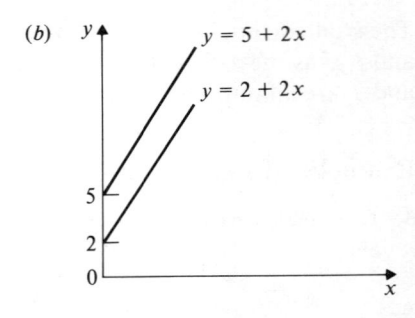

(a)
- $y = 2 + 2x$
- $(\bar{x}, \bar{y}) = (2, 6)$
- $y = 10 - 2x$

(b)
- $y = 5 + 2x$
- $y = 2 + 2x$

Figure 3-10

simultaneous-equation system, consisting of the two equations (3-28) and (3-27) in the two (unknown) endogenous variables Y and C, was solved to yield the *unique* solution values of Y and C. These two examples would tend to convey the impression that equality between the number of endogenous variables (or unknowns) and the number of equations will ensure the existence of a unique solution. Unfortunately, however, this is *not* the case, as will be demonstrated by some examples.

The two simultaneous-equation systems, given in (*a*) and (*b*) below, are both systems with two equations in the two unknowns x and y:

(a) $y = 2 + 2x$
    $y = 10 - 2x$

(b) $y = 2 + 2x$
    $y = 5 + 2x$

If we graph system (*a*) in Fig. 3-10*a* and system (*b*) in Fig. 3-10*b*, then it is immediately apparent that while system (*a*) has a unique solution (as shown by the intersection of the two lines in Fig. 3-10*a*), system (*b*) has no solution (as shown by the non-intersection of the two parallel lines in Fig. 3-10*b*). The reason that system (*b*) has no solution is that its two equations are *inconsistent*. Clearly, if y is equal to the sum of 2 plus $2x$, then it cannot simultaneously be equal to the sum of 5 plus $2x$. By way of contrast, the two equations of system (*a*) are *consistent*.

As a further example, consider the two simultaneous-equation systems given in (*c*) and (*d*) below. System (*c*), which contains two equations in

(c) $y = 2 + 2x$
    $2y = 4 + 4x$

(d) $y = 2 + 2x$
    $2y = 4 + 4x$
    $y = 10 - 2x$

the two unknowns x and y, is a case where the two equations are *functionally dependent*, meaning that one equation can be derived from the other. Thus, in (*c*), the second equation can be derived by multiplying the first equation by two. This means that since the second equation tells us nothing that the first equation cannot tell us, then the second equation is redundant and can be dropped from the system. If we do this, we are left with one equation (or graphically, one line), $y = 2+2x$, in two unknowns. Clearly, since many ordered pairs (x, y) will satisfy $y = 2+2x$, then the solution of (c) is not unique. By way of contrast, the two equations of system (a) are *functionally independent*.

An examination of system (d), which contains more equations than unknowns, indicates that its first and second equations are functionally dependent. Consequently, if we drop the second equation, system (d) reduces to system (a) with a unique solution at $(\bar{x}, \bar{y}) = (2, 6)$. This demonstrates that a system containing more equations than unknowns may still have a unique solution due to the existence of functional dependence among its equations.

The above examples indicate that, for an equation system to possess a unique solution, it is not sufficient to have equality between the number of equations and the number of unknowns. Rather, to the procedure to counting equations and unknowns, we must add the requirement that the equations are *consistent* with and *functionally independent* of one another. This result must always be borne in mind when attempting to construct economic models with unique solutions.

In Chapter 4 we shall encounter a method of testing the existence of a unique solution to a system of linear equations.

3-7 A NONLINEAR MARKET MODEL

In this section we shall examine how to find (partial) equilibrium in the following nonlinear market model:

$$\begin{aligned} Q_d &= Q_s \\ Q_d &= 9 - P^2 \\ Q_s &= -3 + 4P \end{aligned} \quad (3\text{-}37)$$

Note that (3-37) differs from previous (linear) market models in that the demand function is a quadratic function.

Solution by Graphical Methods

As in previous market models, the procedure for solving (3-37) consists of (a) the elimination of variables Q_d and Q_s, via substitution, to obtain a single equation in P which can be solved to give the equilibrium value of P (denoted by $\bar{P}$), and (b) the substitution of $\bar{P}$ back into Q_d (or Q_s) to obtain the equilibrium value of Q (denoted by $\bar{Q}$). Applying step (a) to (3-37) gives

$$Q_d = Q_s$$
$$\text{or} \quad 9 - P^2 = -3 + 4P$$
$$\therefore \quad P^2 + 4P - 12 = 0 \quad (3\text{-}38)$$

We now have a single (quadratic) equation in P, but how do we solve it for $\bar{P}$?

To solve (3-38), note firstly that its left-hand side can be rewritten as the quadratic function

$$f(P) = P^2 + 4P - 12 \qquad (3\text{-}39)$$

This indicates that our problem is to find the value(s) of P for which this function has the particular value of zero. In other words, we have to find P such that

$$f(P) = P^2 + 4P - 12 = 0 \qquad (3\text{-}40)$$

To do this, we can graph (3-39), as is done in Fig. 3-11, using the values of P and $f(P)$ given in the following table:

P	−7	−6	−5	−4	−3	−2	−1	0	1	2	3
$f(P)$	9	0	−7	−12	−15	−16	−15	−12	−7	0	9

An examination of Fig. 3-11 indicates that $f(P)$ is zero when it intersects the horizontal axis at $P = -6$ and $P = 2$. These two values of P are therefore the solution values or *roots* of the quadratic equation (3-40). [*Note*: a quadratic equation, such as (3-40), generally yields two solution values whereas a linear equation, such as (3-14), will yield only one solution

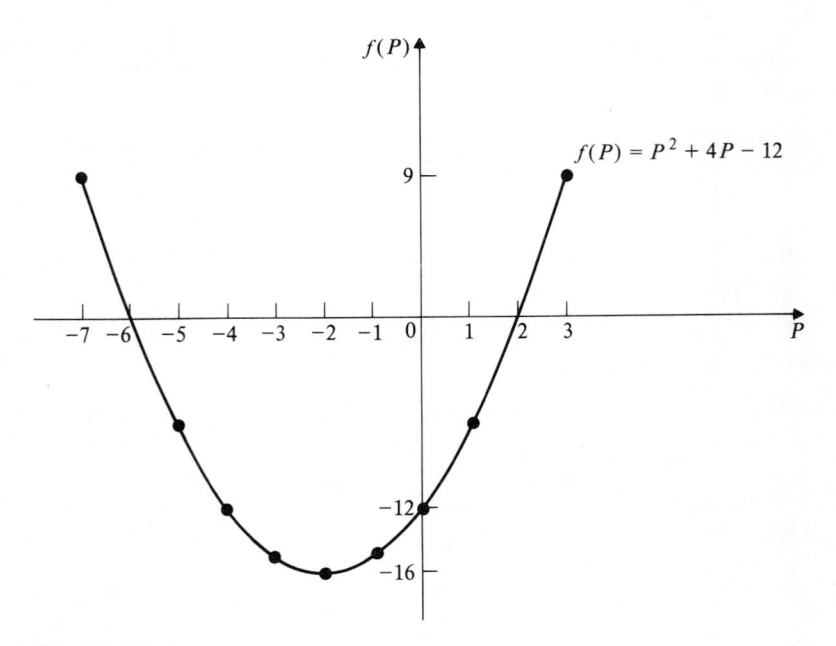

Figure 3-11

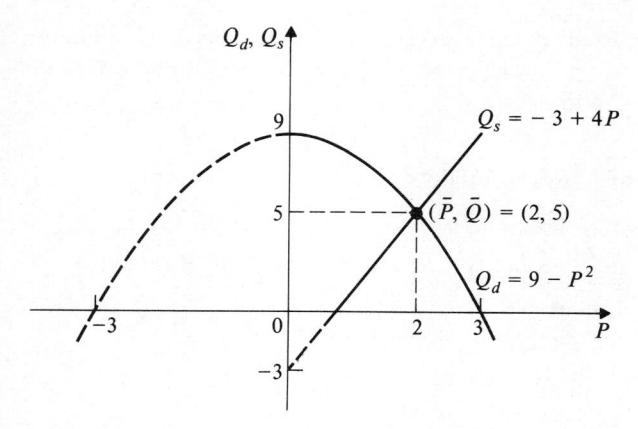

Figure 3-12

Q_d, Q_s axis with curves: $Q_s = -3 + 4P$ and $Q_d = 9 - P^2$, intersecting at $(\bar{P}, \bar{Q}) = (2, 5)$.

value.] Clearly, since $P = -6$ does not make economic sense, $P = 2$ is the economically meaningful equilibrium price (denoted as $\bar{P} = 2$).

Substitution of $\bar{P} = 2$ into Q_s (or Q_d) gives

$$\bar{Q} = \bar{Q}_s (= \bar{Q}_d) = -3 + 4\bar{P} = -3 + 4(2) = 5$$

Thus $(\bar{P}, \bar{Q}) = (2, 5)$.

The same solution can also be obtained graphically by the intersection of the demand and supply functions, as shown in Fig. 3-12.

Solution by Algebraic Method

If we have a quadratic equation of the form

$$ax^2 + bx + c = 0 \quad (a \neq 0) \tag{3-41}$$

its two roots can be obtained from the following *quadratic formula*:

$$x = \frac{-b \pm \sqrt{b^2 - 4ac}}{2a} \tag{3-42}$$

For example, in (3-38), where $a = 1$, $b = 4$, $c = -12$ and $x = P$, the application of the quadratic formula gives

$$P = \frac{-4 \pm \sqrt{16 + 48}}{2} = \frac{-4 \pm 8}{2} = -6 \text{ or } 2$$

which is the same solution for P as was obtained above. Substitution of $\bar{P} = 2$ into Q_s (or Q_d) will then give $\bar{Q} = 5$ as above.

It should be noted that, in keeping with Sec. 3-6, there is a method for testing the existence of a solution to a nonlinear equation system. Unfortunately, however, this method is beyond the scope of this book.

58 STATIC-EQUILIBRIUM MODELS

Students who are interested in this method should consult A. C. Chiang, *Fundamental Methods of Mathematical Economics*, McGraw-Hill, 2nd edition, 1974, Chapters 7 and 8.

Examples of Nonlinear Market Models

3-11 Given the following nonlinear market models:
(a) $Q_d = Q_s$
$Q_d = 7 - 3P^2$
$Q_s = -2 + 6P$

(b) $Q_d = Q_s$
$Q_d = 12 - 4P$
$Q_s = -4 + 2P^2$

Find the economically meaningful equilibrium solution in each case.

SOLUTION
(a) $\qquad Q_d = Q_s$
or $\quad 7 - 3P^2 = -2 + 6P$
$\therefore \quad 3P^2 + 6P - 9 = 0 \Rightarrow P = -3$ or 1 (via quadratic formula)
Substitution of $\bar{P} = 1$ into Q_s (or Q_d) gives $\bar{Q} = 4$. Thus $(\bar{P}, \bar{Q}) = (1, 4)$.

(b) $\qquad Q_d = Q_s$
or $\quad 12 - 4P = -4 + 2P^2$
$\therefore \quad 2P^2 + 4P - 16 = 0 \Rightarrow P = -4$ or 2 (via quadratic formula)
Substitution of $\bar{P} = 2$ into Q_s (or Q_d) gives $\bar{Q} = 4$. Thus $(\bar{P}, \bar{Q}) = (2, 4)$.

3-E PRACTICE PROBLEMS

3-12 Given the following nonlinear market models:

(a) $Q_d = Q_s$
$Q_d = 11 - 2P^2$
$Q_s = -5 + 2P^2$

(b) $Q_d = Q_s$
$Q_d = 9 - 2P^2$
$Q_s = -5 + 3P$

Find the economically meaningful equilibrium solution in each case.

3-8 ADDITIONAL PROBLEMS

3-13 The market demand function for a good is $Q_d = f(P) = 36 - \frac{1}{3}P$. Find
(a) the quantity demanded when the price of the good is (i) 3 (ii) 9 (iii) 99;
(b) the price of the good when the quantity demanded is (i) 27 (ii) 20 (iii) 2;
(c) the quantity demanded when the good is free;
(d) the highest price that would be paid for this good;
(e) the economically meaningful domain and range of the function;
(f) the change in quantity demanded per unit change in the price of the good.

3-14 The market supply function for a good is $Q_s = g(P) = -10 + 7P$. Find
(a) the quantity supplied when the price of the good is (i) 2 (ii) 5 (iii) 13;
(b) the price of the good when the quantity supplied is (i) 2 (ii) 11 (iii) 88;
(c) the set of prices for which this good will be supplied;
(d) the economically meaningful domain and range of the function;
(e) the change in the quantity supplied per unit change in the price of the good.

3-15 The market demand function for a good is given by $Q_d = a - bP$, where $a, b > 0$ and the quantity is measured in pounds weight. If the quantity is converted to kilograms, what effect will this conversion have on the parameters a and b?

3-16 For each of the following market models find $\bar{P}$ and $\bar{Q}$:
(a) $Q_d = Q_s$
$Q_d = 34 - P$
$Q_s = -2 + 2P$

(b) $Q_d = Q_s$
$Q_d = 9 - 2P$
$Q_s = -9 + P$

In each case check your result graphically. Also, comment on your result for (b).

3-17 For the market model given in Prob. 3-16a, find the excess demand when
(a) $P = 14$ and (b) $P = 2$.

3-18 For each of the following market models find $\bar{P}$ and $\bar{Q}$. Also, state what assumptions are necessary to ensure that $\bar{P}, \bar{Q} > 0$.
(a) $Q_d = Q_s$
$Q_d = a + bP \quad (a, b > 0)$
$Q_s = -c + dP \quad (c, d > 0)$

(b) $Q_d = Q_s$
$Q_d = a - bP \quad (a, b > 0)$
$Q_s = c + dP \quad (c, d > 0)$

Graph your result for each case. Also comment on the economic meaningfulness of the demand function in (a) and the supply function in (b).

3-19 For the market model given in Prob. 3-16a, find the effect on $\bar{P}$ and $\bar{Q}$ of the imposition of an excise tax of amount $t = 3$. Is the price increase, due to the imposition of the excise tax, less than $t = 3$?

3-20 Use the results of Probs. 3-16a and 3-19 to find the proportion of the tax per unit borne by (a) consumers and (b) suppliers. [*Hint*: for (a) compare the price per unit paid by consumers before and after tax; for (b) compare the price per unit received by suppliers before the tax with the price per unit (minus the tax per unit paid to the government) received after the imposition of the tax.]

3-21 Given the following national–income models:
(a) $Y = C + I + G$
$C = \alpha + \beta Y \quad (\alpha > 0; 0 < \beta < 1)$

(b) $Y = C + I + G$
$C = \beta(Y - T) \quad (0 < \beta < 1)$
$T = \gamma + tY \quad (\gamma > 0; 0 < t < 1)$

Find $\bar{Y}$ and $\bar{C}$ in (a) and $\bar{Y}, \bar{C}$ and $\bar{T}$ in (b).

3-22 Given the following market models:
(a) $Q_d = Q_s$
$Q_d = 16 - 3P^2$
$Q_s = -4 + 2P^2$

(b) $Q_d = Q_s$
$Q_d = 11 - 4P^2$
$Q_s = -1 + 8P$

Find the economically meaningful equilibrium in each case.

3-23 If saving S is defined as the amount of national income Y not devoted to consumption C, then a linear saving function can be written as

$$S = Y - C = Y - (\alpha + \beta Y) = -\alpha + (1 - \beta)Y \quad (\alpha > 0; 0 < \beta < 1)$$

Assuming investment expenditure to be exogenously determined, and given by the constant I, graph both the linear saving function and the constant investment expenditure (putting S and I on the vertical axis and Y on the horizontal axis). Compare the graph obtained with Fig. 3-9 and explain why the equilibrium level of income $\bar{Y}$, in Fig. 3-9, is identical to the level of income at which $I = S$ in the new graph.

CHAPTER
FOUR
MATRIX ALGEBRA

In Chapter 3 we saw how a linear market model, for one good, can be expressed as a system of simultaneous (linear) equations and solved to yield equilibrium price and quantity. Thus the linear market models that we encountered were of the form

$$\begin{aligned} Q_d &= Q_s \\ Q_d &= f(P) = a_0 + a_1 P \\ Q_s &= g(P) = b_0 + b_1 P \end{aligned} \quad (4\text{-}1)$$

with certain restrictions imposed upon the parameters a_0, a_1, b_0 and b_1 so as to make economic sense. Having dealt with such models, we are now in a position to construct a linear market model for more than one good.

As an example, let us assume that there are two goods and that the demand and supply functions for each of these goods have the form

$$\begin{aligned} Q_{d1} &= Q_{d1}(P_1, P_2) = a_0 + a_1 P_1 + a_2 P_2 \\ Q_{s1} &= Q_{s1}(P_1, P_2) = b_0 + b_1 P_1 + b_2 P_2 \\ Q_{d2} &= Q_{d2}(P_1, P_2) = c_0 + c_1 P_1 + c_2 P_2 \\ Q_{s2} &= Q_{s2}(P_1, P_2) = d_0 + d_1 P_1 + d_2 P_2 \end{aligned} \quad (4\text{-}2)$$

Note that each of the four functions in (4-2) is a *linear* function, since every variable in each function is raised to the first power only. Also, in (4-2), note that while no restrictions have been imposed upon the *a, b, c* and *d* parameters, certain restrictions may be necessary to represent particular forms of demand and supply behaviour and to ensure that the equilibrium prices and quantities are positive. However, for the moment, let us merely note that (4-2) contains four *linear* equations. If we now add, for each good, the equilibrium condition that the quantity demanded equals the quantity supplied, we have the further two equations:

$$Q_{d1} = Q_{s1} \quad \text{and} \quad Q_{d2} = Q_{s2} \qquad (4\text{-}3)$$

Thus we now have a *linear* market model, for two goods, consisting of a system of six linear equations, given by (4-2) and (4-3), in six variables $(Q_{d1}, Q_{d2}, Q_{s1}, Q_{s2}, P_1, P_2)$. Note that this system involves twelve parameters.

If we proceeded to introduce a third good into the linear market model, then the model would consist of a system of nine linear equations (i.e., the three demand and three supply functions plus an equilibrium condition for each of the three goods) in nine variables $(Q_{d1}, Q_{d2}, Q_{d3}, Q_{s1}, Q_{s2}, Q_{s3}, P_1, P_2, P_3)$. This system would involve twenty-four parameters. In a similar fashion, an n good model would consist of a system of $3n$ linear equations (i.e., the n demand and n supply functions plus an equilibrium condition for each of the n goods) in $3n$ variables $(Q_{d1}, Q_{d2}, \ldots, Q_{dn}, Q_{s1}, Q_{s2}, \ldots, Q_{sn}, P_1, P_2, \ldots, P_n)$. This system would involve $2n(n+1)$ parameters (of which some may be zero). Clearly, as we introduce more goods (and thus move from *partial-equilibrium* analysis to *general-equilibrium* analysis) the number of equations, variables and parameters, in the linear market model, increases greatly.

This immediately raises several important questions if we wish to analyse a multi-good linear market model:

1. Must we tediously write out a large system of extremely lengthy equations, or is there a more compact way of writing such a large equation system?
2. How do we test the existence of a unique solution to such a linear-equation system?
3. If a unique solution exists, how do we solve such a seemingly unwieldy equation system in order to find the solution or equilibrium prices and quantities?

The answer to each of these questions is found in *matrix algebra* which, as will be seen in this chapter and in the next, enables us (*a*) to write out even a very large (linear) equation system in a compact way, (*b*) to test the existence of a unique solution to a linear-equation system, and (*c*) to solve for equilibrium prices and quantities. This, in turn, raises another very pertinent question: is matrix algebra difficult to understand and to manipulate? The answer to this question is that while matrix algebra is different from ordinary algebra, and somewhat unusual at first sight, the extent and level of our introduction to matrix algebra will be such as to ensure that it can be both understood and manipulated by even the weaker student after a little practice.

Before proceeding to discuss matrix algebra (which is also known as *linear algebra*) it should be noted that matrix algebra is applicable only to *linear* simultaneous-equation systems. This restriction, however, should not be regarded as totally unrealistic. In some cases the actual nonlinear economic relationships can be closely approximated by assuming a linear relationship, while in other cases a nonlinear relationship can be transformed (for example by taking logarithms as in (2-19)) into a linear relationship. Consequently, in such cases, the assumption of linear relationships in economic models is not unreasonable.

4-1 MATRICES DEFINED

As a preliminary to the definition of matrices, let us note that the following linear-equation system can be written either as

$$\begin{array}{ll} x_1 = 3 - x_2 & \quad x_1 + x_2 = 3 \\ x_1 = 5 - 2x_2 & \text{or} \quad x_1 + 2x_2 = 5 \end{array} \qquad (4\text{-}4)$$

Also, note that a linear-equation system such as (4-4) can be written in the more general form

$$\begin{array}{l} a_{11}x_1 + a_{12}x_2 = b_1 \\ a_{21}x_1 + a_{22}x_2 = b_2 \end{array} \qquad (4\text{-}5)$$

where each of the subscripts can be given a specific interpretation. To demonstrate this interpretation, note firstly that in each equation of (4-5) the variable x_1 is always written first and the variable x_2 is always written second. In other words, the subscript on each variable indicates the exact 'column' location of the variable in the equation system (4-5). Thus, in general, the variable x_j is always located in the jth column (on the left-hand side) of the equation system. Secondly, note in (4-5) that the a coefficients are all double-subscripted. The reason for this is that the double subscript denotes the specific location of each coefficient. For example, a_{12} is the coefficient in the first equation, attached to the variable x_2. Thus, in general, a_{ij} denotes the coefficient in the ith equation, attached to the variable x_j. Lastly, note that the b parameters in (4-5) can also be given a 'location' interpretation. For example, b_2 is the constant term on the right-hand side of the second equation. Thus, in general, b_i represents the constant term on the right-hand side of the ith equation. This demonstrates that the various subscripts in (4-5) all have a specific interpretation in terms of the locations of the variables and parameters in (4-5).

The linear-equation system (4-5) can readily be extended to the case of

m equations and n variables. For example, the latter linear-equation system can be written as

$$a_{11}x_1 + a_{12}x_2 + \ldots + a_{1n}x_n = b_1$$
$$a_{21}x_1 + a_{22}x_2 + \ldots + a_{2n}x_n = b_2$$
$$\ldots \ldots \ldots \ldots \ldots \ldots \ldots \ldots \ldots \ldots$$
$$a_{m1}x_1 + a_{m2}x_2 + \ldots + a_{mn}x_n = b_m$$
(4-6)

where the subscripts in (4-6) have the same interpretation as already noted in relation to (4-5).

Since, in (4-6), m and n can be very large numbers, we now want to see how (4-6) can be written in a more compact way. To do this, note that (4-5) and (4-6), in common, consist of (i) the set of a coefficients, (ii) the set of x variables, and (iii) the set of b constant terms. It is essentially these three component parts of (4-5) and (4-6) that enable us to write a linear-equation system in a more compact way. Thus, if we write these three sets in the format of rectangular arrays, labelled as A, x and b, respectively, we have for (4-5)

$$A = \begin{bmatrix} a_{11} & a_{12} \\ a_{21} & a_{22} \end{bmatrix} \quad x = \begin{bmatrix} x_1 \\ x_2 \end{bmatrix} \quad b = \begin{bmatrix} b_1 \\ b_2 \end{bmatrix} \quad (4\text{-}7)$$

and for (4-6)

$$A = \begin{bmatrix} a_{11} & a_{12} \ldots a_{1n} \\ a_{21} & a_{22} \ldots a_{2n} \\ \ldots \ldots \ldots \ldots \\ a_{m1} & a_{m2} \ldots a_{mn} \end{bmatrix} \quad x = \begin{bmatrix} x_1 \\ x_2 \\ \vdots \\ x_n \end{bmatrix} \quad b = \begin{bmatrix} b_1 \\ b_2 \\ \vdots \\ b_m \end{bmatrix} \quad (4\text{-}8)$$

If we now define a *matrix* as a rectangular array of numbers, parameters or variables, then it can be seen that each of the three rectangular arrays in (4-7), and each of the three rectangular arrays in (4-8), is a matrix.

In a similar fashion, if we write (4-1) in the format of (4-6):

$$1Q_d - 1Q_s + 0P = 0$$
$$1Q_d + 0Q_s - a_1 P = a_0$$
$$0Q_d + 1Q_s - b_1 P = b_0$$
(4-9)

then, as in (4-7) and (4-8), we can write

$$A = \begin{bmatrix} 1 & -1 & 0 \\ 1 & 0 & -a_1 \\ 0 & 1 & -b_1 \end{bmatrix} \quad x = \begin{bmatrix} Q_d \\ Q_s \\ P \end{bmatrix} \quad b = \begin{bmatrix} 0 \\ a_0 \\ b_0 \end{bmatrix} \quad (4\text{-}10)$$

Note, in (4-10), that matrix A contains the coefficients of the variables in the equation system (4-9). For this reason, matrix A is known as a *coefficient matrix*.

Before we extend our description of a matrix, let us note immediately (without proof) that the large equation system (4-6) can be written compactly as

$$Ax = b \qquad (4\text{-}11)$$

where, A, x and b are the matrices defined as in (4-8). Since, in (4-6), m and n can be very large numbers, the compactness of matrix notation is immediately obvious. However, while (4-11) demonstrates very clearly the power of matrix notation, it begs several questions. For example, how do we multiply the two matrices A and x? What does equality between Ax and b mean? How do we find the solution of (4-11)? These questions will be duly answered as we proceed through this chapter.

Returning to our description of matrices, note that the members of each rectangular array, such as the numbers in matrix A in (4-10), are known as the *elements* of the matrix and are usually enclosed by brackets [ ], parentheses ( ) or double vertical lines ‖ ‖. Also, note that since the elements of matrix A in (4-10), and likewise the elements of matrix A in (4-8), appear in a particular location (given, in matrix A in (4-8), by the subscripts of the elements) each matrix represents an ordered set.

The Dimension of a Matrix

The *dimension* or *order* of a matrix is defined in terms of the number of rows and the number of columns it contains. For example, since matrix A in (4-8) contains m rows and n columns, it is said to be an $m \times n$ (read m by n) matrix or a matrix of dimension (order) $m \times n$. Note that it is conventional to refer to rows first, then columns. Also note that when $m = n$, as in the 3×3 matrix A in (4-10), the matrix is known as a *square matrix*.

The dimension indicator for a matrix is generally written under a matrix. Thus matrices A in (4-8) and (4-10) can be written, respectively, as

$$\underset{(m \times n)}{A} \quad \text{and} \quad \underset{(3 \times 3)}{A} \qquad (4\text{-}12)$$

Vectors

A matrix which contains only one column is known as a *column vector*. For example, matrices x in (4-8) and (4-10) are column vectors of dimension $n \times 1$ and 3×1, respectively. Similarly, a matrix which contains only one row is called a *row vector*. For example, the $1 \times n$ matrix

$$x' = [x_1 x_2 \ldots x_n] \qquad (4\text{-}13)$$

is a row vector, with the prime notation being used to distinguish the row vector in (4-13) from the column vector in (4-8).

4-A PRACTICE PROBLEMS

4-1 Rearrange the following linear market models as in (4-9) and then write out the coefficient matrix A, the variable vector x, and the constant vector b:

(a) $Q_d = Q_s$
$Q_d = 20 - 7P$
$Q_s = -4 + 5P$

(b) $Q_d = Q_s$
$Q_d = a - bP$
$Q_s = -c + dP$

4-2 Rearrange the national-income model

$$Y = C + I$$
$$C = \alpha + \beta Y$$

so that the endogenous variables appear in the order Y, C, on the left-hand side of the equation system and the exogenous variable I and the constant α appear on the right-hand side of the equation system. Then write out the coefficient matrix A, the variable vector x, and the constant vector b.

4-2 THE ALGEBRA OF MATRICES

In Sec. 4-1 we saw that a matrix is an array of numbers, rather than a single number, treated as a mathematical entity. This raises the interesting question: since single numbers have an algebra characterized by the familiar operations of addition, subtraction, multiplication and division, what form does the algebra of arrays of numbers or of matrices take? The answer to this question will be found in the following discussion of the matrix operations of addition, subtraction, multiplication and division.

As a preliminary, let us note that it is conventional to write the matrices

$$B = \begin{bmatrix} b_{11} & b_{12} \\ b_{21} & b_{22} \end{bmatrix} \quad \text{and} \quad C = \begin{bmatrix} c_{11} & c_{12} \\ c_{21} & c_{22} \end{bmatrix}$$

in the shorthand notation

$$B = [b_{ij}] \quad \text{and} \quad C = [c_{ij}] \quad \begin{pmatrix} i = 1, 2 \\ j = 1, 2 \end{pmatrix}$$

Similarly, matrix A in (4-8) can be written as

$$A = [a_{ij}] \quad \begin{pmatrix} i = 1, 2, \ldots, m \\ j = 1, 2, \ldots, n \end{pmatrix}$$

Equality of Matrices

Two matrices A and B are said to be *equal* if and only if they have the same dimension and every element of B is identical to the corresponding element in A. Alternatively, $A = B$ or $[a_{ij}] = [b_{ij}]$ iff $a_{ij} = b_{ij}$ for all values of i and j. For example

$$\begin{bmatrix} 5 & 2 \\ -1 & 0 \end{bmatrix} = \begin{bmatrix} 5 & 2 \\ -1 & 0 \end{bmatrix} \quad \text{but} \quad \begin{bmatrix} 0 & 3 \\ 2 & -4 \end{bmatrix} \neq \begin{bmatrix} 3 & 0 \\ -4 & 2 \end{bmatrix}$$

This definition of equality also holds for vectors. Thus

$$\begin{bmatrix} 3 \\ 5 \end{bmatrix} = \begin{bmatrix} 3 \\ 5 \end{bmatrix} \quad \text{and} \quad [2 \quad 6] = [2 \quad 6]$$

Addition of Matrices

Two matrices can be added if and only if they have the same dimension. If two matrices A and B have the same dimension, they are said to be *comformable* for addition and their addition is defined as the addition of each pair of corresponding elements in A and B. For example

$$\begin{bmatrix} 5 & 3 \\ 2 & -1 \end{bmatrix} + \begin{bmatrix} 0 & 2 \\ 3 & 3 \end{bmatrix} = \begin{bmatrix} 5+0 & 3+2 \\ 2+3 & -1+3 \end{bmatrix} = \begin{bmatrix} 5 & 5 \\ 5 & 2 \end{bmatrix}$$

Or, in general, we have

$$\begin{bmatrix} a_{11} & a_{12} \\ a_{21} & a_{22} \end{bmatrix} + \begin{bmatrix} b_{11} & b_{12} \\ b_{21} & b_{22} \end{bmatrix} = \begin{bmatrix} a_{11}+b_{11} & a_{12}+b_{12} \\ a_{21}+b_{21} & a_{22}+b_{22} \end{bmatrix}$$

which can be written in shorthand form as

$$[a_{ij}] + [b_{ij}] = [c_{ij}] \quad \text{where} \quad c_{ij} = a_{ij} + b_{ij}$$

This addition operation also holds for vectors. Thus

$$\begin{bmatrix} 2 \\ 0 \end{bmatrix} + \begin{bmatrix} 3 \\ -2 \end{bmatrix} = \begin{bmatrix} 5 \\ -2 \end{bmatrix} \quad \text{and} \quad [1 \quad 7] + [3 \quad 2] = [4 \quad 9]$$

Note, in each case, that the resulting sum matrix (vector) $[c_{ij}]$ always has the same dimension as $[a_{ij}]$ and $[b_{ij}]$, the matrices (vectors) which are being added.

Matrix (vector) addition also obeys the following rules:

$$A + B = B + A \tag{4-14}$$
$$(A + B) + C = A + (B + C) \tag{4-15}$$

The demonstration of these rules is left for the student to do in Prob. 4-4 in Sec. 4-B.

Subtraction of Matrices

The operation of subtraction can be defined in a manner analogous to the addition of matrices. Thus the subtraction of two matrices A and B is defined if and only if A and B have the same dimension. The subtraction operation $A - B$ is, in general, given by

$$[a_{ij}] - [b_{ij}] = [c_{ij}] \quad \text{where} \quad c_{ij} = a_{ij} - b_{ij}$$

For example

$$\begin{bmatrix} 12 & 3 \\ 0 & 3 \end{bmatrix} - \begin{bmatrix} 10 & 5 \\ 0 & 2 \end{bmatrix} = \begin{bmatrix} 12-10 & 3-5 \\ 0-0 & 3-2 \end{bmatrix} = \begin{bmatrix} 2 & -2 \\ 0 & 1 \end{bmatrix}$$

This subtraction operation also holds for vectors. Thus

$$\begin{bmatrix} 4 \\ 3 \end{bmatrix} - \begin{bmatrix} 2 \\ 4 \end{bmatrix} = \begin{bmatrix} 2 \\ -1 \end{bmatrix} \quad \text{and} \quad [3 \ 0] - [1 \ 2] = [2 \ -2]$$

Scalar Multiplication

When a matrix is multiplied by a number (which, in the context of matrix algebra, is equivalently termed a *scalar*), *every* element in that matrix is multiplied by the scalar. For example,

$$3\begin{bmatrix} 2 & 4 \\ -2 & 0 \end{bmatrix} = \begin{bmatrix} 6 & 12 \\ -6 & 0 \end{bmatrix} \quad \text{and} \quad -2\begin{bmatrix} 0 & -3 \\ 4 & 1 \end{bmatrix} = \begin{bmatrix} 0 & 6 \\ -8 & -2 \end{bmatrix}$$

In general

$$k[a_{ij}] = [ka_{ij}] = [a_{ij}]k \tag{4-16}$$

where k is a scalar. Note, in (4-16), that it is immaterial whether $[a_{ij}]$ is pre- or post-multiplied by k. Scalar multiplication also holds for vectors. Thus

$$4\begin{bmatrix} -2 \\ 3 \end{bmatrix} = \begin{bmatrix} -8 \\ 12 \end{bmatrix} \quad \text{and} \quad \tfrac{1}{3}[6 \ -3] = [2 \ -1]$$

Finally, note that there is no conformability condition for scalar multiplication.

4-B PRACTICE PROBLEMS

4-3 Given $A = \begin{bmatrix} 3 & 1 \\ 0 & -2 \end{bmatrix}$, $B = \begin{bmatrix} 2 & -4 \\ 1 & 0 \end{bmatrix}$, and $C = \begin{bmatrix} 5 & 7 \\ -2 & -1 \end{bmatrix}$, find

(a) $A+B$ (b) $A-B$ (c) $B+A$ (d) $A-C$
(e) $B+C$ (f) $3B$ (g) $-2A$ (h) $3B-2A$

4-4 For A, B and C in Prob. 4-3, demonstrate that
(a) $A+B = B+A$ (b) $(A+B)+C = A+(B+C)$

4-5 Given $u = \begin{bmatrix} 3 \\ 1 \end{bmatrix}$, $v = \begin{bmatrix} 2 \\ -6 \end{bmatrix}$, $u' = [3 \ 1]$, and $v' = [2 \ -6]$, find

(a) $u+v$ (b) $u'+v'$ (c) $u-v$ (d) $v'-u'$ (e) $4u+3v$ (f) $\tfrac{1}{2}v' - 2u'$

Matrix Multiplication

Before we can find the matrix product AB, of two matrices A and B, a conformability condition must be met. This conformability condition states that the matrix product AB is defined if and only if A is of dimension $m \times n$ and B is of dimension $n \times p$. In other words, the matrix product AB is defined if and only if the number of columns in A is equal to the number of rows in B. For example, the products

$$\underset{(2 \times 2)}{A} \underset{(2 \times 3)}{B} \quad \text{and} \quad \underset{(7 \times 5)}{A} \underset{(5 \times 4)}{B}$$

are defined since the conformability condition is met in each case. Conversely, the products

$$\underset{(2 \times 2)}{A} \underset{(3 \times 3)}{B} \quad \text{and} \quad \underset{(9 \times 2)}{A} \underset{(6 \times 5)}{B}$$

are *not* defined since the conformability condition is violated in each case.

It should be noted that when the product AB is defined, the reverse product BA may *not* be defined. For example, if A is a 2×2 matrix and B is a 2×3 matrix, then the reverse product

$$\underset{(2 \times 3)}{B} \underset{(2 \times 2)}{A}$$

is *not* defined since the conformability condition is not met. In contrast, AB is defined.

If A is an $m \times n$ matrix and B an $n \times p$ matrix, then the product matrix AB (which is defined) will be an $m \times p$ matrix. In other words, the product AB will have the same number of rows as A and the same number of columns as B. For example, assuming $AB = C$, we have

$$\underset{(2 \times 2)}{A} \underset{(2 \times 3)}{B} = \underset{(2 \times 3)}{C} \quad \text{and} \quad \underset{(7 \times 5)}{A} \underset{(5 \times 4)}{B} = \underset{(7 \times 4)}{C}$$

Note how the dimension indicators provide both a check of conformability for multiplication and an indication of the dimension of the product matrix C:

$$\text{conformability condition}$$
$$(2 \times \overbrace{2)(2} \times 3)$$
$$\underbrace{}_{\text{dimension of } C}$$

This result helps to explain the matrix notation $Ax = b$ in (4-11). Since, from (4-8), A is an $m \times n$ matrix and b is an $m \times 1$ column vector, then the conformability condition requires x to be a column vector (rather than a row vector) in (4-11) so that

$$\underset{(m \times n)}{A} \underset{(n \times 1)}{x} = \underset{(m \times 1)}{b}$$

The next step is to define the procedure for matrix multiplication. To do this, let us assume $AB = C$, so that

$$\underset{(2 \times 2)}{A} \underset{(2 \times 2)}{B} = \begin{bmatrix} a_{11} & a_{12} \\ a_{21} & a_{22} \end{bmatrix} \begin{bmatrix} b_{11} & b_{12} \\ b_{21} & b_{22} \end{bmatrix} = \begin{bmatrix} c_{11} & c_{12} \\ c_{21} & c_{22} \end{bmatrix} = \underset{(2 \times 2)}{C} \quad (4\text{-}17)$$

Given (4-17), the elements of C are defined as

$$[c_{ij}] = \begin{bmatrix} c_{11} & c_{12} \\ c_{21} & c_{22} \end{bmatrix} = \begin{bmatrix} a_{11}b_{11}+a_{12}b_{21} & a_{11}b_{12}+a_{12}b_{22} \\ a_{21}b_{11}+a_{22}b_{21} & a_{21}b_{12}+a_{22}b_{22} \end{bmatrix} \quad (4\text{-}18)$$

To explain this procedure, consider element $c_{11} = a_{11}b_{11} + a_{12}b_{21}$ which contains the elements of row 1 in A and the elements of column 1 in B. Note that the first subscript of c_{11} tells us to use *row* 1 of A, and the second subscript of c_{11} tells us to use *column* 1 of B, in the multiplication procedure. With the row and column thus marked out, the elements of the row and column are then paired sequentially (i.e., a_{11} with b_{11} and a_{12} with b_{21}) and the elements in each of these pairs multiplied together (to give $a_{11}b_{11}$ and $a_{12}b_{21}$). Finally, the sum of these products (which is given by $a_{11}b_{11} + a_{12}b_{21}$) gives c_{11} as in (4-18).

As a further example, note how we obtain element c_{21} in (4-18). Since the first subscript is 2 and the second subscript is 1, this means that we use *row* 2 of A and *column* 1 of B. Then, with the left index finger moving across (from left to right) row 2 of A and, simultaneously, the right index finger moving down (from top to bottom) column 1 of B, we form the sum of products $a_{21}b_{11} + a_{22}b_{21} = c_{21}$. Therefore, in general, the procedure to obtain element c_{ij} is: (i) take row i of A and column j of B, (ii) sequentially pair the elements therein, (iii) multiply together the elements in each of these pairs, and (iv) take the sum of products thus formed. This 'row by column' rule of multiplication can be applied to multiply any two matrices which meet the conformability condition for multiplication.

The above procedure for matrix multiplication may appear somewhat complicated at first sight, but a little practice will reveal it to be quite straightforward. Before illustrating matrix multiplication with numerical examples, it should be noted that both the conformability condition for multiplication and the multiplication procedure also hold for the multiplication of vectors.

Examples of Matrix Multiplication

4-6 Given $A = \begin{bmatrix} 2 & 3 \\ 1 & 2 \end{bmatrix}$, $B = \begin{bmatrix} 0 & -2 \\ -3 & 1 \end{bmatrix}$, $C = \begin{bmatrix} 1 & 2 & 3 \\ 0 & 4 & 1 \end{bmatrix}$, and $b = \begin{bmatrix} 5 \\ 2 \end{bmatrix}$, find

(a) AB (b) BA (c) Ab (d) BC

SOLUTION

(a) $\begin{bmatrix} 2 & 3 \\ 1 & 2 \end{bmatrix}\begin{bmatrix} 0 & -2 \\ -3 & 1 \end{bmatrix} = \begin{bmatrix} 2(0)+3(-3) & 2(-2)+3(1) \\ 1(0)+2(-3) & 1(-2)+2(1) \end{bmatrix} = \begin{bmatrix} -9 & -1 \\ -6 & 0 \end{bmatrix}$

(b) $\begin{bmatrix} 0 & -2 \\ -3 & 1 \end{bmatrix}\begin{bmatrix} 2 & 3 \\ 1 & 2 \end{bmatrix} = \begin{bmatrix} 0(2)-2(1) & 0(3)-2(2) \\ -3(2)+1(1) & -3(3)+1(2) \end{bmatrix} = \begin{bmatrix} -2 & -4 \\ -5 & -7 \end{bmatrix}$

(c) $\begin{bmatrix} 2 & 3 \\ 1 & 2 \end{bmatrix}\begin{bmatrix} 5 \\ 2 \end{bmatrix} = \begin{bmatrix} 2(5)+3(2) \\ 1(5)+2(2) \end{bmatrix} = \begin{bmatrix} 16 \\ 9 \end{bmatrix}$

(d) $\begin{bmatrix} 0 & -2 \\ -3 & 1 \end{bmatrix}\begin{bmatrix} 1 & 2 & 3 \\ 0 & 4 & 1 \end{bmatrix} = \begin{bmatrix} 0(1)-2(0) & 0(2)-2(4) & 0(3)-2(1) \\ -3(1)+1(0) & -3(2)+1(4) & -3(3)+1(1) \end{bmatrix}$
$= \begin{bmatrix} 0 & -8 & -2 \\ -3 & -2 & -8 \end{bmatrix}$

Note, in Examples 4-6a and 4-6b, that while BA is defined, $AB \neq BA$. This example, with $AB \neq BA$ demonstrates how important it is to specify the order of multiplication. Thus, in the product AB, matrix A is often referred to as the 'lead' matrix and matrix B as the 'lag' matrix. Alternatively, in the product AB, matrix B is said to be 'premultiplied' by matrix A or, equivalently, matrix A is said to be 'postmultiplied' by matrix B. In general, $AB \neq BA$. [*Warning*: unlike ordinary algebra, $AB = AC$ does *not* imply $B = C$.]

4-7 Given $u = \begin{bmatrix} 2 \\ 1 \end{bmatrix}$, $v = \begin{bmatrix} -1 \\ 3 \end{bmatrix}$, and $u' = \begin{bmatrix} 2 & 1 \end{bmatrix}$, find

(a) uu' (b) vu' (c) $u'u$

SOLUTION

(a) $\begin{bmatrix} 2 \\ 1 \end{bmatrix}\begin{bmatrix} 2 & 1 \end{bmatrix} = \begin{bmatrix} 2(2) & 2(1) \\ 1(2) & 1(1) \end{bmatrix} = \begin{bmatrix} 4 & 2 \\ 2 & 1 \end{bmatrix}$

(b) $\begin{bmatrix} -1 \\ 3 \end{bmatrix}\begin{bmatrix} 2 & 1 \end{bmatrix} = \begin{bmatrix} -1(2) & -1(1) \\ 3(2) & 3(1) \end{bmatrix} = \begin{bmatrix} -2 & -1 \\ 6 & 3 \end{bmatrix}$

(c) $\begin{bmatrix} 2 & 1 \end{bmatrix}\begin{bmatrix} 2 \\ 1 \end{bmatrix} = [2(2)+1(1)] = [5]$

Note, in Examples 4-7a and 4-7c, that $uu' \neq u'u$. Also, in Example 4-7c, note that $u'u$ is a 1×1 matrix. Such 1×1 matrices have exactly the same multiplication and addition properties as scalars. Thus, $[2][3] = [6]$ and $[2]+[3] = [5]$, just as $2(3) = 6$ and $2+3 = 5$. However, while a 1×1 matrix can be regarded as a scalar, a scalar can only be replaced by a 1×1 matrix, and used in matrix operations, when the 1×1 matrix meets the relevant conformability conditions for those operations.

4-8 For the matrix A and vector x, given in (4-7), find Ax. If we then write $Ax = b$, where b is also given in (4-7), is $Ax = b$ an equivalent way of writing the equation system (4-5)?

SOLUTION

$$\underset{(2\times 2)}{A}\underset{(2\times 1)}{x} = \underset{(2\times 2)}{\begin{bmatrix} a_{11} & a_{12} \\ a_{21} & a_{22} \end{bmatrix}}\underset{(2\times 1)}{\begin{bmatrix} x_1 \\ x_2 \end{bmatrix}} = \underset{(2\times 1)}{\begin{bmatrix} a_{11}x_1 + a_{12}x_2 \\ a_{21}x_1 + a_{22}x_2 \end{bmatrix}} = \underset{(2\times 1)}{\begin{bmatrix} b_1 \\ b_2 \end{bmatrix}} = \underset{(2\times 1)}{b}$$

Note that Ax is a 2×1 *column vector*. Since $Ax = b$, this implies (by the definition of matrix equality) that not only have Ax and b the same dimension but also that the corresponding elements of Ax and b are identical. Hence

$\begin{bmatrix} a_{11}x_1 + a_{12}x_2 \\ a_{21}x_1 + a_{22}x_2 \end{bmatrix} = \begin{bmatrix} b_1 \\ b_2 \end{bmatrix}$ is equivalent to $\begin{aligned} a_{11}x_1 + a_{12}x_2 &= b_1 \\ a_{21}x_1 + a_{22}x_2 &= b_2 \end{aligned}$ as in (4-5)

4-9 Taking A, x and b as defined in (4-8), demonstrate that $Ax = b$ is an equivalent way of writing the linear-equation system (4-6).

SOLUTION

$$Ax = \begin{bmatrix} a_{11} & a_{12} \cdots a_{1n} \\ a_{21} & a_{22} \cdots a_{2n} \\ \cdots\cdots\cdots\cdots \\ a_{m1} & a_{m2} \cdots a_{mn} \end{bmatrix} \begin{bmatrix} x_1 \\ x_2 \\ \vdots \\ x_n \end{bmatrix} = \begin{bmatrix} a_{11}x_1 + a_{12}x_2 + \ldots + a_{1n}x_n \\ a_{21}x_1 + a_{22}x_2 + \ldots + a_{2n}x_n \\ \cdots\cdots\cdots\cdots\cdots\cdots\cdots \\ a_{m1}x_1 + a_{m2}x_2 + \ldots + a_{mn}x_n \end{bmatrix}$$
$$(m \times n) \qquad (n \times 1) \qquad\qquad (m \times 1)$$

Since $Ax = b$, the definition of matrix equality implies that

$$\begin{bmatrix} a_{11}x_1 + a_{12}x_2 + \ldots + a_{1n}x_n \\ a_{21}x_1 + a_{22}x_2 + \ldots + a_{2n}x_n \\ \cdots\cdots\cdots\cdots\cdots\cdots \\ a_{m1}x_1 + a_{m2}x_2 + \ldots + a_{mn}x_n \end{bmatrix} = \begin{bmatrix} b_1 \\ b_2 \\ \vdots \\ b_m \end{bmatrix} \text{ is equivalent to } \begin{array}{l} a_{11}x_1 + a_{12}x_2 + \ldots + a_{1n}x_n = b_1 \\ a_{21}x_1 + a_{22}x_2 + \ldots + a_{2n}x_n = b_2 \\ \cdots\cdots\cdots\cdots\cdots\cdots \\ a_{m1}x_1 + a_{m2}x_2 + \ldots + a_{mn}x_n = b_m \end{array}$$
$$(m \times 1) \qquad\qquad (m \times 1)$$

as in (4-6).

Matrix Division

Having discussed the operations of addition, subtraction and multiplication for matrices, we naturally want to know whether or not there is a division operation for matrices. The answer is that the operation of division is not defined for matrices. This means, for two matrices A and B, that we cannot unambiguously write A/B. Similarly, given a simultaneous-equation system $Ax = b$, we cannot unambiguously write its solution as $x = b/A$. However, this does not mean that we cannot solve $Ax = b$. In Sec. 4-5 we shall see that the solution of $Ax = b$ is given by $x = A^{-1}b$, where A^{-1} is known as the *inverse* of matrix A. For the moment, until we discuss inverse matrices in 4-5, it is important to note that since A^{-1} may or may not exist, it cannot be unambiguously written as $1/A$.

4-C PRACTICE PROBLEMS

4-10 Given A, B and C, find the following products (if defined) and state the dimension of each product:
$\quad (2 \times 3) \quad (3 \times 2) \quad (7 \times 3)$

(a) AB (b) BA (c) AC (d) CA (e) BC (f) CB

4-11 Given u, v, u' and v', find the following products (if defined) and state the
$\quad\quad\quad\quad (5 \times 1) \ (3 \times 1) \ (1 \times 5) \quad\quad (1 \times 3)$
dimension of each product:

(a) uv (b) vu (c) vu' (d) uv' (e) vv' (f) $u'u$

4-12 Given $b = \begin{bmatrix} 2 \\ 1 \\ -3 \end{bmatrix}$, $y = \begin{bmatrix} y_1 \\ y_2 \\ y_3 \end{bmatrix}$, $b' = [2 \ \ 1 \ \ -3]$, and $z' = [z_1 \ \ z_2]$, find

(a) yb' (b) bz' (c) $b'b$ (d) bb' (e) by (f) $z'y$

4-13 Given $A = \begin{bmatrix} 3 & 0 \\ 2 & -1 \\ -1 & 4 \end{bmatrix}$, $B = \begin{bmatrix} 5 & 0 & -2 \\ 3 & 2 & 1 \end{bmatrix}$, $x = \begin{bmatrix} r \\ s \\ t \end{bmatrix}$, and $b' = [2 \ \ -3 \ \ 7]$, find

(a) AB (b) BA (c) Bx (d) $b'A$ (e) xb' (f) $b'x$ (g) $b'B$ (h) Ax

72 MATRIX ALGEBRA

4-14 Given $A = \begin{bmatrix} 1 & -2 \\ 0 & 3 \end{bmatrix}$, $B = \begin{bmatrix} 0 & 1 \\ 2 & 1 \end{bmatrix}$, $C = \begin{bmatrix} 3 & 2 \\ 1 & 0 \\ -1 & 2 \end{bmatrix}$, $D = \begin{bmatrix} 1 & 1 & 2 \\ 3 & 0 & 1 \end{bmatrix}$, and $E = \begin{bmatrix} 3 & 2 \\ 1 & -5 \end{bmatrix}$.

Are each of the following valid?:
(a) $AB = BA$
(b) $A(B+E) = AB + AE$
(c) $(B+E)A = BA + EA$
(d) $(AD)C = A(DC)$
(e) $-3(A+E) = -3A - 3E$
(f) $5B = 2B + 3B$

4-15 For the matrix A and vector x, given in (4-10), find Ax. Is $Ax = b$, where b is also given in (4-10), an equivalent way of writing (4-9)?

4-3 IDENTITY MATRICES AND NULL MATRICES

Identity Matrices

An *identity matrix*, denoted by I, is defined as a *square* matrix with 1s in its *principal diagonal* (which runs from northwest to southeast) and 0s everywhere else. For example, denoting an $n \times n$ identity matrix by I_n, we have

$$I = I_2 = \begin{bmatrix} 1 & 0 \\ 0 & 1 \end{bmatrix} \qquad I = I_3 = \begin{bmatrix} 1 & 0 & 0 \\ 0 & 1 & 0 \\ 0 & 0 & 1 \end{bmatrix}$$

The identity matrix has particular significance in that it plays a role similar to that of the number 1 in ordinary algebra. Thus, for any matrix A, we can write

$$IA = AI = A \tag{4-19}$$

in just the same way as we can write $1(a) = a(1) = a$, where a is any number. It should be noted, in (4-19), that the premultiplication and postmultiplication of A by I may involve identity matrices of different dimensions. For example

$$\underset{(2\times 2)}{I} \underset{(2\times 2)}{A} = \underset{(2\times 2)}{A} \underset{(2\times 2)}{I} = \underset{(2\times 2)}{A} \quad \text{and} \quad \underset{(3\times 3)}{I} \underset{(3\times 2)}{A} = \underset{(3\times 2)}{A} \underset{(2\times 2)}{I} = \underset{(3\times 2)}{A}$$

Also note that (4-19) illustrates an exception to the general rule $AB \neq BA$. [*Warning*: unlike ordinary algebra, $AB = A$ does *not* imply $B = I$.]

Null Matrices

A *null matrix* or *zero matrix*, denoted by 0, is defined as a matrix whose elements are all zero. For example, we can write

$$\underset{(2\times 2)}{0} = \begin{bmatrix} 0 & 0 \\ 0 & 0 \end{bmatrix} \quad \text{and} \quad \underset{(2\times 4)}{0} = \begin{bmatrix} 0 & 0 & 0 & 0 \\ 0 & 0 & 0 & 0 \end{bmatrix}$$

Just as an identity matrix I plays the role of the number 1, a null matrix 0 plays the role of the number 0. Thus, for any matrix A, we can write

$$A_{(m \times n)} + 0_{(m \times n)} = 0_{(m \times n)} + A_{(m \times n)} = A_{(m \times n)} \qquad (4\text{-}20)$$

and

$$A_{(m \times n)} \, 0_{(n \times p)} = 0_{(m \times p)} \quad \text{and} \quad 0_{(q \times m)} \, A_{(m \times n)} = 0_{(q \times n)} \qquad (4\text{-}21)$$

Note, in (4-20) and (4-21), that the conformability conditions for addition and multiplication must be met. Also, note in (4-21) the respective dimensions of each null matrix. [*Warning*: unlike ordinary algebra, $AB = 0$ does *not* imply that either A or B is a null matrix.]

4-D PRACTICE PROBLEMS

4-16 Given $A = \begin{bmatrix} 3 & 2 \\ -1 & 0 \\ 1 & 4 \end{bmatrix}$, $b' = \begin{bmatrix} 3 & -2 \end{bmatrix}$, and $z = \begin{bmatrix} z_1 \\ z_2 \end{bmatrix}$, compute

(a) IA (b) AI (c) $b'I$ (d) Iz (e) IAI
In each case state the dimension of the identity matrix used.

4-17 For matrices A, b' and z in Prob. 4-16, compute

(a) $A + 0$ (b) $0 + b'$ (c) $z - 0$ (d) $\underset{(3 \times 3)}{0} A$ (e) $\underset{(2 \times 3)}{0} A$

4-4 THE TRANSPOSE OF A MATRIX

The *transpose* of a matrix A, denoted by A' or A^T, is obtained by interchanging the rows and columns of A so that if A is an $m \times n$ matrix, then A' is an $n \times m$ matrix. For example, given

$$\underset{(2 \times 2)}{A} = \begin{bmatrix} 0 & 2 \\ -3 & 6 \end{bmatrix}, \quad \underset{(3 \times 2)}{B} = \begin{bmatrix} -1 & 5 \\ 7 & 9 \\ 2 & 3 \end{bmatrix}, \quad \text{and} \quad \underset{(2 \times 1)}{y} = \begin{bmatrix} y_1 \\ y_2 \end{bmatrix}$$

then

$$\underset{(2 \times 2)}{A'} = \begin{bmatrix} 0 & -3 \\ 2 & 6 \end{bmatrix}, \quad \underset{(2 \times 3)}{B'} = \begin{bmatrix} -1 & 7 & 2 \\ 5 & 9 & 3 \end{bmatrix}, \quad \text{and} \quad \underset{(1 \times 2)}{y'} = \begin{bmatrix} y_1 & y_2 \end{bmatrix}$$

If a square matrix $A = [a_{ij}]$ and its transpose $A' = [a_{ji}]$ are equal, so that $a_{ij} = a_{ji}$ for all i and j, then the matrix is said to be *symmetric* (about its principal diagonal). For example

$$C = \begin{bmatrix} 9 & -3 \\ -3 & 2 \end{bmatrix} = C' \quad \text{and} \quad D = \begin{bmatrix} 1 & 0 & 2 \\ 0 & -2 & 7 \\ 2 & 7 & 5 \end{bmatrix} = D'$$

are *symmetric matrices*. Note in $D = D'$ that $a_{12} = a_{21} = 0$, $a_{13} = a_{31} = 2$ and $a_{23} = a_{32} = 7$. Also note that the identity matrix I is a symmetric matrix with $I' = I$.

Transposes possess the following properties:

$$(A')' = A; \quad (A+B)' = A' + B'; \quad (AB)' = B'A' \qquad (4\text{-}22)$$

The demonstration of (4-22), except for the self-evident property $(A')' = A$, is left for the student to do in Prob. 4-18 in Sec. 4-E.

The significance of the somewhat unusual transposition operation will become clear when we come to solve a simultaneous-equation system such as $Ax = b$.

4-5 THE INVERSE OF A MATRIX

In ordinary algebra every nonzero number has a reciprocal. Thus for any number a (where $a \neq 0$), a^{-1} represents the *inverse* or *reciprocal* of a such that

$$aa^{-1} = a^{-1}a = 1 \qquad (4\text{-}23)$$

In matrix algebra, however, the case is rather different in that the inverse of a given matrix may or may not exist. For this reason we must approach the concept of an inverse with caution.

Before defining an inverse matrix, let us note that only a *square* matrix may have an inverse. This, however, does *not* mean that every square matrix has an inverse. In other words, while squareness is a *necessary* condition, it is *not* a *sufficient* condition, for the existence of an inverse. Also note, as a matter of terminology, that if a square matrix A has an inverse, then A is said to be a *nonsingular* matrix. Conversely, if A has no inverse, then A is said to be a *singular* matrix.

The *inverse* of a square matrix A is defined as another square matrix, denoted by A^{-1}, which satisfies the relation

$$AA^{-1} = A^{-1}A = I \qquad (4\text{-}24)$$

(4-24) states that post- or pre-multiplication of A by its inverse yields the same identity matrix. For example, given

$$A = \begin{bmatrix} 1 & 2 \\ 0 & 4 \end{bmatrix}, \quad \text{and} \quad A^{-1} = \tfrac{1}{4}\begin{bmatrix} 4 & -2 \\ 0 & 1 \end{bmatrix}$$

then

$$AA^{-1} = \begin{bmatrix} 1 & 2 \\ 0 & 4 \end{bmatrix}\begin{bmatrix} 4 & -2 \\ 0 & 1 \end{bmatrix}\tfrac{1}{4} = \begin{bmatrix} 4 & 0 \\ 0 & 4 \end{bmatrix}\tfrac{1}{4} = \begin{bmatrix} 1 & 0 \\ 0 & 1 \end{bmatrix} = I$$

and

$$A^{-1}A = \tfrac{1}{4}\begin{bmatrix} 4 & -2 \\ 0 & 1 \end{bmatrix}\begin{bmatrix} 1 & 2 \\ 0 & 4 \end{bmatrix} = \tfrac{1}{4}\begin{bmatrix} 4 & 0 \\ 0 & 4 \end{bmatrix} = \begin{bmatrix} 1 & 0 \\ 0 & 1 \end{bmatrix} = I$$

In relation to (4-24), it is important to note the following:

1. If A is $n \times n$, then A^{-1} must also be $n \times n$ in order to be conformable for both pre- and post-multiplication by A in (4-24). Also, note that (4-24), like (4-19), is an exception to the general rule $AB \neq BA$.
2. If an inverse exists, then it is *unique*.
3. Since an inverse may not exist, (4-24) can only be regarded as an imperfect analogy to (4-23).

Inverses possess the following properties:

$$(A^{-1})^{-1} = A; \quad (AB)^{-1} = B^{-1}A^{-1}; \quad (A')^{-1} = (A^{-1})' \qquad (4\text{-}25)$$

The demonstration of (4-25), except for the self-evident property $(A^{-1})^{-1} = A$, is left for the student to do in Prob. 4-20 in Sec. 4-E. Note also that $(ABC)^{-1} = C^{-1}B^{-1}A^{-1}$ and $I = I' = I^{-1}$.

We are now in a position to demonstrate how the concept of an inverse matrix can be utilized to obtain the solution of a simultaneous-equation system. For example, the linear-equation system

$$2x_1 + 3x_2 = 21$$
$$5x_1 - 2x_2 = 5$$

can be written in matrix notation as

$$\underset{(2 \times 2)}{A} \underset{(2 \times 1)}{x} = \underset{(2 \times 1)}{b} \qquad (4\text{-}26)$$

where

$$A = \begin{bmatrix} 2 & 3 \\ 5 & -2 \end{bmatrix}, \quad x = \begin{bmatrix} x_1 \\ x_2 \end{bmatrix}, \quad \text{and} \quad b = \begin{bmatrix} 21 \\ 5 \end{bmatrix} \qquad (4\text{-}27)$$

Then, if the inverse matrix A^{-1} exists, (4-26) may be rewritten as

$$\underset{(2 \times 2)}{A^{-1}} \underset{(2 \times 2)}{A} \underset{(2 \times 1)}{x} = \underset{(2 \times 2)}{I} \underset{(2 \times 1)}{x} = \underset{(2 \times 2)}{A^{-1}} \underset{(2 \times 1)}{b}$$

or

$$\underset{(2 \times 1)}{x} = \underset{(2 \times 2)}{A^{-1}} \underset{(2 \times 1)}{b} \qquad (4\text{-}28)$$

Since, in (4-28), x is a column vector of variables and the product $A^{-1}b$ is a column vector of given numbers then, by the definition of vector equality, $A^{-1}b$ is a vector of (solution) values of the variables which satisfy (4-26). To see this more clearly, let us assume that A^{-1} exists and is given by

$$A^{-1} = -\tfrac{1}{19} \begin{bmatrix} -2 & -3 \\ -5 & 2 \end{bmatrix}$$

Therefore (4-28) will be

$$\begin{bmatrix} x_1 \\ x_2 \end{bmatrix} = -\tfrac{1}{19} \begin{bmatrix} -2 & -3 \\ -5 & 2 \end{bmatrix} \begin{bmatrix} 21 \\ 5 \end{bmatrix} = \begin{bmatrix} 3 \\ 5 \end{bmatrix} \qquad (4\text{-}29)$$

which gives the solution of (4-26) as $x_1 = 3$, $x_2 = 5$. Note that, since A^{-1} is unique, $x = A^{-1}b$ will be a unique vector of solution values as shown in (4-29). In keeping with earlier notation, we will write (4-28) as $\bar{x} = A^{-1}b$, with $\bar{x}_1 = 3$ and $\bar{x}_2 = 5$.

The above example indicates that the solution of a linear-equation system $Ax = b$, where A is nonsingular, can be found by the product $A^{-1}b$. This, however, leaves unanswered the following important questions: what is the method of testing the existence of the inverse A^{-1} (or, equivalently, what is the method of testing the nonsingularity of A)? also, assuming A^{-1} exists, what is the procedure for its calculation? The answers to these questions cannot be given until we have done some further analysis. In particular, we must first discuss the concept of *determinants*.

Before proceeding to the discussion of determinants, it will be useful at this stage to introduce the Σ notation.

Σ Notation

This notation permits us to express, say, the sum of x_1, x_2, x_3 and x_4, as

$$x_1 + x_2 + x_3 + x_4 = \sum_{j=1}^{4} x_j$$

which is read 'the sum of x_j as j ranges from 1 to 4'. The summation sign Σ (the Greek capital letter sigma) simply means 'the sum of'. The symbol j, which takes only integer values, is called the *summation index*, while the expression x_j is called the *summand*. Summation indices are commonly denoted by i, j or k. Thus

$$\sum_{i=0}^{3} x_i = x_0 + x_1 + x_2 + x_3 \quad \text{and} \quad \sum_{k=1}^{n} x_k = x_1 + x_2 + \ldots + x_n$$

Other examples of the Σ notation are

$$\sum_{k=1}^{5} x_k = (x_1 + x_2 + x_3) + (x_4 + x_5) = \sum_{k=1}^{3} x_k + \sum_{k=4}^{5} x_k$$

$$\sum_{j=1}^{3} bx_j = bx_1 + bx_2 + bx_3 = b(x_1 + x_2 + x_3) = b \sum_{j=1}^{3} x_j$$

$$\sum_{i=0}^{n} a_i x^i = a_0 x^0 + a_1 x^1 + a_2 x^2 + \ldots + a_n x^n = a_0 + a_1 x + a_2 x^2 + \ldots + a_n x^n$$

$$\sum_{j=1}^{4} a_{1j} x_j = a_{11} x_1 + a_{12} x_2 + a_{13} x_3 + a_{14} x_4$$

These examples will suffice to illustrate the compactness of the Σ notation. This notation will be used in our discussion of determinants.

4-E PRACTICE PROBLEMS

4-18 Given $A = \begin{bmatrix} 2 & 1 \\ 3 & 0 \end{bmatrix}$, $B = \begin{bmatrix} 5 & -2 \\ 4 & 7 \end{bmatrix}$, and $C = \begin{bmatrix} 0 & 4 \\ 2 & 1 \end{bmatrix}$, demonstrate that
(a) $(A+B)' = A' + B'$ (b) $(AB)' = B'A'$ (c) $(ABC)' = C'B'A'$

4-19 Given $A = \begin{bmatrix} 2 & 2 \\ 1 & 4 \end{bmatrix}$, $B = \begin{bmatrix} \frac{2}{3} & -\frac{1}{3} \\ -\frac{1}{6} & \frac{1}{3} \end{bmatrix}$, $C = \begin{bmatrix} 3 & 2 \\ 3 & 1 \end{bmatrix}$, and $D = \begin{bmatrix} -\frac{1}{3} & \frac{2}{3} \\ 1 & -1 \end{bmatrix}$, demonstrate that (a) B is the inverse of A (b) D is the inverse of C

4-20 Given $(AB)^{-1} = \frac{1}{10}\begin{bmatrix} 4 & -6 \\ -19 & 31 \end{bmatrix}$, $B^{-1} = \begin{bmatrix} 0 & 1 \\ \frac{1}{2} & -\frac{9}{2} \end{bmatrix}$, $A^{-1} = \begin{bmatrix} -\frac{1}{5} & \frac{4}{5} \\ \frac{2}{5} & -\frac{3}{5} \end{bmatrix}$, and

$(A')^{-1} = \begin{bmatrix} -\frac{1}{5} & \frac{2}{5} \\ \frac{4}{5} & -\frac{3}{5} \end{bmatrix}$, demonstrate that (a) $(AB)^{-1} = B^{-1}A^{-1}$ (b) $(A')^{-1} = (A^{-1})'$

4-21 Write out the following summation expressions in full:
(a) $\sum_{i=1}^{3} x^{i-1}$ (b) $\sum_{i=5}^{9} bx_i$ (c) $\sum_{i=2}^{m} a_i x_i$ (d) $\sum_{i=0}^{3} (x_i + i)$

4-22 Rewrite the following in Σ notation:
(a) $c_{21} = a_{21}b_{11} + a_{22}b_{21}$ (b) $a_1 + 2a_2 + 3a_3 + 4a_4$
(c) $x_1 y^{-1} + x_2 y^{-2} + x_3 y^{-3}$ (d) $a_{11}x_1 + a_{12}x_2 + \ldots + a_{1n}x_n = b_1$
(e) $b_3(x_1 + 6) + b_4(x_2 + 8) + b_5(x_3 + 10)$

4-6 DETERMINANTS

A *determinant* is a single scalar (number) associated with a square matrix. Determinants are defined only for *square* matrices. Thus, given

$$A = \begin{bmatrix} a_{11} & a_{12} \\ a_{21} & a_{22} \end{bmatrix}$$

the determinant of A, denoted by $|A|$, is defined as

$$|A| = \begin{vmatrix} a_{11} & a_{12} \\ a_{21} & a_{22} \end{vmatrix} = a_{11}a_{22} - a_{21}a_{12} \tag{4-30}$$

where $|A| = a_{11}a_{22} - a_{21}a_{12}$ is a scalar. For example, given

$$A = \begin{bmatrix} 2 & 1 \\ 4 & 5 \end{bmatrix} \quad \text{and} \quad B = \begin{bmatrix} -3 & 8 \\ 2 & 7 \end{bmatrix}$$

their determinants are

$$|A| = \begin{vmatrix} 2 & 1 \\ 4 & 5 \end{vmatrix} = 2(5) - 4(1) = 6 \quad \text{and} \quad |B| = \begin{vmatrix} -3 & 8 \\ 2 & 7 \end{vmatrix} = -3(7) - 2(8) = -37$$

Note, in these two examples, that the determinants $|A|$ and $|B|$ are (by definition) *single numbers*. In contrast, matrices A and B are *arrays of numbers* and as such do not have numerical values. Also, note that $|A|$ and $|B|$ are called *second-order determinants* in view of the fact that both A and

Evaluation of Higher-Order Determinants

Determinants of orders higher than 2 can be evaluated in terms of what is called the *Laplace expansion* of a determinant. Thus, given

$$A = \begin{bmatrix} a_{11} & a_{12} & a_{13} \\ a_{21} & a_{22} & a_{23} \\ a_{31} & a_{32} & a_{33} \end{bmatrix},$$

its determinant

$$|A| = \begin{vmatrix} a_{11} & a_{12} & a_{13} \\ a_{21} & a_{22} & a_{23} \\ a_{31} & a_{32} & a_{33} \end{vmatrix}$$

has the value

$$|A| = a_{11}\begin{vmatrix} a_{22} & a_{23} \\ a_{32} & a_{33} \end{vmatrix} - a_{12}\begin{vmatrix} a_{21} & a_{23} \\ a_{31} & a_{33} \end{vmatrix} + a_{13}\begin{vmatrix} a_{21} & a_{22} \\ a_{31} & a_{32} \end{vmatrix}$$

$$= a_{11}(a_{22}a_{33} - a_{32}a_{23}) - a_{12}(a_{21}a_{33} - a_{31}a_{23})$$

$$+ a_{13}(a_{21}a_{32} - a_{31}a_{22}) \quad (4\text{-}31)$$

While, at first sight, (4-31) looks rather complicated, an examination of (4-31) will demonstrate that it is not so difficult to evaluate in practice.

Firstly, note in (4-31) that $|A|$ is the sum of *three* terms, each of which is a product of a first-row element and a certain *second*-order determinant. Also, note that the three second-order determinants in (4-31) are specified by a particular rule. Thus, the first one,

$$\begin{vmatrix} a_{22} & a_{23} \\ a_{32} & a_{33} \end{vmatrix}$$

is a *sub*-determinant of $|A|$ obtained by deleting the *first* row and *first* column of $|A|$. This sub-determinant of $|A|$ is called the *minor* of the element a_{11}, which is at the intersection of the deleted row and column, and is denoted by M_{11}. In a similar fashion, the middle second-order determinant in (4-31) can be seen to be the minor of element a_{12}, denoted by M_{12} and obtained by deleting the *first* row and *second* column of $|A|$. Finally, the last second-order determinant in (4-31) is the minor of a_{13}, denoted by M_{13}, so that we have

$$M_{11} = \begin{vmatrix} a_{22} & a_{23} \\ a_{32} & a_{33} \end{vmatrix}, \quad M_{12} = \begin{vmatrix} a_{21} & a_{23} \\ a_{31} & a_{33} \end{vmatrix}, \text{ and } M_{13} = \begin{vmatrix} a_{21} & a_{22} \\ a_{31} & a_{32} \end{vmatrix}$$

Consequently, (4-31) can be alternatively expressed as

$$|A| = a_{11}M_{11} - a_{12}M_{12} + a_{13}M_{13} \quad (4\text{-}32)$$

For example, given

(i) $|A| = \begin{vmatrix} 3 & 2 & 1 \\ 0 & 2 & 5 \\ 7 & -1 & 2 \end{vmatrix}$ and (ii) $|A| = \begin{vmatrix} 0 & -2 & 1 \\ 3 & 0 & -2 \\ 5 & 3 & 6 \end{vmatrix}$

then

(i) $|A| = a_{11}M_{11} - a_{12}M_{12} + a_{13}M_{13} = 3\begin{vmatrix} 2 & 5 \\ -1 & 2 \end{vmatrix} - 2\begin{vmatrix} 0 & 5 \\ 7 & 2 \end{vmatrix} + 1\begin{vmatrix} 0 & 2 \\ 7 & -1 \end{vmatrix}$

$= 3(9) - 2(-35) + 1(-14) = 83$

(ii) $|A| = a_{11}M_{11} - a_{12}M_{12} + a_{13}M_{13} = 0\begin{vmatrix} 0 & -2 \\ 3 & 6 \end{vmatrix} - (-2)\begin{vmatrix} 3 & -2 \\ 5 & 6 \end{vmatrix} + 1\begin{vmatrix} 3 & 0 \\ 5 & 3 \end{vmatrix}$

$= 0 + 2(28) + 1(9) = 65$

At this point, the student should do practice Prob. 4-23, in Sec. 4-F, to ensure that the evaluation of a third-order determinant is properly understood.

The above procedure of evaluating a third-order determinant in terms of certain second-order determinants is known as the *Laplace expansion* of the determinant. This procedure can also be applied to fourth- and higher-order determinants. To demonstrate this, let us firstly define the concept of a *cofactor*, which is a concept closely related to that of a *minor*. Thus, if M_{ij} represents the minor of element a_{ij}, obtained by deleting the *i*th row and *j*th column of a given determinant, then the *cofactor* of a_{ij}, denoted by C_{ij}, is the minor M_{ij} with a certain algebraic sign attached to it:

$$C_{ij} \equiv (-1)^{i+j} M_{ij} \qquad (4\text{-}33)$$

For example, if $i = 1$ and $j = 2$, then

$$C_{12} = (-1)^{1+2} M_{12} = (-1)^3 M_{12} = -M_{12}$$

Similarly, if $i = 3$ and $j = 3$, then

$$C_{33} = (-1)^{3+3} M_{33} = (-1)^6 M_{33} = M_{33}$$

Clearly, if the sum of the two subscripts *i* and *j* in the minor M_{ij} is even (odd), then the cofactor takes the same (opposite) sign as the minor.

Applying (4-33) to (4-32) we have

$$|A| = a_{11}M_{11} - a_{12}M_{12} + a_{13}M_{13}$$
$$= a_{11}C_{11} + a_{12}C_{12} + a_{13}C_{13} = \sum_{j=1}^{3} a_{1j}C_{1j} \qquad (4\text{-}34)$$

Equation (4-34) thus expresses the third-order determinant $|A|$ as a sum of three terms, each of which is the product of a first-row element and its corresponding cofactor. Note that (4-33) enables us to rewrite (4-32) compactly in Σ notation, as shown in (4-34).

The Laplace expansion of a fourth-order determinant can now be expressed, in terms of cofactors, in a manner analogous to (4-34). Thus, given

$$|A| = \begin{vmatrix} a_{11} & a_{12} & a_{13} & a_{14} \\ a_{21} & a_{22} & a_{23} & a_{24} \\ a_{31} & a_{32} & a_{33} & a_{34} \\ a_{41} & a_{42} & a_{43} & a_{44} \end{vmatrix} = \begin{vmatrix} 1 & 0 & 2 & 4 \\ 0 & -1 & 0 & 1 \\ 3 & 2 & 0 & 7 \\ 1 & 0 & 5 & 2 \end{vmatrix}$$

then, analogous to (4-34), we have

$$|A| = \sum_{j=1}^{4} a_{1j}C_{1j} = a_{11}C_{11} + a_{12}C_{12} + a_{13}C_{13} + a_{14}C_{14}$$
$$= a_{11}M_{11} - a_{12}M_{12} + a_{13}M_{13} - a_{14}M_{14}$$

Hence

$$|A| = 1\begin{vmatrix} -1 & 0 & 1 \\ 2 & 0 & 7 \\ 0 & 5 & 2 \end{vmatrix} - 0\begin{vmatrix} 0 & 0 & 1 \\ 3 & 0 & 7 \\ 1 & 5 & 2 \end{vmatrix} + 2\begin{vmatrix} 0 & -1 & 1 \\ 3 & 2 & 7 \\ 1 & 0 & 2 \end{vmatrix} - 4\begin{vmatrix} 0 & -1 & 0 \\ 3 & 2 & 0 \\ 1 & 0 & 5 \end{vmatrix}$$

Expanding these third-order determinants as before we obtain

$$|A| = 1(45) - 0 + 2(-3) - 4(15) = -21$$

Note, in this example, that the Laplace expansion of a fourth-order determinant involves firstly the evaluation of third-order determinants and then the evaluation of second-order determinants. In general, the Laplace expansion of an nth-order determinant will involve firstly the evaluation of n cofactors of order $n-1$, and then (via the repeated application of the procedure) the evaluation of lower and lower orders of determinants until the second order is reached and the value of the determinant is then found.

It is important to note that while the Laplace expansion procedure has been outlined in terms of the cofactors of the first-row elements, it is also possible to expand a determinant by the cofactors of *any row* or *any column*. For example, given

$$|A| = \begin{vmatrix} 2 & 1 & 0 \\ 3 & 0 & -1 \\ 5 & 0 & 1 \end{vmatrix}$$

expansion by the *second row* gives

$$|A| = \sum_{j=1}^{3} a_{2j}C_{2j} = a_{21}C_{21} + a_{22}C_{22} + a_{23}C_{23}$$
$$= -a_{21}M_{21} + a_{22}M_{22} - a_{23}M_{23}$$

or
$$|A| = -3\begin{vmatrix}1 & 0\\ 0 & 1\end{vmatrix} + 0\begin{vmatrix}2 & 0\\ 5 & 1\end{vmatrix} - (-1)\begin{vmatrix}2 & 1\\ 5 & 0\end{vmatrix} = -3 + 0 - 5 = -8$$

Similarly, expansion by the *second column* gives
$$|A| = \sum_{i=1}^{3} a_{i2}C_{i2} = a_{12}C_{12} + a_{22}C_{22} + a_{32}C_{32}$$
$$= -a_{12}M_{12} + a_{22}M_{22} - a_{32}M_{32}$$

or
$$|A| = -1\begin{vmatrix}3 & -1\\ 5 & 1\end{vmatrix} + 0\begin{vmatrix}2 & 0\\ 5 & 1\end{vmatrix} - 0\begin{vmatrix}2 & 0\\ 3 & -1\end{vmatrix} = -8 + 0 - 0 = -8$$

Clearly, since any row or any column can be chosen to expand the determinant, it is best to choose that row or column with the most 0s or 1s so as to reduce the amount of computation. In the above example, it is easiest to expand $|A|$ by the second column.

In general, the value of an nth-order determinant $|A|$ is given by the Laplace expansion of *any row* or *any column*:

(a) expansion by the ith row: $\quad |A| = \sum_{j=1}^{n} a_{ij}C_{ij}$

(4-35)

(b) expansion by the jth column: $\quad |A| = \sum_{i=1}^{n} a_{ij}C_{ij}$

4-F PRACTICE PROBLEMS

4-23 Use (4-32) to evaluate the following determinants:

(a) $\begin{vmatrix} -1 & 2 & 0 \\ 3 & 1 & 5 \\ 2 & 1 & -2 \end{vmatrix}$ (b) $\begin{vmatrix} a_1 & b_1 & c_1 \\ a_2 & b_2 & c_2 \\ a_3 & b_3 & c_3 \end{vmatrix}$ (c) $\begin{vmatrix} 7 & 3 & 2 \\ 5 & -9 & 3 \\ 2 & 0 & 1 \end{vmatrix}$

(d) $\begin{vmatrix} -1 & 4 & 3 \\ 5 & 9 & -7 \\ -2 & 8 & 6 \end{vmatrix}$ (e) $\begin{vmatrix} 1 & 7 & 2 \\ 0 & 3 & -9 \\ 2 & 0 & 0 \end{vmatrix}$ (f) $\begin{vmatrix} 5 & 2 & 9 \\ 3 & 0 & 2 \\ -1 & 0 & 3 \end{vmatrix}$

4-24 For each of the following cofactors give the corresponding minor:
(a) C_{15} (b) C_{23} (c) C_{41} (d) C_{66} (e) C_{11} (f) C_{ij}

4-25 In Prob. 4-23b, find the cofactor of:
(a) element c_3 (b) element a_2

4-26 Which row (column) would you choose in order to evaluate (e) and (f) in Prob. 4-23?

4-27 Evaluate the following determinants:

(a) $\begin{vmatrix} 1 & 0 & 3 & 0 \\ 7 & -2 & 5 & 9 \\ -3 & 0 & 2 & 0 \\ 4 & 0 & 0 & 7 \end{vmatrix}$ (b) $\begin{vmatrix} 7 & 3 & 2 & 1 \\ 5 & 9 & -4 & 2 \\ 0 & 3 & 0 & 0 \\ 6 & 7 & 2 & 1 \end{vmatrix}$

4-28 Write the following in Σ notation:
  (a) expansion of a 5th-order determinant by the 3rd row,
  (b) expansion of a 7th-order determinant by the 5th column.

4-7 PROPERTIES OF DETERMINANTS

We can now briefly examine three properties of determinants which, as we shall see later, will be useful in testing the nonsingularity of a matrix and in deriving a method for finding an inverse. It should be noted that, while the following properties are given in terms of second- or third-order determinants, they also hold for determinants of all orders.

Property I A determinant is unchanged in value if its rows and columns are interchanged. In other words, the determinant of a matrix A has the same value as that of its transpose A', so that $|A| = |A'|$. Thus

$$|A| = \begin{vmatrix} 2 & 1 \\ 5 & 7 \end{vmatrix} = 9 \quad \text{and} \quad |A'| = \begin{vmatrix} 2 & 5 \\ 1 & 7 \end{vmatrix} = 9$$

Property II If one row (or column) is a multiple of another row (or column), the value of the determinant is zero. Thus

$$\begin{vmatrix} ka & kb \\ a & b \end{vmatrix} = kab - akb = 0 \quad \text{and} \quad \begin{vmatrix} a & ka \\ b & kb \end{vmatrix} = akb - bka = 0$$

Similarly, when two rows (or two columns) are *identical* the determinantal value is zero (or we say that the determinant 'vanishes'):

$$\begin{vmatrix} a & b \\ a & b \end{vmatrix} = ab - ab = 0 \quad \text{and} \quad \begin{vmatrix} 5 & 5 \\ 2 & 2 \end{vmatrix} = 10 - 10 = 0$$

Property III The expansion of a determinant by *alien cofactors* always yields a value of zero. This means that if we expand by some row (or column), but use the cofactors of some other row (or column), then the result will be zero. For example, if we expand

$$|A| = \begin{vmatrix} 3 & 2 & 1 \\ 5 & 0 & -2 \\ 1 & 4 & 0 \end{vmatrix}$$

by its *first*-row elements, but using the cofactors of the *second*-row elements (instead of the cofactors of the first-row elements), we have

$$\sum_{j=1}^{3} a_{1j} C_{2j} = a_{11} C_{21} + a_{12} C_{22} + a_{13} C_{23} = -a_{11} M_{21} + a_{12} M_{22} - a_{13} M_{23}$$

$$= -3 \begin{vmatrix} 2 & 1 \\ 4 & 0 \end{vmatrix} + 2 \begin{vmatrix} 3 & 1 \\ 1 & 0 \end{vmatrix} - 1 \begin{vmatrix} 3 & 2 \\ 1 & 4 \end{vmatrix} = -3(-4) + 2(-1) - 1(10) = 0$$

Similarly, expansion by the *second* column, but using the cofactors of the *third* column, gives

$$\sum_{i=1}^{3} a_{i2}C_{i3} = a_{12}C_{13} + a_{22}C_{23} + a_{32}C_{33} = a_{12}M_{13} - a_{22}M_{23} + a_{32}M_{33}$$

$$= 2\begin{vmatrix}5 & 0\\1 & 4\end{vmatrix} - 0\begin{vmatrix}3 & 2\\1 & 4\end{vmatrix} + 4\begin{vmatrix}3 & 2\\5 & 0\end{vmatrix} = 2(20) - 0 + 4(-10) = 0$$

The significance of this property will be apparent when we examine the method for computing an inverse.

We are now in a position to state a convenient determinantal test of the nonsingularity of a given matrix.

A Determinantal Test of Nonsingularity

In Sec. 4-5 we noted that inverses are only defined for *square* matrices. Also, we noted that if a square matrix A has an inverse A^{-1}, then A is said to be *nonsingular*. Conversely, if the inverse of A does not exist, A is said to be *singular*. Following our discussion of determinants, a convenient test of the nonsingularity (or otherwise) of A can now be given in terms of $|A|$:

1. $|A| \neq 0 \Leftrightarrow A$ is nonsingular.
   Since this means that the inverse A^{-1} will exist, then we can also state:
2. $|A| \neq 0 \Leftrightarrow A^{-1}$ exists.
   On the basis of (2), the determinantal test also provides a test of the existence of a unique solution to an equation system $Ax = b$, where A is a square matrix. Thus, since (2) states that the unique inverse A^{-1} exists, then we can also state:
3. $|A| \neq 0 \Leftrightarrow$ equation system $Ax = b$ has a unique solution $\bar{x} = A^{-1}b$.
   Conversely, when $|A| = 0$, matrix A will be singular. This means that the inverse A^{-1} will not exist, and that no unique solution can be found for the equation system $Ax = b$.

The above determinantal test of the nonsingularity of A, and of the existence of a unique solution to the equation system $Ax = b$, will be encountered once more (in Sec. 4-8) when we discuss the procedure for finding the inverse matrix A^{-1}. For the present, it will be instructive to relate the above discussion to that of Sec. 3-6, which was concerned with the existence of a unique solution to a linear-equation system.

In Sec. 3-6 we noted that, for a system of equations to possess a unique solution, it is not sufficient to have equality between the number of equations and the number of unknowns. Rather, to this we must add the requirement that the equations are consistent with and functionally independent of one another. Thus, in the context of a linear-equation system, the (linear) equations must be consistent with and *linearly* independent of one another to ensure that a unique solution exists. This immediately raises the question: what is the relation between the criteria given in Sec. 3-6, for a unique solution to an equation system, and the determinantal test given above. The answer is that the above determinantal test and the criteria of Sec. 3-6 are equivalent ways of testing the existence of a unique solution to a linear-equation system. To illustrate this, let us write equation system (*a*) of Sec. 3-6, which has a unique solution, in the matrix format $Ax = b$:

$$y = 2 + 2x \quad \text{or} \quad \begin{bmatrix} 1 & -2 \\ 1 & 2 \end{bmatrix} \begin{bmatrix} y \\ x \end{bmatrix} = \begin{bmatrix} 2 \\ 10 \end{bmatrix} \quad (4\text{-}36)$$

Note, in (4-36), that the coefficient matrix A is square as is necessary for the existence of an inverse A^{-1}. Also, note in (4-36) that the number of equations must be equal to the number of unknowns to ensure the squareness of A. Further, note that $|A| = 4 \neq 0$, so that A is nonsingular and a unique solution $\bar{x} = A^{-1}b$ exists. Thus the determinantal test gives the same result as that already obtained in Sec. 3-6.

Similarly, we can write equation system (*b*) of Sec. 3-6, which has no solution due to the *inconsistency* of its equations, in the matrix format $Ax = b$:

$$y = 2 + 2x \quad \text{or} \quad \begin{bmatrix} 1 & -2 \\ 1 & -2 \end{bmatrix} \begin{bmatrix} y \\ x \end{bmatrix} = \begin{bmatrix} 2 \\ 5 \end{bmatrix} \quad (4\text{-}37)$$

Note, in this case, that $|A| = 0$, so that A is singular and no unique solution exists for the equation system (4-37). Thus the determinantal test gives the same result as that already obtained in Sec. 3-6.

Finally, we can write equation system (*c*) of Sec. 3-6, which has no unique solution due to the *linear dependence* of its equations, in the matrix format $Ax = b$:

$$y = 2 + 2x \quad \text{or} \quad \begin{bmatrix} 1 & -2 \\ 2 & -4 \end{bmatrix} \begin{bmatrix} y \\ x \end{bmatrix} = \begin{bmatrix} 2 \\ 4 \end{bmatrix} \quad (4\text{-}38)$$

Note, in this final case, that $|A| = 0$, so that A is singular and no unique solution exists for the equation system (4-38). Thus once more the determinantal test gives the same result as that already obtained in Sec. 3-6.

Returning to (4-37), it is important to note that the coefficient matrix A contains *linearly dependent* rows in the sense that the second row equals k times the first row, where $k = 1$. Also, in (4-38), note that the coefficient matrix A contains linearly dependent rows in the sense that the second row equals k times the first row, where $k = 2$. In both these cases, Property II of determinants ensures that $|A| = 0$ as already found. This illustrates how linear dependence among the rows of the coefficient matrix can cause inconsistency or linear dependence among the equations of the system $Ax = b$. In contrast, the coefficient matrix in (4-36) contains *linearly independent* rows so that, via Property II of determinants, $|A| \neq 0$. In the latter case, the linear independence among the rows of A prevents inconsistency and linear dependence among the equations of the system $Ax = b$.

In general, any pattern (whether obvious or not) of linear dependence among the rows of A will result in $|A| = 0$. Conversely, if the rows of A are linearly independent, then $|A| \neq 0$. Moreover, since $|A| = |A'|$ by Property I of determinants, this general statement will also hold if we replace the word *row* by *column*. Thus, to (1), (2) and (3) above we can add:

4. $|A| \neq 0 \Leftrightarrow$ linearly independent rows (columns) in matrix A.

Therefore, given a square matrix A, a sufficient condition for the nonsingularity of A is that its rows (columns) be linearly independent. This result, based on the above illustrations, should suffice to demonstrate that just as there is a relation between the 'equality of equations and unknowns' and squareness of A, there is also a relation between the requirement of 'consistency and linear independence among equations' and the linear independence of the rows (columns) of A.

The above discussion thus indicates that the value of $|A|$ not only provides a convenient test of the nonsingularity of matrix A, but also of the existence of a unique solution to the linear-equation system $Ax = b$. Note that while the above illustrations consisted of small equation systems, the determinantal test is also valid for large equation systems.

4-G PRACTICE PROBLEMS

4-29 (a) Evaluate $|A| = \begin{vmatrix} 2 & 1 & 0 \\ 3 & -2 & 2 \\ 1 & 2 & 4 \end{vmatrix}$

(b) What is the value of $\sum_{i=1}^{3} a_{i2} C_{i1}$ for this determinant?

4-30 Which of the following matrices are nonsingular?

(a) $\begin{bmatrix} 8 & 3 & 12 \\ 6 & 0 & 9 \\ 10 & 7 & 15 \end{bmatrix}$ (b) $\begin{bmatrix} 9 & -3 & 18 \\ -1 & 0 & 5 \\ 6 & -2 & 12 \end{bmatrix}$ (c) $\begin{bmatrix} 3 & 11 & 0 \\ -1 & -1 & 2 \\ 7 & 23 & 4 \end{bmatrix}$

4-31 Does the following equation system possess a unique solution?

$$\begin{aligned} 5x_1 + 2x_3 &= 13 \\ 3x_1 + x_2 &= 0 \\ -x_1 + 3x_2 + 4x_3 &= 6 \end{aligned}$$

4-8 CALCULATING THE INVERSE MATRIX

In earlier sections we saw how a linear-equation system can be written in matrix notation as $Ax = b$. Also, we saw that if matrix A is nonsingular, then the inverse A^{-1} will exist and the unique solution to the system will be

86 MATRIX ALGEBRA

$\bar{x} = A^{-1}b$. Now that we have discovered how to test the nonsingularity of A via the value of $|A|$, we are at last in a position to outline the procedure for calculating the inverse matrix A^{-1}.

To show how the matrix inversion procedure is derived, we will take the following 3×3 nonsingular matrix as given:

$$\underset{(3 \times 3)}{A} = \begin{bmatrix} a_{11} & a_{12} & a_{13} \\ a_{21} & a_{22} & a_{23} \\ a_{31} & a_{32} & a_{33} \end{bmatrix} = \underset{(3 \times 3)}{[a_{ij}]}$$

Then, replacing element a_{ij} with its cofactor C_{ij}, we can form the matrix of cofactors (denoted by C) as given by

$$\underset{(3 \times 3)}{C} = \begin{bmatrix} C_{11} & C_{12} & C_{13} \\ C_{21} & C_{22} & C_{23} \\ C_{31} & C_{32} & C_{33} \end{bmatrix} = \underset{(3 \times 3)}{[C_{ij}]}$$

Transposing C, we obtain C' which is known as the *adjoint* of A and denoted by adj A:

$$\underset{(3 \times 3)}{C'} = \begin{bmatrix} C_{11} & C_{21} & C_{31} \\ C_{12} & C_{22} & C_{32} \\ C_{13} & C_{23} & C_{33} \end{bmatrix} = \text{adj } A \tag{4-39}$$

The next step is to find the product AC':

$$\underset{(3 \times 3)}{AC'} = \begin{bmatrix} a_{11} & a_{12} & a_{13} \\ a_{21} & a_{22} & a_{23} \\ a_{31} & a_{32} & a_{33} \end{bmatrix} \begin{bmatrix} C_{11} & C_{21} & C_{31} \\ C_{12} & C_{22} & C_{32} \\ C_{13} & C_{23} & C_{33} \end{bmatrix} = \begin{bmatrix} b_{11} & b_{12} & b_{13} \\ b_{21} & b_{22} & b_{23} \\ b_{31} & b_{32} & b_{33} \end{bmatrix}$$

where the b_{11} and b_{12} elements of the product matrix AC' are given by

$$b_{11} = a_{11}C_{11} + a_{12}C_{12} + a_{13}C_{13} = \sum_{j=1}^{3} a_{1j}C_{1j}$$

and

$$b_{12} = a_{11}C_{21} + a_{12}C_{22} + a_{13}C_{23} = \sum_{j=1}^{3} a_{1j}C_{2j}$$

The other elements of AC' can be similarly expressed so that AC' can be rewritten as

$$\underset{(3 \times 3)}{AC'} = \begin{bmatrix} \sum_{j=1}^{3} a_{1j}C_{1j} & \sum_{j=1}^{3} a_{1j}C_{2j} & \sum_{j=1}^{3} a_{1j}C_{3j} \\ \sum_{j=1}^{3} a_{2j}C_{1j} & \sum_{j=1}^{3} a_{2j}C_{2j} & \sum_{j=1}^{3} a_{2j}C_{3j} \\ \sum_{j=1}^{3} a_{3j}C_{1j} & \sum_{j=1}^{3} a_{3j}C_{2j} & \sum_{j=1}^{3} a_{3j}C_{3j} \end{bmatrix} \tag{4-40}$$

Note immediately in (4-40) that the principal diagonal elements are

4-8 CALCULATING THE INVERSE MATRIX

summation expressions representing the expansion of $|A|$ (check with (4-34) and (4-35) that this is so). Also, note in (4-40) that the off-diagonal elements are summation expressions representing the expansion of $|A|$ by *alien cofactors* (check with Property III of determinants that this is so). This means that each of the off-diagonal elements in AC' is zero. Hence AC' can be rewritten as

$$AC'_{(3 \times 3)} = \begin{bmatrix} |A| & 0 & 0 \\ 0 & |A| & 0 \\ 0 & 0 & |A| \end{bmatrix} = |A| \begin{bmatrix} 1 & 0 & 0 \\ 0 & 1 & 0 \\ 0 & 0 & 1 \end{bmatrix} = |A|I$$

Since A is nonsingular, then $|A|$ is a nonzero scalar enabling us to write $AC' = |A|I$ as

$$\frac{AC'}{|A|} = I$$

Then, premultiplying each side by A^{-1}, we obtain

$$\frac{A^{-1}AC'}{|A|} = A^{-1}I$$

Since $A^{-1}A = I$ and $A^{-1}I = A^{-1}$, then we have

$$A^{-1} = \frac{C'}{|A|} \quad \text{or} \quad A^{-1} = \frac{1}{|A|} \text{adj } A \tag{4-41}$$

Thus we now have the following procedure for calculating A^{-1}:

1. Find $|A|$ and proceed only if $|A| \neq 0$. If $|A| = 0$, then A^{-1} does not exist.
2. Find the cofactor matrix $C = [C_{ij}]$.
3. Find $C' \equiv \text{adj } A$.
4. $A^{-1} = (1/|A|) \text{adj } A$.

Although we have only derived this procedure for a 3×3 matrix, it also holds for an $n \times n$ matrix.

Examples of Matrix Inversion

4-32 Find the inverse of $A = \begin{bmatrix} 3 & 2 \\ 1 & 2 \end{bmatrix}$

SOLUTION
(a) Since $|A| = 4 \neq 0$, then A^{-1} exists

(b) $C = \begin{bmatrix} C_{11} & C_{12} \\ C_{21} & C_{22} \end{bmatrix} = \begin{bmatrix} M_{11} & -M_{12} \\ -M_{21} & M_{22} \end{bmatrix} = \begin{bmatrix} 2 & -1 \\ -2 & 3 \end{bmatrix}$

(c) $C' \equiv \text{adj } A = \begin{bmatrix} 2 & -2 \\ -1 & 3 \end{bmatrix}$

(d) $A^{-1} = \frac{1}{|A|} \text{adj } A = \frac{1}{4} \begin{bmatrix} 2 & -2 \\ -1 & 3 \end{bmatrix} = \begin{bmatrix} \frac{1}{2} & -\frac{1}{2} \\ -\frac{1}{4} & \frac{3}{4} \end{bmatrix}$

88 MATRIX ALGEBRA

The student should check the accuracy of this result by showing that it satisfies $A^{-1}A = I_2$.

4-33 Find the inverse of $A = \begin{bmatrix} 3 & 1 & -2 \\ 4 & 0 & 3 \\ -1 & 0 & 3 \end{bmatrix}$

SOLUTION

(a) Since $|A| = -15 \neq 0$, then A^{-1} exists

(b) $C = \begin{bmatrix} C_{11} & C_{12} & C_{13} \\ C_{21} & C_{22} & C_{23} \\ C_{31} & C_{32} & C_{33} \end{bmatrix} = \begin{bmatrix} M_{11} & -M_{12} & M_{13} \\ -M_{21} & M_{22} & -M_{23} \\ M_{31} & -M_{32} & M_{33} \end{bmatrix}$ or

$C = \begin{bmatrix} \begin{vmatrix} 0 & 3 \\ 0 & 3 \end{vmatrix} & -\begin{vmatrix} 4 & 3 \\ -1 & 3 \end{vmatrix} & \begin{vmatrix} 4 & 0 \\ -1 & 0 \end{vmatrix} \\ -\begin{vmatrix} 1 & -2 \\ 0 & 3 \end{vmatrix} & \begin{vmatrix} 3 & -2 \\ -1 & 3 \end{vmatrix} & -\begin{vmatrix} 3 & 1 \\ -1 & 0 \end{vmatrix} \\ \begin{vmatrix} 1 & -2 \\ 0 & 3 \end{vmatrix} & -\begin{vmatrix} 3 & -2 \\ 4 & 3 \end{vmatrix} & \begin{vmatrix} 3 & 1 \\ 4 & 0 \end{vmatrix} \end{bmatrix} = \begin{bmatrix} 0 & -15 & 0 \\ -3 & 7 & -1 \\ 3 & -17 & -4 \end{bmatrix}$

(c) $C' \equiv \operatorname{adj} A = \begin{bmatrix} 0 & -3 & 3 \\ -15 & 7 & -17 \\ 0 & -1 & -4 \end{bmatrix}$

(d) $A^{-1} = \dfrac{1}{|A|} \operatorname{adj} A = -\tfrac{1}{15} \begin{bmatrix} 0 & -3 & 3 \\ -15 & 7 & -17 \\ 0 & -1 & -4 \end{bmatrix}$

which satisfies $A^{-1}A = I_3$.

4-34 Write the following equation system in the matrix format $Ax = b$ and obtain its unique solution $\bar{x} = A^{-1}b$ (if it exists) by matrix inversion:

$$3x_1 + x_2 - 2x_3 = -10$$
$$4x_1 + 3x_3 = 11$$
$$-x_1 + 3x_3 = 16$$

SOLUTION

$Ax = b$ or $\begin{bmatrix} 3 & 1 & -2 \\ 4 & 0 & 3 \\ -1 & 0 & 3 \end{bmatrix} \begin{bmatrix} x_1 \\ x_2 \\ x_3 \end{bmatrix} = \begin{bmatrix} -10 \\ 11 \\ 16 \end{bmatrix}$

Note that matrix A is identical to that given in Example 4-33. Thus, since $|A| = -15 \neq 0$, then a unique solution exists and is given by

$\bar{x} = A^{-1}b = \dfrac{1}{|A|}(\operatorname{adj} A)b = -\tfrac{1}{15}\begin{bmatrix} 0 & -3 & 3 \\ -15 & 7 & -17 \\ 0 & -1 & -4 \end{bmatrix}\begin{bmatrix} -10 \\ 11 \\ 16 \end{bmatrix} = \begin{bmatrix} -1 \\ 3 \\ 5 \end{bmatrix} = \begin{bmatrix} \bar{x}_1 \\ \bar{x}_2 \\ \bar{x}_3 \end{bmatrix}$

where A^{-1} has already been calculated in Example 4-33. Hence $\bar{x}_1 = -1$, $\bar{x}_2 = 3$ and $\bar{x}_3 = 5$.

4-H PRACTICE PROBLEMS

4-35 Find the inverse of each of the following matrices:

(a) $A = \begin{bmatrix} 4 & -1 \\ 3 & 2 \end{bmatrix}$ (b) $B = \begin{bmatrix} 0 & -2 \\ -3 & 7 \end{bmatrix}$ (c) $C = \begin{bmatrix} 9 & 0 \\ 0 & 2 \end{bmatrix}$

4-36 Find the inverse of each of the following matrices:

(a) $A = \begin{bmatrix} 4 & 0 & 5 \\ 3 & 1 & 2 \\ 0 & 7 & -1 \end{bmatrix}$ (b) $B = \begin{bmatrix} 1 & 2 & 0 \\ 0 & -2 & 0 \\ 3 & 0 & -1 \end{bmatrix}$ (c) $C = \begin{bmatrix} 5 & 2 & -2 \\ 0 & 1 & 0 \\ 3 & 0 & 3 \end{bmatrix}$

4-37 Solve the following equation system by matrix inversion:

$$x_1 + 2x_2 - 3x_3 = 8$$
$$5x_2 + 2x_3 = -4$$
$$-2x_1 \quad\quad - 3x_3 = 2$$

4-9 CRAMER'S RULE

In the previous section we saw how a linear-equation system can be solved by the rather laborious method of matrix inversion. In this section we shall see that there is a much simpler method, known as *Cramer's rule*, for solving a linear-equation system.

To derive Cramer's rule, let us note that the solution of the equation system $Ax = b$, where A is a nonsingular 3×3 matrix, can be written as

$$\bar{x} = A^{-1}b = \frac{1}{|A|}(\text{adj } A)b \tag{4-42}$$

With adj A defined as in (4-39), then (4-42) is given by

$$\begin{bmatrix} \bar{x}_1 \\ \bar{x}_2 \\ \bar{x}_3 \end{bmatrix}_{(3 \times 1)} = \frac{1}{|A|} \begin{bmatrix} C_{11} & C_{21} & C_{31} \\ C_{12} & C_{22} & C_{32} \\ C_{13} & C_{23} & C_{33} \end{bmatrix}_{(3 \times 3)} \begin{bmatrix} b_1 \\ b_2 \\ b_3 \end{bmatrix}_{(3 \times 1)}$$

$$= \frac{1}{|A|} \begin{bmatrix} C_{11}b_1 + C_{21}b_2 + C_{31}b_3 \\ C_{12}b_1 + C_{22}b_2 + C_{32}b_3 \\ C_{13}b_1 + C_{23}b_2 + C_{33}b_3 \end{bmatrix}_{(3 \times 1)} = \frac{1}{|A|} \begin{bmatrix} \sum_{i=1}^{3} C_{i1}b_i \\ \sum_{i=1}^{3} C_{i2}b_i \\ \sum_{i=1}^{3} C_{i3}b_i \end{bmatrix}_{(3 \times 1)}$$

which, by vector equality, gives

$$\bar{x}_1 = \frac{1}{|A|} \sum_{i=1}^{3} C_{i1}b_i; \quad \bar{x}_2 = \frac{1}{|A|} \sum_{i=1}^{3} C_{i2}b_i \quad \text{and} \quad \bar{x}_3 = \frac{1}{|A|} \sum_{i=1}^{3} C_{i3}b_i \tag{4-43}$$

The next step is to discover what these Σ terms in (4-43) mean. To do this, let us replace the first column of $|A|$ by the column vector b, but leaving all the other columns unchanged, so that a new determinant $|A_1|$ is obtained:

$$|A_1| = \begin{vmatrix} b_1 & a_{12} & a_{13} \\ b_2 & a_{22} & a_{23} \\ b_3 & a_{32} & a_{33} \end{vmatrix}$$

Note immediately that the Laplace expansion of $|A_1|$ by its first column (which is the b column) is given by

$$|A_1| = b_1 C_{11} + b_2 C_{21} + b_3 C_{31} = \sum_{i=1}^{3} b_i C_{i1} = \sum_{i=1}^{3} C_{i1} b_i \qquad (4\text{-}44)$$

Thus, given (4-44), $\bar{x}_1$ in (4-43) becomes

$$\bar{x}_1 = \frac{1}{|A|} |A_1|$$

In a similar fashion, if we replace the second column of $|A|$ by the column vector b, but keep all the other columns intact, then the expansion of the new determinant $|A_2|$ by its second column (which is the b column) is given by

$$|A_2| = \sum_{i=1}^{3} b_i C_{i2} = \sum_{i=1}^{3} C_{i2} b_i \qquad (4\text{-}45)$$

Thus, given (4-45), $\bar{x}_2$ in (4-43) becomes

$$\bar{x}_2 = \frac{1}{|A|} |A_2|$$

Similarly, $\bar{x}_3$ will be

$$\bar{x}_3 = \frac{1}{|A|} |A_3|$$

Generalizing this result for $Ax = b$, where A is a nonsingular $n \times n$ matrix, we have

$$\bar{x}_j = \frac{|A_j|}{|A|} = \frac{1}{|A|} \begin{vmatrix} a_{11} & a_{12} \ldots b_1 \ldots a_{1n} \\ a_{21} & a_{22} \ldots b_2 \ldots a_{2n} \\ \vdots & \vdots \quad \vdots \quad \vdots \\ a_{n1} & a_{n2} \ldots b_n \ldots a_{nn} \end{vmatrix} \qquad (4\text{-}46)$$

(jth column replaced by b)

which is a statement of Cramer's rule. Thus the procedure for solving by Cramer's rule is:

1. Find $|A|$ and proceed only if $|A| \neq 0$. If $|A| = 0$, then $Ax = b$ does not possess a unique solution $\bar{x} = A^{-1} b$.
2. To find $\bar{x}_j$, form $|A_j|$ by replacing the jth column of $|A|$ with the column vector b.
3. $\bar{x}_j = |A_j|/|A|$.

Examples of Cramer's Rule

4-38 Use Cramer's rule to solve the equation system:
$$3x_1 + 4x_2 = 26$$
$$5x_1 - x_2 = 5$$

Solution

(a) Writing the equation system as $Ax = b$, we can see that a unique solution $\bar{x} = A^{-1}b$ exists since $|A| = \begin{vmatrix} 3 & 4 \\ 5 & -1 \end{vmatrix} = -23 \neq 0$

(b) $|A_1| = \begin{vmatrix} 26 & 4 \\ 5 & -1 \end{vmatrix} = -46$ and $|A_2| = \begin{vmatrix} 3 & 26 \\ 5 & 5 \end{vmatrix} = -115$

(c) $\bar{x}_1 = \dfrac{|A_1|}{|A|} = \dfrac{-46}{-23} = 2$ and $\bar{x}_2 = \dfrac{|A_2|}{|A|} = \dfrac{-115}{-23} = 5$

4-39 Use Cramer's rule to solve the equation system given in practice problem 4-37 in Sec. 4-H.

Solution

(a) Writing the equation system as $Ax = b$, we can see that a unique solution $\bar{x} = A^{-1}b$ exists since $|A| = -53 \neq 0$. Thus

$$|A| = \begin{vmatrix} 1 & 2 & -3 \\ 0 & 5 & 2 \\ -2 & 0 & -3 \end{vmatrix} = -53$$

(b) $|A_1| = \begin{vmatrix} 8 & 2 & -3 \\ -4 & 5 & 2 \\ 2 & 0 & -3 \end{vmatrix} = -106 \quad |A_2| = \begin{vmatrix} 1 & 8 & -3 \\ 0 & -4 & 2 \\ -2 & 2 & -3 \end{vmatrix} = 0$

$$|A_3| = \begin{vmatrix} 1 & 2 & 8 \\ 0 & 5 & -4 \\ -2 & 0 & 2 \end{vmatrix} = 106$$

(c) $\bar{x}_1 = \dfrac{|A_1|}{|A|} = \dfrac{-106}{-53} = 2; \quad \bar{x}_2 = \dfrac{|A_2|}{|A|} = \dfrac{0}{-53} = 0; \quad \bar{x}_3 = \dfrac{|A_3|}{|A|} = \dfrac{106}{-53} = -2$

4-I PRACTICE PROBLEMS

4-40 Use Cramer's rule to solve the following equation systems:

(a) $9x_1 - 4x_2 = -25$
$-15x_1 + 3x_2 = 16$

(b) $7x_1 + 3x_2 = 1$
$-14x_1 - 9x_2 = -4$

(c) $-2x_1 + 3x_2 - 9x_3 = 13$
$2x_2 + 3x_3 = 9$
$3x_1 - x_2 = -10$

(d) $3x_1 - 7x_2 - 5x_3 = 11$
$4x_2 + 2x_3 = -2$
$-2x_1 - x_3 = -7$

The above discussion of matrix algebra has shown how a very large linear-equation system and its solution may be written compactly as $Ax = b$ and $\bar{x} = A^{-1}b$, respectively. Also we have seen how the value of $|A|$ provides a way of testing the existence of a unique solution to the equation system $Ax = b$. Finally, we saw how matrix inversion and Cramer's rule provide us with methods for solving such linear-equation systems.

Before proceeding to examine economic models in matrix form, it is important to note the following points:

(a) In many of the cases illustrated above, the two- or three-equation systems could have been solved much more quickly by the method of successive elimination of variables (via substitution) than by the methods of matrix inversion or Cramer's rule.

(b) While, with larger equation systems, the methods of matrix inversion and Cramer's rule are clearly more efficient than the method of successive elimination of variables, they still represent inefficient computational procedures for solving a linear-equation system. In practice, much more efficient computer alogorithms can be used both to invert a matrix and to solve a linear-equation system.

Points (a) and (b) immediately raise the question: why bother to learn Cramer's rule and the method of matrix inversion outlined above? The simple answer is that these two procedures are extremely useful in analysing economic models (of form $Ax = b$) in which the coefficient matrix A and the constant vector b contain parametric elements (such as a, b, c, etc.) rather than numerical elements (such as 1, 2, -9, etc.). The analysis of such models is the subject of Chapter 5.

CHAPTER
FIVE
LINEAR ECONOMIC MODELS IN MATRIX FORM

In Chapter 3 we encountered, and solved, simple (linear) static-equilibrium models of price determination and national-income determination. In this chapter, we shall return to these models in order to demonstrate how they may be rewritten in matrix form and solved by matrix inversion or by Cramer's rule. Before doing this, however, it should be noted that matrix methods are not necessary for the solution of these simple economic models, which are presented in Secs. 5-1 and 5-2 below. While this is recognized, these models have been deliberately presented in matrix form in order to prepare the student for handling more complex models where the use of matrix methods is essential. In other words, the pedagogic approach is to (*a*) take simple economic models that are familiar to the student from an earlier chapter and demonstrate how these models may be equivalently analysed via matrix methods, and (*b*) then proceed to more complex models, such as those in Secs. 5-3, 5-4 and 5-5, where the merits of matrix algebra are much more obvious.

5-1 A PARTIAL-EQUILIBRIUM MARKET MODEL IN MATRIX FORM

The linear partial-equilibrium market model (3-12), of Sec. 3-3, can be written as

$$
\begin{aligned}
Q_d &= Q_s \\
Q_d &= a - bP \quad \text{or} \\
Q_s &= -c + dP
\end{aligned}
\qquad
\begin{aligned}
1Q_d - 1Q_s + 0P &= 0 \\
1Q_d + 0Q_s + bP &= a \\
0Q_d + 1Q_s - dP &= -c
\end{aligned}
\qquad (5\text{-}1)
$$

where a, b, c, and d are all positive. Rewriting (5-1) in matrix form, we have

$$Ax = b \quad \text{or} \quad \begin{bmatrix} 1 & -1 & 0 \\ 1 & 0 & b \\ 0 & 1 & -d \end{bmatrix} \begin{bmatrix} Q_d \\ Q_s \\ P \end{bmatrix} = \begin{bmatrix} 0 \\ a \\ -c \end{bmatrix} \quad (5\text{-}2)$$

To solve (5-2) by matrix inversion, we proceed as in Sec. 4-8:

1. The first step is to find $|A|$ in order to test the existence of a unique solution to $Ax = b$. Thus

$$|A| = \begin{vmatrix} 1 & -1 & 0 \\ 1 & 0 & b \\ 0 & 1 & -d \end{vmatrix} = 1 \begin{vmatrix} 0 & b \\ 1 & -d \end{vmatrix} - (-1) \begin{vmatrix} 1 & b \\ 0 & -d \end{vmatrix}$$

$$= -b - d = -(d+b) \neq 0$$

Since $|A| \neq 0$, then a unique solution $\bar{x} = A^{-1}b$ exists. This means we can proceed to find A^{-1} and then $\bar{x} = A^{-1}b$.

2. To find A^{-1}, we first find the cofactor matrix C:

$$C = \begin{bmatrix} \begin{vmatrix} 0 & b \\ 1 & -d \end{vmatrix} & -\begin{vmatrix} 1 & b \\ 0 & -d \end{vmatrix} & \begin{vmatrix} 1 & 0 \\ 0 & 1 \end{vmatrix} \\ -\begin{vmatrix} -1 & 0 \\ 1 & -d \end{vmatrix} & \begin{vmatrix} 1 & 0 \\ 0 & -d \end{vmatrix} & -\begin{vmatrix} 1 & -1 \\ 0 & 1 \end{vmatrix} \\ \begin{vmatrix} -1 & 0 \\ 0 & b \end{vmatrix} & -\begin{vmatrix} 1 & 0 \\ 1 & b \end{vmatrix} & \begin{vmatrix} 1 & -1 \\ 1 & 0 \end{vmatrix} \end{bmatrix} = \begin{bmatrix} -b & d & 1 \\ -d & -d & -1 \\ -b & -b & 1 \end{bmatrix}$$

3. Then we find $C' \equiv \text{adj } A$:

$$C' = \begin{bmatrix} -b & -d & -b \\ d & -d & -b \\ 1 & -1 & 1 \end{bmatrix} = \text{adj } A$$

4. Thus A^{-1} is given by

$$A^{-1} = \frac{1}{|A|} \text{adj } A = -\frac{1}{(d+b)} \begin{bmatrix} -b & -d & -b \\ d & -d & -b \\ 1 & -1 & 1 \end{bmatrix}$$

which satisfies $A^{-1}A = I$.

5. Finally, $\bar{x}$ is given by

$$\bar{x} = A^{-1}b = -\frac{1}{(d+b)} \begin{bmatrix} -b & -d & -b \\ d & -d & -b \\ 1 & -1 & 1 \end{bmatrix} \begin{bmatrix} 0 \\ a \\ -c \end{bmatrix}$$

$$= -\frac{1}{(d+b)} \begin{bmatrix} -(ad-bc) \\ -(ad-bc) \\ -(a+c) \end{bmatrix} = \begin{bmatrix} \bar{Q}_d \\ \bar{Q}_s \\ \bar{P} \end{bmatrix}$$

Hence, $\bar{Q}_d = \bar{Q}_s = \bar{Q} = (ad-bc)/(d+b)$ and $\bar{P} = (a+c)/(d+b)$. Note that these $\bar{P}$, $\bar{Q}$ values are exactly those previously obtained in (3-15) and (3-16). Also, note that while $|A| \neq 0$ ensures a unique solution to $Ax = b$, it does not ensure that the solution values are economically meaningful. Consequently, to ensure $\bar{Q} > 0$, we need the additional restriction on the parameters of $ad > bc$.

The demonstration that the same result can be obtained by Cramer's rule is left for the student to do in Prob. 5-1 in Sec. 5-A.

5-A PRACTICE PROBLEMS

5-1 Solve the market model given in (5-2) by Cramer's rule.

5-2 Given the following partial-equilibrium market models:
(a) $Q_d = Q_s$
$Q_d = a_0 + a_1 P \quad (a_0 > 0; a_1 < 0)$
$Q_s = b_0 + b_1 P \quad (b_0 < 0; b_1 > 0)$

(b) $Q_d = Q_s$
$Q_d = -c + dP \quad (c, d < 0)$
$Q_s = e - fP \quad (e, f < 0)$

Solve (a) by matrix inversion and (b) by Cramer's rule.

5-2 A NATIONAL-INCOME MODEL IN MATRIX FORM

The national-income model (3-32), of Sec. 3-5, can be written as

$$
\begin{aligned}
Y &= C + I + G \\
C &= \alpha + \beta(Y - T) \quad \text{or} \\
T &= tY
\end{aligned}
\qquad
\begin{aligned}
1Y - 1C + 0T &= I + G \\
-\beta Y + 1C + \beta T &= \alpha \\
-tY + 0C + 1T &= 0
\end{aligned}
\qquad (5\text{-}3)
$$

where Y, C and T are endogenous variables and I and G are exogenously determined. Also $\alpha > 0$, $0 < \beta < 1$, and $0 < t < 1$. Rewriting (5-3) in matrix form, we have

$$Ax = b \quad \text{or} \quad \begin{bmatrix} 1 & -1 & 0 \\ -\beta & 1 & \beta \\ -t & 0 & 1 \end{bmatrix} \begin{bmatrix} Y \\ C \\ T \end{bmatrix} = \begin{bmatrix} I+G \\ \alpha \\ 0 \end{bmatrix} \qquad (5\text{-}4)$$

Note, in (5-4), that b is a 3×1 column vector. Consequently, the sum $I+G$ represents a single element in the constant vector.

To solve (5-4) by Cramer's rule, we must first test the existence of a unique solution to $Ax = b$ by obtaining $|A|$. Thus

$$|A| = \begin{vmatrix} 1 & -1 & 0 \\ -\beta & 1 & \beta \\ -t & 0 & 1 \end{vmatrix} = \begin{vmatrix} 1 & \beta \\ 0 & 1 \end{vmatrix} - (-1)\begin{vmatrix} -\beta & \beta \\ -t & 1 \end{vmatrix} = 1 - \beta + \beta t = 1 - \beta(1-t) \neq 0$$

Since $|A| \neq 0$, then a unique solution $\bar{x} = A^{-1}b$ exists. Letting $x_1 = Y$, $x_2 = C$, and $x_3 = T$, we then find the following three determinants:

$$|A_1| = \begin{vmatrix} (I+G) & -1 & 0 \\ \alpha & 1 & \beta \\ 0 & 0 & 1 \end{vmatrix} = 1 \begin{vmatrix} (I+G) & -1 \\ \alpha & 1 \end{vmatrix} = \alpha + I + G$$

$$|A_2| = \begin{vmatrix} 1 & (I+G) & 0 \\ -\beta & \alpha & \beta \\ -t & 0 & 1 \end{vmatrix} = 1 \begin{vmatrix} \alpha & \beta \\ 0 & 1 \end{vmatrix} - (I+G) \begin{vmatrix} -\beta & \beta \\ -t & 1 \end{vmatrix}$$

$$= \alpha - (I+G)(-\beta + \beta t) = \alpha + \beta(1-t)(I+G)$$

$$|A_3| = \begin{vmatrix} 1 & -1 & (I+G) \\ -\beta & 1 & \alpha \\ -t & 0 & 0 \end{vmatrix} = -t \begin{vmatrix} -1 & (I+G) \\ 1 & \alpha \end{vmatrix}$$

$$= -t[-\alpha - (I+G)] = t(\alpha + I + G)$$

Hence,

$$\bar{Y} = \bar{x}_1 = \frac{|A_1|}{|A|} = \frac{\alpha + I + G}{1 - \beta(1-t)}$$

$$\bar{C} = \bar{x}_2 = \frac{|A_2|}{|A|} = \frac{\alpha + \beta(1-t)(I+G)}{1 - \beta(1-t)}$$

and

$$\bar{T} = \bar{x}_3 = \frac{|A_3|}{|A|} = \frac{t(\alpha + I + G)}{1 - \beta(1-t)} = t\bar{Y}$$

Note that these $\bar{Y}$, $\bar{C}$ and $\bar{T}$ values are exactly those previously obtained in (3-34), (3-36) and (3-35).

The demonstration that the same result can be obtained by the matrix inversion method is left for the student to do in Prob. 5-3 in Sec. 5-B.

5-B PRACTICE PROBLEMS

5-3 Solve the national-income model given in Eq. (5-4) by matrix inversion.

5-4 Use Cramer's rule to solve the following national-income model:

$$Y = C + I + G$$
$$C = \alpha + \beta(Y - T) \quad (\alpha > 0; \; 0 < \beta < 1)$$
$$T = \gamma + \delta Y \quad\quad\quad\;\; (\gamma > 0; \; 0 < \delta < 1)$$

where Y, C and T are endogenous variables and I and G are exogenously determined.

5-3 EQUILIBRIUM OF AN ECONOMY WITH A GOODS MARKET AND A MONEY MARKET

So far, in our discussion of macroeconomic models, we have only examined equilibrium in the *goods market*. As yet we have not made any allowance for the fact that, in practice, the (aggregate) demand and supply of goods will be affected by the demand and supply of money. Consequently, in this section, we shall (very briefly) consider a linear macroeconomic model which explicitly incorporates interaction between the goods market and the *money market*. To do this, we shall simplify matters by assuming that there is no government expenditure or taxation. Also, for simplicity, we shall assume that foreign trade does not take place.

Before presenting a macroeconomic model which incorporates both a goods market and a money market, we must first define *money*. Hence, in the following analysis, the quantity of money that is demanded or supplied will be defined as the sum of all notes and coin in circulation plus demand deposits at banks. In this respect, it is essential to note that the quantity of money is a *stock* (expressed, for example, as so many pounds sterling or US dollars). In contrast, variables like income or consumption are *flows* (expressed, for example, as so many pounds sterling or US dollars per unit of time).

The model which we shall consider may be written as follows:

(1) $Y = C + I$
(2) $C = \alpha + \beta Y \quad (\alpha > 0; \, 0 < \beta < 1)$
(3) $I = \gamma + \delta r \quad (\gamma > 0; \, \delta < 0)$
(4) $M_d = M_s$
(5) $M_d = \sigma + \lambda Y + \mu r \quad (\sigma, \lambda > 0; \, \mu < 0)$
(6) $M_s = M_0$

where Eqs. (1), (2) and (3) represent the goods market and Eqs. (4), (5) and (6) represent the money market, and where $Y =$ income, $C =$ consumption, $I =$ investment, $r =$ the rate of interest, $M_d =$ the demand for money, $M_s =$ the supply of money, and M_0 is a constant amount of money.

The goods market, which is represented by Eqs. (1), (2) and (3), can be seen to consist of the equilibrium condition (1) plus the two behavioural equations (2) and (3). The equilibrium condition (1) requires equality between the value of planned aggregate output of goods (and services) and the value of planned aggregate expenditure on goods (and services), while the behavioural equations (2) and (3) indicate that consumption expenditure and investment expenditure are assumed to be linear functions of national income and the rate of interest, respectively. Note, in equation (2), that $\Delta C/\Delta Y = \beta > 0$. In other words, C will rise (fall) as Y rises (falls).

Also note, in Eq. (3), that $\Delta I/\Delta r = \delta < 0$. In other words, I will rise (fall) as r falls (rises).

The money market, which is represented by Eqs. (4), (5) and (6), can be seen to consist of the equilibrium condition (4) plus the two behavioural equations (5) and (6). The equilibrium condition (4) requires equality between the demand for and the supply of money, while the behavioural equations (5) and (6) indicate what determines the demand for money and the supply of money, respectively. Although it is not stated explicitly in Eq. (5), we shall assume that the (stock) demand for money consists of two parts (denoted as L_1 and L_2), as given by $L_1 = \lambda Y$ and $L_2 = \sigma + \mu r$. In other words, one part (L_1) of the demand for money is assumed to be directly related to the level of income (as shown by $\Delta L_1/\Delta Y = \lambda > 0$), while the other part (L_2) of the demand for money is assumed to be inversely related to the rate of interest (as shown by $\Delta L_2/\Delta r = \mu < 0$). As regards the supply of money side, we shall simply assume that the supply of money is exogenously determined by central bank policy. Hence, in Eq. (6), we have $M_s = M_0$, where $M_0 > 0$ is the constant amount of money determined by the central bank.

The attainment of equilibrium in the above model requires the simultaneous satisfaction of *both* the equilibrium condition of the goods market and the equilibrium condition of the money market. Hence, if we substitute Eqs. (2) and (3) into Eq. (1) and Eqs. (5) and (6) into Eq. (4), we obtain the following two equations (with the endogenous variables (Y and r) on the left-hand side and the exogenous variable (M_0) and the given parameters (α, γ and σ) on the right-hand side):

$$\begin{matrix}(1-\beta)Y - \delta r = \alpha + \gamma \\ \lambda Y + \mu r = M_0 - \sigma\end{matrix} \quad \text{or} \quad \begin{bmatrix} (1-\beta) & -\delta \\ \lambda & \mu \end{bmatrix}\begin{bmatrix} Y \\ r \end{bmatrix} = \begin{bmatrix} \alpha + \gamma \\ M_0 - \sigma \end{bmatrix} \quad (5\text{-}5)$$

Equation (5-5) can then be solved by Cramer's rule (which, in this case, is much more convenient than solving either by the elimination of one variable via substitution or by matrix inversion) to obtain the equilibrium values of Y and r, denoted as $\bar{Y}$ and $\bar{r}$, which are consistent with equilibrium in *both* the goods market and the money market. Subsequent substitution of $\bar{Y}$ and $\bar{r}$ into Eqs. (2) and (3) will then yield $\bar{C}$ and $\bar{I}$. The solution of (5-5), in order to obtain $\bar{Y}$ and $\bar{r}$, is left for the student to do in Prob. 5-5 in Sec. 5-C.

Before leaving the above model, it should be noted that the first equation of (5-5), which constitutes the equilibrium condition for the goods market, can be written as

$$r = -\frac{\alpha + \gamma}{\delta} + \frac{(1-\beta)}{\delta} Y \quad (5\text{-}6)$$

In other words, the equilibrium condition for the goods market can be expressed as the set of (Y, r) values which satisfy (5-6). This relationship between r and Y, in (5-6), is referred to in macroeconomic texts as the '*IS* function'. Similarly, it should be noted that the second equation of (5-5), which constitutes the equilibrium condition for the money market, can be written as

$$r = \frac{M_0 - \sigma}{\mu} - \frac{\lambda}{\mu} Y \qquad (5\text{-}7)$$

In other words, the equilibrium condition for the money market can be expressed as the set of (Y, r) values which satisfy (5-7). This relationship between r and Y, in (5-7), is referred to in macroeconomic texts as the '*LM* function'.

5-C PRACTICE PROBLEMS

5-5 Use Cramer's rule to solve the macroeconomic model (5-5) for $\bar{Y}$ and $\bar{r}$.

5-6 Rewrite the *IS* function (5-6) and the *LM* function (5-7) in the forms $r = a + bY$ and $r = c + dY$, respectively, where $a, d > 0$ and $b, c < 0$. Then, assuming that $ad > bc$, demonstrate that the general equilibrium of the goods and money markets can be graphically determined by the intersection of the *IS* and *LM* functions.

5-4 A MACRO-MODEL OF n TRADING COUNTRIES

In this section we shall briefly consider an international general equilibrium situation in which changes in the economy of one country have repercussions on the economies of the countries with which it trades.

To simplify the analysis involved, we shall ignore the money market in each country and simply concentrate our attention on the goods market in each country. Also, in addition to assuming that all exchange rates are fixed, we shall assume that there is no government expenditure or taxation in each country.

As a first step, in constructing a simple macro-model of n trading countries, we shall construct a simple macro-model for *three* trading countries. To do this, note firstly that the condition for equilibrium in the level of income in each country can be expressed in equation form as follows:

(1) $Y_1 = C_1 + I_1 + X_1 - M_1$
(2) $Y_2 = C_2 + I_2 + X_2 - M_2$
(3) $Y_3 = C_3 + I_3 + X_3 - M_3$

where the subscripts 1, 2 and 3 denote countries 1, 2 and 3, respectively, and where Y = income, C = consumption, I = investment (assumed to be exogenously determined), X = exports, and M = imports. In other words, the condition for equilibrium in the level of income (output) in each country is that the value of planned aggregate output Y is exactly equal to the value of planned aggregate expenditure $C+I+X-M$ (made up of planned domestic expenditure $(C+I)$ on domestic output plus planned foreign expenditure (X) on domestic output minus planned domestic expenditure (M) which is *not* used to demand domestic output. Alternatively, $C+I+X-M$ can be regarded as planned domestic expenditure $(C+I)$ on domestic output plus *net* planned foreign expenditure $(X-M)$ on domestic output). Also, note that consumption in each country will be assumed to be a positive proportion of the level of income in each country, as given by the following three equations:

(4) $C_1 = c_1 Y_1$ (5) $C_2 = c_2 Y_2$ (6) $C_3 = c_3 Y_3$

where $0 < c_1, c_2, c_3 < 1$. Similarly, expenditure on imports in each country will be assumed to be a positive proportion of the level of income in each country, as given by the following three equations:

(7) $M_1 = m_1 Y_1$ (8) $M_2 = m_2 Y_2$ (9) $M_3 = m_3 Y_3$

where $0 < m_1, m_2, m_3 < 1$. In other words, as the level of income in each country rises, households and business units in that country will spend more on all kinds of goods, including those produced abroad. This means that both C and M are endogenous variables.

It should be noted, in Eqs. (7), (8) and (9), that so far we have simply stated that a country's imports are a function of that country's income. As yet we have not stated the source of these imports. To do this, we will assume that

(10) $M_1 = m_{12} Y_1 + m_{13} Y_1$
(11) $M_2 = m_{21} Y_2 + m_{23} Y_2$
(12) $M_3 = m_{31} Y_3 + m_{32} Y_3$

where $m_1 = m_{12} + m_{13}$, $m_2 = m_{21} + m_{23}$, $m_3 = m_{31} + m_{32}$. Thus, for example, in Eq. (10) the imports of country 1 (M_1) consist of imports from country 2 (given by $m_{12} Y_1$, where m_{12} is the proportion of country 1 income that is spent on imports from country 2) plus imports from country 3 (given by $m_{13} Y_1$, where m_{13} is the proportion of country 1 income that is spent on imports from country 3). Similarly, the imports of country 2 (country 3) consist of the sum of imports from countries 1 and 3 (countries 1 and 2).

Now that we have stated the source of each country's imports, we can readily define each country's exports. Thus, since $m_{21} Y_2$ and $m_{31} Y_3$, in Eqs. (11) and (12), represent the imports demanded from country 1 by country 2 and country 3, respectively, then the exports of country 1 (X_1) can be defined as

5-4 A MACRO-MODEL OF n TRADING COUNTRIES

$$(13) \quad X_1 = m_{21}Y_2 + m_{31}Y_3$$

Similarly, the exports of country 2 and country 3 can be defined as

$$(14) \quad X_2 = m_{12}Y_1 + m_{32}Y_3$$
$$(15) \quad X_3 = m_{13}Y_1 + m_{23}Y_2$$

The above expressions for consumption, exports and imports can now be substituted into the equilibrium conditions to give

$$Y_1 = c_1 Y_1 + I_1 + m_{21}Y_2 + m_{31}Y_3 - m_{12}Y_1 - m_{13}Y_1$$
$$Y_2 = c_2 Y_2 + I_2 + m_{12}Y_1 + m_{32}Y_3 - m_{21}Y_2 - m_{23}Y_2$$
$$Y_3 = c_3 Y_3 + I_3 + m_{13}Y_1 + m_{23}Y_2 - m_{31}Y_3 - m_{32}Y_3$$

or

$$Y_1 = (c_1 - m_{12} - m_{13})Y_1 \quad\quad + m_{21}Y_2 \quad\quad\quad\quad + m_{31}Y_3 + I_1$$
$$Y_2 = \quad\quad m_{12}Y_1 + (c_2 - m_{21} - m_{23})Y_2 \quad\quad + m_{32}Y_3 + I_2$$
$$Y_3 = \quad\quad m_{13}Y_1 \quad\quad + m_{23}Y_2 + (c_3 - m_{31} - m_{32})Y_3 + I_3$$

which can be rewritten in matrix form as

$$\begin{bmatrix} Y_1 \\ Y_2 \\ Y_3 \end{bmatrix} = \begin{bmatrix} (c_1 - m_{12} - m_{13}) & m_{21} & m_{31} \\ m_{12} & (c_2 - m_{21} - m_{23}) & m_{32} \\ m_{13} & m_{23} & (c_3 - m_{31} - m_{32}) \end{bmatrix} \begin{bmatrix} Y_1 \\ Y_2 \\ Y_3 \end{bmatrix} + \begin{bmatrix} I_1 \\ I_2 \\ I_3 \end{bmatrix}$$

or

$$y = By + e \tag{5-8}$$

Since (5-8) can be written equivalently as

$$Iy = By + e \quad \text{or} \quad (I - B)y = e$$

then, if matrix $(I - B)$ is nonsingular, the unique solution to (5-8) will be

$$\bar{y} = (I - B)^{-1} e \tag{5-9}$$

For example, given

$$\begin{aligned} c_1 &= \tfrac{4}{5} & m_{12} &= \tfrac{1}{4} & m_{13} &= \tfrac{1}{5} & I_1 &= 1894 \\ c_2 &= \tfrac{3}{4} & m_{21} &= \tfrac{1}{10} & m_{23} &= \tfrac{1}{5} & I_2 &= 947 \\ c_3 &= \tfrac{2}{3} & m_{31} &= \tfrac{1}{6} & m_{32} &= \tfrac{1}{10} & I_3 &= 2841 \end{aligned}$$

so that

$$(I - B) = \begin{bmatrix} 1 & 0 & 0 \\ 0 & 1 & 0 \\ 0 & 0 & 1 \end{bmatrix} - \begin{bmatrix} \tfrac{7}{20} & \tfrac{1}{10} & \tfrac{1}{6} \\ \tfrac{1}{4} & \tfrac{9}{20} & \tfrac{1}{10} \\ \tfrac{1}{5} & \tfrac{1}{5} & \tfrac{2}{5} \end{bmatrix} = \begin{bmatrix} \tfrac{13}{20} & -\tfrac{1}{10} & -\tfrac{1}{6} \\ -\tfrac{1}{4} & \tfrac{11}{20} & -\tfrac{1}{10} \\ -\tfrac{1}{5} & -\tfrac{1}{5} & \tfrac{3}{5} \end{bmatrix}$$

then, by inverting matrix $(I-B)$, we obtain

$$\begin{bmatrix} \bar{Y}_1 \\ \bar{Y}_2 \\ \bar{Y}_3 \end{bmatrix} = (I-B)^{-1}e = \tfrac{5}{947}\begin{bmatrix} 372 & 112 & 122 \\ 204 & 428 & 128 \\ 192 & 180 & 399 \end{bmatrix}\begin{bmatrix} 1894 \\ 947 \\ 2841 \end{bmatrix} = \begin{bmatrix} 6110 \\ 6100 \\ 8805 \end{bmatrix}$$

Substitution of these $\bar{Y}$ values into Eqs. (10), (11) and (12) will then yield $\bar{M}_1 = 2749.5$, $\bar{M}_2 = 1830$ and $\bar{M}_3 = 2348$. Similarly, substitution of the $\bar{Y}$ values into (13), (14) and (15) yields $\bar{X}_1 = 2077.5$, $\bar{X}_2 = 2408$ and $\bar{X}_3 = 2442$. Note from these $\bar{X}$ and $\bar{M}$ results, that $\bar{X} \neq \bar{M}$ in each country. This serves to emphasize that although it is possible to have $\bar{X} = \bar{M}$ when $Y = \bar{Y}$, in each country, the above model does not require this.

While the above model has been constructed for three trading countries, it can be readily extended to the case of n trading countries. To do this, we simply adjust (5-8) to represent the n-country case rather than the three-country case. Hence, in (5-8), vector y will now become an $n \times 1$ vector containing $Y_1, Y_2, \ldots, Y_n$, instead of a 3×1 vector containing Y_1, Y_2 and Y_3. In a similar fashion, vector e in (5-8) will now become an $n \times 1$ vector containing $I_1, I_2, \ldots, I_n$. Consequently, given these new dimensions of y and e in (5-8), matrix B must now become an $n \times n$ matrix rather than a 3×3 matrix. To see what the elements of B look like, let us denote matrix B as

$$B = [b_{ij}] \quad \begin{pmatrix} i = 1, 2, \ldots, n \\ j = 1, 2, \ldots, n \end{pmatrix}$$

so that the elements of B can be written as

$b_{11} = (c_1 - m_{12} - m_{13} - \ldots - m_{1n}); b_{12}, \ldots, b_{1n} = m_{21}, \ldots, m_{n1}$

$b_{21} = m_{12}; b_{22} = (c_2 - m_{21} - m_{23} - \ldots - m_{2n}); b_{23}, \ldots, b_{2n} = m_{32}, \ldots, m_{n2}$

$\ldots\ldots\ldots\ldots\ldots\ldots\ldots\ldots\ldots\ldots\ldots\ldots\ldots\ldots\ldots\ldots\ldots\ldots\ldots\ldots\ldots\ldots\ldots$

$b_{n1}, \ldots, b_{n(n-1)} = m_{1n}, \ldots, m_{(n-1)n}; b_{nn} = (c_n - m_{n1} - m_{n2} - \ldots - m_{n(n-1)})$

This demonstrates that $y = By + e$, and hence the solution $\bar{y} = (I-B)^{-1}e$, can be readily extended from the case of three trading countries to the case of n trading countries.

5-D PRACTICE PROBLEMS

5-7 Given the following macro-model of two trading countries:
    (a) $Y_1 = C_1 + I_1 + X_1 - M_1$ (d) $Y_2 = C_2 + I_2 + X_2 - M_2$
    (b) $C_1 = \tfrac{4}{5}Y_1$ (e) $C_2 = \tfrac{3}{4}Y_2$
    (c) $M_1 = \tfrac{1}{5}Y_1$ (f) $M_2 = \tfrac{1}{8}Y_2$
where the subscripts 1 and 2 denote countries 1 and 2, respectively, and where $X_1 = M_2$ and $X_2 = M_1$. Assuming that I_1 and I_2 are exogenously determined and equal to 80 and 120, respectively, rewrite this model in the form $y = By + e$ and find $\bar{y} = (I-B)^{-1}e$.

5-8 Assuming that $(I-B)^{-1}$ is unchanged in Prob. 5-7, find the new level of income in each country when I_1 and I_2 are changed to 120 and 400, respectively.

5-5 INPUT–OUTPUT ANALYSIS

To gain an elementary understanding of input–output analysis, we shall assume that the numerous industries of a hypothetical economy can be aggregated into three productive sectors: Agriculture, Manufacturing and Services. This aggregation means, for example, that the outputs (in value terms) of all the many kinds of agricultural goods are summed to obtain the aggregate output (in value terms) of the Agriculture sector. Having made this simplifying assumption (plus the assumption of no foreign trade), we then ask the question: to whom is the output produced by each sector sold? The answer is that the output of each sector is sold to other sectors (including itself), which use its output as an input in their production process, and to final consumers. For example, the output of the Manufacturing sector may be sold:

(a) as an input to the Agriculture sector (e.g., agricultural machinery);
(b) as an input to the Manufacturing sector itself (e.g., machine-tools);
(c) as an input to the Services sector (e.g., hair-dressing equipment);
(d) to final consumers (e.g., cars).

Each sector is therefore characterized by an inflow of inputs purchased from other sectors and by an outflow of its output which is sold to other sectors (including itself) and to final consumers. In addition to this, we shall assume that the production process in each sector requires some labour input (for simplicity, we shall assume that no capital input is required).

The above discussion of intersectoral flows is illustrated in Table 5-1, where all the figures are measured in (the same) money units (for example, hundreds of millions of pounds sterling). Thus an examination of the second row of figures in Table 5-1 shows how the output of the

Table 5-1

Input from \ Output to	Intersectoral demand			Final demand	Total output
	Agriculture	Manufacturing	Services		
Agriculture	4	10	0	6	20
Manufacturing	5	10	5	10	30
Services	0	6	2	2	10
Labour	11	4	3		
Total input	20	30	10		60

Manufacturing sector is disposed of: 5 units are sold as input to the Agriculture sector, 10 units are sold as input to the Manufacturing sector itself, 5 units are sold as input to the Services sector, and 10 units are sold to final consumers. Therefore, the total output of the Manufacturing sector, of 30 units, goes to meet the intersectoral demand of 20 units plus the final demand of 10 units. The first and third rows of figures, in Table 5-1, likewise show how the output of the Agriculture and Services sectors, respectively, are disposed of.

An examination of the second column of figures in Table 5-1 shows what outputs have been used as inputs in the production process of the Manufacturing sector. Thus, the Manufacturing sector has used 10 units of Agriculture output, 10 units of Manufacturing output, and 6 units of Services output as inputs in its production process. In addition, the Manufacturing sector has used 4 units of labour input in its production process. The first and third columns of figures, in Table 5-1, likewise show what inputs have been used in the production processes of the Agriculture and Services sectors, respectively. Note, in Table 5-1, that the row sum for each sector is equal to the column sum for each sector. In other words, the value of output in each sector is equal to the value of the inputs used in the production of that output.

A further consideration of the Manufacturing input column, in Table 5-1, indicates that the amount of each input needed in the production of *one* unit of Manufacturing output can be obtained by simply dividing each element of that column by the total Manufacturing output. Thus, the production of one unit of Manufacturing output requires $1/3$ ($=10/30$) units of Agriculture input, $1/3$ ($=10/30$) units of Manufacturing input, $1/5$ ($=6/30$) units of Services input, and $2/15$ ($=4/30$) units of labour input. The amount of each input needed in the production of one unit of Agriculture (Services) output can likewise be obtained by dividing each element of the Agriculture (Services) input column by the total Agriculture (Services) output. Note, in this calculation, that each sector uses a fixed input ratio for the production of its output.

To transform the above discussion into mathematical terms, let us denote the respective total outputs of Agriculture, Manufacturing, and Services by x_1, x_2, and x_3. Thus, $x_1 = 20$, $x_2 = 30$, and $x_3 = 10$. Also, let us denote the respective final demands for Agriculture, Manufacturing and Services output by d_1, d_2, and d_3. Thus, $d_1 = 6$, $d_2 = 10$, and $d_3 = 2$. With this notation, the first three rows of figures in Table 5-1 can now be expressed as

$$\frac{1}{5}x_1 + \frac{1}{3}x_2 + 0x_3 + d_1 = x_1$$
$$\frac{1}{4}x_1 + \frac{1}{3}x_2 + \frac{1}{2}x_3 + d_2 = x_2 \qquad (5\text{-}10)$$
$$0x_1 + \frac{1}{5}x_2 + \frac{1}{5}x_3 + d_3 = x_3$$

5-5 INPUT–OUTPUT ANALYSIS

where, for example, the first equation of (5-10) is simply

$$\tfrac{1}{5}x_1 + \tfrac{1}{3}x_2 + 0x_3 + d_1 = x_1$$

or

$$\tfrac{1}{5}(20) + \tfrac{1}{3}(30) + 0(10) + 6 = 20$$

Rewriting (5-10) in matrix form, we have

$$Ax + d = x \quad \text{or} \quad \begin{bmatrix} \tfrac{1}{5} & \tfrac{1}{3} & 0 \\ \tfrac{1}{4} & \tfrac{1}{3} & \tfrac{1}{2} \\ 0 & \tfrac{1}{5} & \tfrac{1}{5} \end{bmatrix} \begin{bmatrix} x_1 \\ x_2 \\ x_3 \end{bmatrix} + \begin{bmatrix} d_1 \\ d_2 \\ d_3 \end{bmatrix} = \begin{bmatrix} x_1 \\ x_2 \\ x_3 \end{bmatrix} \quad (5\text{-}11)$$

Or, in more general terms, (5-11) may be written (in the $x = Ax + d$ form) as

$$x = Ax + d \quad \text{or} \quad \begin{bmatrix} x_1 \\ x_2 \\ x_3 \end{bmatrix} = \begin{bmatrix} a_{11} & a_{12} & a_{13} \\ a_{21} & a_{22} & a_{23} \\ a_{31} & a_{32} & a_{33} \end{bmatrix} \begin{bmatrix} x_1 \\ x_2 \\ x_3 \end{bmatrix} + \begin{bmatrix} d_1 \\ d_2 \\ d_3 \end{bmatrix} \quad (5\text{-}12)$$

where the elements of matrix A are known as *input coefficients*. Since matrix A can be written as $A = [a_{ij}]$, then element a_{ij} indicates how much of the ith output is used as an input in the production of each unit of the jth output. For example, in (5-11) and (5-12), the element $a_{12} = \tfrac{1}{3}$ indicates that $\tfrac{1}{3}$ unit of x_1 is used as an input in the production of each unit of x_2.

Although we have only been working with a three-sector economy, Eq. (5-12) indicates that a multi-sector economy can be similarly expressed compactly as $x = Ax + d$. Since (5-12) can be written equivalently as

$$Ix = Ax + d \quad \text{or} \quad (I - A)x = d$$

then, if matrix $(I - A)$ is nonsingular, the unique solution to (5-12) will be

$$\bar{x} = (I - A)^{-1} d \quad (5\text{-}13)$$

Thus, in our example, since

$$(I - A) = \begin{bmatrix} 1 & 0 & 0 \\ 0 & 1 & 0 \\ 0 & 0 & 1 \end{bmatrix} - \begin{bmatrix} \tfrac{1}{5} & \tfrac{1}{3} & 0 \\ \tfrac{1}{4} & \tfrac{1}{3} & \tfrac{1}{2} \\ 0 & \tfrac{1}{5} & \tfrac{1}{5} \end{bmatrix} = \begin{bmatrix} \tfrac{4}{5} & -\tfrac{1}{3} & 0 \\ -\tfrac{1}{4} & \tfrac{2}{3} & -\tfrac{1}{2} \\ 0 & -\tfrac{1}{5} & \tfrac{4}{5} \end{bmatrix}$$

then, by inverting matrix $(I - A)$, we obtain

$$\begin{bmatrix} \bar{x}_1 \\ \bar{x}_2 \\ \bar{x}_3 \end{bmatrix} = (I - A)^{-1} d = \tfrac{25}{7} \begin{bmatrix} \tfrac{13}{30} & \tfrac{4}{15} & \tfrac{1}{6} \\ \tfrac{1}{5} & \tfrac{16}{25} & \tfrac{2}{5} \\ \tfrac{1}{20} & \tfrac{4}{25} & \tfrac{9}{20} \end{bmatrix} \begin{bmatrix} d_1 \\ d_2 \\ d_3 \end{bmatrix} \quad (5\text{-}14)$$

Substitution of $d_1 = 6$, $d_2 = 10$, and $d_3 = 2$, into (5-14) will then give $\bar{x}_1 = 20$, $\bar{x}_2 = 30$, and $\bar{x}_3 = 10$.

Once we have obtained (5-14), we can engage in some very interesting economic analysis with respect to government planning programmes. To demonstrate this, let us assume that all input coefficients (including labour input coefficients) are unchanged over the planning period. Then, assuming that a government development programme desires to achieve a final-demand vector in which $d_1 = 9$, $d_2 = 15$, and $d_3 = 3$, we can use (5-14) to ascertain what the output of each sector must be in order to fulfil this development programme. Thus, we simply substitute $d_1 = 9$, $d_2 = 15$, and $d_3 = 3$ into (5-14) to obtain $\bar{x}_1 = 30$, $\bar{x}_2 = 45$, and $\bar{x}_3 = 15$. Further, to obtain the labour input requirements consistent with this new output mix, we simply multiply each new output level by its respective labour input coefficient. Since, from Table 5-1, the respective labour input coefficients for the Agriculture, Manufacturing, and Services sectors, are 11/20, 4/30, and 3/10, then the new labour input requirements are $(11/20)(30) = 33/2$ for the Agriculture sector, $(4/30)(45) = 6$ for the Manufacturing sector, and $(3/10)(15) = 9/2$ for the Services sector. Finally, although not done here, a knowledge of the (constant) wage rate means that the new labour input requirements can be converted from value terms into employment terms. The latter conversion is obviously very important in the sense that the government development programme will only be feasible if there is sufficient labour available in the economy to produce the new output levels.

Note, in the above example, that as long as the input coefficients remain unchanged, the inverse $(I - A)^{-1}$ remains unchanged. This means that once we have obtained $(I - A)^{-1}$ in (5-14), then we can examine the implications of as many different final-demand vectors as we wish. In this way, we can examine the input–output implications of various government development programmes. Thus, although our discussion of input–output analysis has been very elementary, it will suffice to demonstrate the practical significance of input–output models in analysing both intersectoral relationships and government development programmes.

5-E PRACTICE PROBLEMS

5-9 A three-sector input–output system is represented by the matrix equation $x = Ax + d$, where

$$A = \begin{bmatrix} \frac{1}{2} & 0 & \frac{1}{3} \\ \frac{1}{5} & \frac{1}{2} & \frac{1}{5} \\ 0 & \frac{1}{4} & \frac{1}{5} \end{bmatrix} \quad \text{and} \quad d = \begin{bmatrix} 10 \\ 8 \\ 4 \end{bmatrix}$$

Find the output levels for the three sectors.

5-10 If d in Prob. 5-9 is changed such that $d_1 = 12$, $d_2 = 10$, and $d_3 = 5$, what is the new output level in each sector (assuming that A is unchanged)?

5-6 ADDITIONAL PROBLEMS

5-11 Given the partial-equilibrium market model:
$$Q_d = Q_s$$
$$Q_d = m - nP \quad (m, n > 0)$$
$$Q_s = -r + sP^T \quad (r, s > 0)$$
$$P^T = P - t \quad (t > 0)$$

Rewrite this equation system in the matrix format $Ax = b$, with the variables arranged in the following order: Q_d, Q_s, P, P^T. Then use Cramer's rule to find the solution values of these variables.

5-12 Given the two-good market model:
(1) $Q_{d1} = Q_{s1}$ (4) $Q_{d2} = Q_{s2}$
(2) $Q_{d1} = 20 - 8P_1 + P_2$ (5) $Q_{d2} = 19 + 2P_1 - 4P_2$
(3) $Q_{s1} = -7 + 3P_1$ (6) $Q_{s2} = -11 + 2P_2$

Reduce this model to two equations in the two variables P_1 and P_2 by substituting the second and third equations into the first, and the fifth and sixth equations into the fourth. Then use Cramer's rule to solve the two resulting equations for $\bar{P}_1$ and $\bar{P}_2$. Also, obtain $\bar{Q}_{d1} = \bar{Q}_{s1} = \bar{Q}_1$ and $\bar{Q}_{d2} = \bar{Q}_{s2} = \bar{Q}_2$ by substitution.

5-13 Use Cramer's rule to solve the following national-income model:
$$Y = C + I + G$$
$$C = \alpha + \beta(Y - T) \quad (\alpha > 0; 0 < \beta < 1)$$
$$I = \gamma + \delta Y \quad (\gamma > 0; 0 < \delta < 1)$$
$$T = tY \quad (0 < t < 1)$$

where Y, C, I and T are endogenous variables and G is exogenously determined. Indicate what additional restrictions (if any) are required on the parameters to ensure that $\bar{Y}$, $\bar{C}$, $\bar{I}$ and $\bar{T}$ are all positive.

5-14 Use Cramer's rule to solve the following national-income model:
$$Y = C + I + G + X - M$$
$$C = \alpha + \beta Y \quad (\alpha > 0; 0 < \beta < 1)$$
$$M = n + mY \quad (n < 0; 0 < m < 1)$$

where Y, C and M are endogenous variables and I, G and X are exogenously determined. Indicate what additional restrictions (if any) are required on the parameters to ensure that $\bar{Y}$, $\bar{C}$ and $\bar{M}$ are all positive.

5-15 Given the following national-income model of two trading countries:
$$Y_1 = C_1 + I_1 + X_1 - M_1 \qquad Y_2 = C_2 + I_2 + X_2 - M_2$$
$$C_1 = c_1 Y_1 \quad (0 < c_1 < 1) \qquad C_2 = c_2 Y_2 \quad (0 < c_2 < 1)$$
$$M_1 = m_1 Y_1 \quad (0 < m_1 < 1) \qquad M_2 = m_2 Y_2 \quad (0 < m_2 < 1)$$
$$X_1 = M_2 \qquad X_2 = M_1$$

where the subscripts 1 and 2 denote countries 1 and 2, respectively. Treating I_1 and I_2 as being exogenously determined, rewrite this model in the matrix form $y = By + e$, as in (5-8), and then obtain the equilibrium values of income in each country (denoted as $\bar{Y}_1$ and $\bar{Y}_2$). Are $\bar{Y}_1$ and $\bar{Y}_2$ both positive?

5-16 Given the following model of an economy with a goods market and a money market:
$$Y = C + I + G \qquad\qquad M_d = M_s$$
$$C = \alpha + \beta Y \quad (\alpha > 0; 0 < \beta < 1) \quad M_d = \sigma + \lambda Y + \mu r \quad (\sigma, \lambda > 0; \mu < 0)$$
$$I = \gamma + \delta r \quad (\gamma > 0; \delta < 0) \qquad M_s = M_0$$

where Y, C, I and r are endogenous variables and G and M_0 are exogenously determined. Rewrite the above model in matrix form, as in (5-5), and then use Cramer's rule to solve for the equilibrium values of Y and r.

5-17 A country has the following input–output table:

Input from \ Output to	Intersectoral demand			Final demand	Total output
	Agriculture	Manufacturing	Services		
Agriculture	1	4	2	1	8
Manufacturing	4	2	2	4	12
Services	2	2	2	2	8
Labour	1	4	2		
Total input	8	12	8		28

where the figures are in billions of US dollars. Assuming that the input coefficients remain unchanged, what will be the output level of each sector if the final demand changes to 3 units of Agriculture output, 6 units of Manufacturing output, and 3 units of Services output?

CHAPTER
SIX
DIFFERENTIATION OF A FUNCTION OF ONE VARIABLE

In Chapter 2, we saw how economic relationships can be represented in terms of functions. Thus, for example, the relationship between the quantity demanded (Q_d) and the unit price (P) of a good can be represented by the function $Q_d = f(P)$. Also, in Chapter 2, we noted that if the demand function is given an explicit form, then the specific form of the relationship between Q_d and P can be represented graphically. For example, in Sec. 2-4, the explicit (linear) demand function $Q_d = 10 - 2P$ is graphed in Fig. 2-6 as a downward-sloping straight line. In Chapter 3, this type of linear relationship between Q_d and P was further examined by noting that the change in Q_d per unit of change in P can be measured by the difference quotient $\Delta Q_d/\Delta P$ or, in graphical terms, the slope of the (linear) demand curve. For example, in Fig. 2-6, the slope of the linear demand curve, given by $\Delta Q_d/\Delta P = -2$, informs us (a) that Q_d will decrease (increase) as P increases (decreases) and (b) that a unit increase (decrease) in P will result in a 2 unit decrease (increase) in Q_d. Thus, in Chapter 3, we noted that the difference quotient provides us with information about both the *direction* and the *magnitude* of the change in Q_d in response to a unit change in P.

The discussion of Chapters 2 and 3 has therefore provided an elementary introduction to the notion of the change in one variable in response to the change in another. However, since this notion of change occurs frequently in economics, we must now examine it in more detail. To do this, we shall leave our demand function $Q_d = f(P)$ and instead refer to the general function $y = f(x)$.

6-1 THE DIFFERENCE QUOTIENT AND THE SLOPE OF A CURVE

When we write the linear function

$$y = f(x) = a + bx \quad (a, b > 0) \tag{6-1}$$

we are stating that certain x values can be mapped into their corresponding y values. For example, when $x = x_1$, the corresponding y value is

$$y_1 = f(x_1) = a + bx_1 \tag{6-2}$$

Similarly, if the value of x is changed from $x = x_1$ to $x = x_2$, the corresponding y value will change from y_1 to

$$y_2 = f(x_2) = a + bx_2 \tag{6-3}$$

Thus, as in Sec. 3-1, subtracting (6-2) from (6-3) gives

$$y_2 - y_1 = bx_2 - bx_1 = b(x_2 - x_1)$$
$$\text{or} \quad \Delta y = b \Delta x \tag{6-4}$$

Therefore the difference quotient is

$$\Delta y / \Delta x = b \tag{6-5}$$

which states that the change in y is b units per unit change in x.

In graphical terms, as illustrated in Fig. 6-1, $\Delta y/\Delta x$ measures the slope of the line segment AB. Since the slope of the line segment AB is identical to the slope of the line $y = a + bx$, then $\Delta y/\Delta x$ measures the slope of the line $y = a + bx$.

Note, in Fig. 6-1, that the slope of the line $y = a + bx$ is constant as indicated by $\Delta y/\Delta x$ being equal to the constant b. This means that if we had

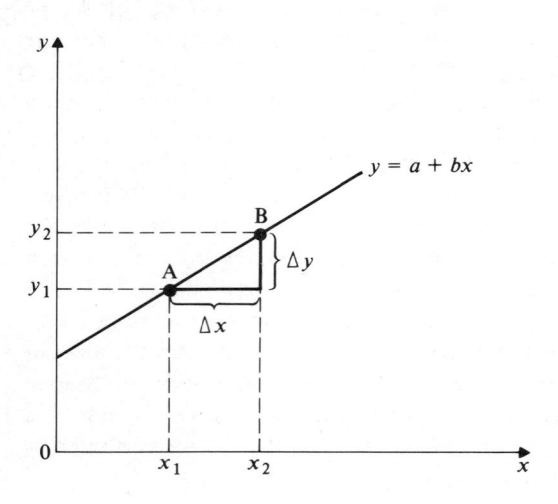

Figure 6-1

6-1 THE DIFFERENCE QUOTIENT AND THE SLOPE OF A CURVE

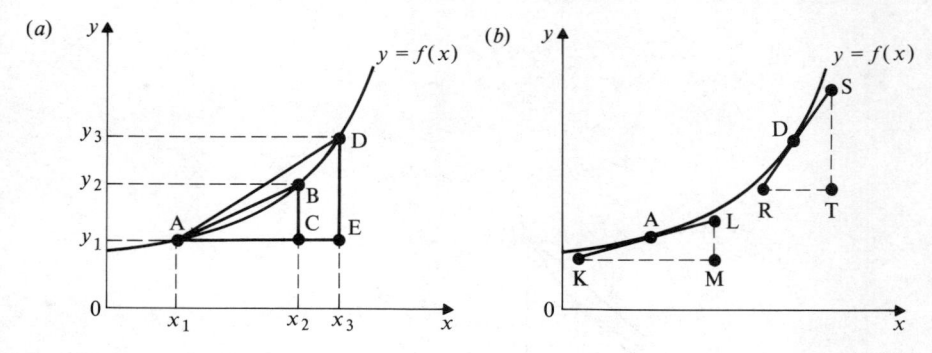

Figure 6-2

taken a smaller (larger) change in x, and thus a corresponding smaller (larger) change in y, the resulting difference quotient $\Delta y/\Delta x$ would still be equal to b in value. In other words, the slope, represented by $\Delta y/\Delta x$, is constant for all values of Δx.

Since the above discussion has been limited to the case of a linear function, we must now examine the case of a nonlinear function. To do this, we shall assume that the graph of a nonlinear function, $y = f(x)$, has the shape portrayed in Fig. 6-2a. In this case, if we take $\Delta x = x_2 - x_1$ and $\Delta y = y_2 - y_1$, then the difference quotient $\Delta y/\Delta x$ will measure the slope of the line AB in Fig. 6-2a. Having done this, we can immediately see the contrast between the linear case of Fig. 6-1 and the nonlinear case of Fig. 6-2a. In Fig. 6-1, the line (segment) AB coincided with the linear curve $y = a + bx$, whereas in Fig. 6-2a the line AB does not coincide with the nonlinear curve $y = f(x)$. Moreover, in contrast to the linear case in Fig. 6-1, the difference quotient $\Delta y/\Delta x$ in Fig. 6-2a is not constant for all values of Δx. To see the latter point, note, in Fig. 6-2a, that if x is changed from x_1 to x_3 (so that $\Delta x = x_3 - x_1$) with a corresponding change in y from y_1 to y_3 (so that $\Delta y = y_3 - y_1$), then $\Delta y/\Delta x = DE/AE$, or the slope of the line AD. Also note, in Fig. 6-2a, that if we decrease the magnitude of Δx to $\Delta x = x_2 - x_1$, with a corresponding decrease in Δy to $\Delta y = y_2 - y_1$, then $\Delta y/\Delta x = BC/AC$, or the slope of the line AB. Since the line AB has a flatter slope than the line AD, then $\Delta y/\Delta x$ is not constant for all values of Δx as was the case in Fig. 6-1.

The obvious conclusion of the discussion of the nonlinear case, shown in Fig. 6-2a, is that we cannot use the difference quotient $\Delta y/\Delta x$ to measure the slope of a nonlinear curve in the way that we used $\Delta y/\Delta x$ to measure the slope of the line $y = a + bx$ in Fig. 6-1. To see how we measure the slope of a nonlinear curve, let us note firstly, in Fig. 6-2b, that the slope of $y = f(x)$ will vary at different points on the curve. For example, in Fig. 6-2b, the slope of the curve at point A is given by the slope of the tangent line KL ($= LM/KM$), while the slope of the curve at point D is given by the slope of

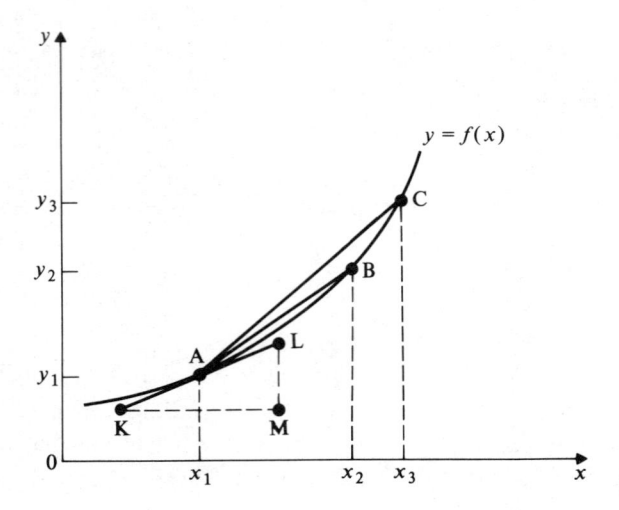

Figure 6-3

the tangent line RS ($=$ ST/RT). This makes it clear that if we wish to measure the slope of a nonlinear curve at a particular point, we must measure the slope of the tangent line to the curve at that point.

Let us now suppose, with reference to Fig. 6-3, that we wish to measure the slope of $y = f(x)$ at point A. Clearly, this can be achieved by measuring the slope of the tangent line KL ($=$ LM/KM) at point A. However, it is interesting to note that this result can also be obtained by using the difference quotient in a particular fashion. To demonstrate this, note in Fig. 6-3 that if $\Delta x = x_3 - x_1$ and $\Delta y = y_3 - y_1$, then $\Delta y/\Delta x$ equals the slope of the line AC. Also, note in Fig. 6-3 that if Δx is reduced to $\Delta x = x_2 - x_1$, with the corresponding reduction in Δy to $\Delta y = y_2 - y_1$, then $\Delta y/\Delta x$ equals the slope of the line AB, which is less than the slope of the line AC. In other words, as Δx has been reduced, the slope given by $\Delta y/\Delta x$ has got closer to the slope of the tangent line KL. This indicates that, as Δx is reduced further and further, the slope given by $\Delta y/\Delta x$ will get closer and closer to the slope of the tangent KL. Therefore, if we wish to obtain an exact measure of the slope of $y = f(x)$, at point A in Fig. 6-3, we can use the difference quotient provided that we make Δx as small as possible so that the slope given by $\Delta y/\Delta x$, for this very small value of Δx, is the same as the slope of the tangent line KL. In doing this, however, it is important to note that we cannot take zero as the smallest possible value of Δx, because the value of $\Delta y/\Delta x$ is undefined when $\Delta x = 0$ (in such a case, $\Delta y/\Delta x$ would have the meaningless form of 0/0). This means we must therefore calculate the value of $\Delta y/\Delta x$ as Δx gets smaller and smaller and approaches (but never actually reaches) zero. This value which $\Delta y/\Delta x$ approaches as Δx approaches zero is known as the *limit* of $\Delta y/\Delta x$ and is expressed symbolically as

$$\lim_{\Delta x \to 0} \frac{\Delta y}{\Delta x} \tag{6-6}$$

The limit of $\Delta y/\Delta x$ as Δx approaches zero defines what is known as the *derivative* of the function $y = f(x)$, and is expressed symbolically as

$$\frac{dy}{dx} = \lim_{\Delta x \to 0} \frac{\Delta y}{\Delta x} \tag{6-7}$$

Note, in relation to (6-7), that dy/dx is a symbol representing the *limit* of $\Delta y/\Delta x$. As such it must be regarded as a single entity, *not* the ratio of one thing (dy) to another (dx).

The above discussion, followed by the definition of the derivative in (6-7), provides an intuitive indication that the slope of $y = f(x)$ at point A, in Fig. 6-3, is measured by the derivative of $y = f(x)$ at that point. However, since the concept of derivative is extensively used in the mathematical analysis of economic models, it is essential that we explore the meaning of this concept in some detail.

6-2 THE DERIVATIVE

An important first point to note about the derivative is that a derivative is a *function*. This point can best be explained by obtaining the derivative dy/dx, as defined in (6-7), of a simple function such as

$$y = f(x) = x^2 \tag{6-8}$$

Before doing this, note that the function (6-8) indicates that a given x value will be associated with a unique corresponding y value. Also, note that if x changes in value, there will be a corresponding change in the value of y. This means that if we denote the change in x by Δx, then we can say that x has changed from some initial value x to a new value $x + \Delta x$. Similarly, if we denote the corresponding change in y by Δy, then we can say that y has changed from some initial value y to a new value $y + \Delta y$. Consequently, if we put these new values into (6-8), we obtain

$$y + \Delta y = f(x + \Delta x) = (x + \Delta x)^2 \tag{6-9}$$
$$\text{or} \quad y + \Delta y = x^2 + 2x\Delta x + (\Delta x)^2 \tag{6-10}$$

Subtraction of (6-8) from (6-10) will then give us

$$\Delta y = 2x\Delta x + (\Delta x)^2$$

which, upon division by Δx, gives us the difference quotient

$$\Delta y/\Delta x = 2x + \Delta x \tag{6-11}$$

An examination of (6-11) indicates that as Δx approaches zero, $(2x + \Delta x)$ will approach the value $2x$. Thus, by taking the limit of (6-11) we obtain the derivative of the function $y = f(x) = x^2$, as given by

$$\frac{dy}{dx} = \lim_{\Delta x \to 0} \frac{\Delta y}{\Delta x} = \lim_{\Delta x \to 0} (2x + \Delta x) = 2x \tag{6-12}$$

Inspection of (6-12) indicates that the derivative $dy/dx = 2x$, like the original function $y = f(x) = x^2$ in (6-8), is a function of the independent variable x. In essence the derivative (6-12) is another function derived from the original function (6-8), with the process of obtaining the derivative dy/dx being known as *differentiation*.

The fact that the derivative is a function means that for each value of x there is a unique corresponding value for the derivative function dy/dx. For example, in (6-12), when $x = 2$, $dy/dx = 4$. Similarly, when $x = -3$ $dy/dx = -6$. To emphasize this fact, an alternative notation for the derivative is frequently employed. Thus, given an original function $y = f(x)$, its derivative may be expressed symbolically as $f'(x)$ or simply f'. Note that this alternative notation emphasizes that the derivative is derived from the original function by denoting the former by f' and the latter by f.

Since the two notations for the derivative of a function $y = f(x)$, are given by

$$dy/dx \equiv f'(x) = \lim_{\Delta x \to 0} \frac{\Delta y}{\Delta x} \tag{6-13}$$

then (6-12) can be rewritten as

$$dy/dx \equiv f'(x) = 2x \tag{6-14}$$

Equation (6-14) not only makes it clear that the derivative is a function of x, but also helps us to see how the derivative is evaluated at different values of x. For example, when $x = 2$, $dy/dx = f'(2) = 4$. Similarly, when $x = -3$, $dy/dx = f'(-3) = -6$.

The preceding point, that the derivative of $y = f(x)$ is itself a function of x, can be further appreciated by reference to Fig. 6-3. Note, in Fig. 6-3, that the slope of the curve $y = f(x)$, at point A, is given by the slope of the tangent line KL at that point. Also, note that the slope of KL represents the limit of $\Delta y/\Delta x$, as Δx approaches zero, when the initial value of x is $x = x_1$. This means that, since the derivative of the function $y = f(x)$ is defined to be the limit of $\Delta y/\Delta x$ as Δx approaches zero, the slope of the curve $y = f(x)$ at point A therefore corresponds to the particular derivative value $f'(x_1)$. In other words, the value of the derivative of the function $y = f(x)$ at point A, given by $f'(x_1)$, equals the slope of the tangent to the curve at point A. Similarly, although not illustrated in Fig. 6-3, the value of the derivative of the function $y = f(x)$ at point B, given by $f'(x_2)$, equals the slope of the tangent to the curve at point B. Consequently, if the different tangent slopes at points A and B, in Fig. 6-3, are associated with particular x values (x_1 and x_2, respectively) then different derivative values (given by $f'(x_1)$ and $f'(x_2)$, respectively) will likewise be associated with these particular x values. Hence the derivative can be seen to be a function of x.

The above result, presented in terms of Fig. 6-3, that the derivative of $y = f(x)$ at a point is the slope of the tangent to the curve at that point, not only helps us to understand that the derivative itself is a function, but also serves to highlight an important requirement for obtaining a derivative. To see this, note in Fig. 6-3 that a *unique* tangent line can be drawn at each point on the curve $y = f(x)$. This means that a derivative can be obtained at each of these points. Note, however, that this result arises from the fact that the curve $y = f(x)$ in Fig. 6-3 has been drawn in such a way that it is both 'continuous' (no gaps) and 'smooth' (no sharp points). In other words, to obtain the derivative of a function $y = f(x)$, the function (curve) must be both continuous and smooth as in Fig. 6-3. When this requirement is met at every point in the domain of a function, then the function is said to possess the property of *differentiability* (meaning that differentiation is possible) at every point in its domain. Since most of the functions which appear in the mathematical analysis of economic models either possess, or are assumed to possess, the property of differentiability at all points, we shall assume all subsequent functions to be differentiable everywhere.

A further important point about the derivative follows from its definition, in (6-7), as the limit of the difference quotient. Since the difference quotient $\Delta y / \Delta x$ measures a rate of change of y in response to a change in x, then the derivative of dy/dx must also measure a rate of change of y. However, while it is true that dy/dx does measure a rate of change of y, it is important to note the exact nature of the rate of change of y that is represented by the derivative. In particular, since the change in x employed in the derivative concept is defined to be infinitesimal (denoted, in (6-7), by $\Delta x \to 0$), then the derivative represents an *instantaneous rate of change* of y.

To explain the concept of an instantaneous rate of change, we shall refer to Fig. 6-2a. Note, in Fig. 6-2a, that $y = f(x)$ changes in the same direction as x changes, increasing as x increases and decreasing as x decreases. Also note, in Fig. 6-2a, that as x is increased from x_1 to x_2, $y = f(x)$ increases by an amount $y_2 - y_1$ to give the *average* rate of increase of y per unit increase in x as $(y_2 - y_1)/(x_2 - x_1) = \Delta y / \Delta x$. Clearly, as the value of Δx becomes smaller, the average rate of increase will approach the limiting value dy/dx, which is termed the instantaneous rate of change (increase) of $y = f(x)$ at the point $x = x_1$. In other words, the derivative dy/dx represents the rate of change of a function $y = f(x)$ *at a point* x. This means, with reference to Fig. 6-2a, that the particular value of instantaneous rate of change will depend upon the particular x value (point on curve) at which it is evaluated. Thus the instantaneous rate of change of a function of x is itself a function of x.

To further illustrate the previous point, note that $y = f(x) = x^2$, in (6-8), has the derivative $dy/dx = 2x$, as given in (6-14). This means that the (instantaneous) rate of change of x^2 is $2x$ when we measure it at the point x. For example, the rate of change of x^2 at the point $x = 2$ is 4, at the point $x = -3$ it is -6, and so on. This indicates that the (instantaneous) rate of change of x^2, at the point x, changes as x changes. In other words, dy/dx is a function of x.

Finally, note that since dy/dx represents a rate of change, it therefore provides information both about the *direction* and the *magnitude* of the change in y resulting from an infinitesimal change in x. For example, the derivative of the function $y = f(x) = x^2$, at the point $x = 2$, is given by $dy/dx = 2x = 4$. Since, at point $x = 2$, $dy/dx = 4 > 0$, this means that y will increase (decrease) in value as x increases (decreases) in value from point $x = 2$. In other words, if dy/dx is positive in value at a point x, then y will change in the *same* direction as x, increasing as x increases and decreasing as x decreases. Also, in this example, with $dy/dx = 4$ at the point $x = 2$, the magnitude of the rate of change of y, at the point $x = 2$, will be 4. In other words, at the point $x = 2$, the value of y is tending to increase (decrease) at the rate of 4 units per unit increase (decrease) in x. Conversely, when $dy/dx = 2x = -6$ at the point $x = -3$, the negative value of dy/dx indicates that y will change in the *opposite* direction to x, decreasing as x increases and increasing as x decreases. In the latter case, the magnitude of the rate of change of y, at the point $x = -3$, will be -6. This means that, at the point $x = -3$, the value of y is tending to decrease (increase) at the rate of 6 units per unit increase (decrease) in x.

In summary, we can now state:

1. The derivative of a function $y = f(x)$, is itself a function of x.
2. The derivative of a function $y = f(x)$, at the point x, is the slope of the tangent to the curve at that point.
3. The derivative of a function $y = f(x)$, at the point x, shows how y changes with x at that point. As such it is an instantaneous rate of change of y with respect to x and provides us with information both about the direction and the magnitude of the change in y resulting from an infinitesimal change in x.

6-3 RULES OF DIFFERENTIATION FOR A FUNCTION OF ONE VARIABLE

In this section, we shall see that there are various rules of differentiation for obtaining the derivatives of various types of (differentiable) functions of a single independent variable. These rules mean that the derivative of a particular type of function can be simply obtained by the application of the appropriate rule of differentiation, instead of having to go through the process of limit-taking as in (6-12).

Before proceeding to discuss various rules of differentiation (which will be presented without proof), note that the derivative of a function $y = f(x)$, which so far has been written as dy/dx or $f'(x)$, can also be written as

$$\frac{d}{dx}[y] \quad \text{or} \quad \frac{d}{dx}[f(x)] \qquad (6\text{-}15)$$

Also note, in the first term of (6-15), that the derivative symbol has been separated into the two parts d/dx and y. In this form, the notation d/dx represents an instruction to perform the operation of differentiation. Hence, d/dx is an operator symbol, like $\sqrt{}$ or Σ (which instruct us to take a square root or obtain a sum, respectively), telling us to differentiate the second part (in this case y) with respect to the variable x.

Power-Function Rule

The derivative of a power function $y = f(x) = ax^n$ is

$$\frac{d}{dx}[ax^n] = nax^{n-1} \quad \text{or} \quad f'(x) = nax^{n-1} \qquad (6\text{-}16)$$

For example, when $y = 3x^2$, then $a = 3$, $n = 2$, and (6-16) gives

$$\frac{d}{dx}[3x^2] = 2 \times 3x^{2-1} = 6x^1 = 6x$$

Similarly, given $y = -5x^{1/2}$, then $a = -5$, $n = 1/2$, and (6-16) gives

$$\frac{d}{dx}[-5x^{1/2}] = \tfrac{1}{2}(-5)x^{(1/2)-1} = -\tfrac{5}{2}x^{-1/2}$$

Examples of the Power-Function Rule

6-1 Find the derivative of each of the following functions:
    (a) $y = 4x^3$ (b) $y = x^{1/2}$ (c) $y = 4x^{-5}$ (d) $y = -2x^{-3/2}$
    (e) $y = \tfrac{1}{2}x^{7/5}$ (f) $y = -7x^7$ (g) $y = 3x$ (h) $y = 7$

SOLUTION
    (a) $dy/dx = 12x^2$ (b) $dy/dx = \tfrac{1}{2}x^{-1/2}$ (c) $dy/dx = -20x^{-6}$
    (d) $dy/dx = 3x^{-5/2}$ (e) $dy/dx = \tfrac{7}{10}x^{2/5}$ (f) $dy/dx = -49x^6$
    (g) $y = 3x = 3x^1$, $dy/dx = 3x^0 = 3$ (h) $y = 7 = 7x^0$, $dy/dx = 0(7)x^{0-1} = 0$
Note that the result obtained in (h) implies that the derivative of a constant function (which is of form $y = f(x) = k$, where k is a constant) is zero. Thus, we may express this result as a separate rule of differentiation.

Constant-Function Rule

The derivative of a constant function $y = f(x) = k$ is

$$\frac{d}{dx}[y] = \frac{d}{dx}[f(x)] = \frac{d}{dx}[k] = 0 \qquad (6\text{-}17)$$

where (6-17) can be equivalently written as $dy/dx = dk/dx = f'(x) = 0$.

Since the graph of a constant function is a horizontal straight line with zero slope throughout (as in Fig. 2-7a), then the derivative (which measures the slope of a function (curve) at a point) of a constant function must also be zero. For example, the derivative of each of the following constant functions: $y = f(x) = a$, $y = f(x) = 12$, and $y = f(x) = -4$, is zero.

Sum-Difference Rule

If y is the sum (difference) of two functions, as given by $y = f(x) \pm g(x)$, then the derivative of this sum (difference) is

$$\frac{d}{dx}[f(x) \pm g(x)] = \frac{d}{dx}[f(x)] \pm \frac{d}{dx}[g(x)] = f'(x) \pm g'(x) \qquad (6\text{-}18)$$

Or, alternatively, letting $u = f(x)$ and $v = g(x)$, (6-18) may be rewritten as

$$\frac{d}{dx}[u \pm v] = \frac{du}{dx} \pm \frac{dv}{dx} \qquad (6\text{-}19)$$

For example, if $y = 7x^{-2} + 3x^{1/3}$, with $u = f(x) = 7x^{-2}$ and $v = g(x) = 3x^{1/3}$, then (6-19) gives

$$\frac{d}{dx}[7x^{-2} + 3x^{1/3}] = \frac{d}{dx}[7x^{-2}] + \frac{d}{dx}[3x^{1/3}] = -14x^{-3} + x^{-2/3}$$

Similarly, if $y = 15x^{1/3} - 2x^2$, with $u = f(x) = 15x^{1/3}$ and $v = g(x) = 2x^2$, then (6-19) gives

$$\frac{d}{dx}[15x^{1/3} - 2x^2] = \frac{d}{dx}[15x^{1/3}] - \frac{d}{dx}[2x^2] = 5x^{-2/3} - 4x$$

Although only stated above in terms of two functions, the sum-difference rule can be readily extended to more than two functions. For example,

$$\frac{d}{dx}[f(x) \pm g(x) \pm h(x)] = f'(x) \pm g'(x) \pm h'(x) \qquad (6\text{-}20)$$

or, alternatively, letting $w = h(x)$, (6-20) may be rewritten as

$$\frac{d}{dx}[u \pm v \pm w] = \frac{du}{dx} \pm \frac{dv}{dx} \pm \frac{dw}{dx} \qquad (6\text{-}21)$$

Hence, if $y = 3x^3 - 2x^{-1/2} + 3x$, with $u = f(x) = 3x^3$, $v = g(x) = 2x^{-1/2}$, and $w = h(x) = 3x$, then (6-21) gives

$$\frac{d}{dx}[3x^3 - 2x^{-1/2} + 3x] = \frac{d}{dx}[3x^3] - \frac{d}{dx}[2x^{-1/2}] + \frac{d}{dx}[3x] = 9x^2 + x^{-3/2} + 3$$

Examples of the Sum-Difference Rule

6-2 Find the derivative of each of the following functions:
  (a) $y = -2x^{-3} + 5x^{1/2} + 4x^{-2}$ (b) $y = 17x^{-1} + 13x^3 + 3x + 4$

SOLUTION
  (a) $dy/dx = 6x^{-4} + \frac{5}{2}x^{-1/2} - 8x^{-3}$
  (b) $dy/dx = -17x^{-2} + 39x^2 + 3 + 0 = -17x^{-2} + 39x^2 + 3$

Product Rule

If y is the product of two functions, as given by $y = f(x)g(x)$, then the derivative of this product is

$$\frac{d}{dx}[f(x)g(x)] = f(x)g'(x) + g(x)f'(x) \qquad (6\text{-}22)$$

Or, alternatively, letting $u = f(x)$ and $v = g(x)$, (6-22) may be rewritten as

$$\frac{d}{dx}[uv] = u\frac{dv}{dx} + v\frac{du}{dx} \qquad (6\text{-}23)$$

For example, if $y = (2x^2 + 5x)(3x^3)$, with $u = f(x) = 2x^2 + 5x$ and $v = g(x) = 3x^3$ so that $du/dx = f'(x) = 4x + 5$ and $dv/dx = g'(x) = 9x^2$, then (6-23) gives

$$\frac{d}{dx}[(2x^2 + 5x)(3x^3)] = (2x^2 + 5x)(9x^2) + (3x^3)(4x + 5) = 30x^4 + 60x^3$$

The product rule can be extended to the case of *three* functions. For example, letting $w = h(x)$, then

$$\frac{d}{dx}[uvw] = uv\frac{dw}{dx} + uw\frac{dv}{dx} + vw\frac{du}{dx} \qquad (6\text{-}24)$$

An example of (6-24) is given in Example 6-3b below.

Examples of the Product Rule

6-3 Find the derivative of each of the following functions:
  (a) $y = (3x^2 + 19)(6x^{-2} + x^3)$ (b) $y = (1 + x)(2x)(3x^2)$

120 DIFFERENTIATION OF A FUNCTION OF ONE VARIABLE

SOLUTION

(a) Letting $u = 3x^2 + 19$ and $v = 6x^{-2} + x^3$, so that $du/dx = 6x$ and $dv/dx = -12x^{-3} + 3x^2$, then via (6-23), the derivative of y is

$$\frac{d}{dx}[uv] = (3x^2 + 19)(-12x^{-3} + 3x^2) + (6x^{-2} + x^3)(6x)$$

$$= 15x^4 + 57x^2 - 228x^{-3}$$

(b) Letting $u = 1 + x$, $v = 2x$ and $w = 3x^2$, so that $du/dx = 1$, $dv/dx = 2$ and $dw/dx = 6x$, then via (6-24), the derivative of y is

$$\frac{d}{dx}[uvw] = (1+x)(2x)(6x) + (1+x)(3x^2)(2) + (2x)(3x^2)(1) = 24x^3 + 18x^2$$

Quotient Rule

If y is the quotient of two functions, as given by $f(x)/g(x)$, then the derivative of this quotient is

$$\frac{d}{dx}\left[\frac{f(x)}{g(x)}\right] = \frac{g(x)f'(x) - f(x)g'(x)}{[g(x)]^2} \tag{6-25}$$

Or, alternatively, letting $u = f(x)$ and $v = g(x)$, (6-25) may be rewritten as

$$\frac{d}{dx}\left[\frac{u}{v}\right] = \frac{v\dfrac{du}{dx} - u\dfrac{dv}{dx}}{v^2} \tag{6-26}$$

For example, if $y = (4x^2 + 3x)/(2x + 1)$, with $u = f(x) = 4x^2 + 3x$ and $v = g(x) = 2x + 1$ so that $du/dx = f'(x) = 8x + 3$ and $dv/dx = g'(x) = 2$, then (6-26) gives

$$\frac{d}{dx}\left[\frac{4x^2 + 3x}{2x + 1}\right] = \frac{(2x+1)(8x+3) - (4x^2 + 3x)(2)}{(2x+1)^2} = \frac{8x^2 + 8x + 3}{(2x+1)^2}$$

Examples of the Quotient Rule

6-4 Find the derivative of each of the following functions:
   (a) $y = x^3/(x^2 + 7)$ (b) $y = (1 + x)/(2x^2 + 1)$

SOLUTION

(a) Letting $u = x^3$ and $v = x^2 + 7$, so that $du/dx = 3x^2$ and $dv/dx = 2x$, then via (6-26), the derivative of y is

$$\frac{d}{dx}\left[\frac{u}{v}\right] = \frac{(x^2+7)(3x^2) - (x^3)(2x)}{(x^2+7)^2} = \frac{x^4 + 21x^2}{(x^2+7)^2}$$

(b) Letting $u = 1 + x$ and $v = 2x^2 + 1$, so that $du/dx = 1$ and $dv/dx = 4x$, then via (6-26), the derivative of y is

$$\frac{d}{dx}\left[\frac{u}{v}\right] = \frac{(2x^2+1)(1) - (1+x)(4x)}{(2x^2+1)^2} = \frac{-2x^2 - 4x + 1}{(2x^2+1)^2}$$

6-5 Given the function $y = (uv)/w$, where $u = f(x)$, $v = g(x)$ and $w = h(x)$, find dy/dx.

SOLUTION In this case we must use a combination of the quotient and product rules. Thus

$$\frac{d}{dx}\left[\frac{uv}{w}\right] = \frac{w\frac{d}{dx}[uv] - (uv)\frac{dw}{dx}}{w^2} = \frac{w\left[u\frac{dv}{dx} + v\frac{du}{dx}\right] - (uv)\frac{dw}{dx}}{w^2}$$
$$\text{(quotient rule)} \qquad \text{(product rule)}$$

In relation to the product and quotient rules, it is important for the student to remember that no matter how complicated the original functional expression may look, it merely represents a relation between certain x values and their (unique) corresponding y values. Also, the student should remember that no matter how complex the differentiation rule may appear, the resulting derivative (which may also look complex) simply provides the information summarized at the end of Sec. 6-2. Finally, the student should take comfort in the fact that the economic applications of differentiation, given in Chapters 7 and 9, involve quite straightforward differentiation. It is for the latter reason that this chapter deliberately avoids the differentiation of complicated functions (such as those which require the combination of several rules of differentiation in order to obtain the respective derivatives).

6-A PRACTICE PROBLEMS

6-6 Find the derivatives of:
  (a) $y = ax^2 + bx + c$ (b) $y = a_0 + a_1x + a_2x^2 + \ldots + a_nx^n$

6-7 Use the product rule to find dy/dx for each of the following functions:
  (a) $y = (4x^{1/2} - 2x^3)(2x^7)$ (b) $y = (2x^3 + 5x)(4x^5 + 2)$ (c) $y = x^3(x^{-2} + 3)$
  (d) $y = 4x^{-7}(3x^2 + 5x)$ (e) $y = (ax^2 + bx)(cx^3)$ (f) $y = (x-2)(3+x)(4-3x)$

6-8 Use the quotient rule to find dy/dx for each of the following functions:
  (a) $y = x^3/(2x^2 + 4x)$ (b) $y = 25/(3x^{-2} + 1)$ (c) $y = f(x)/x$
  (d) $y = xf(x)/g(x)$

Chain Rule

If we have a function $y = y(u)$, where u is in turn a function of another variable x, such that $u = u(x)$, then the derivative of y with respect to x is

$$\frac{dy}{dx} = \frac{dy}{du}\frac{du}{dx} = y'(u)u'(x) \qquad (6\text{-}27)$$

In other words, if y is a function of u where u is a function of x, then dy/dx is the product of the two derivatives dy/du and du/dx.

To understand the *chain rule*, note that a given Δx will result in a corresponding Δu, since u and x are related via the function $u = u(x)$. In turn, this Δu will result in a corresponding Δy, since y and u are related via the function $y = y(u)$. Therefore we have a 'chain reaction' which starts with a change in x, followed by a change in u, and ending with a change in y. Since the change in u per unit of change in x is given by the difference quotient $\Delta u/\Delta x$, and the change in y per unit of change in u is given by the difference quotient $\Delta y/\Delta u$, then the product of these two difference quotients will give us the difference quotient which measures the change in y per unit of change in x:

$$\frac{\Delta y}{\Delta u} \frac{\Delta u}{\Delta x} = \frac{\Delta y}{\Delta x} \tag{6-28}$$

Note, in (6-28), that the Δu cancels itself out. This helps us to understand why $\Delta y/\Delta x$ is the product of $\Delta y/\Delta u$ and $\Delta u/\Delta x$. Also note, in (6-28), that if we take the limit of each difference quotient as $\Delta x \to 0$ (which, via $u = u(x)$, implies $\Delta u \to 0$), each difference quotient becomes a derivative to give $(dy/du)(du/dx) = dy/dx$ as in (6-27).

As an example of the chain rule, let us suppose $y = y(u) = 4u^5$, where $u = u(x) = 2x^2 - 9$. Since $dy/du = 20u^4$ and $du/dx = 4x$, then (6-27) gives

$$\frac{dy}{dx} = \frac{dy}{du}\frac{du}{dx} = (20u^4)(4x) = 20(2x^2 - 9)^4(4x)$$

Similarly, if $z = f(y) = y^3 - 7$, where $y = g(x) = 2x + 3$, then

$$\frac{dz}{dx} = \frac{dz}{dy}\frac{dy}{dx} = (3y^2)(2) = 6(2x+3)^2$$

The usefulness of the chain rule is most readily apparent when we come to differentiate a function such as $y = (x+2)^2$ or $y = (x^{17} - 3x^{1/3} + 7)^{23}$. Clearly, in the case of $y = (x+2)^2$, we can easily expand the terms in the brackets to get $y = x^2 + 4x + 4$ and thus $dy/dx = 2x + 4$. In contrast, in the case of $y = (x^{17} - 3x^{1/3} + 7)^{23}$, it would be extremely laborious and tedious to expand a 23rd power expression. Fortunately, however, this laborious expansion can be avoided by the application of the chain rule. For example, if we define a new *intermediate* variable $u = x^{17} - 3x^{1/3} + 7$, then we have

$$y = y(u) = u^{23} \quad \text{where} \quad u = u(x) = x^{17} - 3x^{1/3} + 7$$

Hence, via (6-27), the derivative dy/dx is given by

$$\frac{dy}{dx} = \frac{dy}{du}\frac{du}{dx} = 23u^{22}(17x^{16} - x^{-2/3}) = 23(x^{17} - 3x^{1/3} + 7)^{22}(17x^{16} - x^{-2/3})$$

Similarly, for the case $y = (x+2)^2$, if we let $u = x+2$, so that $y = u^2$ with $u = x+2$, then

$$\frac{dy}{dx} = \frac{dy}{du}\frac{du}{dx} = 2u(1) = 2(x+2) = 2x+4$$

The chain rule can be readily extended to three (or more) functions.

6-3 RULES OF DIFFERENTIATION FOR A FUNCTION OF ONE VARIABLE

For example, if we have $y = y(u)$, $u = u(x)$, and $x = x(w)$, then

$$\frac{dy}{dw} = \frac{dy}{du}\frac{du}{dx}\frac{dx}{dw} = y'(u)u'(x)x'(w) \qquad (6\text{-}29)$$

Finally, given that y is a function of u where u is a function of x, the chain rule is often referred to as the *function-of-a-function rule*. Similarly, given that $y = y(u)$ where $u = u(x)$, y can be written in the form of a *composite function* (function of a function), as given by $y = y[u(x)]$. Thus the chain rule is also known as the *composite-function rule*.

Examples of the Chain Rule

6-9 (a) If $y = 2u^2 + 5$, where $u = 3x^3 - 7$, find dy/dx (b) if $u = t^2$, where $t = 4w^{1/4} + 3$, find du/dw (c) if $r = r(s)$, $s = s(t)$, $t = t(u)$, and $u = u(w)$, find dr/dw.

SOLUTION

(a) $\dfrac{dy}{dx} = \dfrac{dy}{du}\dfrac{du}{dx} = (4u)(9x^2) = 4(3x^3 - 7)(9x^2) = 36x^2(3x^3 - 7)$

(b) $\dfrac{du}{dw} = \dfrac{du}{dt}\dfrac{dt}{dw} = (2t)(w^{-3/4}) = 2(4w^{1/4} + 3)(w^{-3/4}) = 2w^{-3/4}(4w^{1/4} + 3)$

(c) $\dfrac{dr}{dw} = \dfrac{dr}{ds}\dfrac{ds}{dt}\dfrac{dt}{du}\dfrac{du}{dw}$

6-10 Use the chain rule to find dy/dx for each of the following functions:
(a) $y = (3x^3 - 2x)^{-2}$ (b) $y = 2(4x^{1/2} + 5)^4$

SOLUTION

(a) Let $u = 3x^3 - 2x$ so that $y = u^{-2}$, where $u = 3x^3 - 2x$. Hence

$$\frac{dy}{dx} = \frac{dy}{du}\frac{du}{dx} = (-2u^{-3})(9x^2 - 2) = -2(3x^3 - 2x)^{-3}(9x^2 - 2)$$

(b) Let $u = 4x^{1/2} + 5$ so that $y = 2u^4$, where $u = 4x^{1/2} + 5$. Hence

$$\frac{dy}{dx} = \frac{dy}{du}\frac{du}{dx} = (8u^3)(2x^{-1/2}) = 8(4x^{1/2} + 5)^3(2x^{-1/2})$$

Inverse-Function Rule

If the function $y = f(x)$ represents a one-to-one mapping, such that not only will a given value of x yield a unique corresponding value of y, but also a given value of y will yield a unique corresponding value of x, then the function f will have an *inverse function* $x = g(y)$. For example, the function

$$y = f(x) = 4 + x \qquad (6\text{-}30)$$

has the property that a different x value always yields a different y value. Therefore (6-30) has the inverse function

$$x = g(y) = f^{-1}(y) = y - 4 \qquad (6\text{-}31)$$

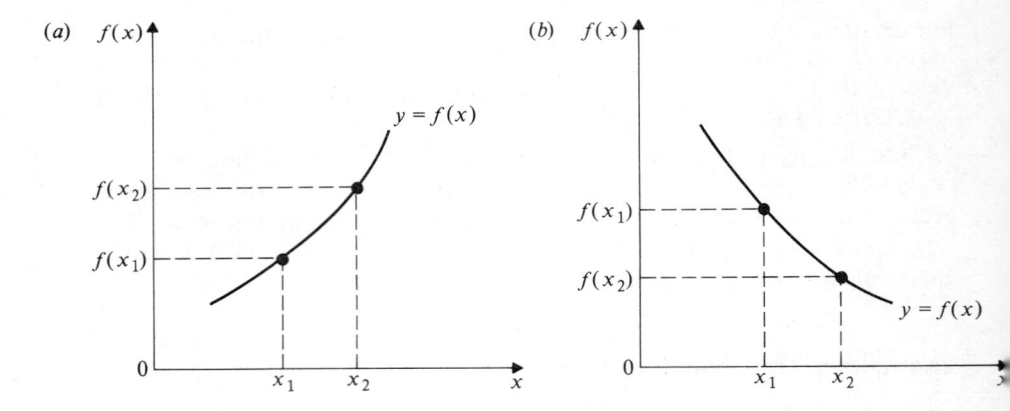

(a) [Figure 6-4a: monotonically increasing curve $y = f(x)$ with points $f(x_1)$ and $f(x_2)$ shown for $x_1 < x_2$]

(b) [Figure 6-4b: monotonically decreasing curve $y = f(x)$ with points $f(x_1)$ and $f(x_2)$ shown for $x_1 < x_2$]

Figure 6-4

with the property that a different y value always yields a different value of x. Note, in (6-31), that the inverse function $x = g(y)$ can also be denoted by $x = f^{-1}(y)$, which is read 'x is an inverse function of y'. [*Note:* in this usage f^{-1} does *not* mean $1/f$.] Since both (6-30) and (6-31) have the property of one-to-one mapping then, not only is f^{-1} the inverse function of f, but f is also the inverse function of f^{-1}.

An examination of Fig. 6-4a and Fig. 6-4b indicates that the property of one-to-one mapping is possessed by functions in which successive increases in x *always* lead to either successive increases in $y = f(x)$, as in Fig. 6-4a, or successive decreases in $y = f(x)$, as in Fig. 6-4b. Such functions, known as *monotonic functions*, are said to be *monotonically increasing* functions if $x_2 > x_1 \Rightarrow f(x_2) > f(x_1)$, as in Fig. 6-4a, and *monotonically decreasing* functions if $x_2 > x_1 \Rightarrow f(x_2) < f(x_1)$, as in Fig. 6-4b. In contrast, a function with a U-shape (and thus not monotonic) does not possess the property of one-to-one mapping, since two x values can yield the same y value. Therefore there is a connection between functions which are monotonic and functions which possess inverse functions. In general, for an inverse function $x = f^{-1}(y)$ to exist, the original function $y = f(x)$ must be monotonic.

The above result means that before we can write $x = f^{-1}(y)$, we must check that $y = f(x)$ is monotonic. Fortunately, such a check is not difficult to make. Since the graph of monotonic functions, such as those depicted in Fig. 6-4, possess a positive or negative slope for all values of x, then the monotonicity of a given function $y = f(x)$ can be ascertained by simply checking that the derivative $f'(x)$ has the same (non-zero) algebraic sign for all values of x.

Given an inverse function $x = f^{-1}(y)$, its derivative is given by the *inverse-function rule* of differentiation:

$$\frac{dx}{dy} = \frac{1}{dy/dx} \qquad (6\text{-}32)$$

that is, the derivative of the inverse function is the reciprocal of the derivative of the original function. For example, given $y = f(x) = 7x + 14$, we first check that $f'(x)$ has the same sign for all x. Thus, since $f'(x) = 7$, which is positive for all x, then $f(x)$ is monotonic and possesses an inverse function. Hence

$$\frac{dx}{dy} = \frac{1}{dy/dx} = \frac{1}{7}$$

In such a case, the inverse function $x = f^{-1}(y) = \frac{1}{7}y - 2$, and thus its derivative $dx/dy = 1/7$, can be easily obtained without recourse to the inverse-function rule. However, the usefulness of the inverse-function rule can best be appreciated when we come to find dx/dy for a more complex function such as $y = f(x) = x^{11} + 19x$. Rather than being faced with the difficult task of solving $y = x^{11} + 19x$ for x, in order to find dx/dy, we simply obtain $dx/dy = 1/(dy/dx)$ via the inverse-function rule. Thus, since $dy/dx = 11x^{10} + 19$, which is positive for all x, then $f(x)$ is monotonic and possesses an inverse function. Hence

$$\frac{dx}{dy} = \frac{1}{dy/dx} = \frac{1}{11x^{10} + 19}$$

Finally, it should be noted that the inverse-function rule may be applied to a non-monotonic function with a restricted domain. For example, $y = f(x) = x^2$ is non-monotonic since $dy/dx = 2x$ has not got the same sign for all x. However, if the domain of $y = f(x) = x^2$ is restricted to $x > 0$, then $dy/dx = 2x$ is positive for all $x > 0$. Consequently, $y = f(x) = x^2$ is monotonic in the restricted domain and $dx/dy = 1/(dy/dx) = 1/2x$ for $x > 0$. The student is encouraged to graph $y = x^2$, firstly for all x and then for $x > 0$, in order to obtain a geometric understanding of this final point.

Examples of the Inverse-Function Rule

6-11 Use the inverse-function rule to find dx/dy for the following functions, checking in each case that the function is monotonic:
(a) $y = f(x) = 3x + \frac{1}{5}x^5 + \frac{1}{7}x^7$ (b) $y = f(x) = 7 - 2x - x^4$ $(x > 0)$

SOLUTION
(a) Since $dy/dx = 3 + x^4 + x^6 > 0$ for all x, then $f(x)$ is monotonic and
$dx/dy = 1/(dy/dx) = 1/(3 + x^4 + x^6)$
(b) Since $dy/dx = -(2 + 4x^3) < 0$ for all $x > 0$, then $f(x)$ is monotonic for $x > 0$ and
$dx/dy = 1/(dy/dx) = -1/(2 + 4x^3)$ for $x > 0$.

6-B PRACTICE PROBLEMS

6-12 Given $y = 2u^5 + 4u^{-2} + 3$, where $u = 7 - 2x$, find dy/dx via the chain rule.
6-13 Use the chain rule to find dy/dx for each of the following functions:
(a) $y = 4(7x^7 - 2x^{1/2})^9$ (b) $y = (3x^2 - 7x)^{-5}$ (c) $v = -3(3x^3 - 2x)^7$

6-14 Use the inverse-function rule to find dx/dy for the following functions, checking in each case that the function is monotonic:
(a) $y = 19x - x^{-3} + \frac{1}{5}x^5 + 7$ (b) $y = 2 - x^8 - 2x^4$ $(x > 0)$

Log-Function Rule

The derivative of the (natural) log function $y = \log_e x = \ln x$ is

$$\frac{d}{dx}[\ln x] = \frac{1}{x} \qquad (6\text{-}33)$$

In the case where $y = \log_a x$, where a is some base other than e, the derivative is

$$\frac{d}{dx}[\log_a x] = \frac{1}{x}\log_a e \qquad (6\text{-}34)$$

Note, in (6-34), that if $a = e$, then $dy/dx = 1/x$ as in (6-33). In theoretical work, it is more common to use natural log functions which, as shown by comparison of (6-33) and (6-34), possess a more convenient derivative.

In the more general case, where $y = \ln u$ with $u = u(x)$, the derivative of y (obtained via the chain rule) is

$$\frac{dy}{dx} = \frac{dy}{du}\frac{du}{dx} = \frac{d}{du}[\ln u]\frac{du}{dx} = \frac{1}{u}\frac{du}{dx} \qquad (6\text{-}35)$$

For example, if $y = \ln x^2$, then we can let $u = x^2$ so that $y = \ln u$ where $u = x^2$. Hence, via (6-35), the derivative is

$$\frac{dy}{dx} = \frac{1}{u}\frac{du}{dx} = \frac{1}{x^2}(2x) = \frac{2}{x}$$

Similarly, if $y = \ln(x^2 + 3x)$, then we can let $u = x^2 + 3x$ so that $y = \ln u$ where $u = x^2 + 3x$. Hence, via (6-35), the derivative is

$$\frac{dy}{dx} = \frac{1}{u}\frac{du}{dx} = \frac{1}{x^2 + 3x}(2x + 3) = \frac{2x + 3}{x^2 + 3x}$$

Examples of the Log-Function Rule

6-15 Find the derivative of each of the following log functions:
(a) $y = \ln w$ (b) $r = \ln t$ (c) $q = \ln p$

SOLUTION
(a) $dy/dw = 1/w$ (b) $dr/dt = 1/t$ (c) $dq/dp = 1/p$

6-16 Use the log-function rule to find dy/dx for each of the following functions:
(a) $y = \ln(4 - 3x^3)$ (b) $y = \ln(x^4 - 2x^3 + 7)$

SOLUTION
(a) Let $u = 4 - 3x^3$ so that $y = \ln u$ with $u = 4 - 3x^3$. Hence, via (6-35),

$$\frac{dy}{dx} = \frac{1}{u}\frac{du}{dx} = \frac{1}{4 - 3x^3}(-9x^2) = -\frac{9x^2}{4 - 3x^3}$$

(b) Let $u = x^4 - 2x^3 + 7$ so that $y = \ln u$ with $u = x^4 - 2x^3 + 7$. Hence, via (6-35),
$$\frac{dy}{dx} = \frac{1}{u}\frac{du}{dx} = \frac{1}{x^4 - 2x^3 + 7}(4x^3 - 6x^2) = \frac{4x^3 - 6x^2}{x^4 - 2x^3 + 7}$$

6-C PRACTICE PROBLEMS

6-17 Find the derivatives of the following log functions:
 (a) $y = \ln(x^2 - 3x + 2)$ (b) $y = 6 \ln t$ (c) $y = \ln(7x^4 - 2x^2)$

6-4 SECOND AND HIGHER DERIVATIVES

In Sec. 6-2, we noted that the derivative $f'(x)$, of a function $y = f(x)$, is also a function of x. This means that $f'(x)$ can itself be differentiated with respect to x (assuming that the function $f'(x)$ is differentiable). The derivative obtained by differentiating $f'(x)$ is called the *second derivative* (or *second-order derivative*) of the function $y = f(x)$, and is denoted either by

$$\frac{d}{dx}[f'(x)] = f''(x) \quad \text{or} \quad \frac{d}{dx}\left[\frac{dy}{dx}\right] = \frac{d^2y}{dx^2} \tag{6-36}$$

For example, if $y = f(x) = x^3$, then $f'(x) = 3x^2$ and

$$\frac{d^2y}{dx^2} \equiv f''(x) = \frac{d}{dx}[f'(x)] = \frac{d}{dx}[3x^2] = 6x$$

Note, in this example, that $f''(x) = 6x$, like $f(x)$ and $f'(x)$, is also a function of x. Hence, the second derivative can also be differentiated with respect to x to yield a *third derivative* (or *third-order derivative*), denoted as $f'''(x)$ or d^3y/dx^3. Thus

$$\frac{d^3y}{dx^3} \equiv f'''(x) = \frac{d}{dx}[f''(x)] = \frac{d}{dx}[6x] = 6$$

In turn, $f'''(x)$ can be differentiated to yield a *fourth derivative*, denoted as $f^{(4)}(x)$ or d^4y/dx^4. Thus

$$\frac{d^4y}{dx^4} \equiv f^{(4)}(x) = \frac{d}{dx}[f'''(x)] = \frac{d}{dx}[6] = 0$$

Repeated differentiation of the fourth derivative will likewise yield the fifth and successively higher derivatives (each of which will be zero since $f^{(n)}(x) = 0$ for all $n \geq 4$).

As a further example, the successive derivatives of $y = f(x) = x^5 - 3x^4 + 2x^2$ are as follows:

$$f'(x) = 5x^4 - 4x^3 + 4x \qquad f^{(4)}(x) = 120x - 24$$
$$f''(x) = 20x^3 - 12x^2 + 4 \qquad f^{(5)}(x) = 120$$
$$f'''(x) = 60x^2 - 24x \qquad f^{(n)}(x) = 0 \text{ for all } n \geq 6$$

The above examples demonstrate that the process of obtaining successive derivatives involves finding the derivative of the previous derivative function. As such, this means that at each stage of differentiation the appropriate rule of differentiation must be used.

6-D PRACTICE PROBLEMS

6-18 Find the first three derivatives of each of the following functions:
(a) $y = (2x^3)(4 - 7x^{-3})$ (b) $y = (2x + 2)/(1 - 3x)$
(c) $y = a_0 + a_1 x + a_2 x^2 + a_3 x^3 + \ldots + a_n x^n$

As already noted, second- and higher-order derivatives, like the original function $y = f(x)$ and the first derivative $f'(x)$, are functions of x. This means that for each value of x there is a unique corresponding value for the particular derivative function under consideration. Thus, in terms of the foregoing example, the second derivative $f''(x) = 20x^3 - 12x^2 + 4$ can be evaluated at, say, $x = 2$ as $f''(2) = 20(2)^3 - 12(2)^2 + 4 = 116$. Similarly, $f^{(4)}(x) = 120x - 24$ can be evaluated at, say, $x = 3$ as $f^{(4)}(3) = 120(3) - 24 = 336$.

In Sec. 6-2, we noted that the first derivative $f'(x)$ measures a rate of change. In a similar fashion, second- and higher-order derivatives also measure a rate of change. Hence, just as the first derivative $f'(x)$ measures the (instantaneous) rate of change of the function $f(x)$, the second derivative $f''(x)$ measures the (instantaneous) rate of change of the function $f'(x)$. This means that $f''(x)$ provides us with information about both the *direction* and the *magnitude* of the change in $f'(x)$ as x changes (infinitesimally). For example, when $f'(x) = 2 > 0$, this means that $f(x)$ increases as x increases, with the value of $f(x)$ tending to increase at the rate of 2 units per unit increase in x. Similarly, when $f''(x) = 3 > 0$, this means that $f'(x)$ increases as x increases, with the value of $f'(x)$ tending to increase at the rate of 3 units per unit increase in x. Therefore, just as $f'(x)$ indicates the direction and the magnitude of the change in $f(x)$ as x changes, so likewise $f''(x)$ indicates the direction and the magnitude of the change in $f'(x)$ as x changes. In turn, $f'''(x)$ indicates the direction and the magnitude of the change in $f''(x)$ as x changes, and so on for higher derivatives.

The preceding interpretation of $f''(x)$ can be illustrated in terms of Figs. 6-5 and 6-6. Note, in Fig. 6-5a, that any tangent line to the curve $f(x)$ will have a positive slope. Thus, $f'(x) > 0$ at all points on the curve. Also, in Fig. 6-5a, note that the slope of any tangent line to the curve will increase as x increases. Therefore, since $f'(x)$ is increasing, as x increases, at all points on the curve, then $f''(x) > 0$ at all points on the curve. Consequently, given a function $y = f(x)$, where $f'(x) > 0$ and $f''(x) > 0$, then its graph will have a shape as shown in Fig. 6-5a, with the value of y increasing at an *increasing*

6-4 SECOND AND HIGHER DERIVATIVES 129

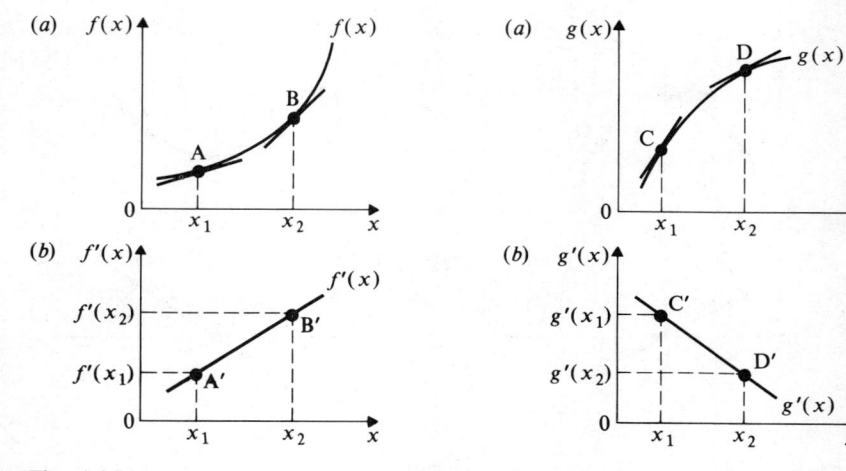

Figure 6-5

Figure 6-6

rate as x increases. In contrast, given a function $y = g(x)$, where $g'(x) > 0$ and $g''(x) < 0$, then its graph will have a shape as shown in Fig. 6-6a, with the value of y increasing at a *decreasing* rate as x increases. The difference between these two cases is further clarified by the graphs of $f'(x)$ and $g'(x)$ in Figs. 6-5b and 6-6b, respectively. Note, in Fig. 6-5b, that since the slope of $f'(x)$ is positive for all x shown, then $f''(x) > 0$. In contrast, in Fig. 6-6b, the slope of $g'(x)$ is negative for all x shown, so that $g''(x) < 0$.

The above discussion, with its graphical illustration, indicates that just as the first derivative informs us about the *slope* of the graph of a function, so the second derivative informs us about the *curvature* of the graph of a function. Thus, in Fig. 6-5a, $f''(x) > 0$, for all x shown, indicates that the graph of $f(x)$ will be *convex* towards the x axis. Similarly, in Fig. 6-6a, $g''(x) < 0$, for all x shown, indicates that the graph of $g(x)$ will be *concave* towards the x axis. Consequently, a knowledge of the signs of the first and second derivatives, at various x values, is a considerable aid in sketching the shape of the graph of a function. For example, the graph of $f(x)$ in Fig. 6-7a embodies the following information:

1. At point E, where $x = x_1, f'(x_1) > 0$ and $f''(x_1) < 0$.
2. At point F, where $x = x_2$, $f'(x_2) = 0$ and $f''(x_2) < 0$. Note, at point F, that $f'(x_2) = 0$ means that the slope of $f(x)$ is horizontal at that point. Also, note that since the tangent slope decreases in value, as x increases, at point F, then $f''(x_2) < 0$.
3. At point G, where $x = x_3, f'(x_3) < 0$ and $f''(x_3) < 0$.

The graph of $f'(x)$, given in Fig. 6-7b, serves to further clarify the information given in Fig. 6-7a. In particular, since $f''(x)$ can be regarded as

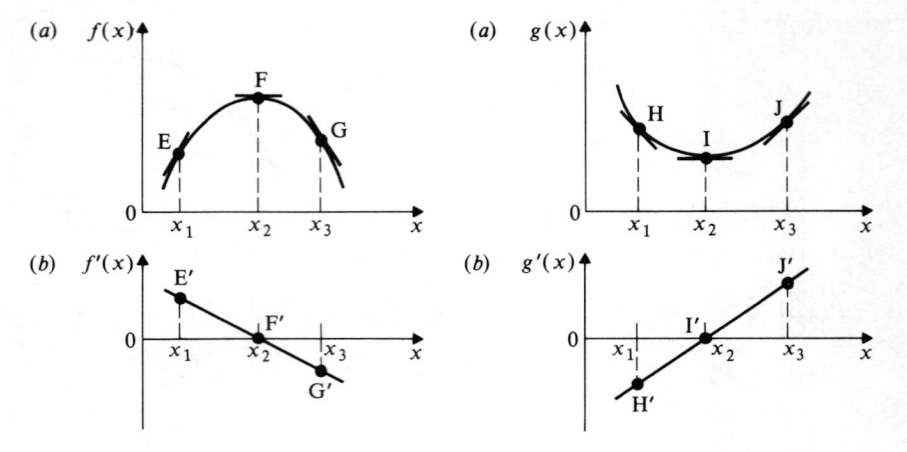

Figure 6-7

Figure 6-8

the slope of $f'(x)$ at a point, then it should be clear from Fig. 6-7b why $f''(x)$ is negative at $x = x_1$, $x = x_2$, and $x = x_3$.

In a similar fashion, the graph of $g(x)$ in Fig. 6-8a embodies the following information:

4. At point H, where $x = x_1$, $g'(x_1) < 0$ and $g''(x_1) > 0$. Note, at point H, that $g''(x_1) > 0$ means that the *negative* slope of $g(x)$ at that point is tending to be *less* steep (for example, changing from -5 to -4) as x increases.
5. At point I, where $x = x_2$, $g'(x_2) = 0$ and $g''(x_2) > 0$.
6. At point J, where $x = x_3$, $g'(x_3) > 0$ and $g''(x_3) > 0$.

The graph of $g'(x)$, given in Fig. 6-8b, serves to further clarify the information given in Fig. 6-8a. In particular, since $g''(x)$ can be regarded as the slope of $g'(x)$ at a point, then it should be clear from Fig. 6-8b why $g''(x)$ is positive at $x = x_1$, $x = x_2$, and $x = x_3$.

6-5 DERIVATIVES AND CURVE-SKETCHING

In this section, we will give a brief example of how derivatives may be used as an aid in sketching the graph of a function. For example, suppose we wish to graph the function

$$y = f(x) = 10 - \frac{12}{2+x} \quad (x \geq 0) \qquad (6\text{-}37)$$

First, note that $f'(x) = 12(2+x)^{-2}$ and $f''(x) = -24(2+x)^{-3}$. Thus, since

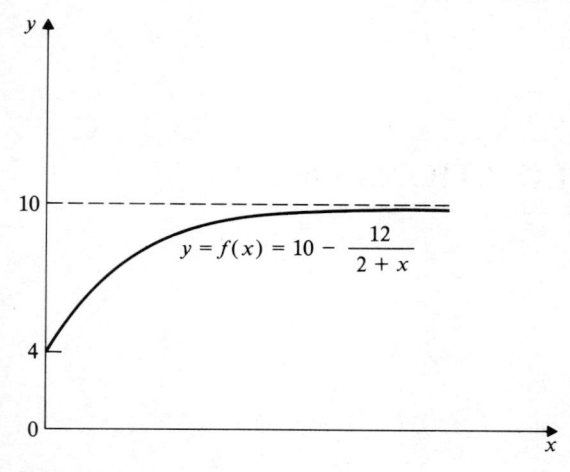

$f'(x) > 0$ and $f''(x) < 0$, for $x \geq 0$, then the graph of (6-37) will have a shape similar to that of $g(x)$ in Fig. 6-6a.

To obtain a more exact sketch of (6-37), note that the y intercept is

$$f(0) = 10 - \frac{12}{2+0} = 4$$

Also, note that if the value of x is increased so that it approaches infinity, then $f(x)$ approaches the limiting value of 10 (since $-12/(2+x)$ approaches zero as x approaches infinity). This means that as x becomes very large, the value of y will come ever closer to the value $y = 10$ but never actually reach it (in other words, the limit of y, as x tends to infinity, is 10). Therefore, combining this information with that provided by $f'(x) > 0$ and $f''(x) < 0$, we can sketch (6-37) as shown in Fig. 6-9.

Note, as a matter of terminology, in Fig. 6-9 the curve $y = f(x)$ is said to approach the (dotted) line $y = 10$ *asymptotically*, with the line $y = 10$ constituting the (horizontal) *asymptote* of $y = f(x)$.

6-E PRACTICE PROBLEMS

6-19 Use the procedure of Sec. 6-5 to sketch the graphs of the following functions:

(a) $y = 3 + \dfrac{32}{4+x}$ $(x \geq 0)$ (b) $y = 20 - \dfrac{18}{1+x}$ $(x \geq 0)$

6-20 Recalling that $\ln x \gtreqless 0$ as $x \gtreqless 1$, sketch the graph of the function $y = \ln x$.

CHAPTER
SEVEN
ECONOMIC APPLICATIONS OF DERIVATIVES

In Chapter 6, we noted that the concept of derivative provides us with information about both the direction and the magnitude of the change in one variable in response to an infinitesimal change in another variable. Consequently, since economics is very much concerned with the question of by how much one variable changes when another variable changes, then it is to be expected that the concept of derivative will have a wide range of economic applications. That this is so, will be very much apparent when we come to analyse maximization and minimization (in Chapter 8) and the economic applications of maximization and minimization (in Chapter 9). In the meantime, in this chapter, we shall briefly examine some elementary economic concepts in terms of derivatives.

7-1 THE DERIVATIVES OF DEMAND AND SUPPLY FUNCTIONS

In Sec. 2-4, we noted that the relationship between the quantity demanded (Q_d) of a good and its unit price (P), per time period, can be represented by a demand function of general form $Q_d = f(P)$. Now that we have encountered the concept of derivative, the responsiveness of the quantity demanded to price changes can now be expressed in terms of the first derivative of the demand function, $dQ_d/dP \equiv f'(P)$. For example, given the nonlinear demand function,

$$Q_d = f(P) = 9 - P^2 \quad (P \geq 0) \tag{7-1}$$

7-1 THE DERIVATIVES OF DEMAND AND SUPPLY FUNCTIONS

which is illustrated in Fig. 7-1a, then the change in Q_d resulting from a change in P is given by the derivative

$$dQ_d/dP \equiv f'(P) = -2P \tag{7-2}$$

Thus, at point A (where $P = 2$) on the demand curve in Fig. 7-1a, the change in Q_d resulting from an infinitesimal change in P is

$$f'(2) = -2(2) = -4 \tag{7-3}$$

This means that (a) since $f'(P) = -4 < 0$, at $P = 2$, then Q_d will change in an *opposite* direction to the change in P, decreasing as P increases and increasing as P decreases (b) since $f'(P) = -4$, at $P = 2$, then the magnitude of the rate of change of Q_d, at point $P = 2$, will be -4. In other words, at point $P = 2$, the value of Q_d is tending to decrease (increase) at the rate of 4 units per unit increase (decrease) in P. [*Note*: $f'(P)$ measures the rate of change of Q_d, with respect to an infinitesimal change in P, *at a point* on the demand curve.]

The responsiveness of the quantity supplied to price changes can be similarly expressed in terms of the first derivative of the supply function. For example, given the nonlinear supply function,

$$Q_s = g(P) = -4 + P^2 \quad (P \geqslant 0) \tag{7-4}$$

which is illustrated in Fig. 7-1b, then the change in Q_s resulting from a change in P is given by the derivative

$$dQ_s/dP \equiv g'(P) = 2P \tag{7-5}$$

Thus, at point B (where $P = 3$) on the supply curve in Fig. 7-1b, the change in Q_s resulting from an infinitesimal change in P is

$$g'(3) = 2(3) = 6 \tag{7-6}$$

This means that (a) since $g'(P) = 6 > 0$, at $P = 3$, then Q_s will change in the *same* direction as the change in P, increasing as P increases and decreasing as P decreases, (b) since $g'(P) = 6$, at $P = 3$, then the magnitude of the rate of change of Q_s, at point $P = 3$, will be 6. In other words, at point $P = 3$, the value of Q_s is tending to increase (decrease) at the rate of 6 units per unit increase (decrease) in P. [*Note*: $g'(P)$ measures the rate of change of Q_s, as P varies infinitesimally, *at a point* on the supply curve.]

In the foregoing demand and supply examples, we simply took the shape of the demand and supply curves as given in Fig. 7-1, and then used the first derivative to measure the responsiveness of either Q_d or Q_s to changes in P. However, now that we have encountered both first and second derivatives, we can now check that Figs. 7-1a and 7-1b have the correct shape. For example, taking the demand function (7-1), the first derivative $f'(P) = -2P < 0$, for $P > 0$, tells us that the demand curve has a negative slope or, equivalently, is downward-sloping to the right, for $P > 0$,

134 ECONOMIC APPLICATIONS OF DERIVATIVES

(a)

Q_d axis, curve with $Q_d = 9 - P^2$ $(P \geqslant 0)$, point A at $(2, 5)$, intercepts at 9 and 3.

(b)

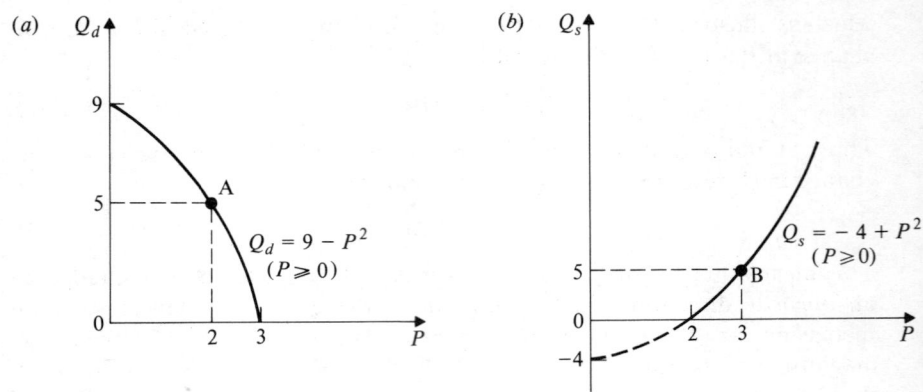

Q_s axis, curve with $Q_s = -4 + P^2$ $(P \geqslant 0)$, point B at $(3, 5)$, intercepts at -4 and 2.

Figure 7-1

as is the case in Fig. 7-1a. Also $f''(P) = -2 < 0$, tells us that the demand curve will be concave towards the P axis or, equivalently, that the negative slope of the demand curve, for $P > 0$, will become steeper as P increases, as is the case in Fig. 7-1a. To complete our check of Fig. 7-1a, the vertical and horizontal intercepts of the demand function (7-1) can be found, respectively, by letting $P = 0$ and $Q_d = 0$. Thus, when $P = 0$, $Q_d = f(0) = 9$, so that the vertical intercept is as shown in Fig. 7-1a. When $Q_d = 0$, $Q_d = 9 - P^2 = 0$ or $P = \pm 3$, so that the (economically meaningful, positive price) horizontal intercept is as shown in Fig. 7-1a.

In a similar fashion, we can check the shape of the supply curve in Fig. 7-1b. Thus, taking the supply function (7-4), the first derivative $g'(P) = 2P > 0$, for $P > 0$, tells us that the supply curve has a positive slope or, equivalently, slopes upward to the right, for $P > 0$, as is the case in Fig. 7-1b. Also, $g''(P) = 2 > 0$, tells us that the supply curve will be convex towards the P axis or, equivalently, the positive slope of the supply curve, for $P > 0$, will become steeper as P increases, as is the case in Fig. 7-1b. To complete the check of Fig. 7-1b, we must also find the vertical and horizontal intercepts of the supply function. Thus, when $P = 0$, $Q_s = g(0) = -4$, so that the (economically meaningless, negative quantity) vertical intercept is as shown in Fig. 7-1b. When $Q_s = 0$, $Q_s = -4 + P^2 = 0$ or $P = \pm 2$, so that the (economically meaningful, positive price) horizontal intercept is as shown in Fig. 7-1b.

Sketching Demand and Supply Functions: Examples

7-1 Sketch the general shape of the supply function

$$Q_s = g(P) = P^2 \quad (P \geqslant 0)$$

SOLUTION Since $g'(P) = 2P > 0$, for $P > 0$, then the supply curve will have a positive slope for $P > 0$. Also, since $g''(P) = 2 > 0$, then the supply curve will be convex towards the P

7-2 ELASTICITY

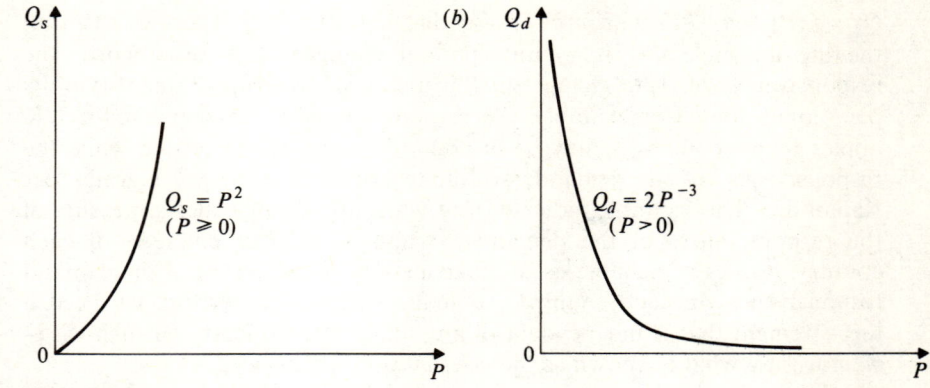

(a) Graph: $Q_s = P^2$ ($P \geq 0$)

(b) Graph: $Q_d = 2P^{-3}$ ($P > 0$)

Figure 7-2

axis. The next step is to find the vertical intercept of the supply function by letting $P = 0$. Thus, when $P = 0$, $Q_s = g(0) = 0$. The horizontal intercept can be similarly found by letting $Q_s = 0$. Thus, when $Q_s = 0$, $Q_s = P^2 = 0$ or $P = 0$. Therefore, the general shape of the supply function will be as shown in Fig. 7-2a.

7-2 Sketch the general shape of the demand function

$$Q_d = f(P) = 2P^{-3} \quad (P > 0)$$

SOLUTION Since $f'(P) = -6P^{-4} = -6/P^4 < 0$, for $P > 0$, then the demand curve will have a negative slope for $P > 0$. Also, since $f''(P) = 24P^{-5} = 24/P^5 > 0$, for $P > 0$, then the demand curve will be convex towards the P axis, for $P > 0$. Note, in this example, that the next step is *not* to find the vertical intercept of the function. The reason for this is that the demand function is defined only for $P > 0$. Instead, in this example, we find the limiting value of Q_d as P approaches zero. Thus, since $Q_d = 2/P^3$, then Q_d will approach infinity as P approaches zero. In addition, we can find the limiting value of Q_d as P approaches infinity. Thus, since $Q_d = 2/P^3$, then Q_d will approach zero as P approaches infinity. Therefore the general shape of the demand function will be as shown in Fig. 7-2b, with the Q_d and P axes constituting, respectively, the vertical and horizontal asymptotes of the demand function.

7-A PRACTICE PROBLEMS

7-3 Sketch the general shape of the following demand functions:
  (a) $Q_d = f(P) = 98 - P^2/2$ ($P \geq 0$) (b) $Q_d = f(P) = aP^{-\alpha}$ ($a, \alpha, P > 0$)

7-4 Sketch the general shape of the following supply functions:
  (a) $Q_s = g(P) = -12 + 4P + P^2$ ($P \geq 0$)
  (b) $Q_s = g(P) = bP^\beta$ ($b > 0; \beta > 1; P \geq 0$)

7-2 ELASTICITY

In the previous section, we used the first derivative of the demand function to measure the responsiveness of Q_d to a change in P. Therefore, if

136 ECONOMIC APPLICATIONS OF DERIVATIVES

$Q_d = f(P) = a - bP$, with $a, b > 0$, so that $dQ_d/dP = -b$, then we say that the rate of change of Q_d is $-b$ units per unit change in P. In other words, the responsiveness of Q_d to changes in P is measured in terms of quantity units per money unit. For example, the responsiveness of the demand for UK apples to price changes may be m pounds weight per £ sterling while the responsiveness of the demand for Italian apples may be n kilograms per Italian lira. This example indicates that while dQ_d/dP provides a measure of the responsiveness of the demand for apples to price changes, in each country, it does not enable us to make a simple comparison of the demand responsiveness in each country. To make such a comparison, we need a measurement that is independent of any units. Consequently, in such cases, we must use what is known as the *price elasticity of demand*.

The *price elasticity of demand* (denoted by E_d), for a demand function $Q_d = f(P)$, is defined as the ratio of the proportional change in the quantity demanded ($\Delta Q_d/Q_d$) to the proportional change in the price ($\Delta P/P$). Hence

$$E_d \equiv -\frac{\Delta Q_d/Q_d}{\Delta P/P} = -\frac{\Delta Q_d}{\Delta P}\frac{P}{Q_d} \qquad (7\text{-}7)$$

When the change in P is infinitesimal, (7-7) can be rewritten as

$$E_d = -\frac{dQ_d}{dP}\frac{P}{Q_d} \qquad (7\text{-}8)$$

It is important to note the following points about E_d, as defined above:

1. Since E_d has been defined in terms of proportional changes, it is therefore independent of units of measurement.
2. Since Q_d usually falls as P increases, so that dQ_d/dP in (7-8) will usually be negative, the negative sign in (7-8) therefore ensures that the (dimensionless) measure of E_d will usually be positive (assuming that P/Q_d is also positive).
3. E_d is evaluated *at a point* on the demand function (curve), as will be seen in the following example.

To give an example of how to find E_d, let us assume that the demand function is $Q_d = f(P) = 20 - 2P$. This means, using (7-8), that

$$E_d = -\frac{dQ_d}{dP}\frac{P}{Q_d} = -(-2)\frac{P}{Q_d} = \frac{2P}{Q_d} \qquad (7\text{-}9)$$

Thus, when $P = 2$ and $Q_d = f(2) = 20 - 2(2) = 16$, then (7-9) gives $E_d = 2P/Q_d = 2(2)/16 = 1/4$. Similarly, when $P = 6$ and $Q_d = f(6) = 20 - 2(6) = 8$, then (7-9) gives $E_d = 2P/Q_d = 2(6)/8 = 3/2$. Note, in each case, that E_d is evaluated at a particular (P, Q_d) point. For this reason, E_d is also known as the *point elasticity* of demand.

To underline the meaning of point elasticity, note that (7-9) can be rewritten as

$$E_d = \frac{2P}{Q_d} = \frac{2P}{20-2P} = \frac{P}{10-P} \qquad (7\text{-}10)$$

Since, in (7-10), E_d is shown as a function of P, then specific price values will determine specific point elasticity values. For example, in Fig. 7-3a, E_d can be seen to vary in value as P varies. Note, in Fig. 7-3a, that since the demand function is linear, dQ_d/dP is constant. This, however, does *not* mean that E_d is constant. Clearly, from (7-9), even if dQ_d/dP is constant, E_d will still vary as P/Q_d varies. Consequently, as can be seen in (7-9), when $P = 0$ (and $Q_d = 20$), $E_d = 0$. Also, in (7-9), when P approaches 10 (and Q_d approaches zero), E_d will approach infinity in value. [*Note*: the student should redraw Fig. 7-3a with the axes reversed, in order to see how E_d varies along a linear demand curve drawn after the fashion of economics textbooks.]

As a further example, given $Q_d = f(P) = aP^{-\alpha}$, where $a, \alpha, P > 0$, then

$$E_d = -\frac{dQ_d}{dP}\frac{P}{Q_d} = -(-\alpha a P^{-\alpha-1})\frac{P}{Q_d} = \frac{\alpha a P^{-\alpha}}{aP^{-\alpha}} = \alpha \qquad (7\text{-}11)$$

Note, for this demand function, that E_d remains constant in value at $E_d = \alpha$, for all $P > 0$. The graph of this constant-elasticity demand function is given in Fig. 7-3b.

Since our discussion of elasticity has so far been limited to the demand side, we will now turn to the supply side and define the *price elasticity of supply* (denoted by E_s), as the ratio of the proportional change in the quantity supplied ($\Delta Q_s/Q_s$) to the proportional change in the price ($\Delta P/P$). Hence

$$E_s \equiv \frac{\Delta Q_s/Q_s}{\Delta P/P} = \frac{\Delta Q_s}{\Delta P}\frac{P}{Q_s} \qquad (7\text{-}12)$$

(b)

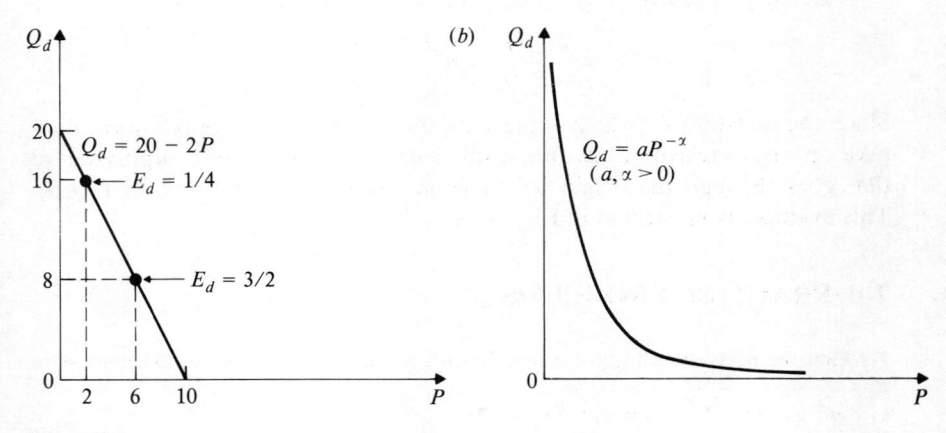

Q_d

20
$Q_d = 20 - 2P$
16 $E_d = 1/4$

8 $E_d = 3/2$

0 2 6 10 P

$Q_d = aP^{-\alpha}$
$(a, \alpha > 0)$

0 P

Figure 7-3

138 ECONOMIC APPLICATIONS OF DERIVATIVES

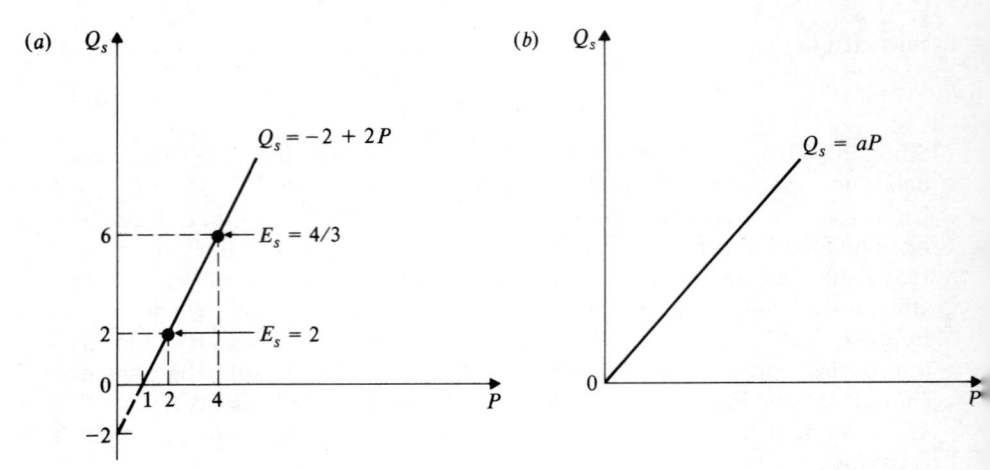

(a) [graph showing $Q_s = -2 + 2P$ with $E_s = 4/3$ at $P=4, Q_s=6$ and $E_s = 2$ at $P=2, Q_s=2$]

(b) [graph showing $Q_s = aP$]

Figure 7-4

When the change in P is infinitesimal, (7-12) can be rewritten as

$$E_s = \frac{dQ_s}{dP} \frac{P}{Q_s} \qquad (7\text{-}13)$$

As an example of how to find E_s, let us assume that the supply function is $Q_s = g(P) = -2 + 2P$. This means, using (7-13), that

$$E_s = \frac{dQ_s}{dP} \frac{P}{Q_s} = 2\frac{P}{Q_s} = \frac{2P}{-2+2P} = \frac{P}{-1+P} \qquad (7\text{-}14)$$

Thus, when $P = 2$ and $Q_s = g(2) = 2$, then (7-14) gives $E_s = 2P/Q_s = 4/2 = 2$. Similarly, when $P = 4$ and $Q_s = g(4) = 6$, then (7-14) gives $E_s = 2P/Q_s = 8/6 = 4/3$. This example is illustrated in Fig. 7-4a.

As a further example, given $Q_s = g(P) = aP$, where $a > 0$, then

$$E_s = \frac{dQ_s}{dP} \frac{P}{Q_s} = a\frac{P}{Q_s} = \frac{aP}{aP} = 1 \qquad (7\text{-}15)$$

Since the constant a (which represents the slope of the supply curve) may take on any positive value, this result means that any linear supply curve that goes through the origin will have an elasticity of one (for all $P > 0$). This example is illustrated in Fig. 7-4b.

7-B PRACTICE PROBLEMS

7-5 Find the price elasticity of demand for each of the following demand functions when $P = 4$:
    (a) $Q_d = 98 - P^2/2$ (b) $Q_d = 14P^{-5}$

7-6 Find the price elasticity of supply for each of the following supply functions when $P = 3$:
    (a) $Q_s = -2 + 5P$ (b) $Q_s = -12 + 4P + P^2$

7-3 TOTAL REVENUE, MARGINAL REVENUE, AND THE PRICE ELASTICITY OF DEMAND

In consumer theory, the demand function is generally written in the form $Q_d = f(P)$. As such, the emphasis is on the quantity demanded at a given price. In contrast, in the theory of the firm, the demand function (facing a firm) is generally written in the form $P = h(Q)$, with the emphasis being on the price per unit obtained when a given quantity of output is sold by the firm. Consequently, in this section, we shall take the demand function facing a firm to be of form $P = h(Q)$.

When a firm sells output, its *total revenue* (R) from this sale of output is simply the product of the unit price (P) of output and the quantity (Q) of output sold. Thus

$$R = PQ \tag{7-16}$$

Note, that if we substitute $P = h(Q)$ into (7-16), we obtain

$$R = h(Q) \cdot Q \tag{7-17}$$

which indicates that R is a function of Q, of form $R = R(Q) = h(Q) \cdot Q$. Also note, from (7-16), that the revenue per unit sold, known as the *average revenue* (AR), is simply $AR = R/Q = PQ/Q = P$. Finally, note that the change in total revenue resulting from an infinitesimal change in the quantity sold is given by the derivative $dR/dQ = R'(Q)$, which is known as *marginal revenue* (MR).

As an example, let us assume a linear demand (or average revenue)

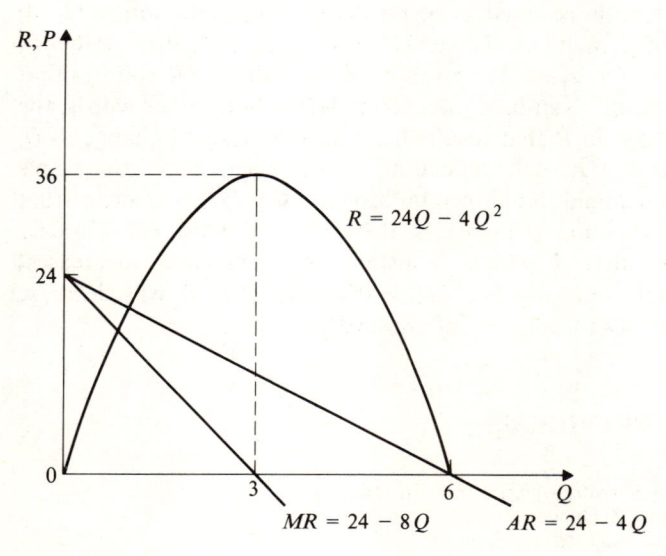

Figure 7-5

function $P = AR = 24 - 4Q$. In this case, the total revenue function will be $R = PQ = (24-4Q)Q = 24Q - 4Q^2$, and the marginal revenue function will be $MR = dR/dQ = 24 - 8Q$. Note in this example, which is illustrated in Fig. 7-5, that the (negative) slope of the MR curve is twice as steep as the (negative) slope of the AR curve (since $d(MR)/dQ = -8$ and $d(AR)/dQ = -4$). Also note, in Fig. 7-5, that the horizontal intercept of the linear AR curve is twice that of the linear MR curve.

Now that we have defined total, average, and marginal revenue, we can derive an interesting relation between marginal revenue (MR) and the price elasticity of demand (E_d). To do this, we first differentiate (7-17), via the product rule, to obtain MR:

$$MR = \frac{dR}{dQ} = \frac{d}{dQ}[h(Q) \cdot Q]$$
$$= h(Q)(1) + Qh'(Q) = h(Q) + Qh'(Q) \qquad (7\text{-}18)$$

or
$$MR = P + Q\frac{dP}{dQ} \qquad (7\text{-}19)$$

Then, since

$$E_d = -\frac{dQ}{dP}\frac{P}{Q} \quad \text{or} \quad Q\frac{dP}{dQ} = -\frac{P}{E_d}$$

(7-19) may be rewritten as

$$MR = P - P/E_d \quad \text{or} \quad MR = P(1 - 1/E_d) \qquad (7\text{-}20)$$

where P and E_d are both assumed to be positive. An examination of (7-20) indicates: (a) that if demand is elastic, as given by $E_d > 1$, then $MR > 0$; (b) that if demand is unit-elastic, as given by $E_d = 1$, then $MR = 0$; (c) that if demand is inelastic, as given by $E_d < 1$, then $MR < 0$. In other words, the direction of the change in R that results from an infinitesimal change in Q, as given by $dR/dQ = MR$, will depend upon the elasticity of the firm's average revenue or demand function. Thus, in case (a), $MR > 0$ means that R will increase (decrease) as Q increases (decreases) infinitesimally. In case (b), $MR = 0$ means that R will be constant as Q increases (decreases) infinitesimally. Finally, in case (c), $MR < 0$ means that R will decrease (increase) as Q increases (decreases) infinitesimally.

7-C PRACTICE PROBLEMS

7-7 Given the demand function $P = h(Q) = 60 - 3Q$, find
(a) the total revenue (R) function
(b) the marginal revenue (MR) function
(c) the price elasticity of demand (E_d) at $Q = 5$.

7-8 If, in Prob. 7-7c, P is measured in US dollars and Q is measured in dozens, what are the units in which E_d is measured?

7-9 Check that the relation (7-20) holds for the case given in Prob. 7-7, when $Q = 5$.

7-4 OTHER DERIVATIVES IN ECONOMICS

In this section we will briefly define some other well-known economic concepts in terms of derivatives.

Marginal Utility

In consumer theory, the individual consumer is assumed to have a *utility function* which relates the level of *total utility* (U), derived by the consumer, to the quantity (Q) of a good he consumes. Thus, given a utility function $U = U(Q)$, the change in total utility resulting from an infinitesimal change in the quantity of the good consumed is given by the derivative $dU/dQ = U'(Q)$, which is known as *marginal utility* (*MU*). In turn, the change in MU resulting from an infinitesimal change in Q is given by the derivative $d(MU)/dQ = d^2U/dQ^2 = U''(Q)$. Clearly, if MU declines as Q increases infinitesimally, then $U''(Q) < 0$, indicating the operation of the *law of diminishing marginal utility*.

Marginal Product

In the short-run analysis of production, the production process is assumed to involve fixed inputs and only *one* variable input, labour services (L). In this case, the *production function*, which relates the level of output (Q) produced to the quantity of labour input, can be written as $Q = g(L)$. This means that the change in output resulting from an infinitesimal change in the quantity of labour input is given by the derivative $dQ/dL = g'(L)$, which is known as the *marginal product* (*MP*) of labour. In turn, the change in MP resulting from an infinitesimal change in L is given by the derivative $d(MP)/dL = d^2Q/dL^2 = g''(L)$. Clearly, if MP declines as L increases infinitesimally, then $g''(L) < 0$, indicating the operation of the *law of diminishing marginal product*.

Marginal Revenue Product

If a firm has a total revenue function $R = R(Q)$, and a production function $Q = g(L)$, then the change in total revenue resulting from an infinitesimal change in the quantity of labour input is given by the derivative dR/dL, which is known as the *marginal revenue product* (*MRP*) of labour. To obtain dR/dL, we use the chain rule as follows:

$$\frac{dR}{dL} = \frac{dR}{dQ}\frac{dQ}{dL} = MR \cdot MP = MRP$$

Marginal Cost

In the theory of cost, the firm is assumed to have a *total cost function* which relates total cost (C) to the level of output (Q) produced by the firm. Thus, given a total cost function $C = C(Q)$, the change in total cost resulting from an infinitesimal change in the quantity of output produced by the firm is given by the derivative $dC/dQ = C'(Q)$, which is known as *marginal cost* (MC).

Marginal Propensity to Consume

In macroeconomics we frequently encounter the concept of a *consumption function*, which relates aggregate consumption expenditure (C) to the level of national income (Y). Thus, given a consumption function $C = C(Y)$, the change in consumption expenditure resulting from an infinitesimal change in the level of national income is given by the derivative $dC/dY = C'(Y)$, which is known as the *marginal propensity to consume* (MPC). Moreover, if saving (S) is defined as the amount of national income not devoted to consumption, then a saving function can be written as $S = Y - C = Y - C(Y) = S(Y)$. This permits us to define the *marginal propensity to save* (MPS) as $dS/dY = S'(Y)$. Finally, in a similar fashion, if we have an import function $M = M(Y)$, which relates the level of imports (M) to the level of national income (Y), then we can define the *marginal propensity of import* as $dM/dY = M'(Y)$.

7-5 ADDITIONAL PROBLEMS

7-10 (a) Sketch the general shape of the demand function $Q_d = f(P) = 16/P^2$, for $P > 0$
  (b) find the price elasticity of demand for this demand function when $P = 5$
  (c) rearrange the demand function into the form $P = h(Q)$, and sketch its general shape for $Q > 0$.

7-11 (a) Sketch the general shape of the supply function $Q_s = g(P) = -27 + 6P + P^2$, for $P \geqslant 0$
  (b) find the price elasticity of supply for this supply function when $P = 3$.

7-12 (a) Find the price elasticity of supply for each of the following supply functions: (i) $Q_s = a$, (ii) $Q_s = bP$, (iii) $P = c$, where a, b, and c are positive constants.
  (b) graph each of the supply functions given in (a), firstly with Q_s on the vertical axis and then with P on the vertical axis.

7-13 (a) Sketch the general shape of the consumption function $C = C(Y) = 1200 - 7200/(9 + Y)$, for $Y \geqslant 0$.
  (b) Find the marginal propensity to consume (MPC) when $Y = 91$.
  (c) Find the marginal propensity to save (MPS) when $Y = 91$.
  (d) Determine whether or not MPC and MPS change in the same direction as Y changes.

7-14 Given a demand function $Q_d = f(P)$, where $f'(P) < 0$. Show that $dR/dP = Q(1 - E_d)$.

7-15 A firm faces a linear AR function $P = h(Q)$, where $h'(Q) < 0$. Show that:
  (a) MR is a linear function of Q

(b) the absolute value of the slope of the MR line is twice that of the AR line
(c) the Q intercept of the AR line is twice the Q intercept of the MR line.

7-16 A firm faces a demand function $P = h(Q) = a/Q$, where $a, Q > 0$. Find:
(a) how the firm's total revenue varies as price varies
(b) the price elasticity of demand for this demand function
(c) use your result in (b) to explain your result in (a). Also, sketch the general shape of the demand function.

7-17 A consumer has a utility function $U = U(Q) = \alpha Q^\beta$, where $\alpha > 0$, $0 < \beta < 1$, and $Q \geq 0$. Does this utility function possess the property of diminishing marginal utility?

7-18 A firm's production and average revenue functions are, respectively, $Q = g(L) = 4L^{1/2}$ and $P = h(Q) = 120 - 2Q$. Find:
(a) the marginal revenue product of labour when $L = 16$
(b) the price at which marginal revenue is zero
(c) the price elasticity of demand when marginal revenue is zero.

7-19 A firm has a production function $Q = g(L) = -\frac{2}{3}L^3 + 10L^2$. Does this production function possess the property of diminishing marginal product of labour?

7-20 For the following total cost functions, state whether marginal cost is an increasing or decreasing function of quantity produced:
(a) $C = C(Q) = 4Q^3 - 240Q^2 + 800Q + 50$ (b) $C = C(Q) = 10Q^2 + 3Q + 9$

7-21 Given equation (3-25), in Chapter 3, find $d\bar{P}/dt$ in order to determine both the direction and the magnitude of the change in $\bar{P}$ resulting from an infinitesimal change in t.

7-22 Given the consumption function (3-27), in Chapter 3, find the marginal propensity to consume. Also, given Eq. (3-30), in Chapter 3, find the investment multiplier $d\bar{Y}/dI$ in order to determine both the direction and the magnitude of the change in $\bar{Y}$ resulting from an infinitesimal change in I.

CHAPTER
EIGHT
MAXIMIZATION AND MINIMIZATION

In economic analysis the decision-maker (whether the individual consumer, the household, the entrepreneur, or the government) is frequently required to make a choice among alternatives in such a way as to *maximize* or to *minimize* something. For example, in the utility theory of consumer demand, the consumer is assumed to have the objective or goal of utility *maximization*; in the theory of cost, the entrepreneur is assumed to have the objective of *minimizing* the cost of producing a given output; in the theory of the firm, the entrepreneur is assumed to have the objective of profit *maximization*. These few examples serve to demonstrate that the concepts of maximization and minimization are not only important but also common features of economic analysis. Consequently, it is essential that the student of economics should become familiar with the mathematics of maximization and minimization.

8-1 RELATIVE AND ABSOLUTE EXTREMA

In mathematical language the collective term for the concepts of maximum and minimum is *extremum*, meaning simply an extreme value. Such extrema may be represented geometrically as the highest and lowest points on a graph. For example, in Fig. 8-1, which represents the graph of a function $y = g(x)$ for nonnegative values of x, point A represents the lowest point on the graph. Consequently, if point A remains the lowest value of y over all (nonnegative) values of x, then A is said to be an *absolute* or *global*

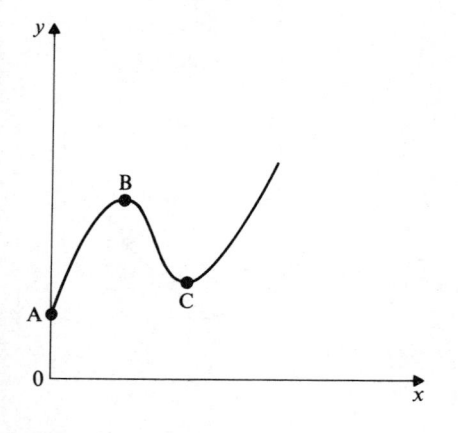

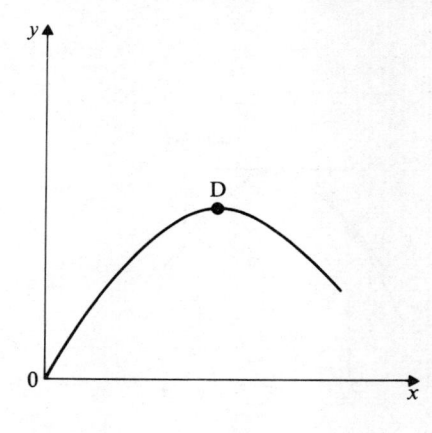

Figure 8-1

Figure 8-2

minimum. In contrast, point C is said to be a *relative* or *local* minimum, in the sense that it represents an extremum in the immediate neighbourhood of point C only. Similarly, point B in Fig. 8-1 is a relative maximum. Note, from Fig. 8-1, that a function may have several relative extrema.

Figure 8-2 represents the graph of a function $y = h(x)$. If, given the nature of the function $y = h(x)$, point D is the highest value of y over all (nonnegative) values of x, then D is both an absolute maximum and a relative maximum. In a similar fashion, if the graph in Fig. 8-2 had been drawn U-shaped, the relative minimum would also be an absolute minimum. Such cases, which (as we shall see in Chapter 9) are not uncommon in economic analysis, are of particular interest since they represent situations where the search for a relative extremum will also yield an absolute extremum.

The following discussion of extrema, in 8-2, will only be concerned with finding relative extrema. Note, however, that since an absolute extremum is either a relative extremum (like point D in Fig. 8-2) or an end point of a function (like point A in Fig. 8-1), we can always find an absolute extremum by simply comparing the relative extrema and end points of a function.

8-2 CRITERIA FOR RELATIVE EXTREMA

In the search for (relative) extrema, the first derivative of a function plays an important role. This can be clearly seen from an examination of Fig. 8-3, where the graphed function has a maximum at the point $x = \bar{x}$. Notice, in Fig. 8-3, that the tangent slopes, evaluated at points E, F and G respectively, change in value from positive (at point E) to zero (at point F), and finally to negative (at point G). Recalling that the first derivative of a

146 MAXIMIZATION AND MINIMIZATION

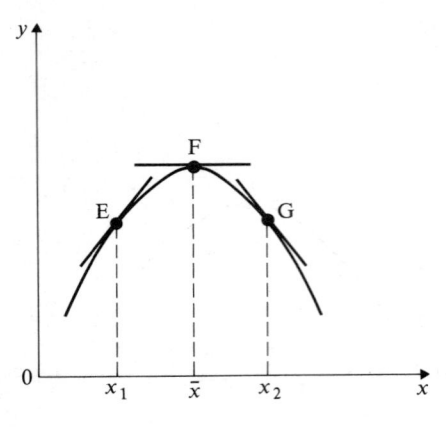

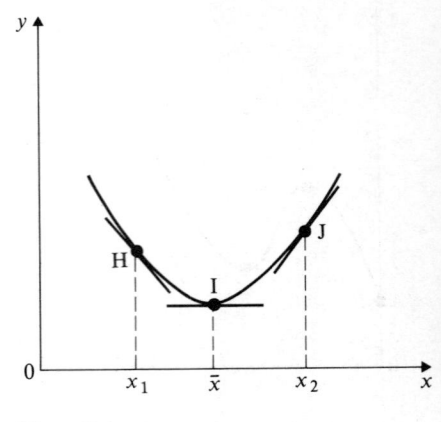

Figure 8-3

Figure 8-4

function permits us to evaluate the tangent slope at any x value, we can use this information in finding a maximum. In particular, note that the maximum occurs at $x = \bar{x}$ where the first derivative is zero (horizontal tangent slope). However, while the condition of a zero first derivative is *necessary* for a maximum, it is *not sufficient* to establish a maximum. Thus, in Fig. 8-4, a minimum is also seen to occur at the value of x for which the first derivative is zero. Clearly, the condition that the first derivative of a function be zero is *not sufficient* to distinguish a maximum from a minimum. Rather this condition, of a zero first derivative at $x = \bar{x}$, only tells us that the function has a *stationary value* at $x = \bar{x}$. This term follows from the fact that momentarily y is neither increasing nor decreasing in value at $x = \bar{x}$. In other words, in the instantaneous sense, y is in a 'standstill' or 'stationary' position at $x = \bar{x}$, so that the first derivative of the function must be zero at $x = \bar{x}$. In Fig. 8-3, or Fig. 8-4, this simply means that the function is horizontal at $x = \bar{x}$.

A *stationary value*, such as F or I in Fig. 8-3 and Fig. 8-4, can be found by finding the value of x for which the first derivative of the function is zero—but we require additional information to distinguish between a maximum and a minimum. It is the first derivative which provides us with exactly this information. Notice in the case of a maximum (Fig. 8-3) that the first derivative changes its sign from positive to negative as x increases from x_1 to x_2. Thus, in Fig. 8-3, the tangent slope changes from positive (at point E) to negative (at point G). In contrast, in the case of a minimum (Fig. 8-4), the first derivative changes its sign from negative to positive as x increases from x_1 to x_2. Graphically, in the case of a *maximum*, the tangent slope decreases as x increases in the neighbourhood of $x = \bar{x}$; in the case of a *minimum*, the tangent slope increases as x increases in the neighbourhood of $x = \bar{x}$. Thus a distinction between a maximum and a minimum can be made by examining the *direction of change* of the first derivative. In summary: given a function $y = f(x)$, whose first derivative $f'(x)$ at point $x = \bar{x}$ is $f'(\bar{x}) = 0$, then the value of the function at this point, $f(\bar{x})$, will be

1. A relative *maximum* if the derivative $f'(x)$ changes its sign from positive to negative as x increases in the neighbourhood of $x = \bar{x}$.
2. A relative *minimum* if the derivative $f'(x)$ changes its sign from negative to positive as x increases in the neighbourhood of $x = \bar{x}$.

The second derivative of a function measures the rate of change of the first derivative. Consequently, the *direction of change* of the first derivative $f'(x)$ can be stated in terms of the *sign of the second derivative* $f''(x)$. Thus when $f'(x)$, or the tangent slope, is decreasing as x increases (as is the case in Fig. 8-3) then $f''(x) < 0$. Similarly, when $f'(x)$, or the tangent slope, is increasing as x increases (Fig. 8-4) then $f''(x) > 0$. Consequently, our summary can now be re-stated as follows:

Summary of Criteria for Relative Extrema

Given a function $y = f(x)$, whose first derivative $f'(x)$ at point $x = \bar{x}$ is $f'(\bar{x}) = 0$, then the value of the function at this point, $f(\bar{x})$, will be

(i) a relative *maximum* if $f''(\bar{x}) < 0$;
(ii) a relative *minimum* if $f''(\bar{x}) > 0$.

The condition $f'(x) = 0$ is clearly a *necessary*, but not *sufficient*, condition to establish a maximum or a minimum. If the *necessary condition* $f'(x) = 0$ is satisfied, then $f''(x) \gtrless 0$ (depending upon whether we have a minimum or a maximum) is a *sufficient condition* to establish a relative extremum. These two conditions are also known, respectively, as the *first-order condition* and the *second-order condition* for a relative extremum.

Examples of Maximization and Minimization

8-1 Find the relative extreme values of the following functions:
   (a) $y = -2x^2 + 20x$
   (b) $y = 3x^2 - 18x + 30$. In each case graph both the function $y = f(x)$, and the first derivative function $f'(x)$, with the graph of $f(x)$ restricted to the positive quadrant.

SOLUTION
   (a) $y = f(x) = -2x^2 + 20x$
We find a stationary value by finding the value of x for which $f'(x) = 0$, thus
$$f'(x) = -4x + 20 = 0 \quad \text{when} \quad x = \bar{x} = 5.$$
To check if this is a maximum or minimum we find $f''(x)$, hence $f''(x) = -4 < 0$, $\therefore y = f(x)$ has a maximum value at $x = 5$, the extreme value being $f(\bar{x}) = f(5) = 50$. The required graphs

148 MAXIMIZATION AND MINIMIZATION

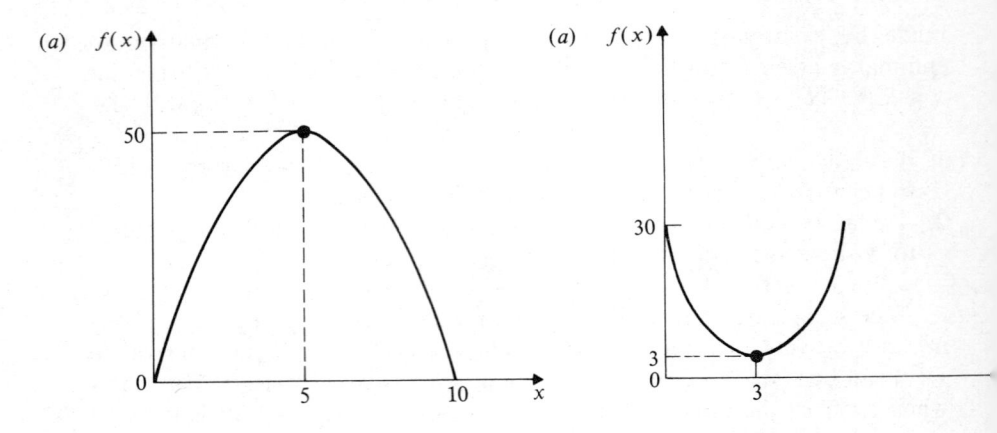

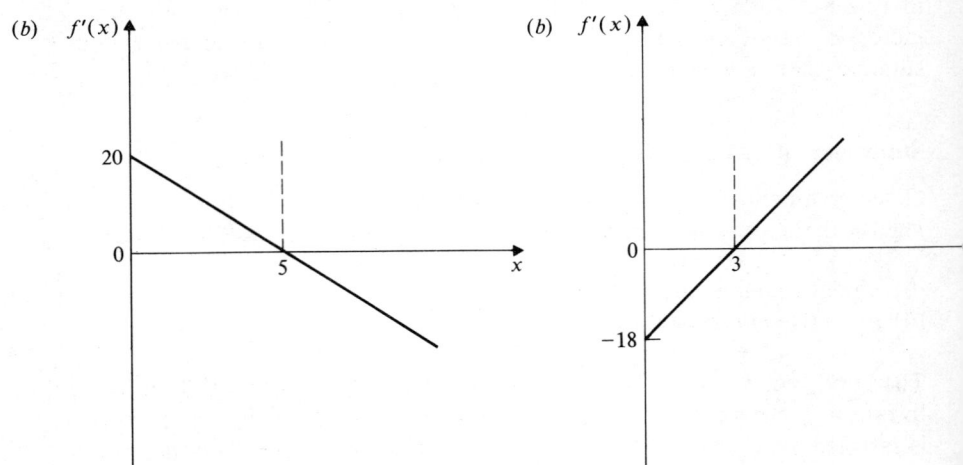

Figure 8-5

Figure 8-6

are shown in Fig. 8-5. Note, in Fig. 8-5, that $f(x)$ has a maximum at that value of x for which $f'(x) = 0$. Also, note that $f'(x) > 0$ for $x < 5$ and $f'(x) < 0$ for $x > 5$, as is required by the first-derivative test for a relative maximum.

(b) $y = f(x) = 3x^2 - 18x + 30$
Stationary value where $f'(x) = 0$, thus

$$f'(x) = 6x - 18 = 0 \quad \text{when} \quad x = \bar{x} = 3$$

$f''(x) = 6 > 0$, $\therefore y = f(x)$ has a minimum value at $x = 3$, the extreme value being $f(\bar{x}) = f(3) = 3$. The required graphs are shown in Fig. 8-6.

8-2 Find the relative extreme value for the function $y = ax^2 + bx + c$.

SOLUTION Stationary value where $f'(x) = 0$, thus

$$f'(x) = 2ax + b = 0 \quad \text{when} \quad x = \bar{x} = -b/2a$$

$$f''(x) = 2a, \text{ therefore}$$

(i) when $a < 0$, $f''(x) < 0$ and $f(x)$ has a maximum value at $x = -b/2a$, the extreme value being $f(\bar{x}) = f(-b/2a) = (4ac - b^2)/4a$;
(ii) when $a > 0$, $f''(x) > 0$ and $f(x)$ has a minimum value at $x = -b/2a$, the extreme value being $f(\bar{x}) = f(-b/2a) = (4ac - b^2)/4a$.

8-3 In Example 8-2, given that $c > 0$, what sign must b have in each case to ensure that the relative extremum occurs at positive values of x and y?

SOLUTION
  (a) For the relative maximum case $(a < 0)$, we require both $\bar{x}$ and $f(\bar{x})$ to be positive, $\therefore$ require $b > 0$ for $\bar{x} = -b/2a > 0$ and $f(\bar{x}) = (4ac - b^2)/4a > 0$.
  (b) For the relative minimum case $(a > 0)$, we require $b < 0$ for $\bar{x} = -b/2a > 0$. However, for $f(\bar{x}) = (4ac - b^2)/4a > 0$ when $a, c > 0$, we also require $4ac > b^2$.

8-4 Find the relative extreme values for the following functions:
  (a) $y = \frac{1}{3}x^3 - 2x^2 + 3x + 5$ (b) $y = -x^3 + 3x - 2$

SOLUTION
  (a) Stationary value where $f'(x) = 0$, thus
$$f'(x) = x^2 - 4x + 3 = 0 \text{ when } x = 3 \text{ or } x = 1 \text{ (quadratic formula)}$$
$$f''(x) = 2x - 4, \text{ therefore}$$
(i) when $x = 3$, $f''(3) = 2 > 0$, $\therefore y = f(x)$ has a minimum value at $x = 3$, the extreme value being $f(3) = 5$.
(ii) when $x = 1$, $f''(1) = -2 < 0$, $\therefore y = f(x)$ has a maximum value at $x = 1$, the extreme value being $f(1) = 19/3$.
  (b) Stationary value where $f'(x) = 0$, thus
$$f'(x) = -3x^2 + 3 = 0 \text{ when } x = \pm 1$$
$$f''(x) = -6x, \text{ therefore}$$
(i) when $x = 1$, $f''(1) = -6 < 0$, $\therefore y = f(x)$ has a maximum value at $x = 1$, the extreme value being $f(1) = 0$,
(ii) when $x = -1$, $f''(-1) = 6 > 0$, $\therefore y = f(x)$ has a minimum value at $x = -1$, the extreme value being $f(-1) = -4$.
Note that the functions given in (a) and (b) have more than one relative extremum.

8-5 Find the relative extreme values for the following functions:
  (a) $y = x + 16x^{-1}$ (b) $y = 16x(x^2 + 4)^{-1}$

SOLUTION
  (a) Stationary value where $f'(x) = 0$, thus
$$f'(x) = 1 - 16x^{-2}$$
$$= (x^2 - 16)/x^2 = 0 \text{ when } x^2 - 16 = 0 \text{ or when } x = \pm 4.$$
$$f''(x) = 32x^{-3}, \text{ therefore}$$
(i) when $x = 4$, $f''(4) = 1/2 > 0$, $\therefore y = f(x)$ has a minimum value at $x = 4$, the extreme value being $f(4) = 8$,
(ii) when $x = -4$, $f''(-4) = -1/2 < 0$, $\therefore y = f(x)$ has a maximum value at $x = -4$, the extreme value being $f(-4) = -8$.
Note that the (x, y) value for the minimum is $(4, 8)$ while the corresponding value for the maximum is $(-4, -8)$. Clearly the 'minimum' exceeds the 'maximum'. This result, however, is not contradictory since these are *relative* extrema. The graph of this function in Fig. 8-7 serves to clarify this apparent contradiction.

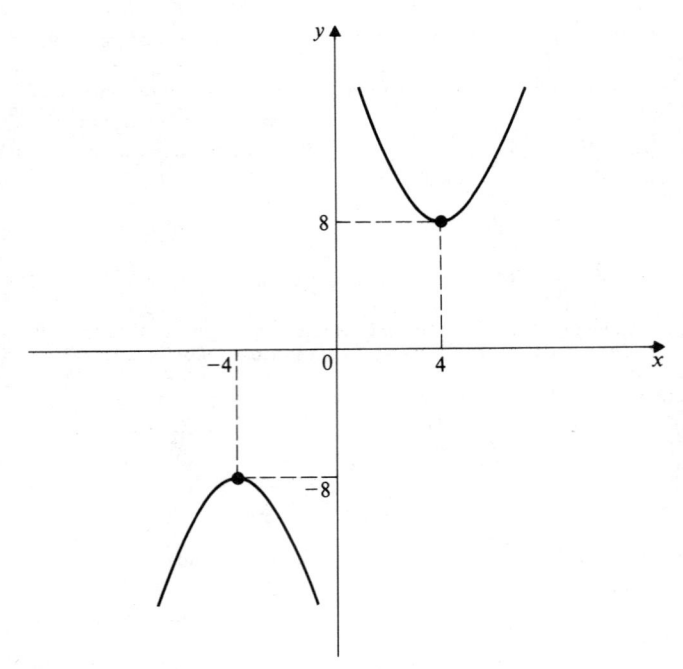

Figure 8-7

(b) Stationary value where $f'(x) = 0$, thus
$$f'(x) = -16x(x^2+4)^{-2}(2x)+(x^2+4)^{-1}(16) \quad \text{(product and chain rules)}$$
$$= (x^2+4)^{-2}[-32x^2+(x^2+4)(16)]$$
$$= (x^2+4)^{-2}[-32x^2+16x^2+64]$$
$$= \frac{64-16x^2}{(x^2+4)^2} = 0 \text{ when } 64-16x^2 = 0 \text{ or when } x = \pm 2$$

Since $f'(x) = (64-16x^2)(x^2+4)^{-2}$ then
$$f''(x) = -2(64-16x^2)(x^2+4)^{-3}(2x) - 32x(x^2+4)^{-2} \quad \text{(product and chain rules)}$$
$$= (x^2+4)^{-3}[-256x+64x^3-32x(x^2+4)]$$
$$= (x^2+4)^{-3}[32x^3-384x]$$
$$= \frac{32(x^3-12x)}{(x^2+4)^3} \quad \text{therefore}$$

(i) when $x = 2$, $f''(2) = -1 < 0$, $\therefore y = f(x)$ has a maximum value at $x = 2$, the extreme value being $f(2) = 4$
(ii) when $x = -2$, $f''(-2) = 1 > 0$, $\therefore y = f(x)$ has a minimum value at $x = -2$, the extreme value being $f(-2) = -4$

8-A PRACTICE PROBLEMS

8-6 Find the relative extreme values of the following functions:
(a) $y = 35x - 3.5x^2 + 2$ (b) $y = 0.2x^2 + 2x - 3$ (c) $y = \frac{1}{2}x^2 - 6x$
(d) $y = -2x^2 + 1/9$ (e) $y = \frac{1}{3}x^3 - 3x^2 + 5x + 3$ (f) $y = 2x^3 + x^2 + 1$
(g) $y = (x+2)x^{-2}$

8-3 POINTS OF INFLECTION

In finding the relative extreme values of a function $y = f(x)$ we proceeded as follows:
(i) if $f'(x) = 0$ at $x = \bar{x}$, $\therefore f(x)$ has a stationary value at $x = \bar{x}$;
(ii) if $f''(\bar{x}) > 0$, $\therefore y = f(x)$ has a minimum value at $x = \bar{x}$, the extreme value being $f(\bar{x})$;
if $f''(\bar{x}) < 0$, $\therefore y = f(x)$ has a maximum value at $x = \bar{x}$, the extreme value being $f(\bar{x})$.

But what happens if *both* $f'(x)$ and $f''(x)$ are equal to zero at $x = \bar{x}$? In such a case we have a stationary value, but a stationary value which is not a maximum or a minimum. Therefore *stationary values may not be relative extrema*. This case, where $f'(\bar{x}) = f''(\bar{x}) = 0$ can be explained in terms of Fig. 8-8.

An examination of Fig. 8-8a indicates that the function $f(x)$ has a stationary value at $x = \bar{x}$, since the tangent slope at this point is zero as shown at point A. The same information is portrayed in Fig. 8-8b, which graphs $f'(x)$, at point A'. If point A was a maximum or a minimum, $f'(x)$ would change its sign from one side of $x = \bar{x}$ to the other. Thus in Fig. 8-5b, which relates to the relative maximum in Fig. 8-5a, $f'(x)$ changes its sign from positive to negative as x increases in the neighbourhood of $x = \bar{x} = 5$, giving $f''(\bar{x}) < 0$. But, in Fig. 8-8b, which relates to Fig. 8-8a, $f'(x)$ does *not* change its sign from one side of $\bar{x}$ to the other, rather $f'(x)$ remains in the nonnegative quadrant. From Figs. 8-8b and 8-8c it can be seen that, for $x < \bar{x}$, $f'(x)$ decreases in value as x increases ($f''(x) < 0$) while, for $x > \bar{x}$, $f'(x)$ increases in value as x increases ($f''(x) > 0$). At $x = \bar{x}$, $f'(x)$ is a minimum ($f''(x) = 0$), as shown by point A'. This case, where $f''(\bar{x}) = 0$ and where $f''(x)$ changes its sign at $x = \bar{x}$, exemplifies what is known as an *inflection point*.

In Fig. 8-9 another example of an inflection point is shown. Thus at point B, in Fig. 8-9a, the tangent slope is zero, while in Fig. 8-9b $f'(x)$ reaches a maximum at $x = \bar{x}$ ($f''(\bar{x}) = 0$), as shown by point B'. Figures 8-8b and 8-9b demonstrate that a characteristic feature of an inflection point is that $f'(x)$ reaches an extreme value at that point. This extreme value of $f'(x)$ may be either a maximum (Fig. 8-9b) or a minimum (Fig. 8-8b).

The two cases illustrated in Figs. 8-8 and 8-9 are examples of what is known as *stationary points of inflection*. In Figs. 8-10 and 8-11 another possibility, known as *non-stationary points of inflection*, is illustrated. Note that while $f''(\bar{x}) = 0$ at points C'' and D'', the tangent slopes are not horizontal at points C and D. Thus, in Figs. 8-10 and 8-11, $f(x)$ has *not* got a stationary value at $x = \bar{x}$. Figures 8-10 and 8-11 serve to illustrate that $f'(x) = 0$, which is a necessary condition for a relative extremum, is *not* required for an inflection point. Points C and D are points of inflection ($f''(\bar{x}) = 0$) yet $f'(\bar{x}) \neq 0$.

152 MAXIMIZATION AND MINIMIZATION

It should be noted, in all the cases illustrated, that $f'(x)$ reaches an extreme value at $x = \bar{x}$ ($f''(\bar{x}) = 0$), whether the point of inflection is stationary or non-stationary. Hence a *necessary condition* for a point of

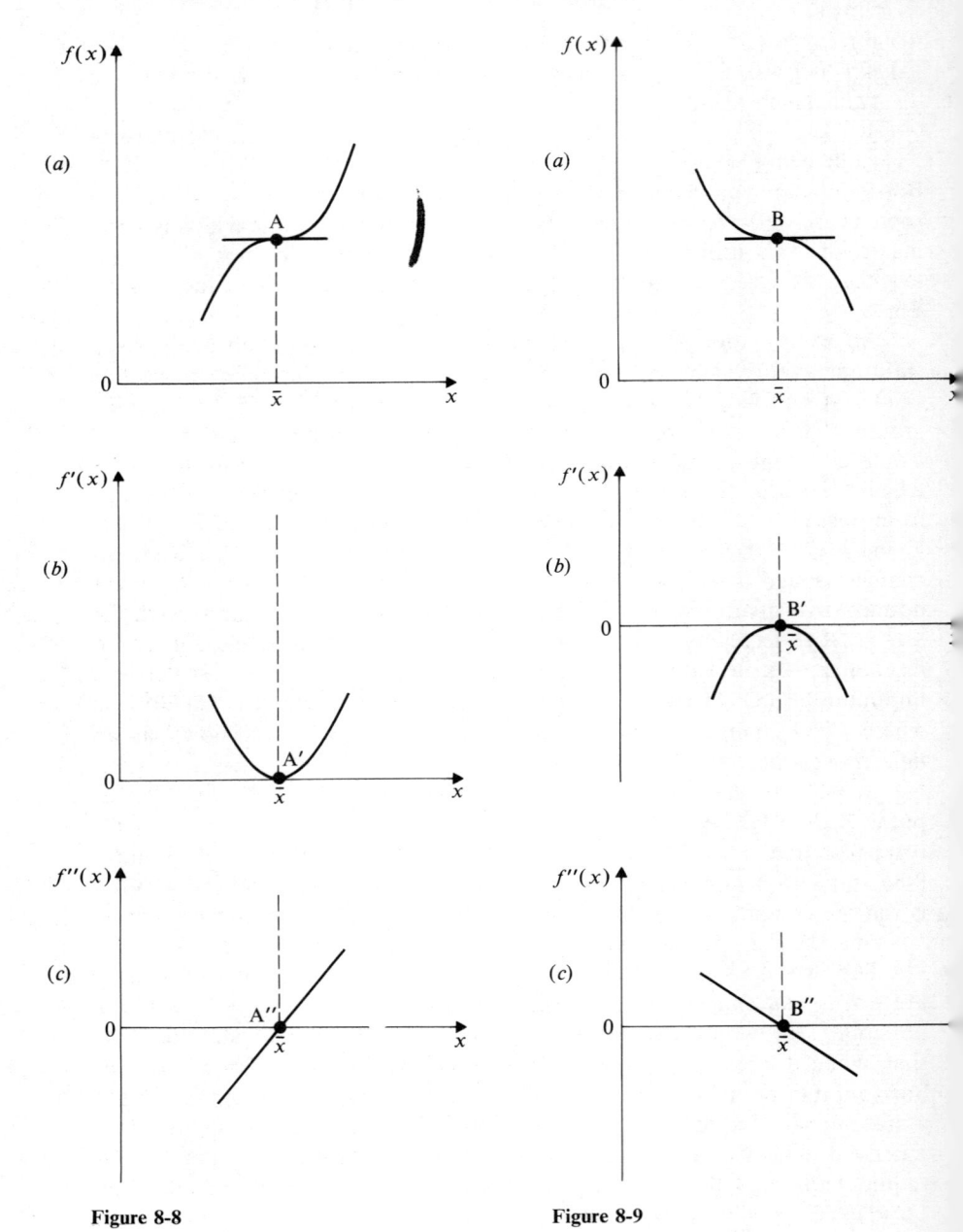

Figure 8-8

Figure 8-9

8-3 POINTS OF INFLECTION 153

inflection is that $f''(x) = 0$. Also, in all the cases shown, $f''(x)$ can be seen to change in sign as x increases through the value $x = \bar{x}$. Since the third derivative, $f'''(x)$, measures the rate of change of the second derivative, then

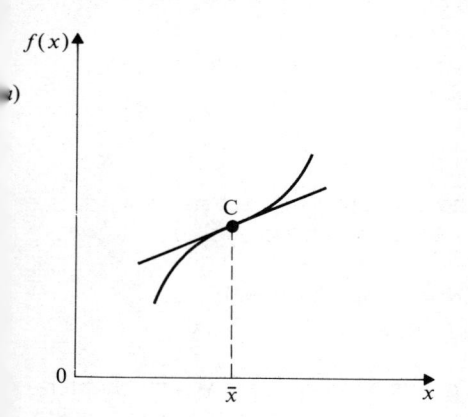

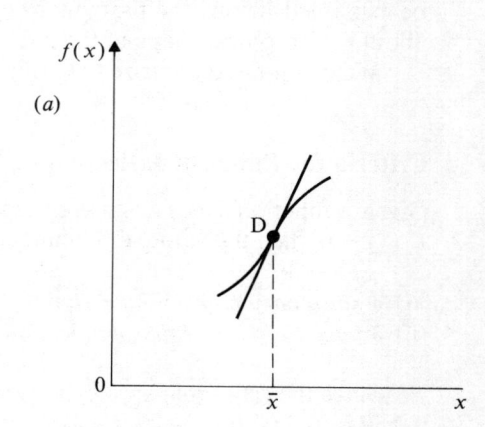

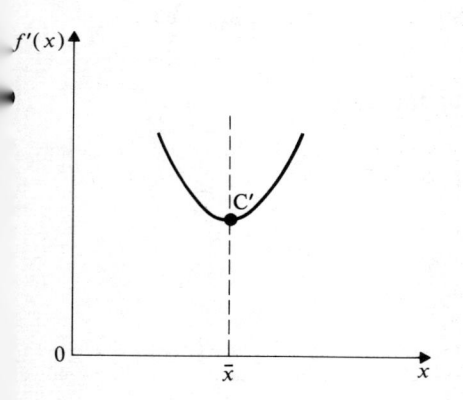

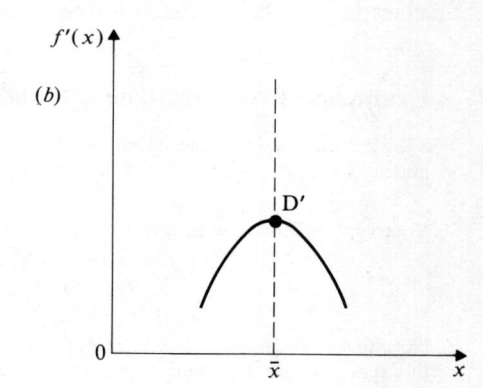

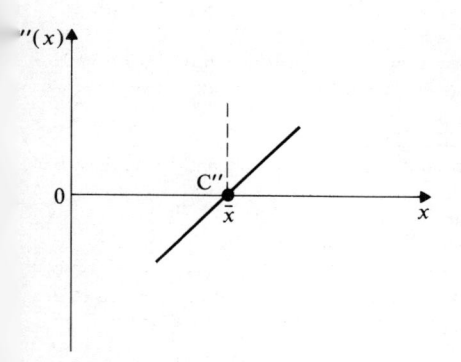

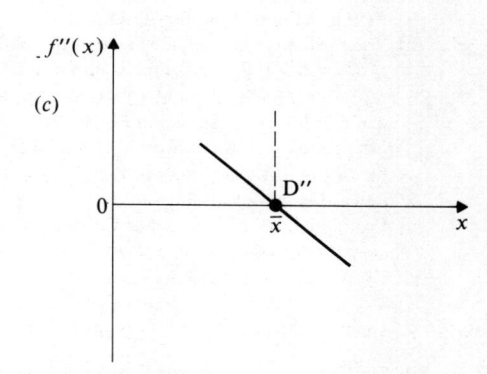

Figure 8-10

Figure 8-11

154 MAXIMIZATION AND MINIMIZATION

the direction of change of $f''(x)$ can be stated in terms of the sign of $f'''(x)$. Consequently, if the *necessary* condition $f''(x) = 0$ is satisfied, then $f'''(x) \neq 0$ is a *sufficient condition* to establish a point of inflection. As will be explained below, the particular sign of $f'''(x)$ also provides information about the graphical shape of the inflection point.

We can now summarize the criteria for points of inflection:

Criteria for Points of Inflection

Given a function $y = f(x)$, whose second derivative $f''(x)$ at point $x = \bar{x}$ is $f''(\bar{x}) = 0$, then the value of the function at this point, $f(\bar{x})$, will be

(i) a *stationary point of inflection* if $f'(\bar{x}) = 0$ and $f'''(\bar{x}) \neq 0$;
(ii) a *non-stationary point of inflection* if $f'(\bar{x}) \neq 0$ and $f'''(\bar{x}) \neq 0$.

Since the economic applications of points of inflection, given in Chapter 9, will only involve *non-stationary points of inflection*, the following worked examples will be restricted to the non-stationary inflection point case.

Examples of Non-Stationary Points of Inflection

8-7 Find the non-stationary point of inflection of the function $y = x^3 - 9x^2 + 30x$. Graph the functions $f(x), f'(x)$ and $f''(x)$, restricting the graph of $f(x)$ to the nonnegative quadrant.

SOLUTION Inflection point where $f''(x) = 0$, thus

$$f'(x) = 3x^2 - 18x + 30$$
$$f''(x) = 6x - 18 = 0 \quad \text{when} \quad x = \bar{x} = 3$$
$$f'''(x) = 6 > 0$$

Note that when $x = \bar{x} = 3$, $f(\bar{x}) = 36$, $f'(\bar{x}) = f'(3) = 3 > 0$, $f''(\bar{x}) = 0$, and $f'''(\bar{x}) > 0$ indicating that $y = f(x)$ has a non-stationary point of inflection at point (3, 36). Figure 8-12 graphs the functions $f(x), f'(x)$ and $f''(x)$. Let us examine how these graphs are obtained:

(i) $f(x)$ has a non-stationary point of inflection at (3, 36), which is plotted in Fig. 8-12a.
(ii) $f'(x)$ will have an extreme value at the point of inflection. Since $f''(x) = 0$ when $x = 3$ and $f'''(3) = 6 > 0$ then $f'(x)$ has a minimum value at point (3, 3) as shown in Fig. 8-12b. Also, $f'(0) = 30$, locating point (0, 30) in Fig. 8-12b. Utilizing this information about $f'(x)$ we can graph $f'(x)$ as shown in Fig. 8-12b.
(iii) $f''(x) = 6x - 18$ is readily graphed as shown in Fig. 8-12c.
(iv) From Fig. 8-12b we can see that $f'(x) > 0$ for all values of x. Consequently, $f(x)$ must be upward-sloping to the right.
(v) From Figs. 8-12b and 8-12c we can see that, for $x < 3$, $f'(x) > 0$ and $f''(x) < 0$. Hence, over this set of values of x, $f(x)$ is concave to the x axis as shown in Fig. 8-12a.
(vi) From Figs. 8-12b and 8-12c we can see that, for $x > 3$, $f'(x) > 0$ and $f''(x) > 0$. Thus, for $x > 3$, $f(x)$ is convex to the x axis as shown in Fig. 8-12a. Hence we have the particular shape of the non-stationary point of inflection as shown in Fig. 8-12a, with $f'''(\bar{x}) > 0$.

8-8 Find the non-stationary point of inflection of the function $y = -\frac{2}{3}x^3 + 10x^2$. Graph the functions $f(x), f'(x)$ and $f''(x)$, restricting the graph of $f(x)$ to the nonnegative quadrant.

8-3 POINTS OF INFLECTION

SOLUTION Inflection point where $f''(x) = 0$, thus
$$f'(x) = -2x^2 + 20x$$
$$f''(x) = -4x + 20 = 0 \quad \text{when} \quad x = \bar{x} = 5$$
$$f'''(x) = -4 < 0$$

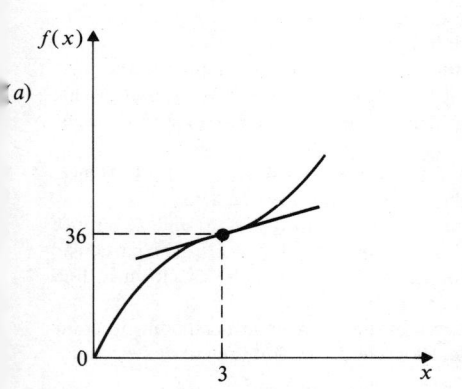

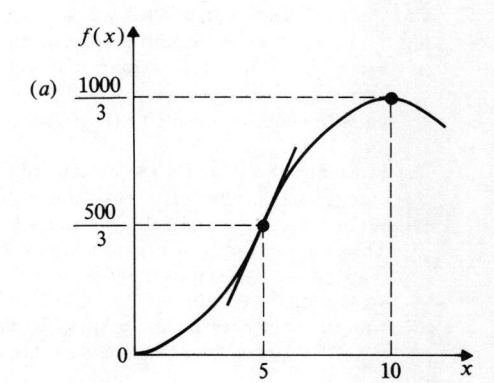

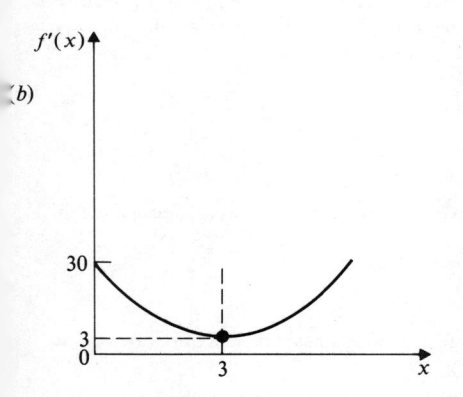

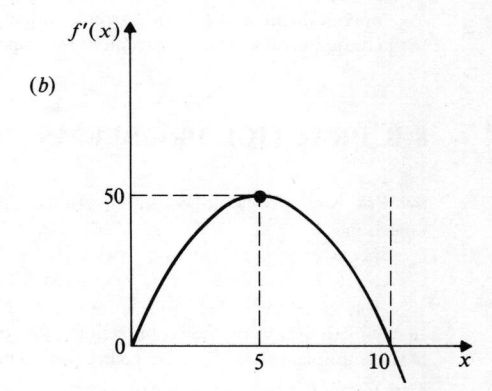

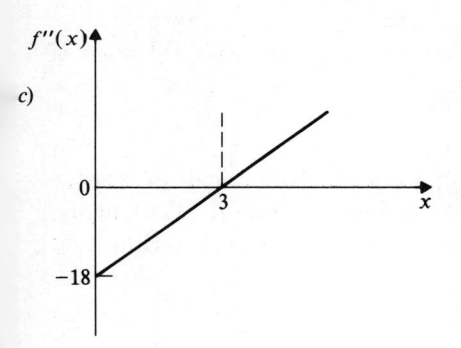

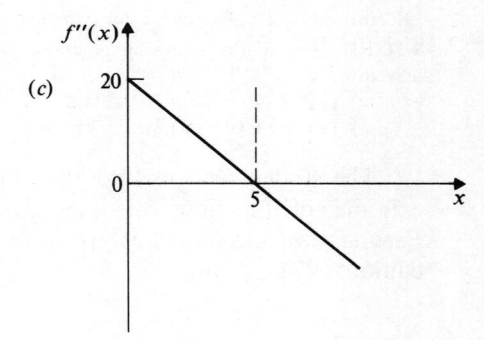

Figure 8-12

Figure 8-13

156 MAXIMIZATION AND MINIMIZATION

Note that when $x = \bar{x} = 5, f(\bar{x}) = \frac{500}{3}, f'(\bar{x}) = f'(5) = 50 > 0, f''(\bar{x}) = 0$, and $f'''(\bar{x}) < 0$ indicating that $y = f(x)$ has a non-stationary point of inflection at point $(5, \frac{500}{3})$. Figure 8-13 graphs the functions $f(x), f'(x)$ and $f''(x)$. Again let us examine how these graphs are obtained:

  (i) The non-stationary point of inflection $(5, \frac{500}{3})$ is plotted in Fig. 8-13a.
 (ii) $f'(x)$ has a maximum at $x = 5$ since $f''(5) = 0$ and $f'''(5) = -4 < 0$. Also, $f'(0) = 0$. The graph of $f'(x)$ will therefore be as shown in Fig. 8-13b.
(iii) $f''(x) = -4x + 20$ is readily graphed as shown in Fig. 8-13c.
 (iv) From Fig. 8-13b, $f'(x) > 0$ for $x < 10$ indicating that $f(x)$ is upward-sloping to the right over these values of x. For $x = 10, f'(x) = 0$ indicating that $f(x)$ is horizontal at this point. Finally, for $x > 10, f'(x) < 0$ indicating that $f(x)$ is downward-sloping to the right for $x > 10$.
  (v) From Figs. 8-13b and 8-13c we can see that, for $x < 5, f'(x) > 0$ and $f''(x) > 0$. Hence, over this set of values of $x, f(x)$ is convex to the x axis as shown in Fig. 8-13a.
 (vi) From Figs. 8-13b and 8-13c we can see that, for $5 < x < 10, f'(x) > 0$ and $f''(x) < 0$. Thus, for $5 < x < 10, f(x)$ is concave to the x axis as shown in Fig. 8-13a. The particular shape of the non-stationary point of inflection at $(5, \frac{500}{3})$ will thus be as shown in Fig. 8-13a, with $f'''(\bar{x}) < 0$.
(vii) Note that, in drawing the graphs, we have established a relative maximum at point $(10, \frac{1000}{3})$. To convince ourselves that this is so, let us check $f(x)$ for a relative extremum:

$$f'(x) = -2x^2 + 20x = 0 \quad \text{when} \quad x = 0 \text{ or } x = 10$$

$f''(x) = -4x + 20$, therefore when $x = 10, f''(10) = -20 < 0, \therefore y = f(x)$ has a relative maximum at $x = 10$, the extreme value being $f(10) = \frac{1000}{3}$. Therefore a function may contain both a relative extremum and a point of inflection.

8-B PRACTICE PROBLEMS

8-9 For each of the following functions, find the relative extreme values and points of inflection:

(a) $y = \frac{1}{3}x^3 - 3x^2 + 8x + 5$ (b) $y = -\frac{1}{3}x^3 + 4x^2 - 26x + 70$
(c) $y = x^3 - 3x + 3$ (d) $y = x^3 - 6x^2 + 9x + 6$
(e) $y = -\frac{1}{3}x^3 + 2x^2 - 4x + \frac{23}{3}$ (f) $y = 2x^3 - 3x^2 - 12x + 4$

In each case graph the function to illustrate your result. (If you have difficulty in drawing any of these graphs re-read Sec. 8-3 before proceeding.)

8-10 Given the function $y = ax^3 + bx^2 + cx + d$, find the values of x for which the function has points of inflection in the following cases:

(a) $a, b, c, d > 0$ and $b^2 < 3ac$ (b) $a, b, c, d > 0$ and $b^2 = 3ac$.

8-11 For each of the following functions, find the relative extreme values and points of inflection:

(a) $y = x^3 - 6x^2 + 9x + 20$ (b) $y = x^3 - 3x^2 + 4$
(c) $y = 3x^3 + 3x^2 + x + \frac{1}{9}$ (d) $y = \frac{2}{3}x^3 - 4x^2 + 6x + 5$

The student who is interested in a more general treatment of relative extrema of functions of one variable should consult A. C. Chiang, *Fundamental Methods of Mathematical Economics*, McGraw-Hill, 2nd edition, 1974, 9.5 and 9.6.

CHAPTER
NINE
ECONOMIC APPLICATIONS OF MAXIMIZATION AND MINIMIZATION

9-1 PROFIT MAXIMIZATION

One of the most obvious applications of maximization in economics is found in the analysis of profit maximization. In the theory of the firm the entrepreneur, or decision-maker, is often assumed to have the objective of profit maximization. Thus the entrepreneur is presented as choosing that output level which will maximize his profit. But this immediately raises the question as to how this profit-maximizing output level is determined. To answer this important question we will apply our knowledge of maximization to the analysis of profit maximization.

Let us define profit (π) as the difference between total revenue (R) and total cost (C):

$$\pi \equiv R - C \qquad (9\text{-}1)$$

Assuming that R and C are functions of output (Q) only, such that $R = R(Q)$ and $C = C(Q)$, then

$$\pi = \pi(Q) = R(Q) - C(Q) \qquad (9\text{-}2)$$

Equation (9-2) indicates that profit is a function of output. This profit function is known as the entrepreneur's *objective function*, since profit (the dependent variable) represents the object of maximization. Also, output (the independent variable) is known as the *choice variable*, since the output level is chosen with a view to maximizing profit.

To obtain the profit-maximizing output level we proceed as in the previous chapter. Firstly, we must satisfy the necessary, or first-order, condition for a maximum that $\pi'(Q) = 0$. Thus differentiating (9-2) with respect to Q, and equating the result to zero, we obtain

$$\pi'(Q) = R'(Q) - C'(Q) = 0 \quad \text{when} \quad R'(Q) = C'(Q) \tag{9-3}$$

Hence the profit-maximizing output ($\bar{Q}$) must satisfy (9-3) such that $\pi'(\bar{Q}) = R'(\bar{Q}) - C'(\bar{Q}) = 0$ or $R'(\bar{Q}) = C'(\bar{Q})$. The first-order condition for profit maximization therefore requires

$$R'(Q) = C'(Q) \quad \text{or} \quad MR = MC \tag{9-4}$$

Equation (9-4) is the familiar 'marginal revenue equals marginal cost' condition. Secondly, to ensure that $\bar{Q}$ represents a profit-maximizing output level we must satisfy the sufficient, or second-order, condition for a maximum that $\pi''(Q) < 0$ when $\pi'(Q) = 0$. Thus differentiating (9-3) with respect to Q, we obtain

$$\pi''(Q) = R''(Q) - C''(Q) < 0 \quad \text{when} \quad R''(Q) < C''(Q) \tag{9-5}$$

The second-order condition therefore requires that output $\bar{Q}$, which satisfies $R'(\bar{Q}) = C'(\bar{Q})$, must also satisfy $R''(\bar{Q}) < C''(\bar{Q})$ to establish it as a profit-maximizing output. In economic terms this means that if the rate of change of MR (given by $R''(Q) \equiv d(MR)/dQ$) is less than the rate of change of MC (given by $C''(Q) \equiv d(MC)/dQ$) at the output where $MR = MC$, then that output will maximize profit.

The first- and second-order conditions for profit maximization can be seen more clearly from an examination of the following figures.

Perfect Competition

Figure 9-1 depicts the revenue, cost and profit functions for a perfectly competitive firm.

Note that the total revenue function (R), in Fig. 9-1a, is a straight line through the origin since $R = R(Q) = \bar{P} \cdot Q$, where $\bar{P}$ is the given price, per unit output, which the price-taking perfectly competitive firm receives. The total cost function, $C = C(Q)$, is also shown in Fig. 9-1a.

The MC function, $MC = C'(Q)$, is presented in Fig. 9-1c. Note that the MC curve has a minimum at $Q = Q_3$, where the total cost function has a non-stationary point of inflection. The MR function, $MR = R'(Q) = \bar{P}$, and the AR function, $AR = R/Q = (\bar{P} \cdot Q)/Q = \bar{P}$, are also presented in Fig. 9-1c.

The profit function, $\pi = \pi(Q) = R(Q) - C(Q)$, is graphed in Fig. 9-1b. Note that Fig. 9-1b is obtained from Fig. 9-1a. Thus at output levels Q_2 and Q_4, where the R and C curves intersect to give $R = C$, π is zero. Where total

9-1 PROFIT MAXIMIZATION

revenue exceeds total cost, as is the case between output levels Q_2 and Q_4, π is positive. Where $R < C$, as is the case when $Q > Q_4$, or when Q lies between zero and Q_2, π is negative. Hence Fig. 9-1b is obtained by simply

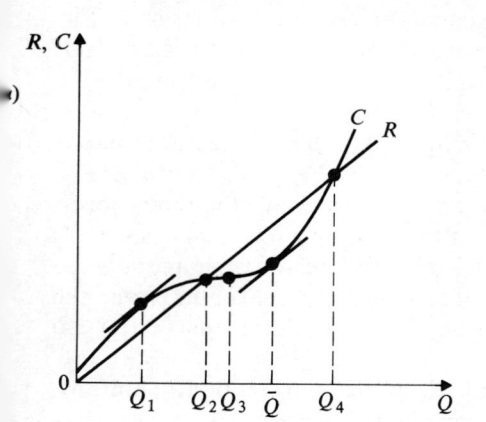

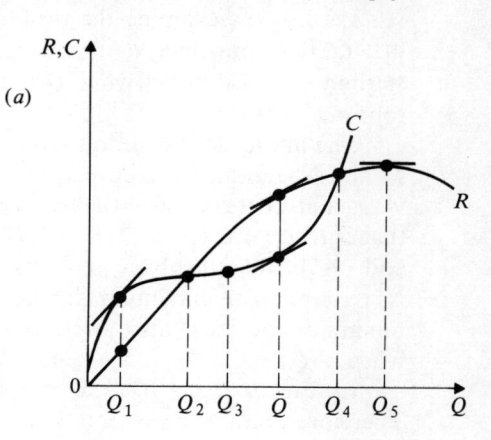

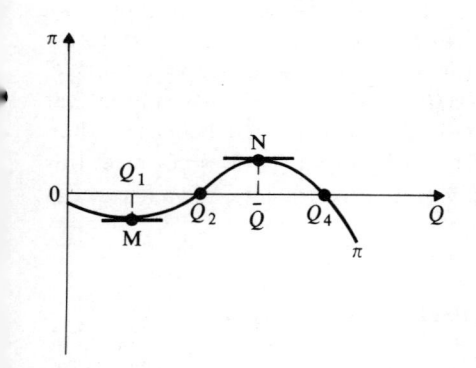

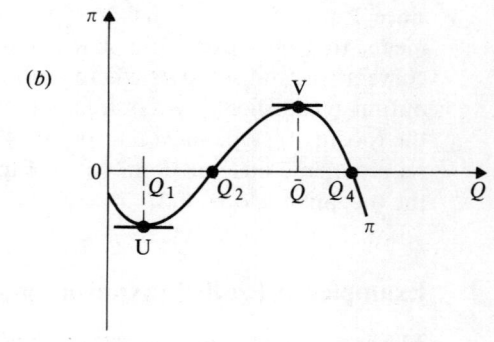

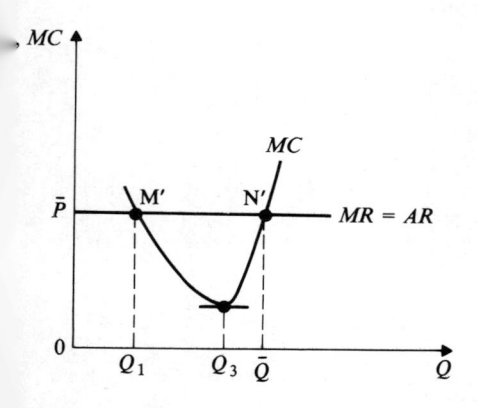

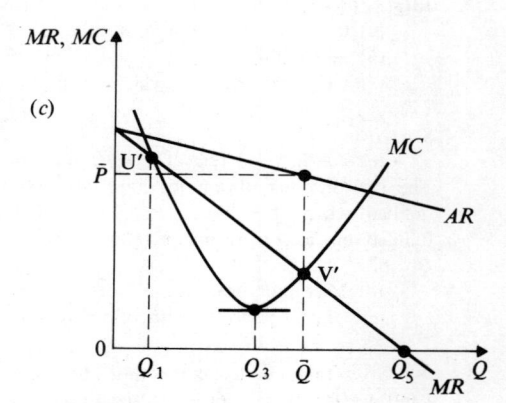

Figure 9-1

Figure 9-2

plotting the vertical distance between the R and C curves, in Fig. 9-1a, for each level of output. Also, substitution of $\bar{Q}$ into the profit function gives the maximum profit, $\pi(\bar{Q})$.

Let us now examine the profit-maximizing conditions in terms of Fig. 9-1, taking note that R, C and π are all in monetary units (e.g., pounds sterling or US dollars) while Q is in units of output per time period (e.g., tons per week).

The first-order condition required $\pi'(Q) = 0$, which is satisfied at points M and N, representing output levels Q_1 and $\bar{Q}$, in Fig. 9-1b. Notice, in Fig. 9-1a, that at these output levels the R and C curves have the same slopes, that is $R'(Q) = C'(Q)$ or $MR = MC$, as is required by $\pi'(Q) = 0$ in Eqs. (9-3) and (9-4). But a problem remains: M is clearly a relative minimum while N is a relative maximum. Thus, to distinguish the maximum from the minimum, we must also apply the second-order condition that $\pi''(Q) < 0$ when $\pi'(Q) = 0$.

In Fig. 9-1b, $\pi''(Q) < 0$ at point N, while $\pi''(Q) > 0$ at point M. Therefore point N represents a relative maximum while point M represents a relative minimum, as distinguished by the second-order condition. Also, since Eq. (9-5) shows that $\pi''(Q) < 0$ is equivalent to $R''(Q) < C''(Q)$, this means that the slope of the MR curve must be less than the slope of the MC curve at the output level where $MR = MC$. From Fig. 9-1c, we can see that output $\bar{Q}$ satisfies this requirement, the (zero) slope of MR being less than the (positive) slope of MC at point N'. Clearly output Q_1 does not meet this requirement, since at point M' in Fig. 9-1c the (zero) slope of MR exceeds the (negative) slope of MC.

Examples of Profit Maximization: Perfect Competition

9-1 Given that a perfectly competitive firm's total revenue and total cost functions are $R(Q) = 18Q$ and $C(Q) = Q^3 - 9Q^2 + 33Q + 10$, respectively, find:
  (a) the profit-maximizing output level
  (b) maximum profit
  (c) the price per unit at which this profit-maximizing output is sold.

SOLUTION
  (a) $\pi = R - C = 18Q - [Q^3 - 9Q^2 + 33Q + 10] = -Q^3 + 9Q^2 - 15Q - 10$
The first-order condition for a profit maximum is $\pi'(Q) = -3Q^2 + 18Q - 15 = 0$ which is fulfilled when $Q = 1$ or $Q = 5$. The second-order condition for a profit maximum is fulfilled only at $Q = 5$ where $\pi''(Q) = -6Q + 18 < 0$. Thus the profit-maximizing output level is $Q = 5$.
  (b) Maximum profit is $\pi(5) = 15$. Note that minimum profit is $\pi(1) = -17$.
  (c) Under perfect competition $R = \bar{P} \cdot Q$. Hence, in this case, $\bar{P} = R/Q = 18$ or $\bar{P} = AR = MR = 18$.

9-2 Given that a perfect competitor's total revenue and total cost functions are $R(Q) = 4Q$ and $C(Q) = \frac{2}{3}Q^3 - 10Q^2 + 36Q + 3$, respectively, find:

(a) the profit-maximizing output level
(b) maximum profit
(c) the price per unit at which this profit-maximizing output is sold.

SOLUTION

(a) $\pi = R - C = 4Q - [\frac{2}{3}Q^3 - 10Q^2 + 36Q + 3] = -\frac{2}{3}Q^3 + 10Q^2 - 32Q - 3$
$\pi'(Q) = -2Q^2 + 20Q - 32 = 0$ when $Q = 2$ or $Q = 8$
$\pi''(Q) = -4Q + 20 < 0$ when $Q = 8$

Thus the profit-maximizing output level is $Q = 8$.

(b) Maximum profit is $\pi(8) = 119/3$. Minimum profit is $\pi(2) = -97/3$.

(c) Under perfect competition $\bar{P} = AR = MR$. Hence, in this case, $\bar{P} = 4$.

Monopoly

Figure 9-2 depicts the revenue, cost and profit functions for a monopolist.

Note, as drawn in Fig. 9-2, that the cost functions are basically the same as those of the perfect competitor represented in Fig. 9-1. The total revenue function is, however, different. Under monopoly the producer faces a downward-sloping demand curve for his product. This means that the price per unit he receives will depend upon his level of output, as shown by his AR function in Fig. 9-2c. If this AR function is given by $P = P(Q) = a - bQ$ where $a, b > 0$, then the corresponding total revenue function will be $R = R(Q) = aQ - bQ^2$, as shown in Fig. 9-2a. The profit function in Fig. 9-2b is obtained once more by simply plotting the vertical distance between the R and C curves, in Fig. 9-2a, for each level of output.

The first-order condition for profit maximization requires $\pi'(Q) = 0$, which is satisfied at points U and V, representing output levels Q_1 and $\bar{Q}$, in Fig. 9-2b. This requirement is equivalently met by $MR = MC$ at points U' and V' in Fig. 9-2c. To distinguish between maximum and minimum profit we must now apply the second-order condition. In Fig. 9-2b, $\pi''(Q) < 0$ at point V, indicating that it is a relative maximum. Point U, with $\pi''(Q) > 0$, is a relative minimum. Hence $\bar{Q}$ is the profit-maximizing output level, and $\pi(\bar{Q})$ the maximum profit. Note that, at $Q = \bar{Q}$, the (positive) slope of MC exceeds the (negative) slope of MR, as shown by point V' in Fig. 9-2c.

Examples of Profit Maximization: Monopoly

9-3 A monopolist has the following total revenue and total cost functions: $R(Q) = 33Q - 4Q^2$ and $C(Q) = Q^3 - 9Q^2 + 36Q + 6$. Find:
   (a) his profit-maximizing output level
   (b) his maximum profit
   (c) his AR function
   (d) the price per unit at which this profit-maximizing output is sold.

SOLUTION

(a) $\pi = R - C = 33Q - 4Q^2 - [Q^3 - 9Q^2 + 36Q + 6]$
$= -Q^3 + 5Q^2 - 3Q - 6$

162 ECONOMIC APPLICATIONS OF MAXIMIZATION AND MINIMIZATION

The first-order condition for a profit maximum is $\pi'(Q) = -3Q^2 + 10Q - 3 = 0$ which is fulfilled when $Q = 1/3$ or $Q = 3$. The second-order condition for a profit maximum is fulfilled only at $Q = 3$ where $\pi''(Q) = -6Q + 10 < 0$. Thus the profit-maximizing output level is $Q = 3$.

    (b) Maximum profit is $\pi(3) = 3$.
    (c) Since $AR = R/Q$, the monopolist's AR function is $P = P(Q) = 33 - 4Q$.
    (d) Substituting the profit-maximizing output level into the AR function gives the price per unit of $P(3) = 33 - 4(3) = 21$.

9-4 A monopolist's total revenue function is $R(Q) = 20Q - 3Q^2$, and his total cost function is $C(Q) = 2Q^2$. Find:
    (a) his profit-maximizing output level
    (b) his maximum profit
    (c) his AR function
    (d) the price per unit at which this profit-maximizing output is sold.

SOLUTION
    (a) $\pi = R - C = 20Q - 3Q^2 - [2Q^2] = -5Q^2 + 20Q$
                $\pi'(Q) = -10Q + 20 = 0$ when $Q = 2$
                $\pi''(Q) = -10 < 0$
Thus the profit-maximizing output level is $Q = 2$.
    (b) Maximum profit is $\pi(2) = 20$.
    (c) The AR function is $P = P(Q) = 20 - 3Q$.
    (d) Price per unit is $P(2) = 20 - 3(2) = 14$.

9-2 REVENUE MAXIMIZATION

In the previous section the entrepreneur was presented as having the objective of profit maximization. An alternative objective, for an imperfectly competitive firm, is that of revenue maximization. Thus the management of such a firm may be envisaged as pursuing a (money) sales, rather than profit, goal. The management cannot, however, pursue revenue maximization irrespective of what happens to profit. Rather the firm must earn, at least, a certain amount of profits which is sufficient to satisfy its shareholders. The implications of such revenue maximization, subject to a profit constraint, can be best understood from an examination of Fig. 9-3. In Fig. 9-3a, the profit-maximizing and revenue-maximizing output levels are, respectively, Q_3 and Q_5. If we assume, for example, that the 'minimum' required profit level is $\pi \geqslant OK$, as shown in Fig. 9-3b, then the revenue-maximizing output level Q_5 can be attained since the profit at $Q = Q_5$, of OM, is more than sufficient to meet the profit constraint. If, however, the 'minimum' required profit level is $\pi \geqslant ON$, in Fig. 9-3b, then the revenue-maximizing output level Q_5 yields insufficient profit to satisfy shareholders. In this case output must be reduced to a level which is compatible with the 'minimum' profit constraint of $\pi \geqslant ON$. Since output levels ranging from Q_2 to Q_4 are compatible with this profit constraint, output Q_4 will then be produced as this gives the highest revenue which management can attain, subject to the 'minimum' profit constraint of $\pi \geqslant ON$.

(a)

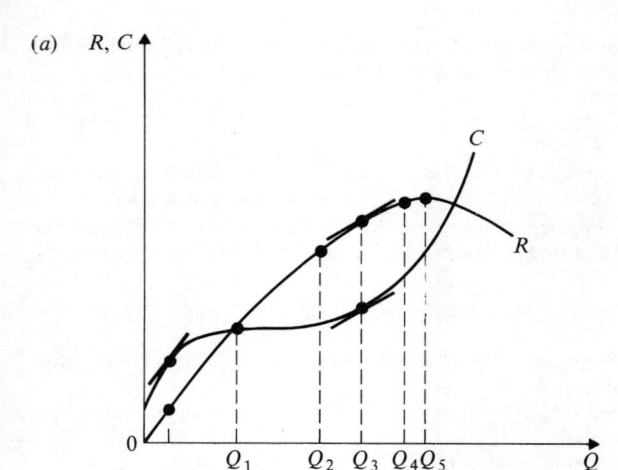

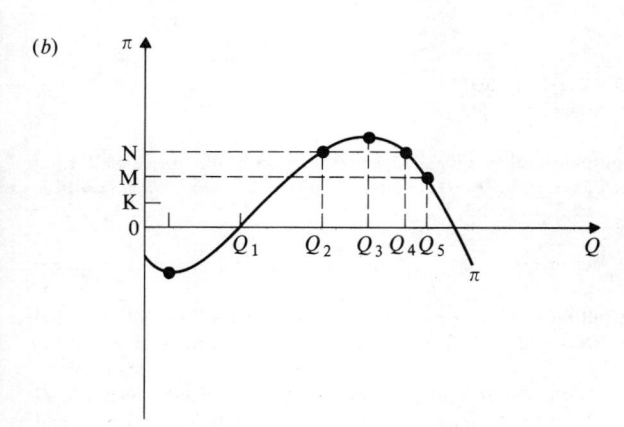

Figure 9-3

Examples of Revenue Maximization

9-5 A firm has a total revenue function $R(Q) = 20Q - Q^2$ and a total cost function $C(Q) = \frac{1}{3}Q^3 - 6Q^2 + 29Q + 15$. Find:

(a) the firm's profit-maximizing output level, and the corresponding values of profit, price and total revenue at this output level

(b) the revenue-maximizing output level, and the corresponding values of profit, price and total revenue at this output level

(c) whether or not the 'minimum' profit constraint of $\pi \geqslant 50$ will prevent the attainment of the revenue-maximizing output level.

SOLUTION

(a) $\quad \pi = R - C = 20Q - Q^2 - [\frac{1}{3}Q^3 - 6Q^2 + 29Q + 15]$
$\quad\quad\quad = -\frac{1}{3}Q^3 + 5Q^2 - 9Q - 15$
$\quad \pi'(Q) = -Q^2 + 10Q - 9 = 0 \quad \text{when} \quad Q = 1 \text{ or } Q = 9$
$\quad \pi''(Q) = -2Q + 10 < 0 \quad \text{when} \quad Q = 9$

164 ECONOMIC APPLICATIONS OF MAXIMIZATION AND MINIMIZATION

Thus the profit-maximizing output level is $Q = 9$. The values of profit, price and total revenue at $Q = 9$ are $\pi(9) = 66$, $P(9) = 20 - (9) = 11$ and $R(9) = 99$, respectively.

(b) $R(Q) = 20Q - Q^2$
$R'(Q) = 20 - 2Q = 0$ when $Q = 10$
$R''(Q) = -2 < 0$

Thus the revenue-maximizing output level is $Q = 10$. The values of profit, price and total revenue at $Q = 10$ are $\pi(10) = 185/3$, $P(10) = 20 - (10) = 10$, and $R(10) = 100$, respectively.

(c) Since profit at the revenue-maximizing output level is $\pi(10) = 185/3$, then the 'minimum' profit constraint of $\pi \geqslant 50$ does not prevent attainment of the revenue-maximizing output level.

9-6 A firm has a total revenue function $R(Q) = 10Q - 1.5Q^2$ and a total cost function $C(Q) = 1.5Q^2$. Find:

(a) the firm's profit-maximizing output level, and the corresponding values of profit, price and total revenue at this output level

(b) the revenue-maximizing output level, and the corresponding values of profit, price and total revenue at this output level

(c) whether or not the 'minimum' profit constraint of $\pi \geqslant 3$ will prevent the attainment of the revenue-maximizing output level.

SOLUTION

(a) $\pi = R - C = 10Q - 1.5Q^2 - [1.5Q^2] = 10Q - 3Q^2$
$\pi'(Q) = 10 - 6Q = 0$ when $Q = 5/3$
$\pi''(Q) = -6 < 0$

Thus the profit-maximizing output level is $Q = 5/3$. The values of profit, price and total revenue at $Q = 5/3$ are $\pi(5/3) = 25/3$, $P(5/3) = 10 - 1.5(5/3) = 7.5$, and $R(5/3) = 12.5$, respectively.

(b) $R(Q) = 10Q - 1.5Q^2$
$R'(Q) = 10 - 3Q = 0$ when $Q = 10/3$
$R''(Q) = -3 < 0$

Thus the revenue-maximizing output level is $Q = 10/3$. The values of profit, price and total revenue at $Q = 10/3$ are $\pi(10/3) = 0$, $P(10/3) = 10 - 1.5(10/3) = 5$, and $R(10/3) = 50/3$, respectively.

(c) Since profit at the revenue-maximizing output level is zero, the profit constraint of $\pi \geqslant 3$ will prevent attainment of the revenue-maximizing output level. If we set $\pi = 3$, and solve $\pi(Q)$ for Q, we can find the output levels which are just compatible with $\pi = 3$ (in the same way as Q_2 and Q_4, in Fig. 9-3b, are just compatible with $\pi = \overline{ON}$).

Thus $\pi = 3$ or $10Q - 3Q^2 = 3$

i.e. $-3Q^2 + 10Q - 3 = 0$

Solving for Q we obtain the two roots $Q = 1/3$ or $Q = 3$. Since $R(1/3) = 19/6$ and $R(3) = 33/2$, the highest revenue which can be achieved, subject to $\pi \geqslant 3$, is thus $R(3) = 33/2$ at output level $Q = 3$. The corresponding values of profit and price are $\pi(3) = 3$, and $P(3) = 10 - 1.5(3) = 5.5$, respectively.

9-3 REVENUE FROM TAXATION

Maximizing Excise-Tax Revenue from a Monopolist

A government may wish to levy an excise tax on the output of a monopolist in such a way as to maximize the tax revenue (T) from this source. The interesting question then posed is: what tax rate (t), in money terms per unit of output sold, should the government choose to ensure that tax revenue from the monopolist is maximized?

The tax revenue obtained by the government will depend upon the monopolist's level of output, $\bar{Q}$, *after* the imposition of the excise tax, since $T = t\bar{Q}$. Thus the first step is to find the monopolist's level of output after taxation. To do this, let us assume that the monopolist maximizes profit and that his total-revenue and total-cost functions are respectively

$$R = R(Q) = \alpha Q - \beta Q^2 \qquad (\alpha, \beta > 0)$$
$$C = C(Q) = aQ^2 + bQ + c \qquad (a, b, c > 0)$$

Before maximizing profit, we must allow for the effect of the excise tax on the monopolist's total cost. Hence the post-tax total-cost function is

$$C^T = C + tQ$$
$$= aQ^2 + bQ + c + tQ = aQ^2 + (b+t)Q + c$$

where tQ is the increase in total cost as a result of the tax, of t per unit output, being levied.

The profit function will therefore be

$$\pi = R - C^T = \alpha Q - \beta Q^2 - [aQ^2 + (b+t)Q + c]$$

To obtain the profit-maximizing output, $\bar{Q}$, we proceed as before:

$$\pi'(Q) = \alpha - 2\beta Q - 2aQ - (b+t) = 0$$
$$= \alpha - [2(\beta + a)]Q - (b+t) = 0 \quad \text{when}$$
$$\bar{Q} = \frac{\alpha - b - t}{2(\beta + a)}$$

Note that $\bar{Q}$ is the monopolist's profit-maximizing output *after* he has made allowance for the effect of the tax levy on his costs of production.

$$\pi''(Q) = -2(\beta + a) < 0 \text{ as required for a profit maximum.}$$

If we substitute the expression for $\bar{Q}$ into the tax-revenue function $T = t\bar{Q}$, we obtain

$$T = t\bar{Q} = \frac{t(\alpha - b - t)}{2(\beta + a)}$$
$$\text{or} \quad T = T(t) = \frac{(\alpha - b)t - t^2}{2(\beta + a)} \qquad (9\text{-}6)$$

Equation (9-6) indicates that the government's tax-revenue function is a function of t only. The government must then choose the value of t which will maximize the tax revenue from the monopolist. To find this value, $\bar{t}$, we maximize the tax-revenue function as follows:

$$T'(t) = \frac{(\alpha-b)-2t}{2(\beta+a)} = 0$$

when $(\alpha-b)-2t = 0$ or $\bar{t} = \frac{\alpha-b}{2}$

$$T''(t) = \frac{-2}{2(\beta+a)} = -\frac{1}{(\beta+a)} < 0$$

as required for a tax-revenue maximum. Thus to maximize tax revenue, from this monopolist, the government must levy an excise tax at the rate of $\bar{t} = (\alpha-b)/2$ per unit of output sold.

Examples of Maximizing Excise-Tax Revenue from a Monopolist

9-7 A monopolist has a total-revenue function of $R(Q) = 40Q - 4Q^2$, and a total-cost function of $C(Q) = 2Q^2 + 4Q + 10$. Find:
  (a) the tax rate, per unit of output sold, which will maximize government excise-tax revenue from this monopolist
  (b) the monopolist's maximum profit after the tax levy
  (c) the price per unit output at which the monopolist's profit-maximizing output is sold.

SOLUTION
(a) $\quad \pi = R - C^T = 40Q - 4Q^2 - [2Q^2 + 4Q + 10 + tQ]$
$\quad\quad\ = -6Q^2 + (36-t)Q - 10$

$\pi'(Q) = -12Q + 36 - t = 0 \quad$ when $\quad \bar{Q} = \dfrac{36-t}{12}$

$\pi''(Q) = -12 < 0$

Thus the monopolist's post-tax profit-maximizing output level is $\bar{Q} = (36-t)/12$.
Government tax revenue from this monopolist is
$$T = t\bar{Q} = (36t - t^2)/12$$

$$T'(t) = \frac{36-2t}{12} = 0 \quad \text{when} \quad 36 - 2t = 0 \text{ or } \bar{t} = 18$$

$$T''(t) = -\tfrac{1}{6} < 0$$

Thus the excise-tax rate which maximizes government tax revenue from this monopolist is $\bar{t} = 18$. When $\bar{t} = 18$, $\bar{Q} = 3/2$, and maximum tax revenue is $\bar{T} = \bar{t}\bar{Q} = 18(3/2) = 27$.
  (b) $\bar{\pi} = -6\bar{Q}^2 + (36-\bar{t})\bar{Q} - 10$ or $\bar{\pi} = -6(3/2)^2 + (36-18)(3/2) - 10 = 7/2$
Thus the monopolist's maximum profit after tax is $\pi(3/2) = 7/2$.
  (c) $\quad R = P \cdot Q = 40Q - 4Q^2$
$\quad\therefore\quad P = P(Q) = 40 - 4Q$
$\quad P(\bar{Q}) = P(3/2) = 40 - 4(3/2) = 34$

9-8 A monopolist faces a linear demand function given by $P = 30 - 3Q$. His total-cost function is given by $C(Q) = Q^2 + 2Q + 2$. If a tax of t per unit of output sold is imposed by the government on this monopolist, find:
  (a) the maximum tax revenue that can be obtained by such taxation
  (b) the monopolist's maximum profit after the tax levy
  (c) the price per unit output at which the monopolist's profit-maximizing output is sold.

9-3 REVENUE FROM TAXATION

SOLUTION
(a) $R = P \cdot Q = 30Q - 3Q^2$
$\pi = R - C^T = 30Q - 3Q^2 - [Q^2 + 2Q + 2 + tQ]$
$= -4Q^2 + (28-t)Q - 2$
$\pi'(Q) = -8Q + 28 - t = 0$ when $\bar{Q} = \dfrac{28-t}{8}$
$\pi''(Q) = -8 < 0$

Thus the monopolist's post-tax profit-maximizing output level is $\bar{Q} = (28-t)/8$. Government tax revenue from this monopolist is

$$T = t\bar{Q} = \dfrac{28t - t^2}{8}$$

$$T'(t) = \dfrac{28 - 2t}{8} = 0 \quad \text{when} \quad \bar{t} = 14$$

$$T''(t) = -\tfrac{1}{4} < 0$$

Thus the excise-tax rate which maximizes government tax revenue from this monopolist is $\bar{t} = 14$. When $\bar{t} = 14$, $\bar{Q} = 7/4$. Maximum tax revenue, in this case, is $\bar{T} = \bar{t}\bar{Q} = 14(7/4) = 49/2$.

(b) $\bar{\pi} = -4\bar{Q}^2 + (28 - \bar{t})\bar{Q} - 2$
$= -4(7/4)^2 + (28 - 14)(7/4) - 2 = 41/4$

Thus the monopolist's maximum profit after tax is $\pi(7/4) = 41/4$.

(c) $P(\bar{Q}) = P(7/4) = 30 - 3(7/4) = 99/4$.

9-9 (a) For the case given in Example 9-8, find the monopolist's maximum profit before the tax levy
(b) also graph the AR, MR, and MC (before and after tax) functions for this case.

SOLUTION
(a) $\pi = R - C = 30Q - 3Q^2 - [Q^2 + 2Q + 2]$
$= -4Q^2 + 28Q - 2$
$\pi'(Q) = -8Q + 28 = 0$ when $\bar{Q} = 7/2$
$\pi''(Q) = -8 < 0$ as required for a profit maximum.

Thus the monopolist's maximum profit before tax is

$\pi(\bar{Q}) = -4\bar{Q}^2 + 28\bar{Q} - 2$
$= -4(7/2)^2 + 28(7/2) - 2 = 47$

(b) $R(Q) = 30Q - 3Q^2$ Also $C(Q) = Q^2 + 2Q + 2$
$\therefore$ $AR = 30 - 3Q$ $\therefore$ $MC = C'(Q) = 2Q + 2$
and $MR = 30 - 6Q$

Similarly $C^T = Q^2 + 2Q + 2 + tQ$ and $MC^T = 2Q + 2 + t = 2Q + 16$ when $\bar{t} = 14$.

Figure 9-4 graphs the AR, MR, MC and MC^T functions. Note that the effect of the excise tax is to decrease output (from 7/2 to 7/4) and hence increase price (from 39/2 to 99/4).

Maximizing Excise-Tax Revenue in a Competitive Market

Let us assume a competitive market of the following form:

$$Q_d = a - bP \quad (a, b > 0)$$
$$Q_s = -c + dP \quad (c, d > 0)$$
$$Q_d = Q_s$$

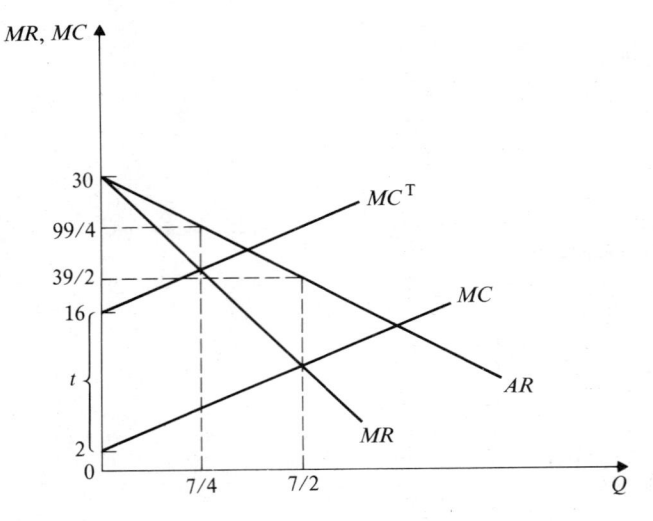

168 ECONOMIC APPLICATIONS OF MAXIMIZATION AND MINIMIZATION

Figure 9-4

If the government imposes a tax of t per unit of output sold, the post-tax supply function will be

$$Q_s = -c + dP^T \quad \text{where} \quad P^T = P - t$$

This means, in the post-tax situation, that for each unit of output sold the producers receive the market price for the good *minus* the amount of the tax. If no tax is levied then the producers receive the whole market price at which the good is sold.

As in the previous monopoly case, the interesting question which arises is: what tax rate, in money terms per unit of output sold, should the government levy to maximize its tax revenue from taxing this good? To answer this question we first need to know the equilibrium quantity ($\bar{Q}$) of the good produced after taxation. To find this we equate Q_d and Q_s in the post-tax situation and solve for $\bar{Q}$:

$$Q_d = Q_s$$

or

$$a - bP = -c + d(P - t)$$

which rearranges as

$$a + c + dt = (d + b)P$$

whence

$$\bar{P} = \frac{a+c}{d+b} + \frac{d}{d+b} t$$

Substituting for $\bar{P}$ in Q_d (or Q_s) we obtain

$$\bar{Q} = \bar{Q}_d (= \bar{Q}_s) = a - b\bar{P} = a - b\left[\frac{a+c}{d+b} + \frac{d}{d+b} t\right]$$

which rearranges to

$$\bar{Q} = \frac{ad-bc}{d+b} - \frac{bd}{d+b}t$$

If we substitute the expression for $\bar{Q}$ into the tax-revenue function, $T = t\bar{Q}$, we obtain

$$T = t\bar{Q} = t\frac{[ad-bc-bdt]}{d+b}$$

or

$$T = T(t) = \frac{(ad-bc)t - bdt^2}{d+b}$$

The value of t which maximizes government tax revenue can then be obtained by maximizing the tax-revenue function as follows:

$$T'(t) = \frac{(ad-bc) - 2bdt}{d+b} = 0$$

when

$$(ad-bc) = 2bdt \quad \text{or} \quad \bar{t} = \frac{ad-bc}{2bd}$$

$$T''(t) = -\frac{2bd}{d+b} < 0$$

as required for a tax-revenue maximum. Thus, to maximize tax revenue from the taxation of this good, the government must levy an excise tax at the rate of $\bar{t} = (ad-bc)/2bd$ per unit of output sold.

Examples of Maximizing Excise-Tax Revenue in a Competitive Market

9-10 Given a competitive market of the following form:

$$Q_d = 18 - 2P$$
$$Q_s = -2 + 2P$$
$$Q_d = Q_s$$

if the government now decides to levy a tax of t per unit of output sold, what value should t be in order to maximize government tax revenue from the taxation of this good?

SOLUTION The post-tax supply function will be

$$Q_s = -2 + 2P^1 \quad \text{where} \quad P^1 = P - t$$

Equilibrium quantity ($\bar{Q}$) in the post-tax situation is found as follows:

$$Q_d = Q_s$$
$$18 - 2P = -2 + 2(P - t)$$

or

$$\bar{P} = \frac{20 + 2t}{4}$$

Substituting for $\bar{P}$ in Q_d (or Q_s) we obtain

$$\bar{Q} = \bar{Q}_d(=\bar{Q}_s) = 18 - 2\bar{P} \quad \text{or} \quad \bar{Q} = 18 - 2\left(\frac{20+2t}{4}\right) = 8 - t$$

Substituting the expression for $\bar{Q}$ into the tax-revenue function gives

$$T = t\bar{Q} = 8t - t^2$$
$$\text{or} \quad T = T(t) = 8t - t^2$$

By maximizing the tax-revenue function $T(t)$ we obtain the value of t which will maximize

$$T'(t) = 8 - 2t = 0 \quad \text{when} \quad \bar{t} = 4$$
$$T''(t) = -2 < 0$$

as required for a tax-revenue maximum. Thus $t = 4$ is the tax rate which will maximize government tax revenue. When $\bar{t} = 4$, $\bar{T} = T(\bar{t}) = 16$.

9-11 (a) For the case given in Example 9-10, find the equilibrium price and quantity values before and after the tax levy

(b) also, for this case, graph the demand and supply functions for both the pre-tax and post-tax situations.

SOLUTION

(a) $\quad Q_d = Q_s$
$\quad 18 - 2P = -2 + 2P$
$\quad \therefore \quad \bar{P} = 5 \qquad$ Also $\bar{Q} = \bar{Q}_d(=\bar{Q}_s) = 18 - 2\bar{P} = 8$

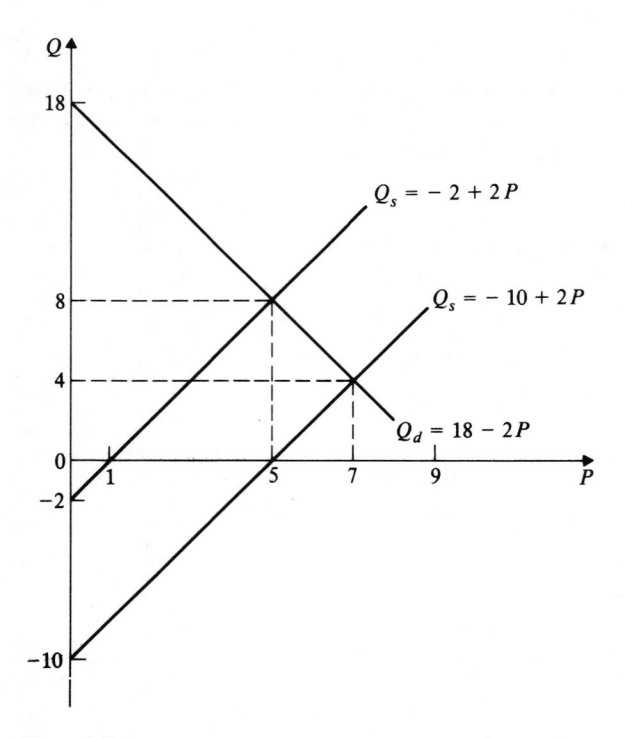

Figure 9-5

Thus the *pre-tax* equilibrium price and quantity values are $\bar{P} = 5$ and $\bar{Q} = 8$. In Example 9-10 we found $\bar{t} = 4$, hence

$$\bar{P} = \frac{20 + 2\bar{t}}{4} = 7 \quad \text{and} \quad \bar{Q} = 8 - \bar{t} = 4$$

Thus the *post-tax* equilibrium price and quantity values are $\bar{P} = 7$ and $\bar{Q} = 4$.

(b) When $\bar{t} = 4$, the post-tax supply function is $Q_s = -2 + 2(P - \bar{t}) = -10 + 2P$. The required graphs are given in Fig. 9-5. Note that, as a result of the tax levy, equilibrium price has risen and equilibrium quantity has fallen.

9-4 THE THEORY OF PRODUCTION

We can also use our knowledge of relative extrema and points of inflection to gain insights into particular aspects of the theory of production. To demonstrate this we shall examine the short-run analysis of production, where the production process involves fixed inputs and only *one* variable input, labour services. In this case the production function can be written as

$$Q = g(L) \tag{9-7}$$

which states that output (Q) is a function of the single variable input, labour services (L).

The production function presented in Eq. (9-7) has no particular form, it is simply stated in general terms. Clearly, however, the production function must be restricted in certain ways so as to make economic sense. For example, the production (or total product) function graphed in Fig. 9-6a is restricted to a particular form so as to embody a particular economic meaning. Similarly, the average product $(AP = Q/L)$ and marginal product $(MP = g'(L))$ functions, in Fig. 9-6b, embody a particular economic meaning that should be familiar to economics students. Thus, in Fig. 9-6b, the MP curve embodies the principle or law of diminishing marginal physical product: as the quantity of the variable input (L) is increased, other inputs being held constant or fixed, a point is reached $(L = \bar{L})$ beyond which marginal product (MP) declines.

The discussion of Fig. 9-6 raises several interesting questions. For example, if we wanted to represent a short-run total product function by a cubic function, how should we restrict the coefficients of the cubic function so as to make economic sense? Also, why do the MP and AP functions have the particular relationship as shown in Fig. 9-6b? We can now use our knowledge of relative extrema and points of inflection to answer these questions.

Restricting the Coefficients of a Cubic Total Product Function

Suppose that we wish to represent a short-run total product function by a cubic function of the following form:

$$Q = g(L) = aL^3 + bL^2 + cL + d \tag{9-8}$$

172 ECONOMIC APPLICATIONS OF MAXIMIZATION AND MINIMIZATION

Clearly, to make economic sense, we must restrict the coefficients a, b, c, and d in certain ways. To see how this may be done, we will first examine the necessary restriction on the coefficient d. Thus, when labour input is zero, we expect output to be zero, that is,

$$g(0) = d = 0$$

Therefore economic sense would require $d = 0$, as is the case in Fig. 9-6a.

To see what restrictions are required on the coefficients a, b and c, let us examine Fig. 9-6b. Firstly, notice that when $L = 0$, $MP = 0$. Therefore the particular production function presented in Fig. 9-6a requires $MP = 0$

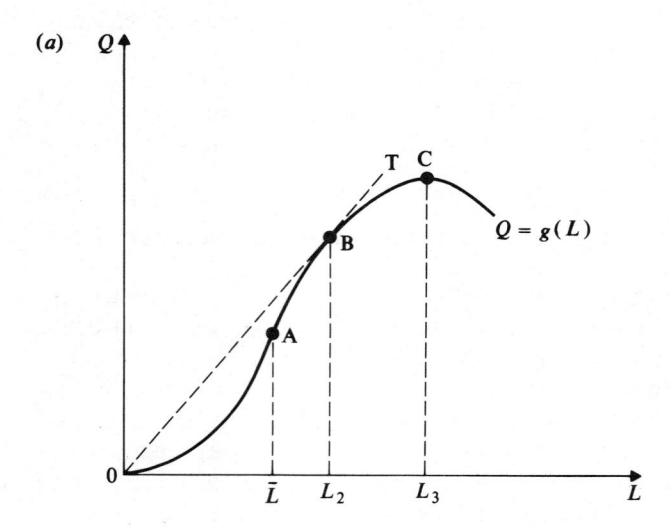

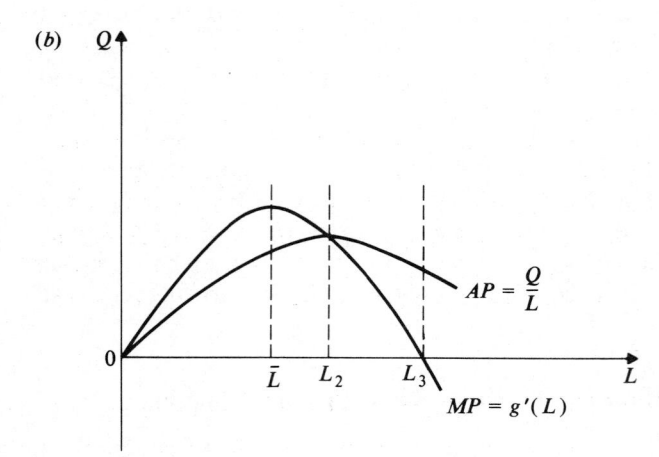

Figure 9-6

when $L = 0$. Since the MP function in this case is
$$MP = g'(L) = 3aL^2 + 2bL + c$$
then
$$g'(0) = c = 0$$

Thus we have another restriction of $c = 0$, which implies that Eq. (9-8) will be of form $Q = aL^3 + bL^2$.

A further examination of Fig. 9-6b reveals that the MP curve has an inverse U-shape, with its (sole) maximum value occurring in the first quadrant. Consequently, we must restrict the coefficients a and b so that the *absolute maximum* (which is identical with the sole relative maximum) of the MP function is *positive*, as in Fig. 9-6b. Hence, from our knowledge of relative extrema, the maximum of MP will occur where

$$\frac{d(MP)}{dL} = g''(L) = 6aL + 2b = 0$$

and

$$\frac{d^2(MP)}{dL^2} = g'''(L) = 6a < 0$$

The first-order condition, $g''(L) = 0$, is satisfied when $L = \bar{L} = -b/3a$. To fulfil the second-order condition we require the restriction of $a < 0$. Also, since we expect $\bar{L} > 0$, we require the restriction that $b > 0$.

The next step is to substitute $\bar{L}$ into the MP function in order to check that $g'(\bar{L}) > 0$. The maximum level of MP, assuming $c = 0$, is

$$MP_{\max} = g'(\bar{L}) = g'\left(-\frac{b}{3a}\right) = 3a\left(-\frac{b}{3a}\right)^2 + 2b\left(-\frac{b}{3a}\right) = -\frac{b^2}{3a} > 0$$

Thus our restrictions, of $a < 0$ and $b > 0$, ensure that the absolute maximum of the MP function is positive, as in Fig. 9-6b.

The above analysis leaves us with the production function

$$Q = g(L) = aL^3 + bL^2 \quad \text{where} \quad a < 0, b > 0 \qquad (9\text{-}9)$$

From this production function we can derive a MP function which has the characteristics shown in Fig. 9-6b.

As a final point, notice that the total product function, in Fig. 9-6a, has a maximum value at $L = L_3$. This raises the question: does our production function in Eq. (9-9) possess such a maximum? To answer this question, let us find its maximum as follows:

$$g'(L) = 3aL^2 + 2bL = 0$$

when

$$L = 0 \quad \text{or} \quad L = -\frac{2b}{3a}$$

$$g''(L) = 6aL + 2b < 0 \quad \text{when} \quad L = -\frac{2b}{3a}$$

Thus the total product function has a maximum at $L = -2b/3a$, which is equivalent to $L = L_3$ in Fig. 9-6a. Note also that $g'(L) = 0$ when $L = 0$ and when $L = -2b/3a$, which are equivalent, respectively, to $L = 0$ and $L = L_3$ in Fig. 9-6b. Finally, before proceeding, it should be noted that our restrictions apply only to the *particular* production function shown in Fig. 9-6a.

Relation between AP and MP

An examination of Fig. 9-6b indicates that the MP curve passes through the maximum point of the AP curve. This particular relationship between MP and AP can be explained in terms of Fig. 9-6a. Thus, when $L = L_2$, the tangent slope (or $g'(L) = MP$) at this point is given by the slope of the ray OT. But the slope of OT is the same as the slope of the ray OB, which measures the average product of labour (Q/L) when $L = L_2$. Hence, when $L = L_2$, $MP = AP$. Also, from Fig. 9-6a, it is clear that the ray OB has the greatest slope of any ray from the origin to a point on the total product curve. This indicates that AP has a maximum value at $L = L_2$.

The relation between AP and MP can also be demonstrated in mathematical terms. Thus if we find the maximum of the AP function, we can then check if $AP = MP$ at that maximum point. From Eq. (9-7) the production function is $Q = g(L)$ and the AP function is

$$AP = \frac{Q}{L} = \frac{g(L)}{L}$$

To find the maximum AP, we obtain the first- and second-order conditions for a maximum as before:

$$\frac{d(AP)}{dL} = \frac{d\left[\frac{g(L)}{L}\right]}{dL} = \frac{L \cdot g'(L) - g(L)}{L^2} = 0 \quad \text{(quotient rule)}$$

when
$$L \cdot g'(L) = g(L) \quad \text{or} \quad g'(L) = \frac{g(L)}{L}$$

Thus the first-order condition for maximum AP is

$$g'(L) = \frac{g(L)}{L} \quad \text{or} \quad MP = AP$$

$$\frac{d^2(AP)}{dL^2} = \frac{L^2[L \cdot g''(L) + g'(L) - g'(L)] - [L \cdot g'(L) - g(L)](2L)}{L^4}$$

(quotient and product rules)

$$= \frac{g''(L)}{L} - \frac{2g'(L)}{L^2} + \frac{2g(L)}{L^3}$$

Substituting the first-order condition that $L \cdot g'(L) = g(L)$, we have

$$\frac{d^2(AP)}{dL^2} = \frac{g''(L)}{L} - \frac{2g'(L)}{L^2} + \frac{2Lg'(L)}{L^3}$$

$$= \frac{g''(L)}{L} < 0 \quad \text{for maximum } AP.$$

Since we expect $L > 0$, at maximum AP, then the second-order condition for maximum AP requires

$$g''(L) < 0 \quad \text{or} \quad \frac{d(MP)}{dL} < 0$$

Therefore, at the point where AP is a maximum, $AP = MP$ and the slope of the MP curve is negative, as shown in Fig. 9-6b.

A further examination of Fig. 9-6b indicates that not only is $MP = AP$ at $L = L_2$, but also that $MP \gtrless AP$ depending upon whether $L \lessgtr L_2$. This relationship can be explained in terms of Fig. 9-6a. For example, at point A, the tangent slope (or MP) is clearly greater than the slope of a ray OA (which measures AP at point A), indicating that $MP > AP$ when $L = \bar{L}$. Also, at point C, the (zero) tangent slope is clearly less than the slope of a ray OC, indicating that $MP < AP$ when $L = L_3$.

This relation, between the MP and AP curves, can also be demonstrated in mathematical terms. Thus

$$MP = \frac{dQ}{dL} = \frac{d[AP \cdot L]}{dL} = AP + L\frac{d(AP)}{dL} \qquad (9\text{-}10)$$

Equation (9-10) provides us with a relation between MP, AP, and the slope of the AP curve. Utilizing this equation we can state the following:

1. When $d(AP)/dL \gtrless 0$, then $MP \gtrless AP$. For example, this is the case when $L = \bar{L}$ and $L = L_3$, respectively, in Fig. 9-6b.
2. When $d(AP)/dL = 0$, then $MP = AP$. This is the case when $L = L_2$ in Fig. 9-6b.

Examples from the Theory of Production

9-12 A firm has the following short-run production function:

$$Q = g(L) = -\tfrac{2}{3}L^3 + 10L^2$$

(a) Does this production function fulfil the coefficient restrictions derived above?
(b) Derive the AP function and show that, where AP is a maximum, $MP = AP$.
(c) Find the value of L for which total product is a maximum. Also, find the maximum total product value.

SOLUTION
(a) The cubic total product function of form

$$Q = aL^3 + bL^2$$

required the restrictions $a < 0$ and $b > 0$. These restrictions are fulfilled in this case since $a = -\frac{2}{3}$ and $b = 10$.

(b) $AP = \dfrac{g(L)}{L} = -\frac{2}{3}L^2 + 10L$

To find maximum AP:

$$\frac{d(AP)}{dL} = -\frac{4}{3}L + 10 = 0 \quad \text{when} \quad L = \frac{15}{2}$$

$$\frac{d^2(AP)}{dL^2} = -\frac{4}{3} < 0 \quad \text{as required for an } AP \text{ maximum.}$$

Thus AP has a maximum value when $L = \frac{15}{2}$. This maximum value is

$$AP = -\frac{2}{3}(\tfrac{15}{2})^2 + 10(\tfrac{15}{2}) = \tfrac{75}{2}$$

The MP function is

$$MP = g'(L) = -2L^2 + 20L$$
$$g'(\tfrac{15}{2}) = -2(\tfrac{15}{2})^2 + 20(\tfrac{15}{2}) = \tfrac{75}{2}$$

Hence, when $L = \frac{15}{2}$, AP has a maximum and $MP = AP$.

(c) To find maximum total product:

$$g'(L) = -2L^2 + 20L = 0 \quad \text{when } L = 0 \text{ or } L = 10$$
$$g''(L) = -4L + 20 < 0 \quad \text{when } L = 10$$

Thus total product is a maximum when $L = 10$. The maximum value of total product is

$$g(10) = -\tfrac{2}{3}(10)^3 + 10(10)^2 = \tfrac{1000}{3}$$

9-13 (a) Demonstrate, using the production function given in Example 9-12, that the total product function has a non-stationary point of inflection at that value of L for which MP is a maximum.

(b) Find the maximum value of MP for this case.

(c) Also, for this case, find the range of values of L for which $d(AP)/dL \gtreqless 0$. Select L values from within this range to demonstrate that when

$$\frac{d(AP)}{dL} \gtreqless 0, MP \gtreqless AP$$

SOLUTION

(a) To find maximum MP:

$$MP = g'(L) = -2L^2 + 20L$$

$$\frac{d(MP)}{dL} = g''(L) = -4L + 20 = 0 \quad \text{when} \quad L = 5$$

$$\frac{d^2(MP)}{dL^2} = g'''(L) = -4 < 0 \quad \text{as required for a } MP \text{ maximum.}$$

Thus the MP function has a maximum at $L = 5$. Note, in obtaining this result, that $g''(5) = 0$, while $g'(5) = 50 \ne 0$ and $g'''(5) = -4 \ne 0$. Hence, by definition, the total product function, $g(L)$, has a non-stationary point of inflection at $L = 5$.

(b) Maximum MP is $g'(5) = 50$

(c) $\dfrac{d(AP)}{dL} = -\tfrac{4}{3}L + 10 \gtreqless 0 \quad \text{as} \quad L \lesseqgtr \tfrac{15}{2}$

Selecting L values within this range gives the following results:

(i) When $L = 6$, $MP = -2(6)^2 + 20(6) = 48$, $AP = -\frac{2}{3}(6)^2 + 10(6) = 36$. Thus when $L = 6$, $d(AP)/dL > 0$ and $MP > AP$.

(ii) When $L = \frac{15}{2}$, $MP = -2(\tfrac{15}{2})^2 + 20(\tfrac{15}{2}) = \tfrac{75}{2}$, $AP = -\tfrac{2}{3}(\tfrac{15}{2})^2 + 10(\tfrac{15}{2}) = \tfrac{75}{2}$. Thus when $L = \tfrac{15}{2}$, $d(AP)/dL = 0$ and $MP = AP$.

(iii) When $L = 9$, $MP = -2(9)^2 + 20(9) = 18$, $AP = -\frac{2}{3}(9)^2 + 10(9) = 36$. Thus when $L = 9$, $d(AP)/dL < 0$ and $MP < AP$.

9-5 THE THEORY OF COST

In the previous discussion of the theory of production, we analysed the relation between inputs and output in terms of the production function. In this section we shall analyse the relation between the cost of production and output.

Let us assume that a firm's short-run total cost function is given by

$$C = C(Q) \tag{9-11}$$

which states that total cost (C) is a function of the level of output (Q). If we substitute the production function of Eq. (9-7) into Eq. (9-11) we obtain

$$C = C(Q) = C[g(L)] \tag{9-12}$$

Equation (9-12) indicates that cost is a function of output which, in turn, is a function of labour input. This equation makes it clear that costs of production arise because output requires inputs and inputs cost money.

The total cost function presented in Eq. (9-11) has no particular form, it is simply stated in general terms. Consequently, to make economic sense, the total cost function must be restricted in certain ways. For example, the total cost function graphed in Fig. 9-7a is restricted to a particular form so as to embody a particular economic meaning. Similarly, the average total cost ($ATC = C/Q$) and marginal cost ($MC = C'(Q)$) functions in Fig. 9-7b embody a particular economic meaning that is common to economics textbooks.

An examination of Fig. 9-7 will help us to appreciate the particular economic meaning embodied in the graphs. For example, in Fig. 9-7a, the total cost function is monotonically increasing, that is, cost always increases as output increases. This means, in Fig. 9-7b, that MC will always be positive. Also, in Fig. 9-7b, the MC curve is seen to be U-shaped. To understand the reason for this U-shape will, however, require some further analysis.

Let us assume that the labour market is perfectly competitive and that the short-run total cost of production is given by

$$C = \bar{w}L + F \tag{9-13}$$

where $\bar{w}$ is the given wage rate of the labour input, L is the number of units of labour input, and F is the fixed costs associated with the fixed inputs. Equation (9-13) permits us to find MC as follows:

$$MC = \frac{dC}{dQ} = \frac{dC}{dL}\frac{dL}{dQ} = \bar{w}\frac{dL}{dQ} = \frac{\bar{w}}{MP} \quad \text{(chain rule)} \tag{9-14}$$

(a)

(b)

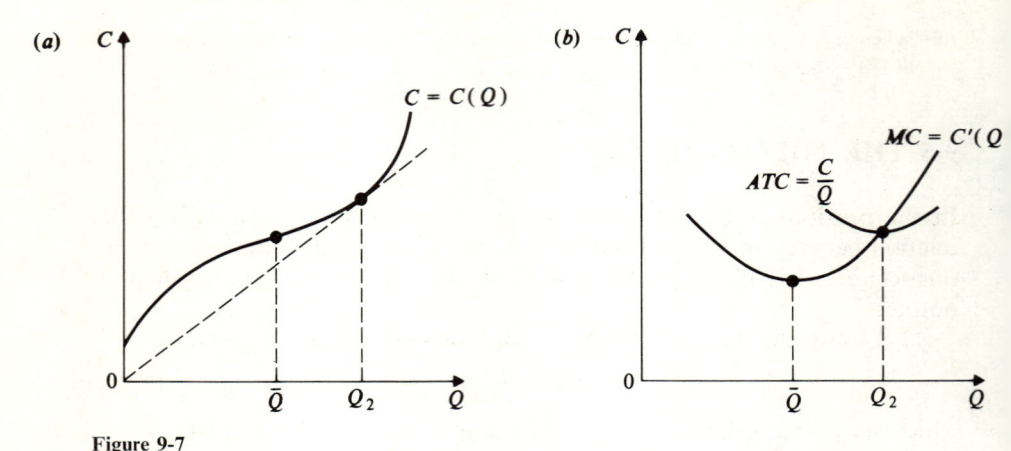

Figure 9-7

Equation (9-14) states that MC is equal to the wage rate divided by MP. This equation provides us with an important link between MC and MP. Since $\bar{w}$ is given, MC will vary inversely with MP. Consequently, we can explain the U-shape of the MC curve in terms of Eq. (9-14) as follows:

1. When MP is increasing in value, MC will be decreasing in value.
2. When MP is at its (sole) maximum, MC is at its (sole) minimum.
3. When MP is decreasing in value, in accordance with the law of diminishing marginal physical product, MC will be increasing in value.

In other words, given the wage rate $\bar{w}$, the shape of the MC curve depends on the shape of the underlying MP curve. This indicates clearly the important relation between the theory of production and the theory of cost. Behind the short-run total cost function, in Fig. 9-7a, lies a short-run production function like that presented in Fig. 9-6a.

The discussion of Fig. 9-7 raises the interesting question: if we wish to represent a short-run total cost function by a cubic function, how should we restrict the coefficients of the cubic function so as to make economic sense? To answer this question we can, once more, use our knowledge of relative extrema and points of inflection. Also, we can analyse why the MC and ATC curves have the particular relationship as shown in Fig. 9-7b.

Restricting the Coefficients of a Cubic Total Cost Function

Suppose that we wish to represent a short-run total cost function by a cubic function of the form

$$C = C(Q) = aQ^3 + bQ^2 + cQ + d \tag{9-15}$$

As in the case of the cubic production function, the coefficients a, b, c, and d will have to be restricted in certain ways so as to make economic sense. For example, the restriction on the coefficient d can be readily obtained since d represents fixed cost and will therefore be positive:

$$C(0) = d > 0$$

To see what restrictions should be placed on the coefficients a, b and c, let us examine Fig. 9-7. In Fig. 9-7a we noted that the total cost function is monotonically increasing or, in Fig. 9-7b, that MC will always be positive. Clearly if MC is U-shaped, with its minimum point in the first quadrant, then MC will always be positive. Consequently, we must restrict the coefficients a, b and c so that the *absolute minimum* (which is identical with the sole relative minimum) of the MC function is *positive*, as in Fig. 9-7b. To do this we must first find where the minimum of MC will occur. Since

$$MC = C'(Q) = 3aQ^2 + 2bQ + c$$

then

$$\frac{d(MC)}{dQ} = C''(Q) = 6aQ + 2b = 0 \quad \text{when} \quad Q = -\frac{b}{3a}$$

and

$$\frac{d^2(MC)}{dQ^2} = C'''(Q) = 6a > 0 \quad \text{when} \quad a > 0$$

Thus the MC function will have a minimum value at $Q = \bar{Q} = -b/3a$. Note that, in order to ensure $C'''(Q) > 0$, we require the restriction $a > 0$. Also note that, since we expect $\bar{Q} > 0$, we require the restriction $b < 0$.

The next step is to substitute $\bar{Q}$ into the MC function in order to check that $C'(\bar{Q}) > 0$. Thus the minimum level of MC is

$$MC_{\min} = C'(\bar{Q}) = 3a\left(-\frac{b}{3a}\right)^2 + 2b\left(-\frac{b}{3a}\right) + c$$

$$= -\frac{b^2}{3a} + c = \frac{3ac - b^2}{3a} \tag{9-16}$$

Equation (9-16) indicates that the restrictions $a > 0$ and $b < 0$ are not sufficient to ensure that the absolute minimum of MC is positive. To ensure this requires the additional restriction $(3ac - b^2) > 0$. This last restriction implies that $c > 0$ and $3ac > b^2$. Note that the restriction on c could have been obtained directly from the requirement that MC must always be positive, even when output is zero. Thus

$$C'(0) = c > 0$$

The above analysis demonstrates how the coefficients of the cubic total cost function, given in Eq. (9-15), can be restricted to embody certain economic meaning. The restrictions required are

$$a, c, d > 0; \quad b < 0; \quad 3ac > b^2 \tag{9-17}$$

Finally, it should be noted that the restrictions apply only to a cubic cost function of the particular form shown in Fig. 9-7a.

Relation between ATC and MC

An examination of Fig. 9-7b indicates that the MC curve passes through the minimum point of the ATC curve. This particular relationship between MC and ATC can be explained in mathematical terms. The procedure is to find the minimum of the ATC function and then to check if $ATC = MC$ at that minimum point. Since

$$ATC = \frac{C}{Q} = \frac{C(Q)}{Q} \tag{9-18}$$

then

$$\frac{d(ATC)}{dQ} = \frac{Q \cdot C'(Q) - C(Q)}{Q^2} = 0 \quad \text{(quotient rule)}$$

when $Q \cdot C'(Q) = C(Q)$ or $C'(Q) = \frac{C(Q)}{Q}$

Thus the first-order condition for minimum ATC is

$$C'(Q) = \frac{C(Q)}{Q} \quad \text{or} \quad MC = ATC$$

$$\frac{d^2(ATC)}{dQ^2} = \frac{Q^2[Q \cdot C''(Q) + C'(Q) - C'(Q)] - [Q \cdot C'(Q) - C(Q)](2Q)}{Q^4}$$

(quotient and product rules)

$$= \frac{C''(Q)}{Q} - \frac{2C'(Q)}{Q^2} + \frac{2C(Q)}{Q^3}$$

Substituting the first-order condition that $Q \cdot C'(Q) = C(Q)$, we have

$$\frac{d^2(ATC)}{dQ^2} = \frac{C''(Q)}{Q} - \frac{2C'(Q)}{Q^2} + \frac{2QC'(Q)}{Q^3}$$

$$= \frac{C''(Q)}{Q} > 0 \quad \text{for minimum } ATC$$

Since we expect $Q > 0$, at minimum ATC, then the second-order condition for minimum ATC requires

$$C''(Q) > 0 \quad \text{or} \quad \frac{d(MC)}{dQ} > 0$$

Therefore, at the point where ATC is a minimum, $ATC = MC$ and the slope of the MC curve is positive, as shown in Fig. 9-7b.

It is interesting to note that the above procedure can also be used to demonstrate that the MC curve passes through the minimum point of the average *variable* cost (AVC) curve. Thus if we define total variable cost (TVC) as the difference between total cost (TC) and total fixed cost (TFC),

$$TVC = TC - TFC$$

then

$$\frac{TVC}{Q} = \frac{TC}{Q} - \frac{TFC}{Q}$$

or

$$AVC = ATC - AFC \qquad (9\text{-}19)$$

where AFC is average fixed cost. Or, in terms of our cubic total cost function given in Eq. (9-15),

$$TC = aQ^3 + bQ^2 + cQ + d \quad \text{where} \quad d = TFC$$

and

$$TVC = aQ^3 + bQ^2 + cQ$$

Hence

$$ATC = aQ^2 + bQ + c + \frac{d}{Q} \quad \text{where} \quad \frac{d}{Q} = AFC$$

and

$$AVC = aQ^2 + bQ + c$$

Also, note that

$$MC = \frac{d(TC)}{dQ} = \frac{d(TVC)}{dQ} = 3aQ^2 + 2bQ + c$$

Consequently, if we let $TVC = V(Q)$ and $AVC = V(Q)/Q$, the application of the above procedure (relating MC and ATC) to MC and AVC will give the following results:

$$\frac{d(AVC)}{dQ} = 0 \quad \text{implies} \quad V'(Q) = \frac{V(Q)}{Q} \qquad (9\text{-}20)$$

and

$$\frac{d^2(AVC)}{dQ^2} > 0 \quad \text{implies} \quad V''(Q) > 0 \qquad (9\text{-}21)$$

Equation (9-20) states that $V'(Q) = V(Q)/Q$ or $MC = AVC$ since $MC = C'(Q) = V'(Q)$. Equation (9-21) states that $V''(Q) > 0$ or $d(MC)/dQ > 0$ as before. Thus, at the point where AVC is a minimum, $AVC = MC$ and the slope of the MC curve is positive (as in Fig. 9-8).

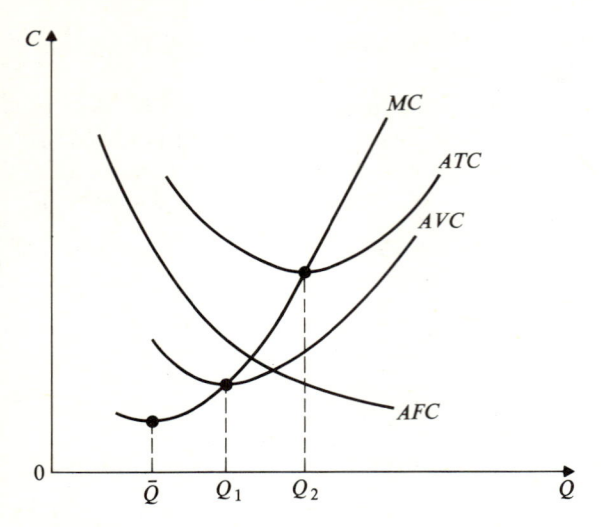

182 ECONOMIC APPLICATIONS OF MAXIMIZATION AND MINIMIZATION

Figure 9-8

It is important to note, however, that minimum ATC will always exceed minimum AVC. This is because ATC equals the sum of AVC and (the always positive) AFC. Thus, to lie on the positive-sloped part of the MC curve, minimum ATC must be above and to the right of minimum AVC, as shown in Fig. 9-8. In economic terms this means that even though AVC is rising beyond $Q = Q_1$, ATC is still falling due to the falling AFC more than offsetting the rising AVC. Once, however, output rises beyond $Q = Q_2$, ATC will begin to rise as rising AVC more than offsets falling AFC.

It is also interesting to note that the shape of the AVC curve reflects the underlying shape of the AP curve. Thus, if we subtract fixed costs (F) from Eq. (9-13), we have TVC expressed as $TVC = \bar{w}L$, whence

$$AVC = \frac{TVC}{Q} = \frac{\bar{w}L}{Q} = \frac{\bar{w}}{AP} \qquad (9\text{-}22)$$

Equation (9-22) shows that AVC will vary inversely with AP. Therefore when AP is at its (sole) maximum, AVC will be at its (sole) minimum. Clearly, since $ATC = AVC + AFC$, the ATC curve will also reflect the underlying production function.

Finally, the relation between the MC and ATC (or AVC) curves can also be demonstrated mathematically. Thus

$$MC = \frac{dC}{dQ} = \frac{d[ATC \cdot Q]}{dQ} = ATC + Q\frac{d(ATC)}{dQ} \qquad (9\text{-}23)$$

Equation (9-23) permits us to state the following:

1. When $d(ATC)/dQ > 0$, then $MC > ATC$. For example, this is the case when $Q > Q_2$ in Fig. 9-8.
2. When $d(ATC)/dQ = 0$, then $MC = ATC$, as is the case when $Q = Q_2$ in Fig. 9-8.
3. When $d(ATC)/dQ < 0$, then $MC < ATC$. For example, this is the case when $Q < Q_2$ in Fig. 9-8.

If we substitute AVC for ATC in Eq. (9-23), we obtain

$$MC = \frac{d(TVC)}{dQ} = \frac{d[AVC \cdot Q]}{dQ} = AVC + Q\frac{d(AVC)}{dQ} \qquad (9\text{-}24)$$

Hence, on the basis of Eq. (9-24) we can state the following:

when $\quad \dfrac{d(AVC)}{dQ} \gtreqless 0, \quad \text{then} \quad MC \gtreqless AVC$

Examples from the Theory of Cost

9-14 A firm has the following short-run total cost function:
$$C = C(Q) = Q^3 - 9Q^2 + 30Q + 25$$

(a) Does this cost function fulfil the restrictions derived above?
(b) Derive the AVC function and show that, when AVC is a minimum, $MC = AVC$.
(c) Derive the ATC function and check that, where $Q = 5$, ATC is a minimum and $MC = ATC$.
(d) Compare the minimum values of AVC and ATC.

SOLUTION
(a) The cubic total cost function of form
$$C(Q) = aQ^3 + bQ^2 + cQ + d$$
required the restrictions $a, c, d > 0$; $b < 0$; $3ac > b^2$. These restrictions are fulfilled in this case since $a = 1, c = 30, d = 25, b = -9$, and $(3ac - b^2) = 9$.

(b) $TVC = TC - TFC = Q^3 - 9Q^2 + 30Q$

$$AVC = \frac{TVC}{Q} = Q^2 - 9Q + 30$$

To find minimum AVC:
$$\frac{d(AVC)}{dQ} = 2Q - 9 = 0 \quad \text{when} \quad Q = \tfrac{9}{2}$$

$$\frac{d^2(AVC)}{dQ^2} = 2 > 0 \quad \text{as required for an } AVC \text{ minimum.}$$

Thus AVC has a minimum value when $Q = \tfrac{9}{2}$. This minimum value is
$$AVC = (\tfrac{9}{2})^2 - 9(\tfrac{9}{2}) + 30 = 9\tfrac{3}{4}$$

The MC function is
$$MC = C'(Q) = 3Q^2 - 18Q + 30$$
$$C'(\tfrac{9}{2}) = 3(\tfrac{9}{2})^2 - 18(\tfrac{9}{2}) + 30 = 9\tfrac{3}{4}$$

Hence, when $Q = \tfrac{9}{2}$, AVC has a minimum and $MC = AVC$.

(c) $ATC = \dfrac{C(Q)}{Q} = Q^2 - 9Q + 30 + \dfrac{25}{Q}$

To see if ATC has a minimum at $Q = 5$, we first find the following derivatives:

$$\dfrac{d(ATC)}{dQ} = 2Q - 9 - \dfrac{25}{Q^2}$$

$$\dfrac{d^2(ATC)}{dQ^2} = 2 + \dfrac{50}{Q^3}$$

When $Q = 5$, $d(ATC)/dQ = 0$ and $d^2(ATC)/dQ^2 = \tfrac{12}{5} > 0$, indicating that ATC has a minimum value when $Q = 5$. This minimum value is

$$ATC = (5)^2 - 9(5) + 30 + \dfrac{25}{(5)} = 15$$

Also, when $Q = 5$, the value of MC is

$$C'(5) = 3(5)^2 - 18(5) + 30 = 15$$

Hence, when $Q = 5$, ATC has a minimum and $MC = ATC$.

(d) The minimum value of ATC exceeds the minimum value of AVC. If we plotted these minimum points as $(5, 15)$ and $(\tfrac{9}{2}, \tfrac{39}{4})$, respectively, then the minimum ATC point would lie above and to the right of the minimum AVC point, as in Fig. 9-8.

9-15 (a) Demonstrate, using the total cost function given in Example 9-14, that the total cost function has a non-stationary point of inflection at that value of Q for which MC is a minimum.

    (b) Find the minimum value of MC for this case.

    (c) Also, for this case, find the range of values of Q for which $d(AVC)/dQ \gtreqless 0$. Select Q values from within this range to demonstrate that when $d(AVC)/dQ \gtreqless 0$, $MC \gtreqless AVC$.

    (d) Demonstrate, for this case, that when $Q \gtreqless 5$, $d(ATC)/dQ \gtreqless 0$ and $MC \gtreqless ATC$.

SOLUTION

(a) To find minimum MC:

$$MC = C'(Q) = 3Q^2 - 18Q + 30$$

$$\dfrac{d(MC)}{dQ} = C''(Q) = 6Q - 18 = 0 \quad \text{when} \quad Q = 3$$

$$\dfrac{d^2(MC)}{dQ^2} = C'''(Q) = 6 > 0 \quad \text{as required for a } MC \text{ minimum.}$$

Thus the MC function has a minimum at $Q = 3$. Note, in obtaining this result, that $C''(3) = 0$, while $C'(3) = 3 \neq 0$ and $C'''(3) = 6 \neq 0$. Hence, by definition, the total cost function has a non-stationary point of inflection at $Q = 3$.

(b) Minimum MC is $C'(3) = 3$.

(c) $\dfrac{d(AVC)}{dQ} = 2Q - 9 \gtreqless 0$ as $Q \gtreqless \tfrac{9}{2}$

Selecting Q values within this range gives the following results:

(i) When $Q = 3$, $MC = 3(3)^2 - 18(3) + 30 = 3$, $AVC = (3)^2 - 9(3) + 30 = 12$. Thus when $Q = 3$, $d(AVC)/dQ < 0$ and $MC < AVC$.

(ii) When $Q = \tfrac{9}{2}$, $MC = \tfrac{39}{4}$, $AVC = \tfrac{39}{4}$. Thus when $Q = \tfrac{9}{2}$, $d(AVC)/dQ = 0$ and $MC = AVC$.

(iii) When $Q = 5$, $MC = 15$, $AVC = 10$. Thus when $Q = 5$, $d(AVC)/dQ > 0$ and $MC > AVC$.

(d) $\dfrac{d(ATC)}{dQ} = 2Q - 9 - \dfrac{25}{Q^2} \gtreqless 0$ as $Q \gtreqless 5$.

Selecting Q values to demonstrate this:
(i) When $Q = 3$, $d(ATC)/dQ = -\frac{52}{9}$, $MC = 3$, and $ATC = \frac{61}{3}$. Thus when $Q = 3$, $d(ATC)/dQ < 0$ and $MC < ATC$.
(ii) When $Q = 5$, $d(ATC)/dQ = 0$, $MC = 15$ and $ATC = 15$. Thus when $Q = 5$, $d(ATC)/dQ = 0$ and $MC = ATC$. Note that, when $Q = 5$, $ATC - AVC = 15 - 10 = 5 = AFC$.
(iii) When $Q = 6$, $d(ATC)/dQ = \frac{83}{36}$, $MC = 30$, and $ATC = 16\frac{1}{6}$. Thus when $Q = 6$, $d(ATC)/dQ > 0$ and $MC > ATC$.

9-6 DEMAND FOR A PRODUCTIVE SERVICE

Let us consider the case of a *perfectly competitive* producer whose production process involves fixed inputs and one variable productive service, labour (L). The production function may then be written as

$$Q = g(L) \tag{9-25}$$

Equation (9-25) states that output is a function of the single variable productive service, labour. If we assume that the labour market is *perfectly competitive*, then the total cost function can be written as

$$C = \bar{w}L + F \tag{9-26}$$

where $\bar{w}$ is the given price (wage rate) of labour (as determined by equality of labour demand and labour supply in the perfectly competitive labour market), L is the number of labour units, and F is the fixed costs associated with fixed inputs. The total cost function in Eq. (9-26) is thus a function of labour input only, with the constant term (F) representing fixed costs.

The perfectly competitive producer faces a given product price ($\bar{P}$). Thus, given his production function in Eq. (9-25), his total revenue function is

$$R = \bar{P} \cdot Q = \bar{P} \cdot g(L) \tag{9-27}$$

Equations (9-26) and (9-27) now permit us to express the profit function in terms of labour input:

$$\pi = R - C = \bar{P} \cdot g(L) - \bar{w}L - F \tag{9-28}$$

This puts us in a position to answer the interesting question: how should the entrepreneur adjust his usage of labour so as to maximize profit? The answer is obtained by maximizing the profit function, given in Eq. (9-28), as follows:

$$\pi'(L) = \bar{P} \cdot g'(L) - \bar{w} = 0 \quad \text{when}$$

$$\bar{P} \cdot g'(L) = \bar{w} \tag{9-29}$$

$$\pi''(L) = \bar{P} \cdot g''(L) < 0 \quad \text{for a } \pi \text{ maximum} \tag{9-30}$$

Let us examine what Eqs. (9-29) and (9-30) mean in economic terms.

In words, Eq. (9-29) simply states that:

(price of product) (marginal product of labour) = wage rate (9-31)

In other words, the profit-maximizing entrepreneur will employ units of the variable productive service until the point is reached at which the value of the marginal product of the input (denoted as $VMP = \bar{P} \cdot g'(L)$) is exactly equal to the input price ($\bar{w}$).

In Eq. (9-30), the second-order condition for a profit maximum requires $g''(L) < 0$, assuming that $\bar{P} > 0$. Since $g'(L)$ is the marginal product of labour (MP) then

$$g''(L) = \frac{d(MP)}{dL} \qquad (9\text{-}32)$$

Therefore diminishing marginal physical productivity of labour ($g''(L) < 0$) will obtain at the profit-maximizing input level.

The above results can be shown graphically, as in Fig. 9-9. Note that the VMP curve has a shape similar to that of the MP curve of Fig. 9-6b. This is because $VMP = \bar{P} \cdot MP$. Also, note that if the entrepreneur only hired L_1 units of labour, then $VMP = 0w_1 > 0\bar{w}$ (the wage rate). Hence, at input level L_1, an additional unit of labour adds more to total revenue than to total cost. This is because

$$\frac{dR}{dL} = \bar{P} \cdot g'(L) = VMP \quad \text{exceeds} \quad \frac{dC}{dL} = \bar{w} = \text{wage rate} \qquad (9\text{-}33)$$

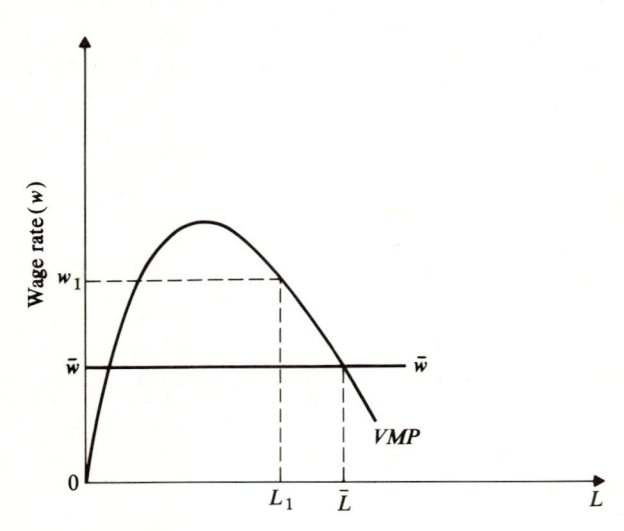

Figure 9-9

Therefore a profit-maximizing entrepreneur would increase his usage of labour beyond L_1. For input levels above $\bar{L}$, where $VMP < \bar{w}$, the entrepreneur would decrease his labour input. Thus the profit-maximizing input level is $\bar{L}$ where $VMP = \bar{w}$, as required by Eq. (9-29).

Examples of Demand for a Productive Service

9-16 A *perfectly competitive* producer has a production function of form $Q = g(L) = 40L^{1/2}$. The output he produces is sold at a price of £5 per unit. His costs of production consist of £50 fixed costs per period plus £25 per period for each unit of labour he employs. Find:
    (a) the profit-maximizing input level of labour
    (b) the maximum profit.

SOLUTION
(a) $R = \bar{P} \cdot Q = 5 \times 40L^{1/2} = 200L^{1/2}$
$C = \bar{w}L + F = 25L + 50$

Hence
$$\pi = R - C = 200L^{1/2} - 25L - 50$$
$$\pi'(L) = 100L^{-1/2} - 25 = 0 \quad \text{when} \quad L = 16$$
$$\pi''(L) = -50L^{-3/2} < 0 \quad \text{for} \quad L = 16$$

Thus the profit-maximizing input level of labour is $L = 16$.
    (b) $\pi(16) = 350$.

9-17 In the previous example check that, when $L = 16$, the value of the marginal product of labour (VMP) is equal to the wage rate.

SOLUTION
$$VMP = \bar{P} \cdot g'(L) = 5 \times 20L^{-1/2} = 25 \text{ when } L = 16, \text{ which is equal to the wage rate.}$$

9-18 A monopolist possesses a production function and a cost function which are given by Eqs. (9-25) and (9-26), respectively. The demand curve he faces is $P = h(Q)$, where $h'(Q) < 0$. Find the monopolist's first-order condition for a profit maximum (i.e., $\pi'(L) = 0$) and interpret it economically. (The second-order condition, $\pi''(L) < 0$, is assumed given as required for a π maximum.)

SOLUTION $\pi = R - C = P \cdot Q - \bar{w}L - F = h[g(L)] \cdot g(L) - \bar{w}L - F = \pi(L)$

$$\pi'(L) = P\frac{dQ}{dL} + Q\frac{dP}{dL} - \bar{w} = 0$$
(product rule)
$$= P\frac{dQ}{dL} + Q\frac{dP}{dQ}\frac{dQ}{dL} - \bar{w} = 0$$
(chain rule)

or $\left[P + Q\frac{dP}{dQ}\right]\frac{dQ}{dL} = \bar{w}$ which may be written as

$$[h(Q) + Qh'(Q)]g'(L) = \bar{w}$$

To interpret this equation economically, let us first find an expression for marginal revenue (MR) in this case. Hence
$$R = P \cdot Q = h(Q) \cdot Q$$
$$MR = \frac{dR}{dQ} = \left[P + Q\frac{dP}{dQ}\right] = [h(Q) + Qh'(Q)]$$

This expression for MR permits us to restate our first-order condition as
$$MR \cdot g'(L) = MR \cdot MP = \bar{w}$$
Once in this form, we can see that the monopolist, who purchases labour in a perfectly competitive market (as shown by the given wage rate $\bar{w}$), will employ units of labour up to the point at which the marginal revenue product of the input (denoted as $MRP = MR \cdot MP$ with $MRP = dR/dL = (dR/dQ)(dQ/dL)$ via the chain rule) equals the input price ($\bar{w}$).

9-A PRACTICE PROBLEMS

9-19 A monopolist has an average revenue function $P = P(Q) = a - bQ$, $(a, b > 0)$, and a cost function $C = C(Q) = \frac{1}{3}Q^3 - 7Q^2 + 100Q + 50$. His profits are maximized when $MR = 67$, $E_d = \frac{89}{22}$, and $dR/dP = -\frac{67}{2}$. Find the monopolist's level of output and derive his profit function to check whether or not this output level is the profit-maximizing output level.

9-20 A profit-maximizing monopolist has an average revenue function $P = P(Q) = a - bQ$, $(a, b > 0)$, and a cost function $C = C(Q) = \alpha Q^2 + \beta Q + \gamma$, $(\alpha, \beta, \gamma > 0)$. Assuming that the government imposes an excise tax on the monopolist's output, demonstrate that (once the tax is imposed) an increase in the tax rate will produce an increase in monopoly price and a decrease in monopoly output which, in each case, is less than half the increase in the tax rate. Also, indicate the tax rate which will maximize government tax revenue from the monopolist.

9-21 A consumer spends all his food budget (M) on two types of food, x and y, whose prices are p_x and p_y. If his utility function is $U = Ax^\alpha y^\beta$ $(\alpha, \beta > 0)$, what quantities of x and y must he purchase (consume) so as to maximize his utility? (Assume that the second-order condition for a utility maximum is fulfilled.) Check your answer by substituting the utility-maximizing values of x and y into the consumer's budget constraint.

9-22 Assume that a consumer is in the position of being able to allocate his total daily hours (H) to either work (W) or leisure (L). With an hourly wage rate of r, his income from work (Y) will be rW. If his utility function, which represents his preferences for work and leisure, is $U = aLY - bY^2 - cL^2$, $(a, b, c > 0)$, how many hours will he work each day in order to maximize his utility? Also, show what adjustment must be made to your answer as a result of an income tax of rate t (where $0 < t < 1$) being imposed.

9-23 A monopolist produces output (Q) with a single variable factor, labour (L). His production function is given by $Q = g(L)$, and the demand curve for his product by $P = h(Q)$. Since he obtains labour in an imperfectly competitive labour market, he faces a labour supply function $w = w(L)$, where w is the wage rate. If the elasticity of labour supply is $\theta = (dL/dw)(w/L)$, and the monopolist maximizes profit, use the first-order condition for a profit maximum to derive a relation between marginal revenue product, wage rate and the elasticity of labour supply (ignore fixed cost).

9-24 A firm has a total revenue function $R(Q) = 24Q - 2Q^2$ and a total cost function $C(Q) = Q^2 + 5$.
(i) If the firm's objective is to maximize profit, find (a) the firm's profit-maximizing output level, and the corresponding values of profit, price and total revenue at this output level; (b) how these results are affected by the imposition of a lump-sum tax of 30.
(ii) If the firm's objective is to maximize total revenue subject to 'minimum' profit constraint of $\pi \geq 10$, find (a) the firm's revenue-maximizing output level, and the corresponding values of profit, price and total revenue at this output level; (b) how these results are affected by the imposition of a lump-sum tax of 30.

9-25 A perfectly competitive firm has a total revenue function $R(Q) = 9Q$, and a total cost function $C(Q) = Q^3 - 9Q^2 + 33Q + 10$. Find:

(a) the profit-maximizing output level and the value of profit at that output level
(b) whether or not the firm will produce the profit-maximizing output level
(c) what the price must exceed to ensure production.

9-7 ADDITIONAL PROBLEMS

9-26 A business-man decides to open a well in the Sahara to sell water to passing camel trains. His only costs are the initial fixed costs of digging the well. He then proceeds to charge that price at which $E_d = 1$. Assuming that the second-order condition for a profit maximum is fulfilled, show that he maximizes his profit.

9-27 A monopolist producing motor cars is faced with a linear average revenue function. Initially he produces 100 cars per week, which he sells at £2500 each. At this price the elasticity of demand is 5. The monopolist can increase production at an average total cost of £$(1800 + 40,000/Q)$ per car, per week. What is the monopolist's profit-maximizing output level? Also, calculate his maximum profit and the price per car at which his profit-maximizing output is sold.

9-28 A profit-maximizing monopolist has a total cost function which is a monotonically increasing function of output ($Q \geqslant 0$). Show why he will not produce output for which demand is inelastic. (Assume that the second-order condition for a profit maximum is fulfilled.)

9-29 (i) A monopolist's total revenue function is $R(Q) = 20Q - 3Q^2$, and his total cost function is $C(Q) = 2Q^2 + 2$. Find (a) his profit-maximizing output level; (b) his maximum profit; (c) the price at which his profit-maximizing output is sold.
(ii) If the government requires this monopolist to equate price with marginal cost, how will this affect the monopolist's price, output and profit?

9-30 Assume that a consumer's utility (U) depends on income (Y) and leisure (L), with his utility function given by $U = AL^\alpha Y^\beta$, ($\alpha, \beta > 0$). Also, assume that the consumer may use the hours available each day (H) for work (W) or leisure. If the hourly wage rate is r, and the consumer maximizes his utility, how many hours will he work each day? Also, indicate the required adjustment to your answer as a result of the imposition of an income tax of rate t, ($0 < t < 1$). Comment on the economic realism of your result. (Assume $U''(W) < 0$ when $U'(W) = 0$.)

9-31 A consumer spends all her cosmetics budget of £30 on two types of cosmetics, x and y, whose prices are £2 and £3, respectively. If her utility function is $U = 2x^{1/2}y^{1/3}$, what quantities of x and y must she purchase so as to maximize her utility? (Assume that the second-order condition for a utility maximum is fulfilled.)

9-32 A perfectly competitive firm produces output (Q) with a single variable input, labour (L), the production function being $Q = g(L)$. The market in which labour is obtained is imperfect, the labour supply function being $w = w(L)$, where w is the wage rate. If the elasticity of labour supply is constant and equal to θ, find:
(a) the first-order condition for a profit maximum (i.e., $\pi'(L) = 0$) and interpret this condition in economic terms
(b) the second-order condition for maximum profit and indicate the relevance of the sign of $g''(L)$ to this condition.

9-33 A monopolist has the following total revenue and total cost functions: $R(Q) = 43Q - 4Q^2$ and $C(Q) = Q^3 - 9Q^2 + 46Q + 4$. Find:
(a) the output level for which his AVC is a minimum
(b) the profit-maximizing output level and the value of profit at that output level. If the output level found under (b) is less than that found under (a), indicate why the monopolist will still produce at the lower output level.

9-34 (a) A firm has a total revenue function $R(Q)$ and a total cost function $C(Q)$. Derive the first- and second-order conditions for profit maximization and interpret your results in economic terms. Illustrate your answer for the cases of perfect competition and monopoly by graphing MR and MC curves.

(b) A firm has a total revenue function of $R(Q) = Q$, and a total cost function of $C(Q) = 4 + Q^{2/3}$. What happens if this firm attempts to maximize its profits? Assess the economic realism of this example, illustrating your answer with graphs of R, C, MR and MC. [Note: $\pi(8) = 0$.]

9-35 (a) A firm has a production function $Q = g(L)$. Demonstrate that $AP = MP$ when AP is at a maximum.

(b) Demonstrate why the difference between marginal cost and average cost (whether average total cost or average variable cost) has always the same sign as the slope of the average cost curve.

(c) Demonstrate, for a profit-maximizing monopolist, that $(P - MC)/P = 1/E_d$. (Assume that the second-order condition for a profit maximum is fulfilled.)

9-36 The demand and supply functions in a competitive market are $Q_d = 20 - 2P$ and $Q_s = 3P$, respectively. If the government imposes a tax of rate t per unit of output sold, find:

(a) the tax rate that will maximize government tax revenue

(b) the effect of changes in t on (post-tax) equilibrium price and quantity.

CHAPTER
TEN
PARTIAL AND TOTAL DIFFERENTIATION

In Chapter 6, we discussed the concept of a derivative, and the techniques of differentiation, of a function of a single independent variable. As such, the differentiation of functions of more than one variable was not considered. This means that while we have learnt how to find the derivative of, for example, a one-variable demand function (such as $Q_d = f(P)$, which relates the quantity demanded of a good, Q_d, to its unit price, P) we do not as yet know how to find the derivative of a multi-variable demand function (such as $Q_{d1} = Q_{d1}(P_1, P_2, \ldots, P_n, Y)$, which relates Q_{d1}, the quantity demanded of good 1, to the prices of goods $1, 2, \ldots, n$ (denoted by $P_1, P_2, \ldots, P_n$) and income, Y). Thus, as yet, we do not know how to find the change in Q_{d1} resulting from a change in one independent variable, such as P_1, when all other prices and income are held constant. Nor do we know how to find the change in Q_{d1} resulting from a simultaneous change in all the independent variables $P_1, P_2, \ldots, P_n$, and Y. Consequently, in this chapter, we must now consider the differentiation of a function of more than one variable.

10-1 PARTIAL DIFFERENTIATION

Let us assume an *n*-variable function

$$y = f(x_1, x_2, \ldots, x_n) \tag{10-1}$$

where the variables $x_1, x_2, \ldots, x_n$ are all *independent* of each other in the sense that each can vary by itself without producing a resulting variation in the others. Given function (10-1), a change in the value of variable x_1, with variables $x_2, \ldots, x_n$ all unchanged or fixed in value, will produce a corresponding change in the value of y. Thus, if we denote the change in x_1 by Δx_1, then we can say that x_1 has changed from some initial value x_1 to a new value $x_1 + \Delta x_1$. Similarly, if we denote the corresponding change in y by Δy, then we can say that y has changed from some initial value y to a new value $y + \Delta y$. Consequently, if we put these new values into (10-1) we obtain

$$y + \Delta y = f(x_1 + \Delta x_1, x_2, \ldots, x_n) \tag{10-2}$$

If we then subtract (10-1) from (10-2), and divide the result by Δx_1, we obtain the difference quotient

$$\frac{\Delta y}{\Delta x_1} = \frac{f(x_1 + \Delta x_1, x_2, \ldots, x_n) - f(x_1, x_2, \ldots, x_n)}{\Delta x_1} \tag{10-3}$$

which measures the rate of change of y with respect to a change in x_1, when all the other independent variables $x_2, \ldots, x_n$ are held *constant*.

The limit of $\Delta y / \Delta x_1$ as Δx_1 approaches zero defines what is known as the *partial derivative* of $y = f(x_1, x_2, \ldots, x_n)$ with respect to x_1, and is expressed symbolically as

$$\frac{\partial y}{\partial x_1} = \lim_{\Delta x_1 \to 0} \frac{\Delta y}{\Delta x_1} \tag{10-4}$$

Note that the particular derivative defined in (10-4) is called the *partial derivative of y with respect to x_1*, because it measures the rate of change of y with respect to an infinitesimal change in x_1 when all the other $n-1$ independent variables in the function (10-1) are held *constant*. Also note, in relation to (10-4), that $\partial y / \partial x_1$ must be regarded as a single entity, *not* the ratio of one thing (∂y) to another (∂x_1).

The partial derivative of y with respect to x_2 can be similarly defined as

$$\frac{\partial y}{\partial x_2} = \lim_{\Delta x_2 \to 0} \frac{\Delta y}{\Delta x_2} \tag{10-5}$$

In the latter case, $\partial y / \partial x_2$ measures the rate of change of y with respect to an infinitesimal change in x_2 when all the other $n-1$ independent variables in the function (10-1) are held constant. Similar partial derivatives can be defined for infinitesimal changes in each of the other $n-2$ independent variables in the function (10-1). In each case, the process of finding the respective partial derivative is called *partial differentiation*.

Since the above definition of a partial derivative indicates that it is a particular type of derivative, then it should be clear that the partial derivative $\partial y / \partial x_1$ measures an instantaneous rate of change of y with respect to an infinitesimal change in x_1. As such, $\partial y / \partial x_1$ will then provide information about both the *direction* and the *magnitude* of the change in y

resulting from an infinitesimal change in x_1 alone. This point will be enlarged in the examples below.

As a matter of notation for partial derivatives, the following points should be noted:

1. Partial derivatives are expressed in terms of the symbol ∂ rather than the letter d (which was used, for example, in the ordinary derivative dy/dx).
2. Just as the ordinary derivative dy/dx, of the function $y = f(x)$, can be written as

$$\frac{d}{dx}[y]$$

so the partial derivative $\partial y/\partial x_1$, of the function (10-1), can be written as

$$\frac{\partial}{\partial x_1}[y]$$

with $\partial/\partial x_1$ representing an operator symbol telling us to find the partial derivative of y with respect to x_1. Alternatively, given the function (10-1), $\partial y/\partial x_1$ may be written as

$$\frac{\partial}{\partial x_1}[f]$$

or simply $\partial f/\partial x_1$.

3. Just as the ordinary derivative dy/dx, of the function $y = f(x)$, can be written as $f'(x)$ or f', so the partial derivative $\partial y/\partial x_1$, of the function (10-1), can be written as f_1, with the subscript indicating the particular independent variable (in this case x_1) which is being varied. Similarly $\partial y/\partial x_2$ can be written as f_2. Or, if the function is of form $z = f(x, y, w)$, then $\partial z/\partial x = f_x$, $\partial z/\partial y = f_y$, and $\partial z/\partial w = f_w$.

10-2 TECHNIQUES OF PARTIAL DIFFERENTIATION

In this section, it will be seen that the techniques of partial differentiation are very similar to those of ordinary differentiation in Sec. 6-3. The reason for this is that the process of partial differentiation involves varying *one* independent variable while holding the other $n-1$ independent variables *constant*. This means, in the actual process of finding a partial derivative, that we can simply treat the other $n-1$ independent variables as *constants* and proceed as in ordinary differentiation.

Before proceeding to examples of partial differentiation, the student should take comfort in the fact that the economic applications of partial differentiation, given in Chapters 11, 12 and 13, involve quite straightforward partial differentiation. It is for this reason that this section

194 PARTIAL AND TOTAL DIFFERENTIATION

deliberately avoids the partial differentiation of complicated functions (such as those which require the combination of several rules of partial differentiation in order to obtain the respective partial derivative).

Examples of Partial Differentiation

10-1 Given $z = f(x,y) = 3x^2 + 4y^3 + 10$, find f_x and f_y.

SOLUTION When finding $f_x \equiv \partial z/\partial x$, we treat y as a constant during differentiation. This means essentially that $z = 3x^2 + k$, where the constant k equals the sum $4y^3 + 10$. Thus

$$f_x \equiv \partial z/\partial x = 6x$$

Similarly, when finding $f_y \equiv \partial z/\partial y$, we treat x as a constant during differentiation. Thus

$$f_y \equiv \partial z/\partial y = 12y^2$$

This example shows that, with such a function, we proceed in a manner analogous to the sum-difference rule of ordinary differentiation.

10-2 Given $z = f(x,y) = x^3 + 2xy + 3y^2$, find f_x and f_y.

SOLUTION Treating y as a constant we obtain

$$f_x \equiv \partial z/\partial x = 3x^2 + 2y$$

Note, in this case, by treating y as a constant, the function has the form $z = x^3 + bx + c$, where the constants b and c equal $2y$ and $3y^2$, respectively. Hence, in finding $\partial z/\partial x$, the *multiplicative* constant (given by $b = 2y$) will remain, while the *additive* constant (given by $c = 3y^2$) will drop out, as in ordinary differentiation.

Similarly, treating x as a constant, we obtain

$$f_y \equiv \partial z/\partial y = 2x + 6y$$

This example makes it clear that the partial derivatives f_x and f_y, like the original function f, are themselves functions of the variables x and y. Consequently, in this case, f_x and f_y can be written as the two derived functions

$$f_x = f_x(x,y) = 3x^2 + 2y \quad \text{and} \quad f_y = f_y(x,y) = 2x + 6y \tag{10-6}$$

Equation (10-6) not only makes it clear that each partial derivative is a function of x and y, but also emphasizes that each partial derivative is always evaluated at some particular (x,y) point or value. For example, when $x = 2$ and $y = 3$, then

$$f_x = f_x(2,3) = 3(2)^2 + 2(3) = 18 \quad \text{and} \quad f_y = f_y(2,3) = 2(2) + 6(3) = 22$$

Since at point $(x,y) = (2,3)$, $f_x \equiv \partial z/\partial x = 18$, this means that z will increase (decrease) in value as x increases (decreases) in value from point $(x,y) = (2,3)$, with the magnitude of the rate of change of z being 18 units per unit change in x. Similarly, at point $(x,y) = (2,3)$, $f_y \equiv \partial z/\partial y = 22$ means that z will increase (decrease) in value as y increases (decreases) in value from point $(x,y) = (2,3)$, with the magnitude of the rate of change of z being 22 units per unit change in y. In other words, the partial derivatives f_x and f_y provide information about both the direction and the magnitude of the changes in z that result from infinitesimal changes in x alone and y alone, respectively.

Before leaving this example, note that if $y = f(x_1, x_2, \ldots, x_n)$, then each partial derivative $f_i (i = 1, 2, \ldots, n)$, like the original function f, will be a function of the variables $x_1, x_2, \ldots, x_n$. For example, $f_3 \equiv \partial y/\partial x_3 = f_3(x_1, x_2, \ldots, x_n)$.

10-3 Given $z = f(x,y) = (x - 7y)(3x + 5y^2)$, find f_x and f_y.

SOLUTION In this case we use a modified form of the product rule to find f_x and f_y. Thus, if we let $u = u(x,y) = x - 7y$ and $v = v(x,y) = 3x + 5y^2$, so that $z = uv$, then

$$f_x \equiv \partial z/\partial x = u\frac{\partial v}{\partial x} + v\frac{\partial u}{\partial x} = (x-7y)(3) + (3x+5y^2)(1) = 6x - 21y + 5y^2$$

and

$$f_y \equiv \partial z/\partial y = u\frac{\partial v}{\partial y} + v\frac{\partial u}{\partial y} = (x-7y)(10y) + (3x+5y^2)(-7) = 10xy - 21x - 105y^2$$

10-4 Given $z = f(x, y) = (2x+4y)/(x^2-3y)$, find f_x and f_y.

SOLUTION In this case we use a modified form of the quotient rule to find f_x and f_y. Thus, if we let $u = u(x, y) = 2x + 4y$ and $v = v(x, y) = x^2 - 3y$, so that $z = u/v$, then

$$f_x \equiv \frac{\partial z}{\partial x} = \frac{v\dfrac{\partial u}{\partial x} - u\dfrac{\partial v}{\partial x}}{v^2} = \frac{(x^2-3y)(2) - (2x+4y)(2x)}{(x^2-3y)^2} = -\frac{(2x^2+6y+8xy)}{(x^2-3y)^2}$$

and

$$f_y \equiv \frac{\partial z}{\partial y} = \frac{v\dfrac{\partial u}{\partial y} - u\dfrac{\partial v}{\partial y}}{v^2} = \frac{(x^2-3y)(4) - (2x+4y)(-3)}{(x^2-3y)^2} = \frac{4x^2+6x}{(x^2-3y)^2}$$

10-5 Given $z = f(x, y) = (x^2+4xy+y^2)^{13}$, find f_x and f_y.

SOLUTION In this case we use a modified form of the chain rule to find f_x and f_y. Thus, if we let $u = u(x, y) = x^2 + 4xy + y^2$, then $z = z(u) = u^{13}$ with $u = x^2 + 4xy + y^2$. Hence

$$f_x \equiv \frac{\partial z}{\partial x} = \frac{dz}{du}\frac{\partial u}{\partial x} = 13u^{12}(2x+4y) = 13(x^2+4xy+y^2)^{12}(2x+4y)$$

and

$$f_y \equiv \frac{\partial z}{\partial y} = \frac{dz}{du}\frac{\partial u}{\partial y} = 13u^{12}(4x+2y) = 13(x^2+4xy+y^2)^{12}(4x+2y)$$

10-6 Given $z = f(x, y) = \ln(x^2+2xy-y^3)$, find f_x and f_y.

SOLUTION In this case we use a modified form of the log-function rule. Thus, if we let $u = u(x, y) = x^2 + 2xy - y^3$, then $z = z(u) = \ln u$ with $u = x^2 + 2xy - y^3$. Hence

$$f_x \equiv \frac{\partial z}{\partial x} = \frac{dz}{du}\frac{\partial u}{\partial x} = \frac{1}{u}\frac{\partial u}{\partial x} = \frac{1}{(x^2+2xy-y^3)}(2x+2y) = \frac{2x+2y}{x^2+2xy-y^3}$$

and

$$f_y \equiv \frac{\partial z}{\partial y} = \frac{dz}{du}\frac{\partial u}{\partial y} = \frac{1}{u}\frac{\partial u}{\partial y} = \frac{1}{(x^2+2xy-y^3)}(2x-3y^2) = \frac{2x-3y^2}{x^2+2xy-y^3}$$

It should be noted that while all the above examples relate to the case $z = f(x, y)$, the same procedure also holds for the partial differentiation of functions of more than two variables.

10-A PRACTICE PROBLEMS

10-7 Find $\partial y/\partial x_1$ and $\partial y/\partial x_2$ for each of the following functions:
(a) $y = 3x_1^{-2} + 6x_1x_2^2 + 7x_2^3$
(b) $y = 4x_1x_2 - x_2^2x_3 + x_3^4 + x_4^5$
(c) $y = (x_1x_2 + 3x_2^2)(x_2^3 - 2)$
(d) $y = (3x_1^3 - 2x_2)/(x_1^2 + 2x_2^2)$
(e) $y = (x_1^2x_2 + x_1^3x_3^2 + x_2^2x_3)^{-5}$
(f) $y = \ln(2x_1x_2^2 - 3x_1^2x_2 + 10)$

10-8 Find f_x and f_y for each of the following functions:
(a) $f(x, y, z) = 2x^2 - 7xy^2 + z^2 - 2$ (b) $f(x, y) = \ln x^2 y^3$
(c) $f(x, y, w) = (3x + w^2)(w - y^2)$ (d) $f(x, y) = 2(x^2 y^3)^{-11}$

10-9 Given $z = f(x, y) = 2x^2 y - xy^3$, find the value of f_x at the point $(x, y) = (2, 1)$. Explain the meaning of your result.

10-3 SECOND-ORDER PARTIAL DERIVATIVES

In the previous section, we noted that the partial derivatives f_x and f_y, of a function $z = f(x, y)$, are themselves functions of x and y. This means that f_x and f_y can be differentiated partially with respect to x and y to yield *second-order* (or *second*) *partial derivatives*. Thus, given $z = f(x, y)$, the first-order partial derivative $\partial z/\partial x \equiv f_x$ can be differentiated partially with respect to x to give the second-order partial derivative

$$\frac{\partial}{\partial x}\left[\frac{\partial z}{\partial x}\right] = \frac{\partial^2 z}{\partial x^2} \quad \text{or} \quad \frac{\partial}{\partial x}[f_x] = f_{xx} \qquad (10\text{-}7)$$

Note that the second-order partial derivative, in (10-7), measures the rate of change of f_x with respect to x while y is held *constant*. Also, note that the second-order partial derivative with respect to x can be denoted by either $\partial^2 z/\partial x^2$ or f_{xx} (where the latter notation, which is common in economic models, indicates that the original function f has been differentiated partially with respect to x twice). The second-order partial derivative with respect to y is similarly defined as

$$\frac{\partial}{\partial y}\left[\frac{\partial z}{\partial y}\right] = \frac{\partial^2 z}{\partial y^2} \quad \text{or} \quad \frac{\partial}{\partial y}[f_y] = f_{yy} \qquad (10\text{-}8)$$

Note, by definition in (10-8), that $\partial^2 z/\partial y^2 \equiv f_{yy}$ measures the rate of change of f_y with respect to y while x is held *constant*.

Since f_x is a function of y as well as x, just as f_y is a function of x as well as y, then we can define two more second partial derivatives:

$$\frac{\partial}{\partial x}\left[\frac{\partial z}{\partial y}\right] = \frac{\partial^2 z}{\partial x \partial y} \quad \text{or} \quad \frac{\partial}{\partial x}[f_y] = f_{xy} \qquad (10\text{-}9)$$

and

$$\frac{\partial}{\partial y}\left[\frac{\partial z}{\partial x}\right] = \frac{\partial^2 z}{\partial y \partial x} \quad \text{or} \quad \frac{\partial}{\partial y}[f_x] = f_{yx} \qquad (10\text{-}10)$$

The second partial derivatives in (10-9) and (10-10) are known as *cross* (or *mixed*) partial derivatives, with f_{xy} measuring the rate of change of f_y with respect to x while y is held constant and f_{yx} measuring the rate of change of f_x with respect to y while x is held constant.

Examples of Second-Order Partial Derivatives

10-10 Given $z = f(x, y) = 2x^4y + 5xy^3 + 3xy + 13$, find f_{xx}, f_{yy}, f_{xy} and f_{yx}.

SOLUTION First, we must obtain f_x and f_y:
$$f_x = 8x^3y + 5y^3 + 3y \quad \text{and} \quad f_y = 2x^4 + 15xy^2 + 3x$$
Then we differentiate once more to obtain

$$\frac{\partial}{\partial x}(f_x) = f_{xx} = 24x^2y; \frac{\partial}{\partial y}(f_y) = f_{yy} = 30xy; \frac{\partial}{\partial x}(f_y) = f_{xy} = 8x^3 + 15y^2 + 3 = f_{yx} = \frac{\partial}{\partial y}(f_x)$$

Note that this example illustrates two important points about second-order partial derivatives. Firstly, note that f_{xx}, f_{yy}, f_{xy}, and f_{yx}, like the original function f and the first-order partial derivatives f_x and f_y, are also functions of the variables x and y. This emphasizes that the second-order partial derivatives, like first-order partial derivatives, are always evaluated at some particular (x, y) point or value. Secondly, note that $f_{xy} = f_{yx}$. This result, known as *Young's theorem*, holds provided that certain conditions relating to the continuity of the function are fulfilled (as will always be assumed in our partial differentiation).

It should be noted that the above two points also apply to functions of more than two variables. For example, given $y = f(x_1, x_2, x_3)$, each of the second partial derivatives (given by $f_{11}, f_{12}, f_{13}, f_{21}, f_{22}, f_{23}, f_{31}, f_{32}$, and f_{33}) are functions of the variables x_1, x_2, and x_3. Also, via Young's theorem, $f_{12} = f_{21}, f_{13} = f_{31}$, and $f_{23} = f_{32}$.

10-11 Given $y = f(x_1, x_2, x_3) = 3x_1^3 x_2 + 5x_3^5 x_2$, find the nine second-order partial derivatives.

SOLUTION $f_1 = 9x_1^2 x_2; f_2 = 3x_1^3 + 5x_3^5; f_3 = 25x_3^4 x_2$. Thus

$$f_{11} = \frac{\partial}{\partial x_1}(f_1) = 18x_1 x_2; \quad f_{22} = \frac{\partial}{\partial x_2}(f_2) = 0; \quad f_{33} = \frac{\partial}{\partial x_3}(f_3) = 100x_3^3 x_2;$$

$$f_{12} = \frac{\partial}{\partial x_1}(f_2) = \frac{\partial}{\partial x_2}(f_1) = f_{21} = 9x_1^2; \quad f_{13} = \frac{\partial}{\partial x_1}(f_3) = \frac{\partial}{\partial x_3}(f_1) = f_{31} = 0;$$

$$f_{23} = \frac{\partial}{\partial x_2}(f_3) = \frac{\partial}{\partial x_3}(f_2) = f_{32} = 25x_3^4.$$

Before leaving this section, it should be noted that second partial derivatives may be repeatedly differentiated to obtain third- and higher-order partial derivatives.

10-B PRACTICE PROBLEMS

10-12 Find the four second-order partial derivatives of each of the following:
  (a) $f(x, y) = x^{-3}y + 4y^3 x^2 - 2x$ (b) $f(x, y) = 2x^{1/2}y^3 - 3x^3 y^5 + 5$

10-13 Find the nine second-order partial derivatives of each of the following:
  (a) $f(x_1, x_2, x_3) = x_1^9 x_3 - 2x_2 x_3^2 + x_1 x_2$ (b) $f(x_1, x_2, x_3) = x_3^2 x_2^3 + x_1^5 x_3 + 6$

10-4 DIFFERENTIALS AND TOTAL DIFFERENTIALS

In Sec. 10-1, we noted that the partial derivative f_x, of a function $z = f(x, y)$, measures the rate of change of z with respect to an infinitesimal change in x while y is held constant. Similarly, we noted that f_y measures the rate of change of z with respect to an infinitesimal change in y while x is held constant. Having examined such changes in z, the obvious next step is to examine the change in z resulting from infinitesimal changes in *both* x and y simultaneously. Consequently, in this section, we shall examine the *total* change in z in terms of what is known as the *total differential* of the z function. To do this, we shall first consider the concept of *differentials* and then the concept of *total differentials*.

Differentials

If we have a function $y = f(x)$, then an arbitrary change in x (denoted by Δx) will produce a corresponding change in y (denoted by Δy), with the change in y per unit change in x being measured by the difference quotient $\Delta y/\Delta x$. This means we can then write

$$\Delta y = \left(\frac{\Delta y}{\Delta x}\right)\Delta x \qquad (10\text{-}11)$$

In other words, if we have actual values for $(\Delta y/\Delta x)$ and Δx, then the magnitude of Δy can be obtained from (10-11).

If we now consider Δx to be infinitesimal, then (via $y = f(x)$) Δy will also be infinitesimal and the difference quotient $\Delta y/\Delta x$, in (10-11), will become the derivative dy/dx. Also, if the infinitesimal changes in x and y are denoted, respectively, by dx and dy (instead of Δx and Δy), then (10-11) can be rewritten as

$$dy = \left(\frac{dy}{dx}\right)dx \quad \text{or} \quad dy = f'(x)dx \qquad (10\text{-}12)$$

where the symbols dx and dy represent what are known as the *differentials* of x and y, respectively.

Note that if we divide the expressions in (10-12) by dx we obtain

$$\frac{(dy)}{(dx)} = \left(\frac{dy}{dx}\right) \quad \text{or} \quad \frac{(dy)}{(dx)} = f'(x) \qquad (10\text{-}13)$$

In other words, the derivative $(dy/dx) = f'(x)$, which was regarded as a single entity in Chapter 6, can now be reinterpreted as the ratio of the two differentials dy and dx.

Since, as shown in (10-12), the differential dy is simply $f'(x)$ times dx, then the process of finding dy is quite straightforward. For example, given $y = f(x) = 5x^2$, then the required differential is simply

$$dy = f'(x)dx = (10x)dx \qquad (10\text{-}14)$$

Thus, given a specific x value, and the given value of dx (measured from this x value), we can evaluate the dy expression in (10-14).

Total Differentials

The concept of differentials can also be applied to functions of more than one independent variable. Thus, given a function $z = f(x, y)$, the total change in z resulting from arbitrary, infinitesimal, changes in *both* x and y simultaneously is given by

$$dz = \frac{\partial z}{\partial x} dx + \frac{\partial z}{\partial y} dy \quad \text{or} \quad dz = f_x dx + f_y dy \qquad (10\text{-}15)$$

which is called the *total differential* of the z function.

To appreciate the meaning of (10-15), note that if x changes while y is held constant, so that $dy = 0$, then the total differential in (10-15) reduces to $dz = (\partial z/\partial x)dx$. In other words, the change in z due to a very small change in x, while y remains constant, is measured by the first term in (10-15). Similarly, if y changes while x is held constant, so that $dx = 0$, then the total differential in (10-15) reduces to $dz = (\partial x/\partial y)dy$. Thus the second term in (10-15) measures the change in z due to a very small change in y, while x is held constant. Consequently, the expression for dz in (10-15) can be seen to be the *sum* of the changes in z from each of these sources. It is for this reason that $dz = f_x dx + f_y dy$ is called the *total differential* of the z function, and the process of finding such a total differential is called *total differentiation*.

In the more general case of a function $y = f(x_1, x_2, \ldots, x_n)$, the total differential can be written as

$$dy = \frac{\partial y}{\partial x_1} dx_1 + \frac{\partial y}{\partial x_2} dx_2 + \ldots + \frac{\partial y}{\partial x_n} dx_n \qquad (10\text{-}16)$$

or

$$dy = f_1 dx_1 + f_2 dx_2 + \ldots + f_n dx_n = \sum_{i=1}^{n} f_i dx_i \qquad (10\text{-}17)$$

Note that the actual process of finding the total differential dz, of a function $z = f(x, y)$, merely involves finding the partial derivatives f_x and f_y and substituting these into Eq. (10-15). For example, given the function

$$z = f(x, y) = 2x^2 y + 3y^5 x^3$$

where $f_x = 4xy + 9y^5 x^2$ and $f_y = 2x^2 + 15y^4 x^3$, then

$$dz = f_x dx + f_y dy = (4xy + 9y^5 x^2) dx + (2x^2 + 15y^4 x^3) dy \qquad (10\text{-}18)$$

Thus, given a specific (x, y) value or point, and the given values of dx and dy (measured from this point), we can evaluate the dz expression in (10-18). The resulting value of dz will then provide information about both the direction and the magnitude of the change in z.

In Chapters 12 and 13, the concept of total differential will be seen to be extremely useful in analysing economic problems involving the optimization of functions of more than one variable.

10-C PRACTICE PROBLEMS

10-14 Find the differential dy for each of the following functions:
  (a) $y = 3x^3 - 7x^2 + 6$ (b) $y = (x^2 + 2x)(x^3 - 3)$ (c) $y = (x^3 - 4)^5$

10-15 Find the total differential dz for each of the following functions:
  (a) $z = f(x, y) = x^3 y^2 - 7yx^2 + 2$ (b) $z = f(x_1, x_2) = 2x_1^2 x_2^3 + x_1^3 x_2 + x_2^2$

10-5 TOTAL DERIVATIVES

In the previous section we considered z to be a function of two *independent* variables x and y. Now, in this section, we shall consider the case where x and y are *not* independent of each other. For example, in the function

$$z = f(x, y) \quad \text{where} \quad y = g(x) \qquad (10\text{-}19)$$

it can be seen that x and y are not independent, but are related via the function g. In such a case, a change in x will not only affect z directly (via the function f), but will also affect z indirectly by changing y (via the function g), which in turn will affect z (via the function f). Thus the rate of change of z with respect to x, which is known as the *total derivative* of z with respect to x, is given by

$$\frac{dz}{dx} = f_x \frac{dx}{dx} + f_y \frac{dy}{dx} \qquad (10\text{-}20)$$

or

$$\frac{dz}{dx} = \frac{\partial z}{\partial x} + \frac{\partial z}{\partial y} \frac{dy}{dx} \quad \text{since} \quad \frac{dx}{dx} = 1 \qquad (10\text{-}21)$$

Note that to obtain the total derivative dz/dx in (10-20), we simply find the total differential $dz = f_x dx + f_y dy$ and then divide each side of this equation by dx to obtain dz/dx as in (10-20). [This procedure indicates that the statement $dz = f_x dx + f_y dy$ holds regardless of whether or not x and y are independent (though, of course, when x and y are dependent, as in (10-19), dx and dy are no longer arbitrary variations in x and y but are related in the sense that $y = g(x)$ means $dy = g'(x) dx$).]

To appreciate the meaning of (10-21), note that the first term $(\partial z/\partial x)$ in (10-21) measures the change in z resulting from the change in x while y is held constant. Consequently, the first term in (10-21) only measures the *direct* effect of x on z. In contrast, the second term $(\partial z/\partial y)(dy/dx)$ measures the change in z resulting from the change in y (the $(\partial z/\partial y)$ part) with this change in y in turn resulting from the initial change in x (the (dy/dx) part). Thus the second term in (10-21) measures the *indirect* effect of x on z.

As an example, let us find the total derivative dz/dx of the function

$$z = f(x, y) = 2x^2 + y^2 \quad \text{where} \quad y = g(x) = x^3 - 2$$

Thus, applying (10-20) or (10-21), we have

$$\frac{dz}{dx} = \frac{\partial z}{\partial x} + \frac{\partial z}{\partial y}\frac{dy}{dx} = 4x + 2y(3x^2) = 4x + 6x^5 - 12x^2$$

If we take a more complicated case, such as

$$z = f(x_1, x_2) \quad \text{where} \quad \begin{cases} x_1 = g(t) \\ x_2 = h(t) \end{cases} \tag{10-22}$$

then a change in t will affect z indirectly through two channels: (1) by changing x_1 (via the function g), which in turn will affect z (via the function f), and (2) by changing x_2 (via the function h), which in turn will affect z (via the function f). Thus, in this case, the total derivative dz/dt is

$$\frac{dz}{dt} = f_1 \frac{dx_1}{dt} + f_2 \frac{dx_2}{dt} = \frac{\partial z}{\partial x_1}\frac{dx_1}{dt} + \frac{\partial z}{\partial x_2}\frac{dx_2}{dt} \tag{10-23}$$

where (10-23) is obtained by finding the total differential dz and dividing both sides by dt. For example, given the function

$$z = f(x_1, x_2) = 3x_1^5 + 2x_2^3$$

where

$$x_1 = g(t) = 2t - 2 \quad \text{and} \quad x_2 = h(t) = t^2$$

then, via (10-23), the total derivative of z with respect to t is

$$\frac{dz}{dt} = \frac{\partial z}{\partial x_1}\frac{dx_1}{dt} + \frac{\partial z}{\partial x_2}\frac{dx_2}{dt} = 15x_1^4(2) + 6x_2^2(2t) = 30(2t-2)^4 + 12t^5$$

An even more complicated case occurs when

$$z = f(x_1, x_2) \quad \text{where} \quad \begin{cases} x_1 = g(t, w) \\ x_2 = h(t, w) \end{cases} \tag{10-24}$$

In this case, the rate of change of z with respect to t, while w is held constant, is given by

$$\left.\frac{dz}{dt}\right|_{w \text{ constant}} = \frac{\partial z}{\partial x_1}\frac{\partial x_1}{\partial t} + \frac{\partial z}{\partial x_2}\frac{\partial x_2}{\partial t} \tag{10-25}$$

Similarly, the rate of change of z with respect to w, while t is held constant, is

$$\left.\frac{dz}{dw}\right|_{t \text{ constant}} = \frac{\partial z}{\partial x_1}\frac{\partial x_1}{\partial w} + \frac{\partial z}{\partial x_2}\frac{\partial x_2}{\partial w} \tag{10-26}$$

10-D PRACTICE PROBLEMS

10-16 Given $z = 4xy + x^2$, where $x = 3y + 5$, find the total derivative dz/dy.
10-17 Given $z = x^2 - y^2$, where $x = 2w + 3$ and $y = w^2$, find the total derivative dz/dw.
10-18 Given $z = 7xy - 2x^2$, where $x = 2u - 3v$ and $y = u^2 + v$, find

$$\left.\frac{dz}{du}\right|_{v \text{ constant}} \quad \text{and} \quad \left.\frac{dz}{dv}\right|_{u \text{ constant}}$$

10-6 DERIVATIVES OF IMPLICIT FUNCTIONS

A function which is written in the form $y = f(x)$, such as

$$y = f(x) = 2x^2 + 5 \tag{10-27}$$

is called an *explicit function* because the variable y is explicitly expressed as a function of x. Note, however, that if (10-27) is rewritten in the equivalent form

$$y - 2x^2 - 5 = 0 \tag{10-28}$$

then, although we no longer have the explicit function (10-27), the function (10-27) is *implicitly* defined by (10-28). Consequently, if we are given an equation in the form of (10-28) then the function $y = f(x)$ which it implies is known as an *implicit function*. For example, the equation

$$xy - y - 2x^2 = 0 \tag{10-29}$$

implicitly defines y as a function of x, even though in this case the implicit function $y = f(x) = 2x^2/(x-1)$ is not so immediately apparent.

If equations in the form of (10-28) and (10-29) are denoted in general by $F(x, y) = 0$, then the derivatives of the implicit functions that they define can be found by: (1) solving $F(x, y)$ for $y = f(x)$, and (2) finding dy/dx in the usual way. However, this immediately raises the interesting question: can we still find the derivative dy/dx in the case where an implicit function (or several such functions) $y = f(x)$ is assumed to be defined by an equation $F(x, y) = 0$, despite the fact that $F(x, y) = 0$ cannot be solved for y explicitly? Fortunately, the answer to this question is yes, as will be shown by reference to the *implicit-function rule*.

Implicit-Function Rule

If we are given an equation $F(x, y) = 0$, for which an implicit function $y = f(x)$ is assumed to exist, then by taking the differentials of both sides of $F(x, y) = 0$ we obtain

$$\frac{\partial F}{\partial x} dx + \frac{\partial F}{\partial y} dy = 0 \quad \text{or} \quad F_x dx + F_y dy = 0$$

which, upon division by dx, yields

$$\frac{\partial F}{\partial x} + \frac{\partial F}{\partial y}\frac{dy}{dx} = 0 \quad \text{or} \quad F_x + F_y \frac{dy}{dx} = 0 \qquad (10\text{-}30)$$

From (10-30) we obtain the general result

$$\frac{dy}{dx} = -\frac{F_x}{F_y} = -\frac{\partial F/\partial x}{\partial F/\partial y} \qquad (10\text{-}31)$$

which is known as the *implicit-function rule*. In other words, given $F(x, y) = 0$, the derivative dy/dx, of the implicit function $y = f(x)$, is the negative of the ratio of the two partial derivatives F_x and F_y. For example, given $F(x, y) = xy - y - 2x^2 = 0$, as in (10-29), then

$$\frac{dy}{dx} = -\frac{F_x}{F_y} = -\frac{(y-4x)}{(x-1)}$$

The implicit-function rule can readily be extended to the general case where the equation $F(y, x_1, x_2, \ldots, x_n) = 0$ is assumed to define the implicit function (or functions) $y = f(x_1, x_2, \ldots, x_n)$. Thus, if we take differentials of both sides of $F(y, x_1, x_2, \ldots, x_n) = 0$ we obtain

$$F_y dy + F_1 dx_1 + F_2 dx_2 + \ldots + F_n dx_n = 0 \qquad (10\text{-}32)$$

Supposing now that only y and x_1 are allowed to vary, so that $dx_2 = dx_3 = \ldots = dx_n = 0$, then (10-32) reduces to

$$F_y dy + F_1 dx_1 = 0$$

which, upon division by dx_1 and solving for dy/dx_1, yields

$$\left.\frac{dy}{dx_1}\right|_{x_2,\ldots,x_n \text{constant}} \equiv \frac{\partial y}{\partial x_1} = -\frac{F_1}{F_y}$$

In an analogous fashion, we can obtain all the other partial derivatives of the implicit function f. Hence, in this general case, the implicit-function rule states that

$$\frac{\partial y}{\partial x_i} = -\frac{F_i}{F_y} \quad (i = 1, 2, \ldots, n) \qquad (10\text{-}33)$$

For example, assuming that the equation

$$F(x, y, z) = x^3 y + yz^2 + xyz - 32 = 0$$

defines an implicit function $y = f(x, z)$, then the derivative $\partial y/\partial x$ is given by (10-33) as

$$\frac{\partial y}{\partial x} = -\frac{F_x}{F_y} = -\frac{(3x^2 y + yz)}{(x^3 + z^2 + xz)}$$

10-E PRACTICE PROBLEMS

10-19 Assuming that each of the following equations, of form $F(x, y) = 0$, defines an implicit function $y = f(x)$, find dy/dx by the implicit-function rule:
  (a) $2x^2 - y^3x + x^3y - 18 = 0$ (b) $xy + y^5x^2 - 10yx^3 - 14 = 0$

10-20 Assuming that the equation $F(w, x, y, z) = w^5x^2 + 2yx^4 - z^3y^7 - 3y^3 - 19 = 0$ defines an implicit function $y = f(w, x, z)$, find $\partial y/\partial w$ and $\partial y/\partial z$.

CHAPTER ELEVEN
ECONOMIC APPLICATIONS OF PARTIAL AND TOTAL DIFFERENTIATION

In this chapter, we shall briefly examine some economic applications of partial and total differentiation. The brief discussion of this chapter will then be followed, in Chapters 12 and 13, by a much fuller examination of the economic applications of these concepts.

11-1 COMPARATIVE-STATIC ANALYSIS

In Chapter 3, we saw how static-equilibrium market models, and static-equilibrium national-income models, can be constructed in terms of simultaneous-equation systems. Also, in Chapter 3, we saw how such models can be solved in order to obtain the equilibrium values of the respective endogenous variables in terms of the given parameters and exogenous variables. Now, in this section, we will use our knowledge of partial differentiation to extend our analysis of such models. In particular, we shall proceed to a *comparative-static analysis* of such models by examining how the equilibrium value of an endogenous variable changes when there is a change in the value of some parameter or exogenous variable.

A Linear Partial-Equilibrium Market Model

In Chapter 3, we encountered the linear partial-equilibrium market model:

$$Q_d = Q_s$$
$$Q_d = a - bP \quad (a, b > 0) \tag{11-1}$$
$$Q_s = -c + dP \quad (c, d > 0)$$

with solutions

$$\bar{P} = \frac{a+c}{d+b} \quad \text{and} \quad \bar{Q} = \bar{Q}_d = \bar{Q}_s = \frac{ad-bc}{d+b} \tag{11-2}$$

Note, in (11-2), that the equilibrium values $\bar{P}$ and $\bar{Q}$ $(= \bar{Q}_d = \bar{Q}_s)$, of the three endogenous variables P, Q_d, and Q_s, are expressions in terms of the given parameters a, b, c, and d.

If we now wish to find how an infinitesimal change in one of the parameters will affect the value of $\bar{P}$ (or $\bar{Q}$), then we simply differentiate the $\bar{P}$ (or $\bar{Q}$) expression, in (11-2), partially with respect to the parameter that has changed. For example, the change in the value of $\bar{P}$ when parameter a changes is given by

$$\frac{\partial \bar{P}}{\partial a} = \frac{1}{d+b} \quad \left[\text{since } \bar{P} = \frac{a+c}{d+b} = a\left(\frac{1}{d+b}\right) + \frac{c}{d+b} \right]$$

Thus, since $\partial \bar{P}/\partial a = 1/(d+b) > 0$, then $\bar{P}$ will change in the same direction as a changes, increasing (decreasing) as a increases (decreases), with the magnitude of the rate of change of $\bar{P}$ being $1/(d+b)$ units per unit change in a. Similarly, the change in the value of $\bar{P}$ when parameter b changes is given by

$$\frac{\partial \bar{P}}{\partial b} = \frac{(d+b)(0) - (a+c)(1)}{(d+b)^2} = -\frac{(a+c)}{(d+b)^2} \quad \text{[quotient rule]}$$

Since $\partial \bar{P}/\partial b = -(a+c)/(d+b)^2 < 0$, then $\bar{P}$ will change in the opposite direction as b changes, decreasing (increasing) as b increases (decreases), with the magnitude of the rate of decrease (increase) of $\bar{P}$ being $(a+c)/(d+b)^2$ units per unit increase (decrease) in b.

A better appreciation of the meaning of $\partial \bar{P}/\partial a > 0$ and $\partial \bar{P}/\partial b < 0$ can be obtained by an examination of Figs. 11-1a and 11-1b, which show the changes in a and b, respectively. Thus, in Fig. 11-1a, it can be seen that an increase in the intercept parameter of the demand function, from a to a', will lead to a parallel upward shift of the demand curve from Q_d to Q'_d. The intersection of the new demand curve Q'_d and the (unchanged) supply curve Q_s will then determine a new equilibrium price $\bar{P}'$, which can be seen to be greater than the initial equilibrium price $\bar{P}$. Note that this graphical result indicates that *any* increase in a, including the infinitesimal increase implied

11-1 COMPARATIVE-STATIC ANALYSIS

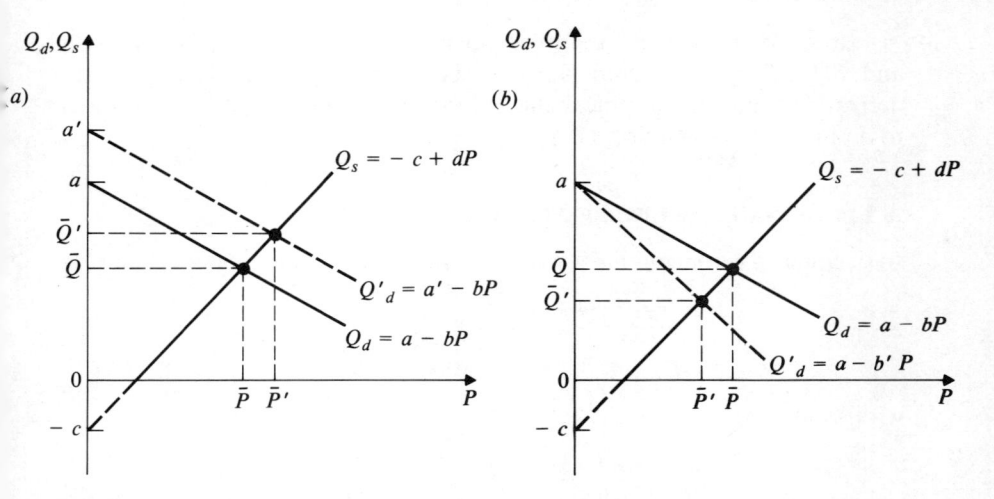

Figure 11-1

(a) Q_d, Q_s axes showing $Q_s = -c + dP$, $Q_d = a - bP$, $Q'_d = a' - bP$, with equilibrium shifting from $\bar{P}$ to $\bar{P}'$ and $\bar{Q}$ to $\bar{Q}'$.

(b) Q_d, Q_s axes showing $Q_s = -c + dP$, $Q_d = a - bP$, $Q'_d = a - b'P$, with equilibrium shifting from $\bar{P}$ to $\bar{P}'$.

by $\partial \bar{P}/\partial a$, will result in an increase in the equilibrium price. Consequently, the graphical result confirms the mathematical result that $\partial \bar{P}/\partial a > 0$. Also, note that the graphical analysis serves to emphasize that comparative-static analysis (or comparative statics for short) is concerned with a comparison of the initial (*pre*change) static-equilibrium and the final (*post*change) static-equilibrium.

In Fig. 11-1b, an increase in the slope parameter of the demand function, from b to b', will make the (negative-sloped) demand curve become steeper, as can be seen by comparison of Q_d and Q'_d. Thus, in Fig. 11-1b, the equilibrium price has fallen from $\bar{P}$ to $\bar{P}'$ as a result of the increase in b, which is in keeping with the mathematical result that $\partial \bar{P}/\partial b < 0$.

Note, in Fig. 11-1a, that an increase in a results in an increase in equilibrium quantity from $\bar{Q}$ to $\bar{Q}'$. Also note, in Fig. 11-1b, that an increase in b results in a decrease in equilibrium quantity from $\bar{Q}$ to $\bar{Q}'$. This implies that $\partial \bar{Q}/\partial a > 0$ and $\partial \bar{Q}/\partial b < 0$. To check this, let us differentiate $\bar{Q}$ in (11-2) partially with respect to a and then with respect to b to obtain

$$\frac{\partial \bar{Q}}{\partial a} = \frac{d}{d+b} > 0 \quad \left[\text{since } \bar{Q} = \frac{ad-bc}{d+b} = a\left(\frac{d}{d+b}\right) - \frac{bc}{d+b}\right]$$

and

$$\frac{\partial \bar{Q}}{\partial b} = \frac{(d+b)(-c) - (ad-bc)(1)}{(d+b)^2} = -\frac{d(a+c)}{(d+b)^2} < 0 \quad \text{[quotient rule]}$$

Since $\partial \bar{Q}/\partial a > 0$ and $\partial \bar{Q}/\partial b < 0$, then the above graphical results are confirmed by these mathematical results.

In a similar fashion, the other partial derivatives, $\partial \bar{P}/\partial c$, $\partial \bar{P}/\partial d$, $\partial \bar{Q}/\partial c$, and $\partial \bar{Q}/\partial d$, can be obtained from (11-2). The finding of these partial derivatives (and the graphical checking of the results) is left for the student to do in Prob. 11-1 of Sec. 11-A.

A Linear National-Income Model

In Chapter 3, we encountered the linear national-income model:

$$\begin{aligned} Y &= C + I + G \\ C &= \alpha + \beta(Y - T) \quad (\alpha > 0; 0 < \beta < 1) \\ T &= tY \quad (0 < t < 1) \end{aligned} \quad (11\text{-}3)$$

with solutions

$$\bar{Y} = \frac{\alpha + I + G}{1 - \beta(1-t)}, \quad \bar{C} = \frac{\alpha + \beta(1-t)(I+G)}{1 - \beta(1-t)},$$
$$\text{and} \quad \bar{T} = \frac{t(\alpha + I + G)}{1 - \beta(1-t)} \quad (11\text{-}4)$$

Note, in (11-4), that the equilibrium values $\bar{Y}$, $\bar{C}$, and $\bar{T}$, of the three endogenous variables Y, C, and T, are expressions in terms of the given parameters (α, β, and t) and the exogenous variables (I and G).

If we wish to find how an infinitesimal change in one of the parameters, or in one of the exogenous variables, will affect the value of $\bar{Y}$ (or $\bar{C}$ or $\bar{T}$), then we simply differentiate the $\bar{Y}$ (or $\bar{C}$ or $\bar{T}$) expression in (11-4) partially with respect to the parameter or exogenous variable that has changed. For example, if the government is interested (for policy purposes) in knowing how $\bar{Y}$ will be affected by changes in: (1) private investment expenditure I, (2) government expenditure G, and (3) the income-tax rate t, then we find the three partial derivatives:

$$\frac{\partial \bar{Y}}{\partial I} = \frac{1}{1 - \beta(1-t)} > 0 \quad (11\text{-}5)$$

$$\frac{\partial \bar{Y}}{\partial G} = \frac{1}{1 - \beta(1-t)} > 0 \quad (11\text{-}6)$$

$$\frac{\partial \bar{Y}}{\partial t} = -\frac{\beta(\alpha + I + G)}{[1 - \beta(1-t)]^2} = -\frac{\beta \bar{Y}}{1 - \beta(1-t)} < 0 \quad (11\text{-}7)$$

which provide us with information about both the direction and the magnitude of the changes in $\bar{Y}$ resulting from the (infinitesimal) changes in I, G and t, respectively. These three important partial derivatives are known, respectively, as the *investment multiplier*, the *government-expenditure multiplier*, and the *income-tax-rate multiplier*.

The above comparative-static analysis, in terms of partial derivatives, can be readily extended to models involving many endogenous variables. Note, in such cases, that although we cannot resort to graphical analysis, the mathematical analysis in terms of partial derivatives can still be applied.

11-A PRACTICE PROBLEMS

11-1 Given $\bar{P}$ and $\bar{Q}$ in (11-2), find the partial derivatives $\partial \bar{P}/\partial c$, $\partial \bar{P}/\partial d$, $\partial \bar{Q}/\partial c$, and $\partial \bar{Q}/\partial d$. In each case, check your result by graphical analysis.

11-2 Given $\bar{Y}$ in (11-4), find the partial derivatives $\partial \bar{Y}/\partial \alpha$ and $\partial \bar{Y}/\partial \beta$. Also, indicate the information provided by each of these partial derivatives.

11-2 PARTIAL ELASTICITIES

In Chapter 7, we encountered the concept of *elasticity* for functions of one independent variable. Now, in this section, we can use our knowledge of partial differentiation to define what are known as *partial elasticities* for functions of more than one independent variable.

To illustrate the concept of partial elasticity, let us assume that Q_1, the quantity demanded of good 1, is a function of the prices of goods 1 and 2 (denoted by P_1 and P_2), and consumers' income (denoted by Y). Hence, the (market) demand function for Q_1 may be written as

$$Q_1 = Q_1(P_1, P_2, Y) \qquad (11\text{-}8)$$

For this demand function the following three *partial elasticities of demand* can be defined:

1. The *own* (or *direct*) *price elasticity of demand*

$$E_{11} = -\frac{\partial Q_1}{\partial P_1} \frac{P_1}{Q_1}$$

which measures the ratio of the proportional change in the quantity demanded of good 1 to the proportional (infinitesimal) change in the price of good 1, *with the price of good 2 and income held constant*.

2. The *cross price elasticity of demand*

$$E_{12} = \frac{\partial Q_1}{\partial P_2} \frac{P_2}{Q_1}$$

which measures the ratio of the proportional change in the quantity demanded of good 1 to the proportional (infinitesimal) change in the price of good 2, *with the price of good 1 and income held constant*. Note that if $E_{12} < 0$, then goods 1 and 2 bear a complementary relationship to each other. Conversely, if $E_{12} > 0$, then goods 1 and 2 bear a substitute

relationship to each other. Also, note that if the absolute value of E_{12} is close to zero, then goods 1 and 2 bear little relation to each other.
3. The *income elasticity of demand*

$$E_{1Y} = \frac{\partial Q_1}{\partial Y} \frac{Y}{Q_1}$$

which measures the ratio of the proportional change in the quantity demanded of good 1 to the proportional (infinitesimal) change in consumers' income, *with the prices of goods* 1 *and* 2 *held constant*.

Note that each of the above elasticity measures is defined in terms of the change in *one* of the independent variables only. Hence the name *partial elasticities*.

As an example, let us assume that the demand function is linear and given by

$$Q_1 = Q_1(P_1, P_2, Y) = 12 - 4P_1 + 3P_2 + \tfrac{1}{10}Y$$

The partial elasticities, E_{11}, E_{12}, and E_{1Y}, when $P_1 = 2$, $P_2 = 4$, and $Y = 200$, can then be found as follows:

$$E_{11} = -\frac{\partial Q_1}{\partial P_1} \frac{P_1}{Q_1} = -(-4)\frac{P_1}{Q_1} = \frac{4(2)}{36} = \frac{2}{9}$$

where $Q_1(2, 4, 200) = 36$. Similarly,

$$E_{12} = \frac{\partial Q_1}{\partial P_2} \frac{P_2}{Q_1} = 3\frac{P_2}{Q_1} = \frac{3(4)}{36} = \frac{1}{3}$$

and

$$E_{1Y} = \frac{\partial Q_1}{\partial Y} \frac{Y}{Q_1} = \frac{1}{10}\frac{Y}{Q_1} = \frac{1}{10}\frac{200}{36} = \frac{5}{9}$$

Note that $E_{12} = \tfrac{1}{3} > 0$, indicating that goods 1 and 2 are substitutes. Also, in each case, note that (*a*) the resulting elasticity measure is dimensionless, and (*b*) the respective partial elasticity is evaluated at some (P_1, P_2, Y) point.

As a further example, let us assume that the equation

$$F(Q_1, P_1, P_2, Y) = Q_1^2 P_1^{2/3} P_2^{2/3} Y^{-5} - 32 = 0$$

defines an implicit demand function $Q_1 = Q_1(P_1, P_2, Y)$. In this example, in finding E_{11}, E_{12}, and E_{1Y}, we will first make use of the implicit-function rule in order to obtain the required partial derivatives $\partial Q_1/\partial P_1$, $\partial Q_1/\partial P_2$, and $\partial Q_1/\partial Y$. Thus,

$$\frac{\partial Q_1}{\partial P_1} = -\frac{\partial F/\partial P_1}{\partial F/\partial Q_1} = -\frac{\tfrac{2}{3}Q_1^2 P_1^{-1/3} P_2^{2/3} Y^{-5}}{2Q_1 P_1^{2/3} P_2^{2/3} Y^{-5}} = -\frac{1}{3}\frac{Q_1}{P_1}.$$

Hence,
$$E_{11} = -\frac{\partial Q_1}{\partial P_1}\frac{P_1}{Q_1} = \frac{1}{3}.$$

$$\frac{\partial Q_1}{\partial P_2} = -\frac{\partial F/\partial P_2}{\partial F/\partial Q_1} = -\frac{\frac{2}{3}Q_1^2 P_1^{2/3} P_2^{-1/3} Y^{-5}}{2Q_1 P_1^{2/3} P_2^{2/3} Y^{-5}} = -\frac{1}{3}\frac{Q_1}{P_2}.$$

Hence,
$$E_{12} = \frac{\partial Q_1}{\partial P_2}\frac{P_2}{Q_1} = -\frac{1}{3}.$$

Since $E_{12} = -\frac{1}{3} < 0$, goods 1 and 2 are complements.

$$\frac{\partial Q_1}{\partial Y} = -\frac{\partial F/\partial Y}{\partial F/\partial Q_1} = \frac{5Q_1^2 P_1^{2/3} P_2^{2/3} Y^{-6}}{2Q_1 P_1^{2/3} P_2^{2/3} Y^{-5}} = \frac{5}{2}\frac{Q_1}{Y}.$$

Hence,
$$E_{1Y} = \frac{\partial Q_1}{\partial Y}\frac{Y}{Q_1} = \frac{5}{2}.$$

Partial elasticities can also be defined for other functions. For example, given an investment function

$$I = I(r, Y)$$

where I = aggregate investment expenditure, r = rate of interest, and Y = national income, the partial elasticities for this function may be written as

$$E_{Ir} = \frac{\partial I}{\partial r}\frac{r}{I} \quad \text{and} \quad E_{IY} = \frac{\partial I}{\partial Y}\frac{Y}{I}$$

11-B PRACTICE PROBLEMS

11-3 Find the own price elasticity, the cross price elasticity, and the income elasticity of demand for each of the following demand functions at point $(P_1, P_2, Y) = (4, 32, 100)$. In each case, state whether the goods referred to are complements or substitutes:
 (a) $Q_1 = 2 - 2P_1 - \frac{1}{8}P_2 + \frac{1}{5}Y$ (b) $Q_1 = \frac{1}{100}P_1^{-1/2}P_2^{1/5}Y^{3/2}$

11-4 Assuming that the equation $F(Q_1, P_1, P_2, Y) = 10P_1Q_1 + 5Q_1 - 2P_2 - 4Y - 18 = 0$ defines an implicit demand function $Q_1 = Q_1(P_1, P_2, Y)$, find E_{11}, E_{12}, and E_{1Y} at point $(Q_1, P_1, P_2, Y) = (4, 2, 1, 10)$.

11-5 If the supply function of good A is $Q_A = Q_A(P_A, S)$, where P_A and S denote the price of good A and hours of sunshine, respectively, write out the expressions for
 (a) the price elasticity of supply E_{AA}, and
 (b) the sunshine elasticity of supply E_{AS}.

11-3 DIFFERENTIALS AND ELASTICITY

In Chapter 10, we noted that a derivative can be reinterpreted as the ratio of two differentials. For example, the derivative dQ_d/dP, of a demand function $Q_d = f(P)$, can be regarded as the ratio of the two differentials dQ_d and dP. This means that the expression for the price elasticity, of a demand function $Q_d = f(P)$, can be written either as

$$E_d = -\frac{dQ_d}{dP}\frac{P}{Q_d} \quad \text{or} \quad E_d = -\frac{dQ_d/Q_d}{dP/P} \qquad (11\text{-}9)$$

To obtain a further expression for price elasticity of demand, recall that if $y = \ln x$, then the log-function rule of differentiation gives $dy/dx = d(\ln x)/dx = 1/x$ or, treating the derivative as the ratio of two differentials, $dy = d(\ln x) = dx/x$. This result enables us, by analogy, to write

$$d(\ln Q_d) = dQ_d/Q_d \quad \text{and} \quad d(\ln P) = dP/P \qquad (11\text{-}10)$$

Therefore, substituting (11-10) into (11-9), we have

$$E_d = -\frac{dQ_d}{dP}\frac{P}{Q_d} = -\frac{dQ_d/Q_d}{dP/P} = -\frac{d(\ln Q_d)}{d(\ln P)} \qquad (11\text{-}11)$$

The elasticity expression in (11-11) is very convenient for finding the elasticity of a function which comes in the form of a multiplicative or divisional expression. For example, given $Q_d = f(P) = \alpha P^{-\beta}$ or, equivalently, $Q_d = \alpha/P^\beta$, where $\alpha, \beta > 0$, we simply take logs to obtain $\ln Q_d = \ln \alpha - \beta \ln P$ and then differentiate to find

$$E_d = -\frac{d(\ln Q_d)}{d(\ln P)} = \beta$$

In the case of a demand function of more than one independent variable, such as $Q_1 = Q_1(P_1, Y)$, we can define the *partial* price elasticity of demand as follows:

$$E_{11} = -\frac{d(\ln Q_1)}{d(\ln P_1)}\bigg|_{Y \text{ constant}} = \left(-\frac{dQ_1}{dP_1}\frac{P_1}{Q_1}\right)_{Y \text{ constant}}$$

or

$$E_{11} = -\frac{\partial(\ln Q_1)}{\partial(\ln P_1)} = -\frac{\partial Q_1}{\partial P_1}\frac{P_1}{Q_1}$$

Similarly, the *partial* income elasticity of demand is

$$E_{1Y} = \frac{d(\ln Q_1)}{d(\ln Y)}\bigg|_{P_1 \text{ constant}} = \left(\frac{dQ_1}{dY}\frac{Y}{Q_1}\right)_{P_1 \text{ constant}}$$

or

$$E_{1Y} = \frac{\partial(\ln Q_1)}{\partial(\ln Y)} = \frac{\partial Q_1}{\partial Y}\frac{Y}{Q_1}$$

Thus, for example, given the demand function $Q_1 = AP_1^{-\alpha} P_2^{\beta} Y^{\gamma}$, where $A, \alpha, \beta, \gamma > 0$, we simply take logs to obtain $\ln Q_1 = \ln A - \alpha \ln P_1 + \beta \ln P_2 + \gamma \ln Y$ and then differentiate partially to find

$$E_{11} = -\frac{\partial (\ln Q_1)}{\partial (\ln P_1)} = \alpha, \quad E_{12} = \frac{\partial (\ln Q_1)}{\partial (\ln P_2)} = \beta,$$

and

$$E_{1Y} = \frac{\partial (\ln Q_1)}{\partial (\ln Y)} = \gamma.$$

Note that while the above discussion has been limited to demand functions, it is equally applicable to any function which comes in the form of a multiplicative or divisional expression.

11-C PRACTICE PROBLEMS

11-6 Given the supply function $Q_s = \delta P^{\sigma}$, where $\delta, \sigma > 0$, find the price elasticity of supply (E_s) using logs.

11-7 Given the demand function $Q_1 = \frac{1}{200} P_1^{-3/8} P_2^{-2/5} Y^{5/2}$, find $E_{11}, E_{12},$ and E_{1Y} using logs.

11-4 PRODUCTION FUNCTION ANALYSIS

In this section we shall briefly indicate how partial and total differentiation can be used in the economic analysis of production.

As a first step, we shall assume that output (Q) is a function of the inputs capital (K) and labour (L), so that the production function may be written as

$$Q = f(K, L) \tag{11-12}$$

Given (11-12), we can now use partial differentiation to answer the following, interesting, economic questions:

1. How does output vary as labour input varies, with capital input held constant at some level? To answer this we find $\partial Q/\partial L \equiv f_L$. Similarly, to find how output varies as capital input is varied, with labour input held constant at some level, we find $\partial Q/\partial K \equiv f_K$. These partial derivatives are known, respectively, as the *marginal product of labour* (denoted by $MP_L = f_L$) and the *marginal product of capital* (denoted by $MP_K = f_K$).
2. How does the marginal product of labour vary as labour input is varied, with capital input held constant at some level? To answer this we find $\partial (MP_L)/\partial L = \partial^2 Q/\partial L^2 \equiv f_{LL}$. Similarly, to find how the marginal product of capital varies as capital input varies, with labour input held constant at some level, we find $\partial (MP_K)/\partial K = \partial^2 Q/\partial K^2 \equiv f_{KK}$.
3. How does the marginal product of labour vary as capital input is varied, with labour input held constant at some level? To answer this we find

$\partial(MP_L)/\partial K = \partial^2 Q/\partial K \partial L \equiv f_{KL}$. Similarly, to find how the marginal product of capital varies as labour input is varied, with capital input held constant at some level, we find $\partial(MP_K)/\partial L = \partial^2 Q/\partial L \partial K \equiv f_{LK}(= f_{KL}$ via Young's theorem).

4. What is the proportional change in output resulting from a proportional (infinitesimal) change in labour input, with capital input held constant at some level? To answer this we find the *partial elasticity of output with respect to labour input* $E_{QL} = (\partial Q/\partial L)(L/Q)$. Similarly, to find the proportional change in output resulting from a proportional (infinitesimal) change in capital input, with labour input held constant at some level, we find the *partial elasticity of output with respect to capital input* $E_{QK} = (\partial Q/\partial K)(K/Q)$.

The above analysis can be illustrated by taking a specific production function. For example, a specific production function which is widely used in economic analysis is the *Cobb-Douglas production function*:

$$Q = f(K, L) = AK^\alpha L^\beta \qquad (11\text{-}13)$$

where A is a positive constant and both α and β are positive fractions. Thus, for the Cobb-Douglas production function, the answers to the above four questions are given by:

(1')
$$MP_L = f_L = \beta AK^\alpha L^{\beta-1} = \beta \frac{Q}{L} > 0 \text{ for } K, L > 0$$

and

$$MP_K = f_K = \alpha AK^{\alpha-1} L^\beta = \alpha \frac{Q}{K} > 0 \text{ for } K, L > 0$$

(2')
$$\frac{\partial(MP_L)}{\partial L} = f_{LL} = (\beta-1)\beta AK^\alpha L^{\beta-2} = (\beta-1)\frac{\beta Q}{L^2} < 0 \text{ for } K, L > 0$$

and

$$\frac{\partial(MP_K)}{\partial K} = f_{KK} = (\alpha-1)\alpha AK^{\alpha-2} L^\beta = (\alpha-1)\frac{\alpha Q}{K^2} < 0 \text{ for } K, L > 0$$

(3')
$$\frac{\partial(MP_L)}{\partial K} = f_{KL} = \alpha\beta AK^{\alpha-1} L^{\beta-1} = \frac{\alpha\beta Q}{KL} > 0 \text{ for } K, L > 0$$

and

$$\frac{\partial(MP_K)}{\partial L} = f_{LK} = \alpha\beta AK^{\alpha-1} L^{\beta-1} = \frac{\alpha\beta Q}{KL} > 0 \text{ for } K, L > 0$$

(4')
$$E_{QL} = \frac{\partial Q}{\partial L}\frac{L}{Q} = (\beta AK^\alpha L^{\beta-1})\frac{L}{Q} = \left(\beta\frac{Q}{L}\right)\frac{L}{Q} = \beta$$

and

$$E_{QK} = \frac{\partial Q}{\partial K}\frac{K}{Q} = (\alpha AK^{\alpha-1} L^\beta)\frac{K}{Q} = \left(\alpha\frac{Q}{K}\right)\frac{K}{Q} = \alpha$$

A further interesting question that we may ask in relation to the Cobb-Douglas production function is: if *all* inputs are changed in the same proportion, will the resultant change in output be in a smaller, equal, or greater proportion? To answer this, let us change both K and L by the proportion λ (where λ is a nonzero constant) to, respectively, λK and λL. Thus, output will be changed to

$$A(\lambda K)^\alpha(\lambda L)^\beta = \lambda^{\alpha+\beta}(AK^\alpha L^\beta) = \lambda^{\alpha+\beta}Q$$

In other words, output has changed by the proportion $\lambda^{\alpha+\beta}$. This means that (a) if $\alpha+\beta = 1$, then the proportionate change in output is equal to the proportionate change in both inputs (which, in economic terminology, is the case of *constant returns to scale*), (b) if $\alpha+\beta < 1$, then the proportionate change in output is less than the proportionate change in both inputs (the case of *decreasing returns to scale*), and (c) if $\alpha+\beta > 1$, then the proportionate change in output is greater than the proportionate change in both inputs (the case of *increasing returns to scale*).

As an example, let us suppose that the production function is $Q = f(K,L) = 28K^{1/4}L^{2/3}$ and the proportionate increase in both inputs is $\lambda = 4$. Thus, output will be changed to $28(\lambda K)^{1/4}(\lambda L)^{2/3} = \lambda^{1/4+2/3}(28K^{1/4}L^{2/3}) = \lambda^{11/12}Q = 4^{11/12}Q$. Since $4^{11/12}Q < 4Q$, then the proportionate (less than fourfold) change in output is less than the proportionate (fourfold) change in both inputs. Consequently, output is subject to decreasing returns to scale.

In general, a production function $Q = f(K, L)$ is said to be *homogeneous of degree r* if multiplication of both K and L by a constant λ will alter the value of the production function by the proportion λ^r. That is, if

$$f(\lambda K, \lambda L) = \lambda^r f(K, L)$$

for all values of K, L, and λ for which the function f is defined. Consequently, if the Cobb-Douglas production function has $\alpha+\beta = 1$, so that output is subject to constant returns to scale, then we say that it is homogeneous of degree 1. It is for this reason that the term *linearly homogeneous* (meaning homogeneous of degree one) is often used interchangeably with the term *constant returns to scale*. Similarly, if a production function is homogeneous of degree less than one (greater than one), then output is said to be subject to decreasing (increasing) returns to scale.

Finally, in the case where $Q = f(K, L)$, with both K and L being functions of time (t), the change in output over time can be obtained by finding the total derivative dQ/dt. Thus, given

$$Q = f(K, L) \quad \text{where} \quad \begin{cases} K = g(t) \\ L = h(t) \end{cases}$$

then

$$\frac{dQ}{dt} = \frac{\partial Q}{\partial K}\frac{dK}{dt} + \frac{\partial Q}{\partial L}\frac{dL}{dt}.$$

11-D PRACTICE PROBLEMS

11-8 Given $Q = f(K, L) = 200K^{1/2}L^{2/3}$, find the answers to questions (1) to (4) in Sec. 11-4.

11-9 What is the effect of doubling both factor inputs in the production function given in Prob. 11-8?

11-5 ADDITIONAL PROBLEMS

11-10 Given the expressions for equilibrium price and quantity in (3-25) and (3-26), respectively, find the partial derivatives $\partial \bar{P}/\partial b$, $\partial \bar{Q}/\partial b$, $\partial \bar{P}/\partial c$, and $\partial \bar{Q}/\partial c$. Explain the meaning and determine the sign of each partial derivative.

11-11 Given $\bar{C}$ and $\bar{T}$ in (11-4), find the partial derivatives $\partial \bar{C}/\partial G$ and $\partial \bar{T}/\partial t$. Explain the meaning and determine the sign of each partial derivative.

11-12 The equilibrium value of Y in Prob. 5-14, in Sec. 5-6, is

$$\bar{Y} = (\alpha - n + I + G + X)/(1 - \beta + m)$$

Find the partial derivative $\partial \bar{Y}/\partial m$. Also, explain the meaning and determine the sign of $\partial \bar{Y}/\partial m$.

11-13 The equilibrium values of Y and r in Prob. 5-16, in Sec. 5-6, are

$$\bar{Y} = \frac{(\alpha + \gamma + G)\mu + \delta(M_0 - \sigma)}{(1 - \beta)\mu + \lambda\delta} \quad \text{and} \quad \bar{r} = \frac{(1 - \beta)(M_0 - \sigma) - \lambda(\alpha + \gamma + G)}{(1 - \beta)\mu + \lambda\delta}$$

Find the partial derivatives $\partial \bar{Y}/\partial G$, $\partial \bar{r}/\partial G$, $\partial \bar{Y}/\partial M_0$, and $\partial \bar{r}/\partial M_0$. Explain the policy significance of these partial derivatives and determine their signs.

11-14 Given the utility function $U = U(Q_1, Q_2, Q_3)$, where $Q_2 = g(Q_1)$ and $Q_3 = h(Q_1)$, find the change in utility resulting from a change in Q_1 (i.e., find dU/dQ_1).

11-15 Assuming that the equation $F(Q_1, P_1, P_2, P_3, Y) = 6P_1Q_1 + 3Q_1 - 2P_2 + 4P_3 - 5Y = 0$ defines an implicit demand function $Q_1 = Q_1(P_1, P_2, P_3, Y)$, use the implicit-function rule of differentiation to find:

(a) the own price elasticity of demand E_{11}
(b) the cross price elasticities of demand E_{12} and E_{13}
(c) the income elasticity of demand E_{1Y},

at point $(Q_1, P_1, P_2, P_3, Y) = (4, 2, 2, 1, 12)$.

11-16 Given the production function $Q = 18K^{2/5}L^{1/2}$, use logs to find:

(a) the partial elasticity of output with respect to capital input
(b) the partial elasticity of output with respect to labour input

11-17 Given the production function $Q = f(K, L, R) = AK^\alpha L^\beta R^\gamma$, where R is raw material input, A is a positive constant, and the parameters α, β and γ are positive fractions, demonstrate that:

(a) $\alpha + \beta + \gamma < 1$ implies decreasing returns to scale
(b) $\alpha + \beta + \gamma = 1$ implies constant returns to scale
(c) $\alpha + \beta + \gamma > 1$ implies increasing returns to scale
(d) α, β and γ are, respectively, the partial elasticities of output with respect to capital, labour, and raw material inputs.

11-18 Given the production function $Q = f(K, L) = (\alpha K^{-\rho} + \beta L^{-\rho})^{-1/\rho}$, where α, β, and ρ are constants, demonstrate that output is subject to constant returns to scale.

11-19 A certain production function is said to possess:

(a) the property of diminishing marginal product of labour (capital) as labour (capital) input increases, with capital (labour) input held constant at some level
(b) the property of increasing returns to scale. Are (a) and (b) contradictory? Illustrate your answer by reference to the Cobb-Douglas production function.

CHAPTER
TWELVE
UNCONSTRAINED EXTREMA

In Chapter 8, maximization and minimization were analysed within the context of a function of one independent variable. While such an analysis is both useful and important for certain problems in economics, it is inadequate for many other problems. For example, it is incapable of handling the following selection of problems: (i) profit maximization by a multi-product firm; (ii) profit maximization by a firm selling its output in more than one market; (iii) profit maximization by a firm producing its output in more than one plant; (iv) finding a firm's profit-maximizing input combination when output is produced by more than one input. To handle such problems requires a knowledge of maximization for cases which involve a function of two or more independent variables. Consequently, in this chapter, we will examine how to find the relative extrema of a function of more than one variable. While our discussion will be confined to the two-variable case, the analysis which will be developed can be readily extended to the more-than-two-variable case.

It should be noted that the above selection of problems all involve *unconstrained maximization*. However, not all problems in economics are of this nature. For example, in the theory of consumer choice, a consumer is presented as maximizing his utility subject to a given budget constraint. Also, in the theory of production and cost, an entrepreneur may be presented as maximizing his output subject to a given cost constraint, or minimizing his cost subject to a given output constraint. Consequently we need to develop a way of handling problems which involve *constrained maximization* or *constrained minimization*. Thus *unconstrained extrema* will be the subject of this chapter, and *constrained extrema* the subject of the next.

12-1 UNCONSTRAINED EXTREMA OF A FUNCTION OF TWO VARIABLES: GRAPHICAL ANALYSIS

A function of two independent variables, such as $z = f(x, y)$, can be represented graphically with the aid of a three-dimensional figure. Thus, in Fig. 12-1a, the locus of points such as (x_1, y_1, z_1) and (x_2, y_2, z_2) constitutes the graph of the function f. In Fig. 12-1b it can be seen that this locus takes the form of a *surface*—drawn here as a dome-shaped surface. Point A, in Fig. 12-1b, at the highest point of the dome, represents a *maximum*, since the value of z at this point exceeds that at any other point in its immediate neighbourhood. If we had drawn the surface as an inverted dome, then the lowest point of the inverted dome would represent a *minimum*, since the value of z at this point is smaller than at any other point in its immediate neighbourhood.

12-2 THE FIRST-ORDER CONDITION FOR A RELATIVE EXTREMUM: $z = f(x, y)$

In the case of a function of one independent variable, such as $y = f(x)$, with an extreme value at $x = \bar{x}$, the first-order condition for a relative extremum is that the first derivative of the function be zero at $x = \bar{x}$. This means that the function has a stationary value at $x = \bar{x}$, so that momentarily y is neither increasing nor decreasing in value at $x = \bar{x}$. In terms of differentials, the previous sentence simply states that the differential dy is zero at $x = \bar{x}$. Thus, at $x = \bar{x}$, we have

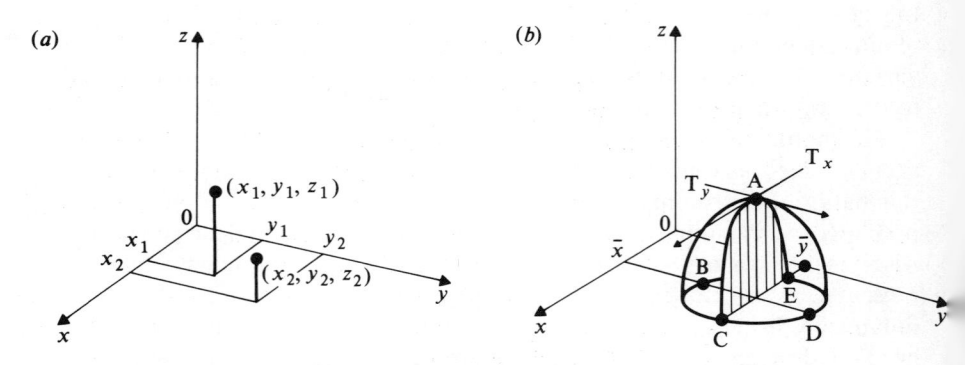

$$dy = f'(x)dx = 0 \qquad (12\text{-}1)$$

Figure 12-1

12-2 THE FIRST-ORDER CONDITION FOR A RELATIVE EXTREMUM: $z = f(x, y)$

Equation (12-1) indicates that to guarantee a zero dy for any arbitrary (nonzero) variation dx, it is necessary that $f'(x) = 0$, which is the familiar first-order condition for a relative extremum. Thus $dy = 0$ and $f'(x) = 0$ are equivalent conditions.

The first-order condition, for the case of a function with two independent variables, can be expressed in an analogous fashion. Thus for z to attain an extreme value at, for example, point A in Fig. 12-1(b), it is necessary that the function has a stationary value at this point. In other words, z must be in a 'standstill' position at point A, so that momentarily z is neither increasing nor decreasing in value at this point. Expressed in terms of differentials, the previous sentence simply states that the total differential dz is zero at point A, that is

$$dz = f_x dx + f_y dy = 0 \qquad (12\text{-}2)$$

at point A. Equation (12-2) indicates that to guarantee a zero dz for any arbitrary variations dx and dy (both nonzero), it is necessary that $f_x = f_y = 0$. Thus $dz = 0$ and $f_x = f_y = 0$ are equivalent conditions. This condition, $dz = 0$ or equivalently $f_x = f_y = 0$, constitutes the *first-order condition* for a relative extremum.

The requirement that f_x and f_y be simultaneously equal to zero at an extremum can be intuitively grasped from an examination of Fig. 12-1b. Since point A represents a maximum, this means that the tangent line T_x, drawn through point A parallel to the xz plane, has a zero slope. Similarly, the tangent line T_y, drawn through point A parallel to the yz plane, has a zero slope. The tangent lines T_x and T_y are thus parallel to the x axis and y axis, respectively. If we now cut the surface from point A by a plane (shown in Fig. 12-1b with the base CE) parallel to the xz plane, we obtain the cross-section view of the surface shown in Fig. 12-2a. In a similar fashion, the

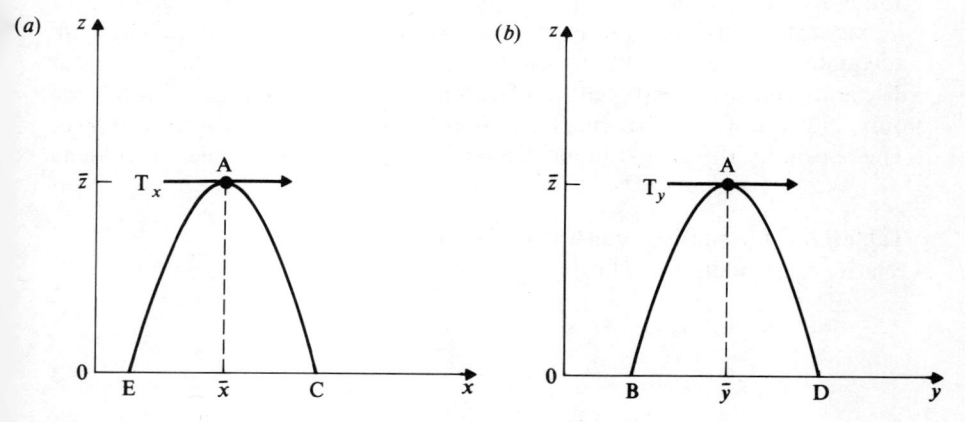

Figure 12-2

cross-section curve in Fig. 12-2b is obtained by cutting the surface from point A by a plane (with base BD in Fig. 12-1b) parallel to the *yz* plane. Note that if we had drawn the surface as an inverted dome, the analogous cross-section curves (obtained by cutting the inverted dome from its lowest point by planes parallel to the *xz* and *yz* planes, respectively) would be U-shaped.

An inspection of the cross-section curves in Fig. 12-2 should make it intuitively clear why T_x and T_y are required to have zero slopes at point A. In addition, an inspection of Fig. 12-1b indicates that, in drawing T_x parallel to the *xz* plane, we are holding the value of *y* fixed at $y = \bar{y}$. The slope of T_x is therefore the rate of change of *z* with respect to a change in *x*, with *y* held constant—in other words, the partial derivative $\partial z/\partial x$. The zero slope of T_x thus means that $\partial z/\partial x = f_x = 0$ at point A. Similarly, the zero slope of T_y means that $\partial z/\partial y = f_y = 0$ at point A. Therefore to state that a relative extremum, such as point A in Fig. 12-1b, will have zero tangent slopes (given by the slopes of T_x and T_y) is equivalent to stating that $f_x = f_y = 0$, which is the *first-order condition* for a relative extremum.

While the above discussion has indicated how the first-order condition of $dz = 0$, or equivalently $f_x = f_y = 0$, enables us to locate a stationary value of *z* (and it should be noted that *z* may have more than one stationary value), it is important to recognize the limited information provided by this condition. In particular, it should be noted that the first-order condition (summarized in Table 12-1) does not enable us to distinguish between a maximum and a minimum. That this is so should be evident from the fact that the zero tangent slopes may locate either the highest point of a dome-shaped surface or the lowest point of an inverted dome-shaped surface. In other words, while the first-order condition is *necessary* it is *not sufficient* to establish a relative extremum.

In order to ascertain whether a stationary value of *z* is a maximum or a minimum (or neither), we need knowledge of a *sufficient condition* or *second-order condition* for a relative extremum. Unfortunately, since an adequate discussion of this condition is beyond the scope of this book, our discussion must be restricted to a consideration of the first-order condition only. Note, however, that this restriction is not as serious as it may appear. The reason for this is that in most economic applications of relative extrema

Table 12-1 First-order condition for a relative extremum: $z = f(x, y)$

$$f_x = f_y = 0$$
or
$$dz = 0$$

for arbitrary dx and dy

12-2 THE FIRST-ORDER CONDITION FOR A RELATIVE EXTREMUM: $z = f(x, y)$

the second-order condition is either satisfied, or (by making certain assumptions about the objective function) assumed to be satisfied.

The student who is interested in the second-order condition and the more-than-two-variable case should consult A. C. Chiang, *Fundamental Methods of Mathematical Economics*, 2nd edition, McGraw-Hill, 1974, Chapter 11.

Examples of Unconstrained Extrema: $z = f(x, y)$

12-1 Find the relative extreme value(s) of $z = x^2 + xy + 2y^2 - 2x - y$.

SOLUTION We find the stationary value(s) of z by finding the values of x and y which satisfy the first-order condition $f_x = f_y = 0$. Thus

$$f_x = 2x + y - 2 = 0$$
$$f_y = x + 4y - 1 = 0$$

The single solution which satisfies these two equations simultaneously is $\bar{x} = 1$, $\bar{y} = 0$. To ascertain whether the stationary value $\bar{z} = f(\bar{x}, \bar{y}) = f(1, 0) = -1$ is a maximum or a minimum (or neither) requires application of a second-order condition.

12-2 Find the relative extreme value(s) of $z = -5x^2 + 2xy - y^2 + 12x + 4y + 10$.

SOLUTION The first-order condition is $f_x = f_y = 0$. Thus

$$f_x = -10x + 2y + 12 = 0$$
$$f_y = 2x - 2y + 4 = 0$$

which is satisfied by the single solution $\bar{x} = 2$, $\bar{y} = 4$. Once more to ascertain whether the stationary value $\bar{z} = f(\bar{x}, \bar{y}) = f(2, 4) = 30$ is an extremum requires application of a second-order condition.

12-3 Find the relative extreme value(s) of $z = -\frac{8}{3}x^3 + 4xy - 2x^2 + 2y^2$.

SOLUTION The first-order condition is $f_x = f_y = 0$. Thus

$$f_x = -8x^2 + 4y - 4x = 0$$
$$f_y = 4x + 4y = 0$$

Note that $f_y = 0$ implies that $y = -x$. Substituting this into $f_x = 0$ gives $-8x^2 - 8x = 0$, which can be solved via the quadratic formula to obtain the pair of solutions $x = 0$ or $x = -1$. Hence, when $x = 0$, then $y = -x = 0$ and $z = f(0, 0) = 0$. Similarly, when $x = -1$, then $y = -x = 1$ and $z = f(-1, 1) = -\frac{4}{3}$. Thus, in this case, we have two stationary values of z: one at $z = 0$ and the other at $z = -\frac{4}{3}$. To say whether either of these values is an extremum requires application of a second-order condition.

12-4 Find the relative extreme value(s) of $z = -2x^3 + 2xy - 2y^2 - \frac{13}{2}x^2$.

SOLUTION The first-order condition is $f_x = f_y = 0$. Thus

$$f_x = -6x^2 + 2y - 13x = 0$$
$$f_y = 2x - 4y = 0$$

Since $f_y = 0$ implies that $2y = x$, substitution of this into $f_x = 0$ gives $-6x^2 - 12x = 0$ which (via quadratic formula) yields the pair of solutions $x = 0$ or $x = -2$. Hence, when $x = 0$, then $y = \frac{1}{2}x = 0$ and $z = f(0, 0) = 0$. Similarly, when $x = -2$, then $y = \frac{1}{2}x = -1$ and $z = f(-2, -1) = -8$. To say whether either of these two stationary values of z is an extremum requires application of a second-order condition.

12-5 Find the relative extreme value(s) of $z = -3x^3 + y^3 + 36x - 27y + 100$.

SOLUTION The first-order condition is $f_x = f_y = 0$. Thus
$$f_x = -9x^2 + 36 = 0$$
$$f_y = 3y^2 - 27 = 0$$
The first equation yields $x = \pm 2$, while the second equation yields $y = \pm 3$. Thus, in this case, we have four solutions: $(2, 3)$, $(2, -3)$, $(-2, 3)$, and $(-2, -3)$.

Hence, the four corresponding stationary values of z will be $z = 94$, $z = 202$, $z = -2$, and $z = 106$, respectively. To ascertain whether any one of these stationary values of z is an extremum requires application of a second-order condition.

12-A PRACTICE PROBLEMS

12-6 For each of the following functions, find the stationary values of z:
(a) $z = -3x^2 - 2y^2 + 4xy + 2x + 4$
(b) $z = 2x^2 + y^2 + 4xy - 28x - 22y + 99$
(c) $z = 6x^2 - 5.5y^2 + 11xy - 45x + 22y + 0.5$
(d) $z = -x^2 + 7y^2 + 6x - 28y - 1$
(e) $z = \frac{4}{3}x^3 - 2y^2 + 2xy + \frac{7}{2}x^2$
(f) $z = \frac{3}{2}x^2 + \frac{1}{3}y^3 + 3xy - \frac{3}{2}y^2 - 8$

12-3 ECONOMIC APPLICATIONS OF UNCONSTRAINED EXTREMA

The foregoing analysis of unconstrained extrema, with its restriction to the first-order condition, can now be applied to the four economic problems listed in the introductory section of this chapter.

Profit Maximization by a Multi-Product Firm: Perfect Competition

In Chapter 9 we dealt with firms which produce only one product. Since almost all firms produce a variety of products, we shall now examine the case of a multi-product firm.

Firstly, let us assume that the output levels (per time period) of a firm's two products are given by Q_1 and Q_2, respectively. Secondly, while the output levels Q_1 and Q_2 are assumed to be independent of one another, let us assume that the two products are technically interdependent in the sense that the firm's total cost will depend on the *joint* level of production of Q_1 and Q_2. Consequently, the firm's total (joint) cost function may be written as

$$C = C(Q_1, Q_2)$$

with $MC_1 \equiv \partial C / \partial Q_1 = C_1(Q_1, Q_2)$ representing the marginal cost of the first product and $MC_2 \equiv \partial C / \partial Q_2 = C_2(Q_1, Q_2)$ representing the marginal cost of the second product. Note in particular that the MC of one product is partly affected by the output of the other product (assuming that

$\partial^2 C/\partial Q_1 \partial Q_2 = \partial^2 C/\partial Q_2 \partial Q_1 \neq 0$). This particular form of the MC functions is the result of our assumption that the two products are technically related in production.

Finally, let us assume that the firm is *perfectly competitive*, so that the prices of the two products are given to the firm. These prices are denoted by $\bar{P}_1$ and $\bar{P}_2$, respectively. Thus the firm's total revenue function is

$$R = \bar{P}_1 Q_1 + \bar{P}_2 Q_2$$

with $MR_1 \equiv \partial R/\partial Q_1 = \bar{P}_1$ representing the marginal revenue of the first product and $MR_2 \equiv \partial R/\partial Q_2 = \bar{P}_2$ representing the marginal revenue of the second product.

The profit function of this multi-product firm can now be written as

$$\pi = R - C = \bar{P}_1 Q_1 + \bar{P}_2 Q_2 - C(Q_1, Q_2) \tag{12-3}$$

Equation (12-3) indicates that profit is a function of the two choice variables Q_1 and Q_2. The next step is to find the levels of Q_1 and Q_2 which, in combination, will maximize $\pi = \pi(Q_1, Q_2)$.

The first-order condition for a π maximum is $\pi_1 = \pi_2 = 0$. Thus

$$\pi_1 \equiv \frac{\partial \pi}{\partial Q_1} = \bar{P}_1 - \frac{\partial C}{\partial Q_1} = MR_1 - MC_1 = 0$$

$$\pi_2 \equiv \frac{\partial \pi}{\partial Q_2} = \bar{P}_2 - \frac{\partial C}{\partial Q_2} = MR_2 - MC_2 = 0$$

The solution of these two simultaneous equations, which contain the two choice variables (Q_1 and Q_2) plus the two price parameters ($\bar{P}_1$ and $\bar{P}_2$), will yield $\bar{Q}_1$ and $\bar{Q}_2$. Substitution of $\bar{Q}_1$ and $\bar{Q}_2$ into the profit function gives $\bar{\pi} = \pi(\bar{Q}_1, \bar{Q}_2)$. Hence, assuming that the second-order condition for a profit maximum is satisfied, $\bar{\pi}$ therefore represents maximum profit.

We can now examine what the first-order condition means in economic terms. To do this, note that at the profit-maximizing output levels ($\bar{Q}_1$ and $\bar{Q}_2$), given by the first-order condition, the price (equals marginal revenue) of each product is equal to its respective marginal cost. In other words, the firm will produce that quantity of each product for which its marginal revenue is exactly equal to its marginal cost (as indicated by $MR_1 = MC_1$ and $MR_2 = MC_2$).

Example of Profit Maximization by a Multi-Product Firm: Perfect Competition

12-7 A perfectly competitive firm's total revenue and total cost functions are $R(Q_1, Q_2) = \bar{P}_1 Q_1 + \bar{P}_2 Q_2 = 4Q_1 + 8Q_2$ and $C(Q_1, Q_2) = Q_1^2 + 2Q_1 Q_2 + 3Q_2^2 + 2$, respectively. Assuming that the second-order condition for a profit maximum is satisfied, find the firm's profit-maximizing output level of each product and its maximum profit.

SOLUTION $\pi = R - C = 4Q_1 + 8Q_2 - Q_1^2 - 2Q_1Q_2 - 3Q_2^2 - 2$
The first-order condition for a π maximum is $\pi_1 = \pi_2 = 0$. Thus

$$\begin{aligned}\pi_1 \equiv \partial\pi/\partial Q_1 = 4 - 2Q_1 - 2Q_2 = 0\\ \pi_2 \equiv \partial\pi/\partial Q_2 = 8 - 2Q_1 - 6Q_2 = 0\end{aligned}\quad \text{or} \quad \begin{cases} 2Q_1 + 2Q_2 = 4 \\ 2Q_1 + 6Q_2 = 8 \end{cases}$$

The solution of these two simultaneous equations is $\bar{Q}_1 = \bar{Q}_2 = 1$. Substitution of $\bar{Q}_1$ and $\bar{Q}_2$ into the profit function gives $\bar{\pi} = \pi(\bar{Q}_1, \bar{Q}_2) = 4$. Given the above assumption, $\bar{\pi} = 4$ represents maximum profit.

Profit Maximization by a Multi-Product Firm: Monopoly

Once we come to examine the multi-product monopolist we must take into account the fact that he does not face given prices for his products—rather the price per unit of each product will vary with their output levels. For example, let us assume that a monopolist has the following AR functions: $AR_1 \equiv P_1 = 20 - 2Q_1$ and $AR_2 \equiv P_2 = 20 - Q_2$. The total revenue function is therefore

$$\begin{aligned}R &= P_1 Q_1 + P_2 Q_2 \\ &= (20 - 2Q_1)Q_1 + (20 - Q_2)Q_2 = 20Q_1 - 2Q_1^2 + 20Q_2 - Q_2^2\end{aligned}$$

If we assume that the total cost function is

$$C(Q_1, Q_2) = Q_1^2 + 2Q_1Q_2 + Q_2^2 + 10$$

then the profit function will be

$$\begin{aligned}\pi = R - C &= 20Q_1 - 2Q_1^2 + 20Q_2 - Q_2^2 - Q_1^2 - 2Q_1Q_2 - Q_2^2 - 10 \\ &= 20Q_1 - 3Q_1^2 + 20Q_2 - 2Q_2^2 - 2Q_1Q_2 - 10\end{aligned}$$

The first-order condition for a π maximum is $\pi_1 = \pi_2 = 0$. Thus

$$\begin{aligned}\pi_1 = 20 - 6Q_1 - 2Q_2 = 0\\ \pi_2 = 20 - 2Q_1 - 4Q_2 = 0\end{aligned}\quad \text{or} \quad \begin{cases} 6Q_1 + 2Q_2 = 20 \\ 2Q_1 + 4Q_2 = 20 \end{cases}$$

These two equations yield the solution $\bar{Q}_1 = 2$ and $\bar{Q}_2 = 4$. Upon substitution into the profit function we obtain $\bar{\pi} = \pi(\bar{Q}_1, \bar{Q}_2) = 50$. Assuming that the second-order condition for a profit maximum is satisfied, $\bar{\pi} = 50$ represents maximum profit.

Example of Profit Maximization by a Multi-Product Firm: Monopoly

12-8 A multi-product monopolist has the following AR functions: $AR_1 \equiv P_1 = 70 - 2Q_1 - 3Q_2$ and $AR_2 \equiv P_2 = 110 - 3Q_1 - 5Q_2$. His total cost function is

$$C(Q_1, Q_2) = 2Q_1^2 - 2Q_1Q_2 + Q_2^2 + 37.5$$

Assuming that the second-order condition for a profit maximum is satisfied, find the monopolist's profit-maximizing output levels for each product and his maximum profit.

SOLUTION Note that in this case the AR functions contain both Q_1 and Q_2.
$$\pi = R - C = P_1 Q_1 + P_2 Q_2 - C(Q_1, Q_2)$$
$$= (70 - 2Q_1 - 3Q_2)Q_1 + (110 - 3Q_1 - 5Q_2)Q_2 - 2Q_1^2 + 2Q_1 Q_2 - Q_2^2 - 37.5$$
The first-order condition for a π maximum is $\pi_1 = \pi_2 = 0$. Thus
$$\left. \begin{array}{l} \pi_1 = 70 - 8Q_1 - 4Q_2 = 0 \\ \pi_2 = 110 - 4Q_1 - 12Q_2 = 0 \end{array} \right\} \quad \text{or} \quad \begin{cases} 8Q_1 + 4Q_2 = 70 \\ 4Q_1 + 12Q_2 = 110 \end{cases}$$
These two equations yield the solution $\bar{Q}_1 = 5$ and $\bar{Q}_2 = \frac{15}{2}$. Upon substitution into the profit function we obtain $\bar{\pi} = \pi(\bar{Q}_1, \bar{Q}_2) = 550$. Given the above assumption, $\bar{\pi} = 550$ represents maximum profit. Also, from the AR functions we find that $\bar{P}_1 = 70 - 2\bar{Q}_1 - 3\bar{Q}_2 = 37.5$ and $\bar{P}_2 = 110 - 3\bar{Q}_1 - 5\bar{Q}_2 = 57.5$.

Price Discrimination

An interesting economic application of unconstrained extrema arises in the case where a *single-product* firm sells its output in more than one market. For example, a monopoly producer of electricity can usually sell his output in distinctly separate markets, such as the two distinct markets formed by industrial and residential purchasers of electricity. The interesting question which then arises is how much output should the monopolist sell in each market, and consequently what price should he charge in each market, in order to maximize his profit? To answer this question we shall examine the case of a monopolist selling a single product in two separate markets.

Firstly, as a matter of terminology, the monopolist's total output is
$$Q = Q_1 + Q_2$$
where Q_1 and Q_2 represent the quantities of the *single* product sold in the first and second market, respectively. Clearly, the quantity of the product sold in each market will vary with its price in each market—the particular relation between price and quantity in each market reflecting the (different) demand conditions in each market. The monopolist's total revenue function can therefore be written as
$$R = R_1(Q_1) + R_2(Q_2)$$
where R_1 and R_2 represent the revenue functions of the first and second market, respectively. The total cost function is
$$C = C(Q) \quad \text{where} \quad Q = Q_1 + Q_2$$
Note that there is only one cost function since production of the *single* product takes place in the single firm for both markets. Also, note that
$$\frac{\partial [C(Q)]}{\partial Q_1} = \frac{dC}{dQ} \frac{\partial Q}{\partial Q_1} = \frac{dC}{dQ} = C'(Q) \quad \text{since} \quad \frac{\partial Q}{\partial Q_1} = 1$$
Similarly
$$\frac{\partial [C(Q)]}{\partial Q_2} = \frac{dC}{dQ} \frac{\partial Q}{\partial Q_2} = C'(Q) \quad \text{since} \quad \frac{\partial Q}{\partial Q_2} = 1$$

This simply means that the *MC* of output to be sold in market one or market two is exactly the same as the *MC* of the total output Q. This is to be expected since there is only one product being produced by the single firm.

The profit function can now be written as

$$\pi = R_1(Q_1) + R_2(Q_2) - C(Q) \tag{12-4}$$

It is important to note that even though there is only one product involved in (12-4), the profit function has been deliberately formulated in terms of the two choice variables Q_1 and Q_2. The profit-maximizing problem thus consists of finding the values of Q_1 and Q_2 which maximize the monopolist's profit.

The first-order condition for a π maximum is $\pi_1 = \pi_2 = 0$. Thus

$$\pi_1 = R_1'(Q_1) - C'(Q)\frac{\partial Q}{\partial Q_1} = R_1'(Q_1) - C'(Q) = 0$$

$$\pi_2 = R_2'(Q_2) - C'(Q)\frac{\partial Q}{\partial Q_2} = R_2'(Q_2) - C'(Q) = 0$$

The solution of these two simultaneous equations will yield $\bar{Q}_1$ and $\bar{Q}_2$. Hence $\bar{Q} = \bar{Q}_1 + \bar{Q}_2$. Substitution of $\bar{Q}_1$ and $\bar{Q}_2$ into (12-4) will yield $\bar{\pi} = \pi(\bar{Q}_1, \bar{Q}_2)$. Assuming that the second-order condition for a profit maximum is satisfied, $\bar{\pi}$ represents maximum profit.

Note that the first-order condition implies that

$$R_1'(Q_1) = R_2'(Q_2) = C'(Q) \quad \text{or} \quad MR_1 = MR_2 = MC \tag{12-5}$$

Thus the levels $\bar{Q}_1$ and $\bar{Q}_2$ are chosen such that the *MR* in each market is equal to the *MC* of the total output $\bar{Q}$. Clearly if $MR_1 \neq MR_2$, the monopolist could increase his total revenue without affecting his total cost by shifting sales from the low *MR* market to the high *MR* market.

Also, it is important to note the implications of (12-5) for the price in each market. Since $R_1 = P_1 Q_1$, then

$$MR_1 \equiv \frac{dR_1}{dQ_1} = P_1 \frac{dQ_1}{dQ_1} + Q_1 \frac{dP_1}{dQ_1}$$

$$= P_1\left(1 + \frac{dP_1}{dQ_1}\frac{Q_1}{P_1}\right) = P_1\left(1 - \frac{1}{E_{d1}}\right)$$

where $E_{d1} = -(dQ_1/dP_1)(P_1/Q_1)$ is the price elasticity of demand in market one. Similarly $MR_2 = P_2(1 - 1/E_{d2})$. In these expressions for *MR* it can be seen that $E_d > 1$ implies $MR > 0$. Since we expect the firm's *MC* to be positive, then (12-5) implies that E_{d1} and E_{d2} are both greater than unity. If we now use (12-5) to equate MR_1 and MR_2, then we have

$$P_1\left(1 - \frac{1}{E_{d1}}\right) = P_2\left(1 - \frac{1}{E_{d2}}\right) \tag{12-6}$$

From (12-6), we can see that P_1 will only be equal to P_2 if $E_{d1} = E_{d2}$. If $E_{d1} < E_{d2}$, at $\bar{Q}_1$ and $\bar{Q}_2$, then (12-6) implies that $P_1 > P_2$. Consequently, if demand conditions differ in the two markets, as indicated by $E_{d1} \neq E_{d2}$, profit maximization will involve the practice of price discrimination.

Examples of Price Discrimination

12-9 A monopolist's total cost function is $C(Q) = 10Q + 6$, where $Q = Q_1 + Q_2$. The AR functions for his product in each of his two markets are $P_1 = 50 - 5Q_1$ and $P_2 = 30 - 2Q_2$, respectively. Assuming that the second-order condition for a profit maximum is satisfied, find his profit-maximizing output in each market, the price he will charge in each market, and his overall profit.

SOLUTION $R_1 = P_1 Q_1 = 50Q_1 - 5Q_1^2$; $R_2 = P_2 Q_2 = 30Q_2 - 2Q_2^2$ and
$$C = 10(Q_1 + Q_2) + 6 = 10Q_1 + 10Q_2 + 6$$

Thus
$$\pi = R - C = 50Q_1 - 5Q_1^2 + 30Q_2 - 2Q_2^2 - 10Q_1 - 10Q_2 - 6 = 40Q_1 - 5Q_1^2 + 20Q_2 - 2Q_2^2 - 6$$

The first-order condition for a π maximum is $\pi_1 = \pi_2 = 0$. Thus
$$\pi_1 = 40 - 10Q_1 = 0$$
$$\pi_2 = 20 - 4Q_2 = 0$$

Hence $\bar{Q}_1 = 4$, $\bar{Q}_2 = 5$ and $\bar{Q} = \bar{Q}_1 + \bar{Q}_2 = 9$. Substitution of these values into the profit function yields $\bar{\pi} = 124$ (which, given the above assumption, represents maximum profit). Similar substitution into the AR functions indicate that the monopolist will charge the discriminatory prices $\bar{P}_1 = 30$ and $\bar{P}_2 = 20$.

12-10 Use the results of Example 12-9 to find the price elasticity of demand in each market.

SOLUTION

$$E_{d1} = -\frac{dQ_1}{dP_1} \frac{\bar{P}_1}{\bar{Q}_1} = -\left(\frac{1}{dP_1/dQ_1}\right) \frac{\bar{P}_1}{\bar{Q}_1} = -\left(\frac{1}{-5}\right) \frac{30}{4} = \frac{3}{2}$$

$$E_{d2} = -\frac{dQ_2}{dP_2} \frac{\bar{P}_2}{\bar{Q}_2} = -\left(\frac{1}{dP_2/dQ_2}\right) \frac{\bar{P}_2}{\bar{Q}_2} = -\left(\frac{1}{-2}\right) \frac{20}{5} = 2$$

Note that $E_{d1} < E_{d2}$ and $\bar{P}_1 > \bar{P}_2$ as implied by (12-6).

Multiplant Monopoly

In this section we shall consider a profit-maximizing monopolist who sells his (single-product) output in a single market, but can produce this output in two separate plants. The profit-maximizing problem in this case consists of finding how much the monopolist should produce in each plant in order to maximize his profit.

Firstly, by way of definition, let us denote total output as $Q = Q_1 + Q_2$, where Q_1 and Q_2 represent the quantities of the *single* product produced in the first and second plant, respectively. If we then assume that cost conditions differ from one plant to another, the monopolist's total cost function can be written as

$$C = C_1(Q_1) + C_2(Q_2)$$

228 UNCONSTRAINED EXTREMA

where C_1 and C_2 represent the cost functions of the first and second plant, respectively. The total revenue function is

$$R = R(Q) \quad \text{where} \quad Q = Q_1 + Q_2$$

Note that there is only one revenue function since the single product is sold in one market.

The profit function can now be written as

$$\pi = R(Q) - C_1(Q_1) - C_2(Q_2) \tag{12-7}$$

The first-order condition for a π maximum is $\pi_1 = \pi_2 = 0$. Thus

$$\pi_1 = R'(Q)\frac{\partial Q}{\partial Q_1} - C'_1(Q_1) = R'(Q) - C'_1(Q_1) = 0 \quad \text{since} \quad \frac{\partial Q}{\partial Q_1} = 1$$

$$\pi_2 = R'(Q)\frac{\partial Q}{\partial Q_2} - C'_2(Q_2) = R'(Q) - C'_2(Q_2) = 0 \quad \text{since} \quad \frac{\partial Q}{\partial Q_2} = 1$$

The solution of these two simultaneous equations yields $\bar{Q}_1$ and $\bar{Q}_2$. Hence $\bar{Q} = \bar{Q}_1 + \bar{Q}_2$. Substitution of $\bar{Q}_1$ and $\bar{Q}_2$ into (12-7) will yield $\bar{\pi}$. Assuming that the second-order condition for a profit maximum is satisfied, $\bar{\pi}$ represents maximum profit.

Note that the first-order condition implies

$$R'(Q) = C'_1(Q_1) = C'_2(Q_2) \quad \text{or} \quad MR = MC_1 = MC_2$$

Thus the levels $\bar{Q}_1$ and $\bar{Q}_2$ are chosen such that the MC in each plant is equal to the MR of the total output $\bar{Q}$. Clearly, if $MC_1 \neq MC_2$, the monopolist can reduce his total cost without affecting his total revenue by shifting production from the high MC plant to the low MC plant.

Example of Multiplant Monopoly

12-11 A monopolist's cost functions for his two plants are $C_1 = 2Q_1^2 + 4$ and $C_2 = 6Q_2^2 + 8$, respectively. The AR function for his product is $P = 88 - 4Q$, where $Q = Q_1 + Q_2$. Assuming that the second-order condition for a profit maximum is satisfied, find his profit-maximizing output, the amount he will produce in each plant, and the price he will charge for his product.

SOLUTION
$$R = PQ = 88Q - 4Q^2 = 88(Q_1 + Q_2) - 4(Q_1 + Q_2)^2 = 88Q_1 + 88Q_2 - 4Q_1^2 - 8Q_1Q_2 - 4Q_2^2$$
$$\pi = R - C = 88Q_1 + 88Q_2 - 4Q_1^2 - 8Q_1Q_2 - 4Q_2^2 - 2Q_1^2 - 4 - 6Q_2^2 - 8$$
$$= 88Q_1 + 88Q_2 - 6Q_1^2 - 8Q_1Q_2 - 10Q_2^2 - 12$$

The first-order condition for a π maximum is $\pi_1 = \pi_2 = 0$. Thus

$$\left.\begin{matrix} \pi_1 = 88 - 12Q_1 - 8Q_2 = 0 \\ \pi_2 = 88 - 8Q_1 - 20Q_2 = 0 \end{matrix}\right\} \quad \text{or} \quad \begin{cases} 12Q_1 + 8Q_2 = 88 \\ 8Q_1 + 20Q_2 = 88 \end{cases}$$

These two equations yield the solution $\bar{Q}_1 = 6$ and $\bar{Q}_2 = 2$. Hence $\bar{Q} = \bar{Q}_1 + \bar{Q}_2 = 8$. Substitution of $\bar{Q}_1$ and $\bar{Q}_2$ into the profit function gives $\bar{\pi} = 340$ (which, given the above assumption, represents maximum profit). Also, $\bar{P} = 88 - 4\bar{Q} = 56$.

Profit Maximization and Input Decisions

Let us consider the case of a *perfectly competitive* producer whose production process involves two variable productive services, labour (L) and capital (K). The production function may then be written as

$$Q = f(K, L) \tag{12-8}$$

Equation (12-8) states that output (Q) is a function of the variable inputs, capital and labour. If we assume that both input or factor markets are *perfectly competitive*, then the total cost function can be written as

$$C = C(K, L) = rK + wL \tag{12-9}$$

where r and w are the given prices of the capital and labour inputs. Since the perfectly competitive producer faces a given price ($\bar{P} > 0$) for his product, his total revenue function is given by

$$R = \bar{P}Q = \bar{P}f(K, L) \tag{12-10}$$

Equations (12-9) and (12-10) now permit us to express the profit function in terms of inputs as follows

$$\pi = R - C = \bar{P}f(K, L) - rK - wL$$

Thus the profit-maximizing problem consists of finding the input levels of K and L which will maximize the producer's profit.

The first-order condition for a π maximum is $\pi_K = \pi_L = 0$. Thus

$$\pi_K = \bar{P}\frac{\partial f}{\partial K} - r = \bar{P}f_K - r = 0$$

$$\pi_L = \bar{P}\frac{\partial f}{\partial L} - w = \bar{P}f_L - w = 0$$

The solution of these two simultaneous equations, which contain the two choice variables (K and L) and the given price parameters ($\bar{P}$, r and w), yields $\bar{K}$ and $\bar{L}$. Substitution of $\bar{K}$ and $\bar{L}$ into the profit function yields $\bar{\pi} = \pi(\bar{K}, \bar{L})$. Assuming that the second-order condition for a profit maximum is satisfied, $\bar{\pi}$ represents maximum profit.

We can now examine what the first-order condition means in economic terms. To do this, note that at the profit-maximizing input levels ($\bar{K}$ and $\bar{L}$), given by the first-order condition, we have

$$\bar{P}f_K = \bar{P} \cdot MP_K = VMP_K = r$$
$$\bar{P}f_L = \bar{P} \cdot MP_L = VMP_L = w \tag{12-11}$$

where MP_K and MP_L are the (positive) marginal products of K and L, and VMP_K and VMP_L are the values of the marginal products of K and L, respectively. Thus, in words, (12-11) simply states, for each input, that

(product price)(marginal product of input) = (input price)

Example of Profit Maximization and Input Decisions

12-12 A firm has a production function $Q = 6K^{1/3}L^{1/2}$. Its product price is $\bar{P} = 2$ and its input prices are $r = 4$ and $w = 3$. Assuming that the second-order condition for a profit maximum is satisfied, find the firm's profit-maximizing input levels, level of output, and maximum profit.

SOLUTION
$$\pi = R - C = \bar{P}Q - rK - wL$$
$$= 12K^{1/3}L^{1/2} - 4K - 3L$$

The first-order condition for a π maximum is $\pi_K = \pi_L = 0$. Thus
$$\left.\begin{array}{l}\pi_K = 4K^{-2/3}L^{1/2} - 4 = 0 \\ \pi_L = 6K^{1/3}L^{-1/2} - 3 = 0\end{array}\right\} \quad \text{or} \quad \left\{\begin{array}{l}K^{-2/3}L^{1/2} = 1 \\ K^{1/3}L^{-1/2} = \frac{1}{2}\end{array}\right.$$

The solution of these two simultaneous equations yields $\bar{K} = 8$ and $\bar{L} = 16$, (i.e., divide first equation by second to get $L = 2K$. Substitute $L = 2K$ into either the first or the second equation to get $\bar{K} = 8$. Hence $\bar{L} = 2\bar{K} = 16$). Substitution of $\bar{K}$ and $\bar{L}$ into the profit function yields $\bar{\pi} = \pi(\bar{K}, \bar{L}) = 16$ (which, given the above assumption, represents maximum profit). Similar substitution into the production function yields the profit-maximizing output level $\bar{Q} = Q(\bar{K}, \bar{L}) = 48$.

12-B PRACTICE PROBLEMS

In each of the following problems, assume that the second-order condition for a profit maximum is satisfied.

12-13 Given the following total revenue and total cost functions, find the firm's profit-maximizing output level of each product and its maximum profit:
(i) $R(Q_1, Q_2) = 42Q_1 + 51Q_2$; $C(Q_1, Q_2) = 1.5Q_1^2 + 3Q_1Q_2 + 2Q_2^2 + 34.5$
(ii) $R(Q_1, Q_2) = 51Q_1 + 76Q_2$; $C(Q_1, Q_2) = 2Q_1^2 + 5Q_1Q_2 + 4Q_2^2$

12-14 A monopolist has the following AR and total cost functions: $AR_1 = 40 - 3Q_1$; $AR_2 = 44 - 2Q_2$; $C = Q_1^2 + 4Q_1Q_2 + 2Q_2^2 + 8$. Find his profit-maximizing output level for each product, his maximum profit, and the selling price of each product.

12-15 The demand functions for a monopolist's two products are $Q_1 = 40 - 2P_1 + P_2$ and $Q_2 = 30 + P_1 - P_2$, respectively. His total cost function is $C = Q_1^2 + 2Q_1Q_2 + Q_2^2 + \frac{95}{2}$. Find his profit-maximizing output level for each product, his maximum profit, and the selling price of each product. [*Hint*: Rewrite the demand functions as $-2P_1 + P_2 = Q_1 - 40$ and $P_1 - P_2 = Q_2 - 30$, respectively. Then, regarding Q_1 and Q_2 as parameters, solve these two equations simultaneously (via Cramer's rule) to obtain $P_1 \equiv AR_1$ and $P_2 \equiv AR_2$.]

12-16 A monopolist sells his output in two markets. His total cost and AR functions are $C(Q) = 12Q + 4$, where $Q = Q_1 + Q_2$; $AR_1 = 60 - 3Q_1$; $AR_2 = 20 - 2Q_2$. Find his profit-maximizing output in each market, his maximum profit, the price he will charge in each market, and the elasticity of demand in each market.

12-17 A monopolist's cost functions for his two plants are $C_1 = 3Q_1^2 + 2Q_1 + 6$ and $C_2 = 2Q_2^2 + 2Q_2 + 4$, respectively. His AR function is $P = 74 - 6Q$, where $Q = Q_1 + Q_2$. Find his profit-maximizing output, the amount produced in each plant, his maximum profit, and the selling price of his product.

12-18 A firm's production function is $Q = 8K^{1/4}L^{1/2}$. Its product price is $P = 4$, and its input prices are $r = 8$ and $w = 4$. Find the firm's profit-maximizing input levels, level of output, and maximum profit.

12-4 ADDITIONAL PROBLEMS

In problems 12-19–12-25, assume that the second-order condition for a profit maximum is satisfied.

12-19 A perfectly competitive firm's total revenue and total cost functions are $R(Q_1, Q_2) = 36Q_1 + 86Q_2$ and $C(Q_1, Q_2) = Q_1^2 + 4Q_1Q_2 + 5Q_2^2 + 23$, respectively. Find the firm's profit-maximizing output level for each product and its maximum profit.

12-20 The demand functions for a monopolist's two products are $Q_1 = 20 - 5P_1 + 3P_2$ and $Q_2 = 10 + 3P_1 - 2P_2$, respectively. His total cost function is $C(Q_1, Q_2) = 2Q_1^2 - 2Q_1Q_2 + Q_2^2 + 37.5$. Find his profit-maximizing output levels for each product and his maximum profit.

12-21 A producer has a monopoly for two types of photo-copy equipment. The demand functions for his two products are $Q_1 = 1700 - \frac{1}{6}P_1$ and $Q_2 = 1533\frac{1}{3} - \frac{1}{3}P_2$, respectively. His total cost function is $C = 3Q_1^2 + 6Q_1Q_2 + Q_2^2 + 10{,}000$. Find his profit-maximizing output level for each product, his maximum profit, and the selling price of each product.

12-22 A monopolist's AR function is $P = 4Q^{-1/2}$. His production function is $Q = 36K^{1/2}L^{1/2}$ and his input prices are $r = \frac{3}{4}$ and $w = 12$. Find his profit-maximizing input levels, level of output, and maximum profit.

12-23 A monopolist's demand function is $Q = Q(P, A)$, where P = price and A = current advertising expenditure. His costs consist of the costs of production, $C = C(Q)$, plus advertising costs, A. Use the first-order condition for a profit maximum to show that $A/PQ = [(\partial Q/\partial A)(A/Q)]/[-(\partial Q/\partial P)(P/Q)] = \eta_A/\eta_P$, where A/PQ is the ratio of advertising expenditure to sales revenue and η_A/η_P is the ratio of the advertising elasticity of demand to the price elasticity of demand.

12-24 A monopolist produces the same chemical in two different plants. His two cost functions are $C_1 = 2Q_1^2 + 16Q_1 + 18$ and $C_2 = Q_2^2 + 32Q_2 + 70$, respectively. The demand function for his product is $Q = 30 - \frac{1}{4}P$, where $Q = Q_1 + Q_2$. Find his profit-maximizing output, the amount he will produce in each plant, the price he will charge for his product, and his maximum profit.

12-25 A monopolist sells his product to both residential and industrial consumers. His demand functions in these two distinct markets are $Q_1 = 103 - \frac{1}{6}P_1$ and $Q_2 = 55 - \frac{1}{2}P_2$, respectively. His total cost function is $C = 18Q + 750$, where $Q = Q_1 + Q_2$. Find his profit-maximizing output in each market, the price he will charge in each market, his overall profit, and the elasticity of demand in each market.

12-26 Given a function
$$S = S(\hat{\alpha}, \hat{\beta}) = \sum_{t=1}^{T} e_t^2 \text{ where } e_t = y_t - \hat{\alpha} - \hat{\beta}x_t, \quad \bar{y} = \sum_{t=1}^{T} y_t/T \text{ and } \bar{x} = \sum_{t=1}^{T} x_t/T.$$
Use the first-order condition for a S minimum to show that the S-minimizing values of $\hat{\alpha}$ and $\hat{\beta}$ are $\hat{\alpha} = \bar{y} - \hat{\beta}\bar{x}$ and
$$\hat{\beta} = \left(\sum_{t=1}^{T} x_t y_t - T\bar{y}\bar{x}\right) \bigg/ \left(\sum_{t=1}^{T} x_t^2 - T\bar{x}^2\right) = \sum_{t=1}^{T} (y_t - \bar{y})(x_t - \bar{x}) \bigg/ \sum_{t=1}^{T} (x_t - \bar{x})^2$$

CHAPTER
THIRTEEN
CONSTRAINED EXTREMA

In Chapter 12 we examined how to find an *unconstrained* extremum of a function of two variables. Also, in Sec. 12-3, we saw that a knowledge of unconstrained extrema enables us to handle many interesting economic problems. However, as noted in the introduction to Chapter 12, not all extremum problems in economics are of an unconstrained nature. Rather, many problems in economics involve finding a *constrained* extremum. For example, in the theory of consumer choice, a consumer is presented as maximizing his utility subject to a given budget constraint. While this consumer choice problem is perhaps the best-known example of constrained extrema in introductory economics, many other examples are to be found in every branch of economics. This is to be expected since economics is very much concerned with 'choice'—whether this is choice by consumers, entrepreneurs, unions or government—and such choice generally involves the very important concept of maximizing or minimizing subject to a constraint. Consequently many of the interesting problems in economics are problems of constrained extrema. It is for this very important reason that the student of economics should have a working knowledge of *constrained extrema*.

In this chapter we will examine how to find a constrained extremum of a function of two variables. While our discussion will be confined to the two-variable case, the analysis which will be developed can be readily extended to the more-than-two-variable case.

13-1 CONSTRAINED EXTREMA OF A FUNCTION OF TWO VARIABLES: GRAPHICAL ANALYSIS

In order to aid our understanding of constrained extrema, we shall examine the well-known consumer choice problem of a consumer maximizing his utility subject to a budget constraint.

To do this, let as assume that a consumer has a utility function given by

$$U = U(x, y) = xy \qquad (13\text{-}1)$$

which indicates that, for all positive amounts of x and y, the consumer can always increase his utility (U) by purchasing more of both goods (x and y). Also, in order to portray (13-1) in graphical terms, we can define an *indifference curve* as the locus of the combinations of x and y that will yield a constant level of U. For example, if we take the constant level of U to be U^0, then (13-1) becomes

$$U^0 = U(x, y) = xy \qquad (13\text{-}2)$$

where U^0 is simply some constant. Equation (13-2) thus represents the equation for an indifference curve which can be plotted in an xy plane to give an indifference curve like U^0 in Fig. 13-1a. Note, in Fig. 13-1a, that while each point on U^0 represents a different (x, y) combination, each of these (x, y) combinations yields the constant level of utility $U = U^0$. In a similar fashion, if we take different (higher) constant levels of U, such as $U = U^1$ or $U = U^2$, we obtain $U^1 = U(x, y) = xy$ or $U^2 = U(x, y) = xy$, which can be plotted like U^1 or U^2 in Fig. 13-1a. Hence, as shown in Fig. 13-1a, the utility function (13-1) can be represented graphically in terms of indifference curves, with each indifference curve representing a constant level of utility and higher indifference curves representing higher (constant) levels of utility.

It should be noted, in relation to Fig. 13-1a, that as yet we have given no mathematical justification for drawing U^0, U^1 and U^2 as negative-sloped, convex-to-the-origin shaped curves. In order to provide such a justification note that, as x and y vary in value along a given indifference

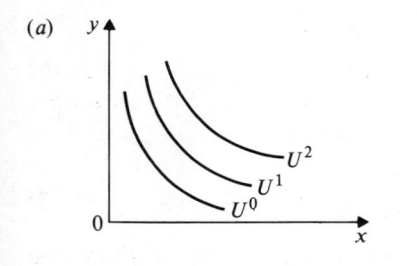

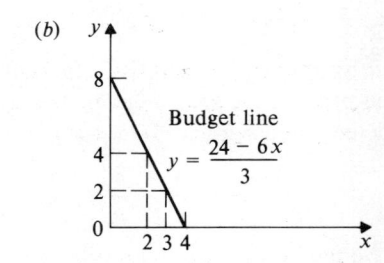

Figure 13-1

curve, the level of U is unchanged or, equivalently, the change in U is zero. Hence on an indifference curve the total differential of (13-1) is zero, that is

$$dU = \frac{\partial U}{\partial x}dx + \frac{\partial U}{\partial y}dy = 0 \quad \text{or} \quad dU = U_x dx + U_y dy = 0 \qquad (13\text{-}3)$$

which implies that $dy/dx = -(\partial U/\partial x)/(\partial U/\partial y) = -U_x/U_y$. This means that any indifference curve plotted in Fig. 13-1a will have a slope given by $dy/dx = -U_x/U_y$. Consequently, given the utility function (13-1), each indifference curve in Fig. 13-1a will have a *negative slope*, as given by $dy/dx = -U_x/U_y = -y/x < 0$ for $x, y > 0$. Also, given $dy/dx = g = g(x, y) = -y/x$, then

$$\frac{d^2y}{dx^2} = \frac{d}{dx}\left[\frac{dy}{dx}\right] = \frac{dg}{dx} = \frac{\partial g}{\partial x}\frac{dx}{dx} + \frac{\partial g}{\partial y}\frac{dy}{dx}$$

or

$$\frac{d^2y}{dx^2} = \frac{y}{x^2}\frac{dx}{dx} + \left(-\frac{1}{x}\right)\frac{dy}{dx} = \frac{y}{x^2} + \left(-\frac{1}{x}\right)\left(-\frac{y}{x}\right) = \frac{2y}{x^2}$$

Since $d^2y/dx^2 = 2y/x^2 > 0$ for $x, y > 0$, this means that all the indifference curves in Fig. 13-1a will be *convex to the origin* for $x, y > 0$ as shown.

Now that we have a graphical representation of the consumer's utility function, we must ask why the consumer cannot attain maximum U (or the highest possible indifference curve) by simply purchasing *infinite* amounts of both goods. The simple answer, of course, is that the consumer cannot afford to purchase infinite amounts of x and y. In other words, the consumer faces an expenditure or budget constraint. Consequently, the consumer's choice problem consists of maximizing his utility subject to this budget constraint.

In order to obtain a graphical representation of the consumer's budget constraint, let us assume that the consumer sets aside a certain sum of money or 'budget', $M = £24$, for his purchases of x and y on a particular date. Also, we will assume that the prices of x and y are $p_x = 6$ and $p_y = 3$, respectively. Hence, assuming that the consumer desires to spend his *whole* budget, his *budget constraint* is given by

$$M = p_x x + p_y y = 6x + 3y = 24 \qquad (13\text{-}4)$$

which simply states that the expenditure on good x (given by $p_x x$) plus the expenditure on good y (given by $p_y y$) is exactly equal to the consumer's predetermined budget, M. Since (13-4) can be rewritten as

$$y = \frac{M}{p_y} - \frac{p_x}{p_y}x \quad \text{or} \quad y = \frac{24}{3} - \frac{6}{3}x = 8 - 2x \qquad (13\text{-}5)$$

the budget constraint can therefore be represented by the straight line (known as a *budget line*) drawn in Fig. 13-1b.

Note, in Fig. 13-1b, that while each point on the budget line represents a different (x, y) combination, the expenditure required to purchase each of these (x, y) combinations is exactly $M = £24$. For example, if he purchases $(x, y) = (2, 4)$, his expenditure is $p_x x + p_y y = (6)(2) + (3)(4) = 24 = M$. Hence, if the consumer desires to spend his *whole* budget, he is restricted to purchasing one of the (x, y) combinations that lie on the budget line. Also, note from (13-5) that the budget line has a negative slope, as given by $dy/dx = -p_x/p_y = -6/3 = -2 < 0$.

We can now put the consumer's indifference curves and budget line on the one diagram, as in Fig. 13-2. This diagram immediately indicates that the highest indifference curve the consumer can attain, while still remaining on his budget line, is U^1. In other words, the consumer's choice problem of maximizing (13-1), subject to the constraint (13-4), is graphically equivalent to the problem of finding the highest indifference curve a consumer can attain, whilst still remaining on his budget line. Consequently, point R in Fig. 13-2 represents a constrained utility maximum.

It is important to note, in relation to finding the (constrained) maximum level of utility U^1, in Fig. 13-2, that it is only the levels of utility associated with those indifference curves (like U^0 and U^1) which either cut or touch the budget line that can be considered. In other words, it is only a restricted range of U values that is relevant to the constrained utility maximization problem. Also, it is important to note, in relation to the budget line in Fig. 13-2, that if more x is bought this means that less y must be bought. In other words, the choice variables, x and y, are no longer independent of one another. This dependence of the choice variables, established in this case via the budget constraint, is an important feature of constrained extremum problems. In contrast, in unconstrained extremum problems, all the choice variables are *independent* of one another.

Before leaving the graphical analysis note, at point R in Fig. 13-2, that

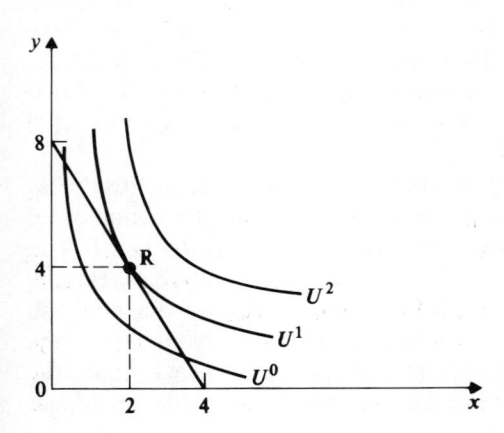

Figure 13-2

the optimal combination of x and y is $(\bar{x}, \bar{y}) = (2, 4)$. Therefore the (constrained) maximum level of utility is $U^1 = U(\bar{x}, \bar{y}) = \bar{x}\bar{y} = (2)(4) = 8$. Also note, at point R in Fig. 13-2, that the slope of the budget line (given by $-p_x/p_y = -2$) and the slope of the indifference curve U^1 (given by $-U_x/U_y = -y/x = -2$ when $(x, y) = (2, 4)$ as at point R) are equal. Hence a constrained utility maximum will be characterized by tangency between an indifference curve and the budget line, as given by

$$-\frac{U_x}{U_y} = -\frac{p_x}{p_y} \quad \text{or} \quad \frac{U_x}{U_y} = \frac{p_x}{p_y} \tag{13-6}$$

Now that we have briefly examined constrained utility maximization in graphical terms, the next step will be to introduce a mathematical method, known as the *Lagrange-multiplier method*, for handling constrained utility maximization. This method, as we shall see below, is essentially a mathematical equivalent of the above graphical analysis in the sense that it will give us exactly the same results as those already obtained from the graphical analysis.

13-2 CONSTRAINED EXTREMA VIA THE LAGRANGE-MULTIPLIER METHOD

To aid our understanding of the following discussion, we shall continue with the consumer choice problem of maximizing a utility function $U = U(x, y)$ subject to the budget constraint $M = p_x x + p_y y$ (with $U = xy$ and $M = 6x + 3y = 24$). In doing so, note that the budget constraint can be written as $h(x, y) = M$ (with $h(x, y) = p_x x + p_y y = 6x + 3y$ and $M = 24$). Also, in order to gain an adequate understanding of the Lagrange-multiplier method, the following discussion will proceed in three stages. First, we will examine the first-order condition for a constrained utility maximum using a total-differential method. Second, we will relate the results of this method to those of the graphical analysis in Sec. 13-1. Third, we will introduce the Lagrange-multiplier method and demonstrate that it yields results identical to those produced by both the total-differential method and the graphical analysis.

As an introduction to the total-differential method, recall (from Sec. 12-2) that the first-order condition for an unconstrained maximum of $U = U(x, y)$ can be stated in terms of the total differential dU as $dU = 0$. Also, recall that, in such a case, x and y are *independent* variables. Having reminded ourselves of the unconstrained extremum case, we can now ask the interesting question: can the total-differential method still be used in the analysis of the constrained utility maximum case, given that the introduction of the budget constraint means that x and y are no longer independent of one another? The answer to this question is yes, as we shall now demonstrate.

In Chapter 10 we noted that, given a function such as $U = U(x, y)$, the total differential $dU = U_x dx + U_y dy$ holds regardless of whether x and y are independent or dependent. Thus the first-order condition

$$dU = U_x dx + U_y dy = 0 \tag{13-7}$$

still holds after a budget constraint $M = h(x, y)$ has been added. While this is so, it should be intuitively clear that if the values of x and y are no longer independent of one another, because of the budget constraint, then the variations dx and dy are no longer independent of one another either. Since x and y are dependent due to $M = h(x, y)$, then dx and dy will be dependent on each other because the budget constraint requires

$$dM = h_x dx + h_y dy = 0 \quad \text{or} \quad dM = p_x dx + p_y dy = 0 \tag{13-8}$$

Therefore when we state the first-order condition for a constrained utility maximum as $dU = 0$, subject to the budget constraint $M = h(x, y)$, we must remember that dx and dy in (13-7) are no longer arbitrary variations, but are dependent via (13-8). This means that $dy = -(h_x/h_y)dx = -(p_x/p_y)dx$, which is implied by (13-8), can be substituted into (13-7) to give $dU = 0$ equivalently as

$$dU = [U_x - U_y(p_x/p_y)] dx = 0 \tag{13-9}$$

Consequently, for $dU = 0$, we require (for $dx \neq 0$)

$$U_x - U_y \left(\frac{p_x}{p_y} \right) = 0 \quad \text{or} \quad \frac{U_x}{p_x} = \frac{U_y}{p_y} \tag{13-10}$$

which may be written as

$$\frac{U_x}{U_y} = \frac{p_x}{p_y} \tag{13-11}$$

Thus the *first-order condition* for a constrained utility maximum can be equivalently written as $dU = 0$, subject to $M = h(x, y)$, or (13-11), subject to $M = h(x, y)$. Either of these two sets of two simultaneous equations, constituting the first-order condition for a constrained utility maximum, can then be solved to yield the values of x and y (our familiar $\bar{x}$ and $\bar{y}$) for which U has a stationary value, subject to $M = h(x, y)$.

The first-order condition for a constrained utility maximum, obtained via the total-differential approach, can now be readily related to the graphical analysis of Sec. 13-1. To do this, recall that the constrained utility maximum was located at point R, in Fig. 13-2, where an indifference curve is tangential to the budget line. Since at point R the slope of U^1 (given by $-U_x/U_y$) is equal to the slope of the budget line (given by $-p_x/p_y$), then at point R we have $U_x/U_y = p_x/p_y$. Also, since point R is on the budget line, then at point R we have $M = p_x x + p_y y$ or $M = h(x, y)$. In other words, at point R in Fig. 13-2, we have the simultaneous satisfaction of the two equations, $U_x/U_y = p_x/p_y$ and $M = h(x, y)$, which constitute the first-order condition for a constrained utility maximum. Hence the total-differential method and the graphical analysis yield exactly the same result.

It is important to note, in relation to Fig. 13-2, that $U_x/U_y = p_x/p_y$ on its own does not provide enough information to enable us to locate point R on the budget line. Clearly, since several indifference curves may have a point where the slope of the indifference curve is $-U_x/U_y = -p_x/p_y$ (for example, in Fig. 13-2, such points will be located where lines parallel to the budget line are tangential to various indifference curves), we need the additional restriction of $M = p_x x + p_y y$ or $M = h(x, y)$ to locate point R.

It is also important to note, in relation to the above discussion, that while the two simultaneous equations, $U_x/U_y = p_x/p_y$ and $M = h(x, y)$, constituting the first-order condition for a constrained utility maximum, enable us to locate point R in Fig. 13-2, they do not permit us to state that point R is a constrained utility maximum. To see why this is so, let us examine Fig. 13-3, which is identical to Fig. 13-2 except for the fact that the indifference curves have been drawn with a *concave*-to-the-origin shape. Note immediately that point R' is a constrained utility *minimum*, since any point on the budget line other than R' will be on a higher indifference curve than indifference curve U^1. Also, note that at point R' we have the simultaneous satisfaction of $U_x/U_y = p_x/p_y$ (given by the tangency of U^1 and the budget line) and $M = h(x, y)$. In other words, while the first-order condition can locate the values of x and y for which U has a stationary value, subject to $M = h(x, y)$, it is *not* sufficient to establish whether that stationary value is a constrained maximum or a constrained minimum (or neither). Consequently, to establish point R, in Fig. 13-2, as a constrained utility maximum (or point R', in Fig. 13-3, as a constrained utility

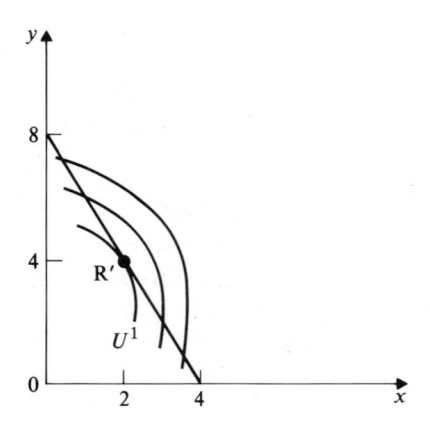

Figure 13-3

minimum) we require knowledge of a second-order condition for a constrained extremum.

Now that we have related the total-differential method to the graphical analysis of Sec. 13-1, we are in a position to introduce the Lagrange-multiplier method. To do this, note that the two simultaneous equations, $U_x/U_y = p_x/p_y$ and $M = h(x, y) = p_x x + p_y y$, constituting the first-order condition for a constrained utility maximum, can be written equivalently as $U_x/p_x = U_y/p_y$ and $M = p_x x + p_y y$. Consequently, if we write

$$U_x/p_x = \lambda \quad \text{and} \quad U_y/p_y = \lambda$$

so that $U_x = \lambda p_x$ and $U_y = \lambda p_y$, then we obtain

$$U_x - \lambda p_x = 0 \quad \text{and} \quad U_y - \lambda p_y = 0$$

where λ represents some as yet undetermined number. Hence the first-order condition for a constrained utility maximum can be rewritten as the following set of three simultaneous equations:

$$\left. \begin{array}{c} M - p_x x - p_y y = 0 \\ U_x - \lambda p_x = 0 \\ U_y - \lambda p_y = 0 \end{array} \right\} \quad (13\text{-}12)$$

Note that (13-12) contains the new variable λ in addition to the choice variables x and y. Therefore (13-12) is a set of three simultaneous equations in the three unknowns x, y, and λ. Also note, given our definition of the new variable λ, that the three simultaneous equations in (13-12) convey precisely the same information as the two simultaneous equations $U_x/U_y = p_x/p_y$ and $M = p_x x + p_y y$. This means that the solution of (13-12), for the three unknowns x, y and λ, will then yield the same stationary value of U, subject to $M = h(x, y) = p_x x + p_y y$, as before. In other words, the solution of (13-12) will yield $\bar{x}$, $\bar{y}$, $\bar{\lambda}$, and therefore $\bar{U}$ (which equals U^1 in Fig. 13-2) via $\bar{U} = U(\bar{x}, \bar{y}) = \bar{x}\bar{y}$. Finally, note that the solution of (13-12) yields the value $\bar{\lambda}$ in addition to the values $\bar{x}$ and $\bar{y}$. This value $\bar{\lambda}$, as we shall see in Sec. 13-3, can be given an interesting economic interpretation.

The next step is to show how (13-12), which represents the first-order condition for a constrained utility maximum, can be obtained directly by an alternative method, known as the *Lagrange-multiplier method*. To do this, we first write out what is known as the *Lagrangian function*:

$$L = L(\lambda, x, y) = U(x, y) + \lambda[M - h(x, y)] \quad (13\text{-}13)$$

or

$$L = L(\lambda, x, y) = U(x, y) + \lambda[M - p_x x - p_y y] \quad (13\text{-}14)$$

where λ is known as a *Lagrange (undetermined) multiplier*. Note that (13-13) incorporates the objective function $U = U(x, y)$, the Lagrange multiplier λ, and the budget constraint $M = h(x, y)$, in the particular form shown.

Secondly, if we differentiate (13-14) partially to find the three equations $L_\lambda = 0$, $L_x = 0$ and $L_y = 0$, we can then form the following set of three simultaneous equations:

$$\begin{aligned} L_\lambda &\equiv \frac{\partial L}{\partial \lambda} = M - p_x x - p_y y = 0 \\ L_x &\equiv \frac{\partial L}{\partial x} = U_x - \lambda p_x = 0 \\ L_y &\equiv \frac{\partial L}{\partial y} = U_y - \lambda p_y = 0 \end{aligned} \quad (13\text{-}15)$$

Note immediately that (13-15) is identical to (13-12). Therefore (13-15), like (13-12), constitutes the first-order condition for a constrained utility maximum.

To see why (13-15) constitutes the first-order condition for a constrained utility maximum, note that the first equation in (13-15), $L_\lambda = M - p_x x - p_y y = 0$ or $M = p_x x + p_y y$, automatically ensures that the budget constraint is satisfied. In terms of Fig. 13-2, this ensures that the stationary value of U, subject to $M = p_x x + p_y y$, will be located at a point on the budget line. Also, note that the last two equations in (13-15), $L_x = 0$ and $L_y = 0$, can be written as $U_x/p_x = \lambda$ and $U_y/p_y = \lambda$ or $U_x/p_x = U_y/p_y$, which upon rearranging can be written as $-U_x/U_y = -p_x/p_y$. In other words, in terms of Fig. 13-2, this ensures that the stationary value of U, subject to $M = p_x x + p_y y$, will be at a point where the slope of an indifference curve is equal to the slope of the budget line. Therefore, when simultaneously satisfied, the three equations of (13-15) enable us to locate point R in Fig. 13-2. Finally, note that if we solve (13-15) for $\bar{x}$, $\bar{y}$ and $\bar{\lambda}$, and then substitute these values into (13-14), we obtain

$$\bar{L} = L(\bar{\lambda}, \bar{x}, \bar{y}) = U(\bar{x}, \bar{y}) + \bar{\lambda}[M - p_x \bar{x} - p_y \bar{y}]$$

or

$$\bar{L} = U(\bar{x}, \bar{y}) = \bar{U}$$

since $[M - p_x \bar{x} - p_y \bar{y}] = 0$, as required by the first equation in (13-15). Hence the Lagrange-multiplier method gives exactly the same results as the total-differential method and the graphical analysis.

To reinforce the demonstration that the Lagrange-multiplier method gives the same results as the graphical analysis, we can substitute $U = xy$ for $U = U(x, y)$ and $24 - 6x - 3y$ for $M - p_x x - p_y y$ in (13-14) to form the Lagrangian function

$$L = L(\lambda, x, y) = xy + \lambda(24 - 6x - 3y) \quad (13\text{-}16)$$

Then, analogous to (13-15), we obtain the following set of simultaneous equations:

13-2 CONSTRAINED EXTREMA VIA THE LAGRANGE-MULTIPLIER METHOD

$$L_\lambda \equiv \frac{\partial L}{\partial \lambda} = 24 - 6x - 3y = 0$$

$$L_x \equiv \frac{\partial L}{\partial x} = y - 6\lambda = 0$$

$$L_y \equiv \frac{\partial L}{\partial y} = x - 3\lambda = 0$$

which can be solved (by substitution or by Cramer's rule) to obtain $\bar{x} = 2$, $\bar{y} = 4$, and $\bar{\lambda} = \frac{2}{3}$. Substitution of these values into (13-16) gives $\bar{L} = \bar{x}\bar{y} + \bar{\lambda}(0) = \bar{U}$ or $\bar{L} = \bar{U} = 8$. Therefore, since $\bar{U} = U^1$ in terms of Fig. 13-2, the Lagrange-multiplier method generates exactly the same results as the graphical analysis. Note, however, that while the Lagrange-multiplier method yields $\bar{U} = U^1 = 8$, it is *not* sufficient to establish $\bar{U}$ as a constrained utility maximum. For this we require knowledge of a second-order condition for a constrained extremum.

Before leaving the above example, note that the Lagrange-multiplier method generates a value for $\bar{\lambda}$ in addition to $\bar{x}$ and $\bar{y}$. This value of $\bar{\lambda}$, as we shall see in Sec. 13-3, is very useful in that it provides information about the sensitivity of $\bar{U}$ to a change in the budget constraint.

The above illustration permits us to make a general statement of the Lagrange-multiplier method for the case of a function of two variables, subject to one constraint (where such a constraint is also known as a *side relation*, a *subsidiary condition*, or simply a *restraint*). Hence given the objective function

$$z = f(x, y)$$

subject to the constraint

$$k = g(x, y) \quad \text{or} \quad k - g(x, y) = 0$$

where k is a constant, the Lagrangian function will be

$$L = L(\lambda, x, y) = f(x, y) + \lambda[k - g(x, y)] \tag{13-17}$$

Then, analogous to (13-15) in the consumer choice problem, we obtain

$$\begin{aligned} L_\lambda &= k - g(x, y) = 0 \\ L_x &= f_x - \lambda g_x = 0 \\ L_y &= f_y - \lambda g_y = 0 \end{aligned} \tag{13-18}$$

which constitutes the *first-order condition* for a constrained extremum of z. Thus, solving (13-18) for $\bar{x}$, $\bar{y}$ and $\bar{\lambda}$, and substituting these values into (13-17), we obtain the value $\bar{L} = \bar{z}$.

It is important to note that $\bar{z}$ represents a stationary value of z (and there may be more than one such stationary value), subject to the constraint $k = g(x, y)$. Consequently, to ascertain whether $\bar{z}$ represents a constrained maximum or a constrained minimum (or neither) of z requires knowledge of a second-order condition for constrained extrema. Unfortunately, since an adequate discussion of this condition is beyond the scope of this book, our discussion will be restricted to the above consideration of the first-order condition for constrained extrema. Note, however, that this restriction is not as serious as it may appear, since in most economic applications of constrained extrema the second-order condition is either satisfied, or (by making certain assumptions about the objective function) assumed to be satisfied.

It should also be noted that, while our discussion has been confined to the two-variable case, the Lagrange-multiplier method can be readily extended to the *more-than-two-variable* case. Also, while we have only dealt with the single constraint case, the Lagrange-multiplier method can be extended to handle the *multi-constraint* case. The student who is interested in these cases should consult A. C. Chiang, *Fundamental Methods of Mathematical Economics*, 2nd edition, McGraw-Hill, 1974, Chapter 12.

Finally, before proceeding to examples of the Lagrange-multiplier method, it will be instructive to demonstrate how the Lagrangian procedure transforms a constrained-extremum problem so as to permit the first-order condition of an unconstrained-extremum problem to be applied. To do this, recall that when faced with the problem of finding an extremum of the objective function $z = f(x, y)$, subject to the constraint $k = g(x, y)$, the first step in the Lagrangian procedure is to introduce a modified version of the objective function that incorporates the constraint. This modified version of the objective function, as we have already noted, is known as the Lagrangian function and is presented in (13-17). Also, recall (from section 12-2) that the first-order condition for an unconstrained extremum of $z = f(x, y)$ is $dz = 0$ or, equivalently, $f_x = f_y = 0$. Finally, although not discussed in chapter 12, note that the first-order condition for an unconstrained extremum of the *three*-variable function $z = f(x, y, w)$ can be analogously expressed as $dz = 0$ or, equivalently, $f_x = f_y = f_w = 0$.

With the above background, we can now see that the first-order condition for an unconstrained extremum of the three-variable function $L = L(\lambda, x, y)$ is $dL = 0$ or, equivalently, $L_\lambda = L_x = L_y = 0$. This, in turn, means that the first-order condition for an unconstrained extremum of the Lagrangian function (13-17), with respect to λ, x and y, will be given by the set of three simultaneous equations in (13-18). Consequently, given an objective function $z = f(x, y)$, subject to the constraint $k = g(x, y)$, we can see that (13-18) not only constitutes the first-order condition for a constrained extremum of the function $z = f(x, y)$, but also constitutes the first-order condition for an unconstrained extremum of the Lagrangian function $L = L(\lambda, x, y) = f(x, y) + \lambda[k - g(x, y)]$. Thus the Lagrangian procedure transforms a constrained-extremum problem, via the modified version of the objective function, in such a way that the first-order condition of an unconstrained-extremum problem can still be applied.

13-2 CONSTRAINED EXTREMA VIA THE LAGRANGE-MULTIPLIER METHOD

It is important, however, to recognize that while (13-18) constitutes both the first-order condition for a constrained extremum of z and the first-order condition for an unconstrained extremum of L, this does *not* mean that when we find an extremum of $z = f(x, y)$, subject to the constraint $k = g(x, y)$, we have also found an unconstrained extremum of $L = L(\lambda, x, y)$. Although the constrained-extremum analysis may show $\bar{L}$ ($= \bar{z}$) to be an extremum of the function $z = f(x, y)$, subject to the constraint $k = g(x, y)$, this does *not* mean that $\bar{L}$ is an unconstrained extremum of the Lagrangian function (13-17). The student who desires more detail on this point should consult the further reading referred to above.

Examples of the Lagrange-Multiplier Method

13-1 Write out the Lagrangian function, and the first-order condition for a constrained extremum of z, when

$$z = 8x + 4xy \quad \text{subject to} \quad x + y = 12$$

SOLUTION The Lagrangian function is

$$L = 8x + 4xy + \lambda(12 - x - y)$$

The first-order condition for a constrained extremum of z is

$$\left. \begin{array}{l} L_\lambda = 12 - x - y = 0 \\ L_x = 8 + 4y - \lambda = 0 \\ L_y = 4x - \lambda = 0 \end{array} \right\} \quad \text{or} \quad \left\{ \begin{array}{rr} -x - y = -12 \\ -\lambda + 4y = -8 \\ -\lambda + 4x = 0 \end{array} \right.$$

Solving by substitution or by Cramer's rule gives $\bar{\lambda} = 28$, $\bar{x} = 7$ and $\bar{y} = 5$. Substitution of these values into L gives $\bar{L} = \bar{z} = 196$.

13-2 Write out the Lagrangian function, and the first-order condition for a constrained extremum of z, when

$$z = x_1^2 - x_1 x_2 + 2x_2^2 + 2 \quad \text{subject to} \quad 8 - x_1 - x_2 = 0$$

SOLUTION The Lagrangian function is

$$L = x_1^2 - x_1 x_2 + 2x_2^2 + 2 + \lambda(8 - x_1 - x_2)$$

The first-order condition for a constrained extremum of z is

$$L_\lambda = 8 - x_1 - x_2 = 0$$
$$L_1 = 2x_1 - x_2 - \lambda = 0$$
$$L_2 = -x_1 + 4x_2 - \lambda = 0$$

Solving by substitution or by Cramer's rule we obtain $\bar{\lambda} = 7$, $\bar{x}_1 = 5$ and $\bar{x}_2 = 3$. Substitution of these values into L gives $\bar{L} = \bar{z} = 30$.

13-3 Write out the Lagrangian function, and the first-order condition for a constrained maximum of U, when

$$U = xy \quad \text{subject to} \quad 24 = 6x + 3y$$

SOLUTION The Lagrangian function is

$$L = xy - \lambda(24 - 6x - 3y)$$

This example is identical to our consumer choice problem, except that λ is now preceded by a *minus* sign. The first-order condition for a constrained maximum of U is

$$L_\lambda = -24 + 6x + 3y = 0$$
$$L_x = y + 6\lambda = 0$$
$$L_y = x + 3\lambda = 0$$

Solving by substitution or by Cramer's rule gives $\bar{\lambda} = -\frac{2}{3}$, $\bar{x} = 2$ and $\bar{y} = 4$. Substitution into L then gives $\bar{L} = \bar{U} = 8$ as before. Note that the only resulting effect of preceding λ by a minus rather than a plus sign is that the sign of λ in the solution is changed.

13-A PRACTICE PROBLEMS

13-4 Use the Lagrange-multiplier method to find the stationary value of z, subject to the given constraint, in each of the following cases:
  (a) $z = x^2 - xy + \frac{3}{2}y^2$ subject to $x + 2y = 3$
  (b) $z = -2x^2 + xy + 3y^2 - 400$ subject to $36 = x + 3y$
  (c) $z = \frac{3}{2}x^2 - 2xy + \frac{1}{2}y^2 + 144$ subject to $2x + 2y = 96$
  (d) $z = 2x^2 + 2xy - 3y^2 - 11$ subject to $3x + 5y = 9$

13-3 ECONOMIC APPLICATIONS OF CONSTRAINED EXTREMA

The foregoing analysis of constrained extrema, with its restriction to the first-order condition, can now be applied to the following economic problems.

Utility Maximization subject to a Budget Constraint

In this section, we shall (briefly) return once more to the consumer choice problem of maximizing utility subject to a budget constraint. However, instead of analysing a specific utility function and a specific budget constraint, the analysis will be conducted in terms of a general utility function and a general budget constraint.

Let us assume that the consumer's utility function is given by

$$U = U(x, y) \tag{13-19}$$

Also, we shall assume that

$$\partial U/\partial x \equiv U_x = U_x(x, y) > 0 \quad \text{and} \quad \partial U/\partial y \equiv U_y = U_y(x, y) > 0 \tag{13-20}$$

for all positive values of x and y. In other words, we shall assume that both goods have positive marginal utility functions, as given by $U_x = U_x(x, y) > 0$ and $U_y = U_y(x, y) > 0$, for $x, y > 0$, respectively. Given (13-19) and the fact that, by definition, the level of U is unchanged along an indifference curve or, equivalently, the change in U is zero along an indifference curve, then on an indifference curve we have

$$dU = U_x dx + U_y dy = 0 \tag{13-21}$$

which implies that $dy/dx = -U_x/U_y$. Since we have assumed that $U_x, U_y > 0$, then $dy/dx < 0$. Note that this means that an indifference curve will have a *negative slope*, as given by $dy/dx = -U_x/U_y$. Hence, it is for this reason that the indifference curves U^0 and U^1 are drawn with negative slopes in Fig. 13-4. Also, note that the convex-to-the-origin shape of U^0 and U^1, in Fig. 13-4, requires the assumption of $d^2y/dx^2 > 0$ at all points on an indifference curve.

In economic terminology, the *negative* of the slope of an indifference curve is called the *marginal rate of substitution* (*MRS*) between the two goods, as given by

$$-\frac{dy}{dx} = \frac{U_x}{U_y} = MRS \qquad (13\text{-}22)$$

Thus, since

$$\frac{d(MRS)}{dx} < 0 \quad \text{or} \quad \frac{d}{dx}\left[-\frac{dy}{dx}\right] < 0$$

is equivalent to $d^2y/dx^2 > 0$, this means that if we wish to have $d^2y/dx^2 > 0$ at all points on an indifference curve we must assume a *diminishing marginal rate of substitution* (or $d(MRS)/dx < 0$) all along that indifference curve.

The consumer's budget constraint will be taken as

$$M = p_x x + p_y y \qquad (13\text{-}23)$$

where M represents his budget (which is *all* spent on x and y), and where p_x and p_y represent the given (positive) prices of x and y, respectively. Hence,

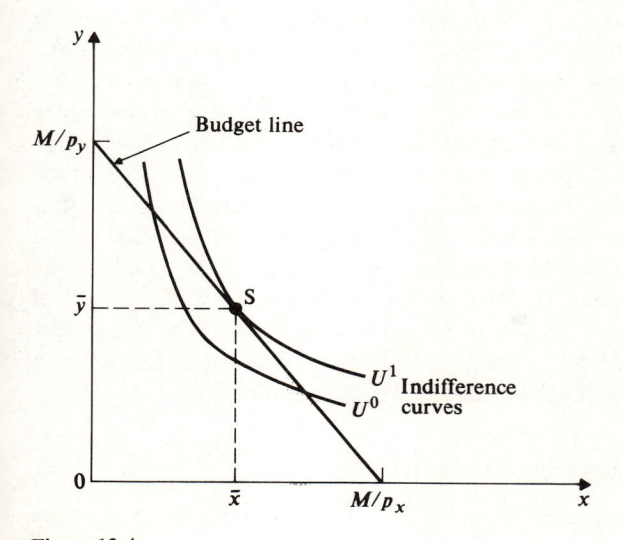

Figure 13-4

rewriting (13-23) as $y = M/p_y - (p_x/p_y)x$, the budget constraint can be plotted as the budget line shown in Fig. 13-4.

The consumer choice problem can now be seen to consist of maximizing (13-19) subject to (13-23). In this case the Lagrangian function is

$$L = U(x, y) + \lambda[M - p_x x - p_y y] \tag{13-24}$$

and the first-order condition for a constrained maximum of U is

$$\left. \begin{aligned} L_\lambda &= M - p_x x - p_y y = 0 \\ L_x &= U_x - \lambda p_x = 0 \\ L_y &= U_y - \lambda p_y = 0 \end{aligned} \right\} \tag{13-25}$$

The solution of this set of simultaneous equations yields $\bar{x}$, $\bar{y}$ and $\bar{\lambda}$. Substitution of these values into (13-24) will then give $\bar{L} = \bar{U}$ (which equals U^1 in Fig. 13-4). Hence, assuming that the second-order condition for a constrained maximum of U is satisfied, $\bar{U}$ will represent a constrained maximum of U.

To see what the first-order condition means in economic terms, note that the first equation in (13-25) implies the satisfaction of the budget constraint. In other words, $\bar{x}$ and $\bar{y}$ are chosen so as to satisfy the budget constraint. In terms of Fig. 13-4, this means that point $(\bar{x}, \bar{y})$ must be located on the budget line. Also, note that the last two equations of (13-25) give

$$\frac{U_x}{p_x} = \frac{U_y}{p_y} = \lambda \quad \text{or} \quad -\frac{U_x}{U_y} = -\frac{p_x}{p_y} \tag{13-26}$$

In terms of Fig. 13-4, this means that point $(\bar{x}, \bar{y})$ must be located where the slope of an indifference curve is equal to the slope of the budget line. Therefore, when simultaneously satisfied, the three equations of (13-25) enable us to locate point S in Fig. 13-4. Assuming that the second-order condition for a constrained U maximum is satisfied, point S will therefore represent a constrained U maximum. Finally, note that (13-26) can be rewritten as $U_x/U_y = p_x/p_y$. Hence, since $U_x/U_y = MRS$, and assuming that the second-order condition for a constrained U maximum is satisfied, point S will be located where the MRS between the two goods is equal to the price ratio of the two goods. In other words, we have the familiar result of consumer theory that, in order to maximize U subject to a budget constraint, the consumer must allocate his budget so that the MRS between the two goods is equal to the price ratio of the two goods.

Interpretation of the Lagrange Multiplier

In the above discussion of constrained utility maximization, the stationary value of U (denoted as $\bar{U}$), subject to the given budget constraint, was obtained by solving the first-order condition (13-25) for $\bar{x}$, $\bar{y}$, and $\bar{\lambda}$, and then substituting these values into the Lagrangian function (13-24) to yield

$$\bar{L} = \bar{U} = U(\bar{x}, \bar{y}) + \bar{\lambda}[M - p_x\bar{x} - p_y\bar{y}]$$

In other words, we have so far only utilized $\bar{\lambda}$ to obtain $\bar{U}$. This, however, does not constitute the only use of $\bar{\lambda}$ since, as noted in Sec. 13-2, the solution value of the Lagrange multiplier ($\bar{\lambda}$) provides a measure of the sensitivity of $\bar{U}$ to changes in the budget constraint. In mathematical terms this means that $\bar{\lambda} = \partial \bar{U}/\partial M$. While a full demonstration of this statement is beyond the scope of this book, we shall illustrate this interpretation of the Lagrange multiplier by reference to a consumer choice problem.

As an example, let us take the case where a consumer wishes to maximize $U = U(x, y) = xy$, subject to the budget constraint $M = h(x, y) = p_x x + p_y y$. In this case, the Lagrangian function is

$$L = xy + \lambda[M - p_x x - p_y y]$$

and the first-order condition for a constrained maximum of U is

$$\left. \begin{array}{l} L_\lambda = M - p_x x - p_y y = 0 \\ L_x = y - \lambda p_x = 0 \\ L_y = x - \lambda p_y = 0 \end{array} \right\} \qquad (13\text{-}27)$$

The solution of (13-27) yields $\bar{x} = M/2p_x$, $\bar{y} = M/2p_y$, and $\bar{\lambda} = M/2p_x p_y$ (that is, $L_x = L_y = 0$ yields $y/p_x = x/p_y = \lambda$ and substitution of $y = (p_x/p_y)x$ into $L_\lambda = 0$ yields $\bar{x} = M/2p_x$. Hence $\bar{y} = (p_x/p_y)\bar{x} = M/2p_y$ and $\bar{\lambda} = \bar{x}/p_y = M/2p_x p_y$). Substitution of these values into the L function gives $\bar{L} = \bar{U} = M^2/4p_x p_y$. Hence, assuming that the second-order condition for a constrained maximum of U is satisfied, $\bar{U}$ will represent a constrained maximum of U.

Now that we have found $\bar{U} = M^2/4p_x p_y$, we can quickly obtain $\partial \bar{U}/\partial M = M/2p_x p_y$. Note immediately that $\partial \bar{U}/\partial M = \bar{\lambda}$ as stated above. Thus $\bar{\lambda}$ measures the change in maximized utility resulting from a change in budget money (M). In other words, $\bar{\lambda}$ can be considered as the gain (loss) in maximized utility resulting from an infinitesimally small increase (decrease) in budget money, prices being held constant. It is for this reason that $\bar{\lambda}$ can be interpreted as the *marginal utility of money* when the consumer's utility is maximized. Expressed in another way, $\bar{\lambda} = \partial \bar{U}/\partial M$ is the *opportunity cost* in utility terms of not having an additional (very small) increase in budget money or, simply, the cost of having to observe the budget constraint. For this reason $\bar{\lambda}$ is also known as a *shadow price* or an *accounting price* (the terminology resulting from the fact that the shadow or accounting price represents an imputed valuation, derived from the constrained utility maximization problem, rather than a market valuation).

In general, for an extremum of $z = f(x,y)$, subject to a constraint $k = g(x,y)$, where k is a constant and where the Lagrangian function is $L = f(x,y) + \lambda[k - g(x,y)]$, we can state (without proof) that $\bar{\lambda} = \partial \bar{z}/\partial k$.

The above interpretation of $\bar{\lambda}$, as the marginal utility of money when the consumer's utility is maximized, can now be utilized to provide us with a better understanding of the Lagrange-multiplier method. In order to do this, note that the consumer choice problem of maximizing $U = U(x,y)$, subject to the budget constraint $M = h(x,y) = p_x x + p_y y$, involves finding the (x,y) combination which will both maximize $U(x,y)$ and satisfy the budget constraint $M = h(x,y)$. Alternatively, given the Lagrangian function $L = L(\lambda, x, y) = U(x,y) + \lambda[M - h(x,y)]$, the consumer choice problem involves finding the (x,y) combination which constitutes a constrained maximum of the utility function $U(x,y)$ or, equivalently, which will both maximize $U(x,y)$ and ensure that $\lambda[M - h(x,y)] = \lambda[0]$. Hence, taking the Lagrangian function $L = L(\lambda, x, y) = U(x,y) + \lambda[M - h(x,y)]$, let us consider the following cases.

Suppose the consumer overspends by choosing an (x,y) combination such that $[M - h(x,y)] < 0$ or $h(x,y) > M$. If $\lambda > 0$, this means that the term $\lambda[M - h(x,y)]$ is negative and therefore represents a deduction from $U(x,y)$. Consequently, since this deduction from $U(x,y)$ is the 'penalty' resulting from the consumer's overspending, we can interpret the term $\lambda[M - h(x,y)] < 0$ as a 'penalty' term.

While the consumer's overspending has resulted in a deduction from $U(x,y)$, via $\lambda[M - h(x,y)] < 0$, this same overspending will permit an increase in $U(x,y)$. Hence, the consumer's overspending will lead to both a utility gain and a 'penalty'. Note, however, that if a large enough value of λ is chosen then the 'penalty' will outweigh the utility gain and the consumer will have an incentive to reduce his overspending. This, in turn, suggests that some value of λ can be chosen so as to ensure that the consumer purchases that (x,y) combination for which $h(x,y) = M$. In particular, the appropriate value of λ must be such that the 'penalty' for overspending exactly offsets the utility gain from overspending and therefore discourages any overspending.

To find the appropriate value of λ, let us rewrite $\lambda[M - h(x,y)]$ as λK, with $K = [M - h(x,y)] < 0$ to indicate overspending. Note that any increase in $|K|$ (that is, any increase in overspending) will imply a higher 'penalty'. In particular, note that if $|K|$ is increased by one very small unit of money (that is, if overspending is increased by one very small unit of money), the 'penalty' will increase by λ, as given by $\partial(\lambda K)/\partial K = \lambda$. Also, note that this increase in overspending, by one very small money unit, will result in a utility gain, as measured by the marginal utility of money $\partial U/\partial M$. Hence if $\lambda = \partial U/\partial M$, then the 'penalty' for overspending by one very small unit of money will exactly offset the utility gain resulting from this extra unit of overspending. Thus, when $\lambda = \partial U/\partial M$, as was the case above when $\bar{\lambda} = \partial \bar{U}/\partial M$, the consumer will have no incentive to overspend or, equivalently, to choose an (x, y) combination for which $h(x, y) > M$.

The above analysis can also be applied, via analogous reasoning, to the case where $\lambda > 0$ and where the consumer *under*spends. In this case, the consumer's underspending will result in both a utility loss and a 'bonus', with the latter addition to $U(x, y)$ being given by $\lambda[M - h(x, y)] > 0$. If, analogous to the overspending case, we choose λ such that $\lambda = \partial U/\partial M$ then the 'bonus' for underspending by one very small unit of money will be exactly offset by the utility loss resulting from this extra unit of underspending. Thus when $\lambda = \partial U/\partial M$, as was the case above when $\bar{\lambda} = \partial \bar{U}/\partial M$, the consumer will have no incentive to underspend or, equivalently, to choose an (x, y) combination for which $h(x, y) < M$.

This discussion of the overspending and underspending cases demonstrates the important role of the variable λ in the Lagrangian procedure for maximizing $U(x, y)$ subject to $M = h(x, y)$. In particular, the appropriate value of the Lagrange multiplier λ must be chosen so as to ensure that it will just be worthwhile for the consumer to choose that (x, y) combination such that $h(x, y) = M$ when maximizing $U(x, y)$. As demonstrated in the consumer choice problem above, the appropriate value of λ is $\bar{\lambda} = \partial \bar{U}/\partial M$.

Examples of Utility Maximization subject to a Budget Constraint

13-5 A consumer's utility function is $U = U(x_1, x_2) = 2 \ln x_1 + \ln x_2$. His budget constraint is $M = p_1 x_1 + p_2 x_2 = 2x_1 + 4x_2 = 36$. Assuming that the second-order condition for a constrained U maximum is satisfied, find:

(a) the levels of x_1 and x_2 that the consumer should purchase in order to maximize his utility, subject to his budget constraint.

(b) the consumer's marginal utility of money when his utility is maximized.

SOLUTION

(a) The Lagrangian function is
$$L = 2 \ln x_1 + \ln x_2 + \lambda[36 - 2x_1 - 4x_2]$$
The first-order condition for a constrained maximum of U is $L_\lambda = L_1 = L_2 = 0$. Thus
$$L_\lambda = 36 - 2x_1 - 4x_2 = 0$$
$$L_1 = \frac{2}{x_1} - 2\lambda = 0$$
$$L_2 = \frac{1}{x_2} - 4\lambda = 0$$
From $L_1 = 0$ and $L_2 = 0$ we obtain $1/x_1 = \lambda = 1/4x_2$ or $4x_2 = x_1$. Substituting $4x_2 = x_1$ into $L_\lambda = 0$ gives $\bar{x}_1 = 12$. Hence $\bar{x}_2 = 3$ and $\bar{\lambda} = \frac{1}{12}$. Substitution of these values into the Lagrangian function gives $\bar{L} = \bar{U} = \ln 432 = 6.07$. Hence, given the above assumption, $\bar{U} = 6.07$ represents a constrained maximum of U.

(b) The consumer's marginal utility of money is given by $\partial \bar{U}/\partial M = \bar{\lambda} = \frac{1}{12}$.

13-6 Find, using the utility function of Example 13-5, the MRS of x_1 for x_2. Does diminishing MRS hold at the optimal levels of purchase $\bar{x}_1$ and $\bar{x}_2$?

SOLUTION Along any indifference curve the change in U is zero. Thus

$$dU = U_1 dx_1 + U_2 dx_2 = \frac{2}{x_1} dx_1 + \frac{1}{x_2} dx_2 = 0$$

which implies that $dx_2/dx_1 = -U_1/U_2 = -2x_2/x_1$. Hence, by definition, $MRS = -dx_2/dx_1 = U_1/U_2 = 2x_2/x_1$. For example, at $(\bar{x}_1, \bar{x}_2) = (12, 3)$ we have $MRS = \frac{1}{2}$.

To check for diminishing MRS at $(\bar{x}_1, \bar{x}_2)$ involves checking the sign of $d(MRS)/dx_1 = -d^2x_2/dx_1^2$. Since $dx_2/dx_1 = g(x_1, x_2) = -2x_2/x_1$, then

$$\frac{d^2x_2}{dx_1^2} = \frac{d}{dx_1}\left[\frac{dx_2}{dx_1}\right] = \frac{dg}{dx_1} = \frac{\partial g}{\partial x_1}\frac{dx_1}{dx_1} + \frac{\partial g}{\partial x_2}\frac{dx_2}{dx_1}$$

or

$$\frac{d^2x_2}{dx_1^2} = \frac{2x_2}{x_1^2}\frac{dx_1}{dx_1} + \left(-\frac{2}{x_1}\right)\frac{dx_2}{dx_1} = \frac{2x_2}{x_1^2} + \left(-\frac{2}{x_1}\right)\left(-\frac{2x_2}{x_1}\right) = \frac{6x_2}{x_1^2}$$

Therefore at $(\bar{x}_1, \bar{x}_2) = (12, 3)$ we have $d^2x_2/dx_1^2 = \frac{1}{8}$. Thus $d(MRS)/dx_1 = -d^2x_2/dx_1^2 = -\frac{1}{8} < 0$ at $(\bar{x}_1, \bar{x}_2)$, indicating that diminishing MRS holds at $(\bar{x}_1, \bar{x}_2)$.

It should be noted in this case that, since $d^2x_2/dx_1^2 > 0$ for $x_1, x_2 > 0$, each of the consumer's indifference curves will be convex to the origin for $x_1, x_2 > 0$. In other words, a diminishing MRS (or $d(MRS)/dx_1 < 0$) holds at all points along each indifference curve.

Cost Minimization subject to an Output Constraint

Let us consider the case of a producer whose production function is given by $Q = f(K, L)$, where both inputs have positive marginal product functions (over the input levels relevant to our analysis), as given by $\partial Q/\partial K \equiv f_K = f_K(K, L) > 0$ and $\partial Q/\partial L \equiv f_L = f_L(K, L) > 0$. The producer's cost function is given by $C = rK + wL$ where r and w are the given (positive) prices of K and L, respectively.

If the producer is now presented with an order for a specified level of output, $Q = Q^1$, this raises the interesting question: what levels of K and L should the producer use in his production process in order to produce Q^1 at minimum cost? In other words, what is the producer's least-cost input combination for the production of Q^1? The answer to this question is to be found by minimizing $C = rK + wL$ subject to $Q^1 = f(K, L)$.

Before proceeding to find minimum C, let us see what this problem looks like graphically. The first point to note is that $Q^1 = f(K, L)$ is an equation similar to the indifference-curve equation $U^1 = U(x, y)$. Thus, by analogy, we can plot $Q^1 = f(K, L)$ in Fig. 13-5a as shown, recognizing that as yet we have no mathematical justification for the negative-sloped, convex-to-the-origin shape of curve Q^1. Since, as drawn, curve Q^1 consists of the locus of the combinations of K and L that will produce a constant level of output $(Q = Q^1)$, it is known as an *isoquant*. To obtain other isoquants, as shown in Fig. 13-5b, we simply take levels of constant output other than Q^1 in just the same way as we took U^0 and U^1 to get the indifference curves in Fig. 13-4. [*Note*: in Fig. 13-5, K has been put on the vertical rather than the horizontal axis. This reversal of the axes is simply to make Fig. 13-5 identical to diagrams in microeconomics textbooks.]

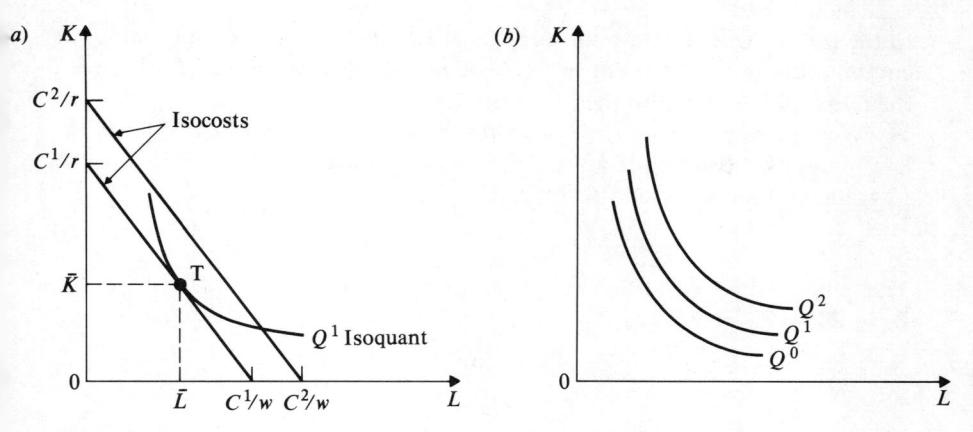

13-3 ECONOMIC APPLICATIONS OF CONSTRAINED EXTREMA

Figure 13-5

To obtain the slope of an isoquant we use the property that the change in Q along an isoquant is zero. Hence on an isoquant we have

$$dQ = f_K \, dK + f_L \, dL = 0$$

which implies that the slope of an isoquant, given by $dK/dL = -f_L/f_K$, is negative as drawn in Fig. 13-5. In economic terminology, the *negative* of the slope of an isoquant is called the *marginal rate of technical substitution* (*MRTS*) between the two inputs, as given by $-dK/dL = f_L/f_K = MRTS$. This means, in relation to Fig. 13-5 (where the convex-to-the-origin shape of each isoquant indicates that $d^2K/dL^2 > 0$ or $d(MRTS)/dL = d(-dK/dL)/dL < 0$ at all points on each isoquant), that we must assume a *diminishing marginal rate of technical substitution* (or $d(MRTS)/dL < 0$) all along each isoquant.

The cost function can also be represented graphically. Thus if we take a given level of cost, $C = C^1$, the cost function can then be rewritten as

$$K = \frac{C^1}{r} - \frac{w}{r} L \qquad (13\text{-}28)$$

which is, in fact, the equation of the straight line with vertical intercept C^1/r in Fig. 13-5a. This line, consisting of the locus of input combinations that entail the same total cost ($C = C^1$), is known as an *isocost*. Note, from (13-28), that the slope of this isocost is $dK/dL = -w/r$. Also, note that if we take a higher level of cost, $C = C^2$, we obtain the (parallel) isocost drawn in Fig. 13-5a with vertical intercept C^2/r.

In terms of Fig. 13-5a, the producer's problem can now be seen as consisting of choosing that input combination which will not only produce $Q = Q^1$, but will also put him on the lowest possible isocost. Clearly, in Fig. 13-5a, this input combination is $(\bar{K}, \bar{L})$, where the isoquant Q^1 is tangential to the isocost with vertical intercept C^1/r. In other words, the optimal input combination is at that point on the isoquant Q^1 where the MRTS between the two inputs is equal to the price ratio of the two inputs.

We can now obtain the above result mathematically. Since the problem consists of minimizing $C = rK + wL$ subject to $Q^1 = f(K, L)$, the Lagrangian function (denoted by Z) is

$$Z = rK + wL + \lambda[Q^1 - f(K, L)] \tag{13-29}$$

The first-order condition for a constrained minimum of C is $Z_\lambda = Z_K = Z_L = 0$. Thus

$$Z_\lambda = Q^1 - f(K, L) = 0$$
$$Z_K = r - \lambda f_K = 0$$
$$Z_L = w - \lambda f_L = 0$$

The solution of these three simultaneous equations yields $\bar{\lambda}$, $\bar{K}$ and $\bar{L}$. Substitution of these values into (13-29) will then give $\bar{Z} = \bar{C}$ (which equals C^1 in Fig. 13-5). Hence, assuming that the second-order condition for a constrained minimum of C is satisfied, $\bar{C}$ will represent a constrained minimum of C.

To see what the first-order condition means in economic terms, note that equation $Z_\lambda = 0$ implies the satisfaction of the output constraint. In other words, $\bar{K}$ and $\bar{L}$ are chosen so as to satisfy the output constraint. In terms of Fig. 13-5, this means that point $(\bar{K}, \bar{L})$ must be located on isoquant Q^1. Also, note that equations $Z_K = 0$ and $Z_L = 0$ together give $r/f_K = w/f_L = \lambda$ (which is therefore positive) or $-f_L/f_K = -w/r$. In terms of Fig. 13-5, this means that point $(\bar{K}, \bar{L})$ must be located where the slope of an isoquant is equal to the slope of the budget line or, equivalently, where the MRTS between the two inputs is equal to the price ratio of the two inputs (since $-f_L/f_K = -w/r$ can be rewritten as MRTS $= f_L/f_K = w/r$). Therefore, when the three equations $Z_\lambda = 0$, $Z_K = 0$ and $Z_L = 0$ are simultaneously satisfied, we can locate point T in Fig. 13-5. Assuming that the second-order condition for a constrained C minimum is satisfied, point T will therefore represent a constrained C minimum. Finally, note that $\partial \bar{C}/\partial Q^1 = \partial C^1/\partial Q^1 = \bar{\lambda}$ can be interpreted as the *marginal cost of production* when the producer's total cost is minimized.

Examples of Cost Minimization subject to an Output Constraint

13-7 A producer's production function is $Q = f(K, L) = 4K^{1/2}L^{1/2}$. His cost function is $C = rK + wL = 2K + 8L$. Assuming that the second-order condition for a constrained C minimum is satisfied, find:
    (a) his least-cost combination of K and L for producing $Q = 32$
    (b) his marginal cost of production when his total cost is minimized.

13-3 ECONOMIC APPLICATIONS OF CONSTRAINED EXTREMA

SOLUTION
(a) The Lagrangian function is
$$Z = 2K + 8L + \lambda[32 - 4K^{1/2}L^{1/2}]$$
The first-order condition for a constrained minimum of C is $Z_\lambda = Z_K = Z_L = 0$. Thus
$$Z_\lambda = 32 - 4K^{1/2}L^{1/2} = 0$$
$$Z_K = 2 - 2\lambda K^{-1/2}L^{1/2} = 0$$
$$Z_L = 8 - 2\lambda K^{1/2}L^{-1/2} = 0$$
Eliminating λ from the last two equations gives $4L = K$. Substituting this into $Z_\lambda = 0$ gives $\bar{L} = 4$. Hence $\bar{K} = 16$ and $\bar{\lambda} = 2$. Substitution of these values into the Lagrangian function gives $\bar{Z} = \bar{C} = 64$ which, given the above assumption, represents a constrained minimum of C.
(b) The producer's marginal cost of production is given by $\partial \bar{C}/\partial Q = \bar{\lambda} = 2$.

13-8 Does the production function of Example 13-7 possess the property of diminishing $MRTS$?

SOLUTION
$$MRTS = -dK/dL = f_L/f_K = 2K^{1/2}L^{-1/2}/2K^{-1/2}L^{1/2} = K/L$$
To check for diminishing $MRTS$ we must find $d(MRTS)/dL = -d^2K/dL^2$. Since $dK/dL = g(K, L) = -K/L$, then
$$\frac{d^2K}{dL^2} = \frac{d}{dL}\left[\frac{dK}{dL}\right] = \frac{dg}{dL} = \frac{\partial g}{\partial K}\frac{dK}{dL} + \frac{\partial g}{\partial L}\frac{dL}{dL}$$
or
$$\frac{d^2K}{dL^2} = \left(-\frac{1}{L}\right)\frac{dK}{dL} + \frac{K}{L^2}\frac{dL}{dL} = \left(-\frac{1}{L}\right)\left(-\frac{K}{L}\right) + \frac{K}{L^2} = \frac{2K}{L^2}$$
Thus $d(MRTS)/dL = -d^2K/dL^2 = -2K/L^2$, which is negative for $K, L > 0$, indicating that $Q = 4K^{1/2}L^{1/2}$ possesses the property of diminishing $MRTS$ for $K, L > 0$.

13-B PRACTICE PROBLEMS

13-9–13-12 In each of these problems, assume that the second-order condition for a constrained utility maximum is satisfied and find the consumer's (a) utility-maximizing purchases of x and y, subject to the budget constraint $M = p_x x + p_y y$, (b) maximum level of utility in this situation, and (c) marginal utility of money when utility is maximized.

13-9 $U = x^{1/2}y$; $M = 48$; $p_x = 1$; $p_y = 4$.
13-10 $U = 9x + 18xy$; $M = 15$; $p_x = 3$; $p_y = 6$.
13-11 $U = 6\ln x + 7\ln y$; $M = 26$; $p_x = 2$; $p_y = 7$.
13-12 $U = x^{1/2}y^{1/3}$; $M = 40$; $p_x = 6$; $p_y = 2$.
13-13 A consumer has a Cobb-Douglas type utility function given by $U = U(x, y) = Ax^\alpha y^\beta$, where A, α and β are constants. His budget constraint is given by $M = p_x x + p_y y$. Assuming that the second-order condition for a constrained U maximum is satisfied, find the consumer's utility-maximizing purchases of x and y. Also, give an economic interpretation of the expressions obtained for optimal purchases of x and y.
13-14–13-17 In each of these problems, assume that the second-order condition for a constrained cost minimum is satisfied and find the producer's (a) cost-minimizing input levels of K and L for producing the given output, (b) minimum level of cost in this situation, and (c) marginal cost of production when cost is minimized.

13-14 $C = 2K + 4L$; $Q = 8K^{1/4}L^{1/2} = 64$.
13-15 $C = 8K + 2L$; $Q = K^{1/3}L^{2/3} = 32$.
13-16 $C = 0.5K + 9L$; $Q = K^{1/2}L = 24$.
13-17 $C = K + 2L$; $Q = \ln K + 2\ln L = \ln 27$.

13-4 ADDITIONAL PROBLEMS

13-18 A consumer's utility function is $U = U(x, y)$, with his expenditure on x and y given by $M = p_x x + p_y y$. Assuming that he desires to minimize his expenditure on x and y, subject to a given level of utility, $U = U^1$, then (i) show, using μ as the Lagrange multiplier, that the first-order condition for constrained expenditure minimization implies $MRS = p_x/p_y$, as obtained for constrained utility maximization, (ii) give $\bar{\mu}$ an economic interpretation and compare it with $\bar{\lambda} = \partial \bar{U}/\partial M$ obtained in relation to Eq. (13-24), and (iii) assuming that the second-order condition for a constrained expenditure minimum is satisfied, illustrate constrained expenditure minimization graphically.

13-19 (i) Minimize $M = p_1 x_1 + p_2 x_2 = 6x_1 + 3x_2$, subject to $U^1 = x_1 x_2 = 8$; (ii) maximize $U = x_1 x_2$, subject to $M = p_1 x_1 + p_2 x_2 = 6x_1 + 3x_2 = 24$; (iii) explain the correspondence between the results obtained for (i) and (ii).

13-20 Minimize $M = p_1 x_1 + p_2 x_2 = 2x_1 + 4x_2$, subject to $U(x_1, x_2) = 2\ln x_1 + \ln x_2 = \ln 432$. Compare your results with those for Example 13-5 in Sec. 13-3.

13-21 A producer's production function is $Q = f(K, L)$, with expenditure on K and L given by $C = rK + wL$. Assuming that he desires to maximize his output, subject to a given level of cost, $C = C^1$, then (i) show, using μ as the Lagrange multiplier, that the first-order condition for output maximization, subject to a cost constraint, implies $MRTS = w/r$ as obtained for cost minimization, subject to an output constraint; (ii) give $\bar{\mu}$ an economic interpretation and compare it with $\bar{\lambda} = \partial C^1/\partial Q^1$ obtained in relation to Eq. (13-29); (iii) assuming that the second-order condition for a constrained output maximum is satisfied, illustrate constrained output maximization graphically.

13-22 Maximize $Q = f(K, L) = 4K^{1/2}L^{1/2}$, subject to $C = rK + wL = 2K + 8L = 64$. Compare your results with those for Example 13-7 in Sec. 13-3.

13-23 A consumer has a utility function $U(x_1, x_2) = Ax_1^\alpha x_2^{1-\alpha}$, and a budget constraint $M = p_1 x_1 + p_2 x_2$. Assuming that the second-order condition for a constrained U maximum is satisfied, find the consumer's demand functions for x_1 and x_2. Then, for the demand functions obtained, derive

(a) the own price elasticities
(b) the cross price elasticities
(c) the income elasticities.

Also, comment on the economic realism of the demand functions obtained.

13-24 For the following production functions, find the *elasticity of substitution* (σ), defined as

$$\sigma \equiv \frac{\text{relative change in } (K/L)}{\text{relative change in } MRTS} = \frac{d(K/L)/(K/L)}{d(MRTS)/MRTS} = \frac{d(K/L)}{d(MRTS)} \cdot \frac{MRTS}{(K/L)}$$

(i) $Q = AK^\alpha L^\beta$ (ii) $Q = \gamma[\delta K^{-\alpha} + (1-\delta)L^{-\alpha}]^{-v/\alpha}$

[*Hint*: $d(K/L)/d(MRTS) = 1/\{d(MRTS)/d(K/L)\}$.]

CHAPTER
FOURTEEN
INTEGRATION AND EXPONENTIAL FUNCTIONS

In Chapter 6, we discussed the mathematical operation of differentiation, for functions of one independent variable. Now, in this chapter, we shall consider the mathematical operation, known as *integration*, which is the exact opposite of differentiation. Thus, instead of finding the derivative $dy/dx \equiv f'(x)$, of a given function $y = f(x)$, we shall now consider the method of finding the function $y = f(x)$ from a given derivative $f'(x)$.

14-1 THE CONCEPT OF INTEGRATION

To help us understand the concept of integration, let us suppose that we have a function $y = f(x) = x^2 + 12x + 20$, which can be differentiated to yield the derivative $dy/dx \equiv f'(x) = 2x + 12$. Since integration is the reverse of differentiation, then the integration of $f'(x) = 2x + 12$ should enable us to get back to the original function $f(x) = x^2 + 12x + 20$. However, at this point a problem arises. If we are only given $f'(x) = 2x + 12$, then this derivative function may have come from many different functions such as $f(x) = x^2 + 12x + 10$, $f(x) = x^2 + 12x + 25$ or, more generally,

$$f(x) = x^2 + 12x + c \qquad (14\text{-}1)$$

where c is an arbitrary constant which may assume any value. In other words, any function of form $f(x) = x^2 + 12x + c$ can produce the derivative function $f'(x) = 2x + 12$. This means that if we are only given $f'(x) = 2x + 12$, then we can only get back to the function (14-1). In order

255

to get back to the original function $f(x) = x^2 + 12x + 20$, we must be given additional information (known as an *initial condition* or *boundary condition*) that enables us to give c the definite value of $c = 20$.

For example, if we are given the additional information that $f(0) = 20$, then we can use this information to give c a definite value. To see this, let us set $x = 0$ in (14-1) to obtain

$$f(0) = (0)^2 + 12(0) + c = c$$

Thus, if we know $f(0) = 20$, then $c = 20$, so that (14-1) becomes

$$f(x) = x^2 + 12x + 20 \qquad (14\text{-}2)$$

This example demonstrates that the initial condition of $f(0) = 20$ enables us to definitize c, so that we can get back from $f'(x) = 2x + 12$ to the original function $f(x) = x^2 + 12x + 20$.

Now that we have some idea of what the concept of integration involves, we can proceed to a more detailed discussion of integration. In doing so, note that we will denote the original and derivative functions, respectively, by $F(x)$ and $f(x)$, instead of $f(x)$ and $f'(x)$. This means, in keeping with our discussion above, that the differentiation of $F(x)$ will yield $F'(x) = f(x)$, and the integration of $F'(x) = f(x)$ will yield $F(x) + c$, where c is an arbitrary constant. Note also, as a matter of terminology, that the function $F(x)$ is referred to as an *integral* (or *antiderivative*) of the function $f(x)$, and c is referred to as an arbitrary *constant of integration*. This, in turn, means that $F(x) + c$ can also be referred to as an integral (or antiderivative) of $f(x)$, in the sense that the differentiation of both $F(x)$ and $F(x) + c$ yield the same derivative function $f(x)$.

14-2 INDEFINITE INTEGRALS

The standard notation to denote the integration of $f(x)$, in order to obtain $F(x) + c$, is

$$\int f(x)dx = F(x) + c \qquad (14\text{-}3)$$

where the symbol $\int$ is called the *integral sign*, $f(x)$ is called the *integrand* (meaning the function to be integrated), and dx simply indicates that the integration operation is to be performed with respect to the variable x. Alternatively, if we write the differential of the original function $F(x)$ as $dF = F'(x)dx = f(x)dx$, then the integral sign $\int$ can be interpreted as an instruction to reverse the differentiation process that produced the differential $dF = f(x)dx$.

Note that since $\int f(x)dx = F(x) + c$, we can refer to $\int f(x)dx$ as an integral of $f(x)$. In particular, since the integral $\int f(x)dx$ is expressed as a function of x (of form $F(x) + c$) with no definite numerical value, it is known as the *indefinite integral* of $f(x)$.

14-2 INDEFINITE INTEGRALS

In the following sub-section, we shall develop some basic rules of integration for obtaining the (indefinite) integral of various types of functions of a single independent variable.

Rules of Integration

To obtain certain basic rules of integration, we shall make use of the fact that integration is the reverse of differentiation. For example, if we let $F(x) = (x^{n+1})/(n+1)$, where $n \neq -1$, then

$$\frac{d}{dx}[F(x)] = \frac{d}{dx}\left[\frac{x^{n+1}}{n+1}\right] = x^n = f(x)$$

Thus, since differentiation of $F(x) = (x^{n+1})/(n+1)$ yields $f(x) = x^n$, then integration of $f(x) = x^n$ must yield $F(x) + c = [(x^{n+1})/(n+1)] + c$. This result gives us the following rule of integration:

I The Power Rule

$$\int x^n dx = \frac{1}{n+1} x^{n+1} + c \qquad (n \neq -1) \qquad (14\text{-}4)$$

The following examples illustrate the application of (14-4):

(i) Find $\int x^7 dx$. In this case, $n = 7$, so that (14-4) gives

$$\int x^7 dx = \tfrac{1}{8} x^8 + c$$

(ii) Find $\int x\,dx$. In this case, $n = 1$, so that (14-4) gives

$$\int x\,dx = \int x^1 dx = \tfrac{1}{2} x^2 + c$$

(iii) Find $\int dx$. Firstly, note that $\int dx = \int 1\,dx = \int x^0 dx$. Thus, since $n = 0$, (14-4) gives

$$\int dx = \int 1\,dx = \int x^0 dx = \frac{1}{0+1} x^{0+1} + c = x + c$$

(iv) Find $\int x^{5/2} dx$. In this case, $n = \tfrac{5}{2}$, so that (14-4) gives

$$\int x^{5/2} dx = \frac{x^{(5/2)+1}}{\tfrac{5}{2}+1} + c = \frac{x^{7/2}}{\tfrac{7}{2}} + c = \tfrac{2}{7} x^{7/2} + c$$

(v) Find $\int x^{-6} dx$. In this case, $n = -6$, so that (14-4) gives

$$\int x^{-6} dx = \frac{x^{-6+1}}{-6+1} + c = -\frac{x^{-5}}{5} + c = -\frac{1}{5x^5} + c$$

(vi) Find $\int x^{-2/3} dx$. In this case, $n = -\tfrac{2}{3}$, so that (14-4) gives

$$\int x^{-2/3} dx = \frac{x^{-(2/3)+1}}{-\tfrac{2}{3}+1} + c = \frac{x^{1/3}}{\tfrac{1}{3}} + c = 3x^{1/3} + c$$

Note, in each of the above examples of integration, that the validity of the result can be checked by differentiation. Thus, if we differentiate the integral obtained in each case, the derivative of the integral should be equal to the integrand. For example, differentiation of the integral $3x^{1/3}+c$, in Example (vi), yields the integrand $x^{-2/3}$ and therefore indicates that our integration is correct.

To obtain a further rule of integration, recall that

$$\frac{d}{dx}[\ln x] = \frac{1}{x} \qquad (x > 0)$$

Thus, since integration is the reverse of differentiation, we have

II The Logarithmic Rule

$$\int \frac{1}{x}dx = \ln x + c \qquad (x > 0) \qquad (14\text{-}5)$$

Note that the integrand in (14-5) is $1/x = x^{-1}$, which is a particular form of the power function x^n with $n = -1$. This indicates that the case of $n = -1$, which was excluded from the power rule, is now dealt with under the logarithmic rule. Also, note that (14-5) requires $x > 0$. This will be implicitly assumed whenever we use this rule. Finally, note that $\int(1/x)dx$ can be equivalently written as $\int dx/x$.

III The Integral of a Sum
The integral of the sum of two functions is the sum of the integrals of the functions:

$$\int [f(x)+g(x)]dx = \int f(x)dx + \int g(x)dx \qquad (14\text{-}6)$$

Since $\int f(x)dx = F(x)+c_1$, and $\int g(x)dx = G(x)+c_2$, where c_1 and c_2 are arbitrary constants of integration, then

$$\int f(x)dx + \int g(x)dx = F(x)+c_1+G(x)+c_2 \qquad (14\text{-}7)$$

If we let $c = c_1 + c_2$, then (14-7) becomes

$$\int f(x)dx + \int g(x)dx = F(x)+G(x)+c \qquad (14\text{-}8)$$

For example, to find $\int(x^7+x^2)dx$, we apply (14-6) to obtain

$$\int(x^7+x^2)dx = \int x^7 dx + \int x^2 dx = \left(\frac{x^8}{8}+c_1\right)+\left(\frac{x^3}{3}+c_2\right) = \frac{x^8}{8}+\frac{x^3}{3}+c$$

Similarly, to find $\int((1/x)+x^4)dx$, we apply (14-6) to obtain

$$\int\left(\frac{1}{x}+x^4\right)dx = \int \frac{1}{x}dx + \int x^4 dx = (\ln x + c_1)+\left(\frac{x^5}{5}+c_2\right) = \ln x + \frac{x^5}{5}+c$$

Note, in relation to this rule, that the constants of integration are generally combined into a single constant in the final answer.

This rule can be generalized for cases of more than two functions. For example,

$$\int \left(x^7 + x^2 + \frac{1}{x} + x^4\right) dx = \int x^7 dx + \int x^2 dx + \int \frac{1}{x} dx + \int x^4 dx$$

$$= \frac{x^8}{8} + \frac{x^3}{3} + \ln x + \frac{x^5}{5} + c$$

where the four constants of integration have been combined into the single constant c.

IV The Integral of a Multiple The integral of a constant (denoted by k) times a function is the constant times the integral of the function:

$$\int k f(x) dx = k \int f(x) dx \qquad (14\text{-}9)$$

For example, to find $\int 3x^3 dx$, we apply (14-9) to obtain

$$\int 3x^3 dx = 3 \int x^3 dx = 3\left(\frac{x^4}{4} + c_1\right) = \frac{3}{4}x^4 + c$$

where $c = 3c_1$. Similarly, to find $\int (9/x) dx$, we apply (14-9) to obtain

$$\int \frac{9}{x} dx = 9 \int \frac{1}{x} dx = 9(\ln x + c_1) = 9 \ln x + c$$

To illustrate the above four rules of integration, note that

$$\int \left(4x^3 + \frac{7}{x} - 5x^{-1/2} + 1\right) dx = 4 \int x^3 dx + 7 \int \frac{1}{x} dx - 5 \int x^{-1/2} dx + \int dx$$

$$= 4\left(\frac{x^4}{4} + c_1\right) + 7(\ln x + c_2)$$

$$- 5\left(\frac{x^{1/2}}{\frac{1}{2}} + c_3\right) + (x + c_4)$$

$$= x^4 + 7 \ln x - 10 x^{1/2} + x + c$$

[*Warning*: Note that whereas the multiplicative *constant* k can be factored out of the integral sign, a *variable* term *cannot* be factored out in this manner.]

It should be noted, in the discussion of the above four rules of integration, that the integrands are relatively straightforward expressions. This immediately raises the question: are there rules for the integration of more complex expressions such as the product or quotient of two functions? The answer, unfortunately, is that there exist no general rules or formulas for obtaining the integrals of such expressions. While it is quite straightforward to differentiate expressions involving the product or

260 INTEGRATION AND EXPONENTIAL FUNCTIONS

quotient of two functions, it is by no means easy to integrate such expressions. It is for this reason that integration is considerably more difficult than differentiation.

In practice, a complex expression is integrated by looking up the answer in prepared tables of integration formulas (known as *standard forms*). If a formula cannot be found to fit the expression, then various techniques are available to transform the expression into a standard form in order to obtain the integral.

A discussion of standard forms and special methods of integration is, however, beyond the scope of this book. In this section, we shall discuss only one further rule of integration (which will prove helpful in our discussion of exponential functions in Sec. 14-5).

To grasp the next rule of integration, let us first do some differentiation involving the chain rule. Thus, given a function $F(u)$ where $u = u(x)$, then by the chain rule

$$\frac{d}{dx}[F(u)] = \frac{d}{du}[F(u)]\frac{du}{dx} = F'(u)\frac{du}{dx} = f(u)\frac{du}{dx}$$

Since $f(u)(du/dx)$ is the derivative of $F(u)$ with respect to x, then the integral (or antiderivative) of $f(u)(du/dx)$, with respect to x, must be $F(u) + c$, that is,

$$\int \left(f(u)\frac{du}{dx} \right) dx = F(u) + c$$

or, since the two dx's cancel out,

$$\int f(u) du = F(u) + c$$

Therefore, we can state the following rule of integration:

V The Substitution Rule The integral of $f(u)(du/dx)$ with respect to the variable x is the integral of $f(u)$ with respect to the variable u:

$$\int \left(f(u)\frac{du}{dx} \right) dx = \int f(u) du = F(u) + c \tag{14-10}$$

For example, suppose we want to find $\int 9x^2(x^3+3)^{11} dx$. In this case, we can use the substitution rule by letting $u = u(x) = x^3 + 3$. This means that $du = u'(x)dx = 3x^2 dx$ or $dx = du/3x^2$. Hence, substitution of u for $x^3 + 3$ and $du/3x^2$ for dx gives

$$\int 9x^2(x^3+3)^{11} dx = \int 9x^2 u^{11} \frac{du}{3x^2}$$

$$= \int 3u^{11} du = 3\int u^{11} du = 3\left(\frac{u^{12}}{12} + c_1\right)$$

$$= \tfrac{1}{4}(x^3+3)^{12} + 3c_1 = \tfrac{1}{4}(x^3+3)^{12} + c$$

Similarly, to find $\int[(6x^2-2)/(x^3-x)]dx$, we let $u = u(x) = x^3 - x$ so that $du = u'(x)dx = (3x^2-1)dx$ or $dx = du/(3x^2-1)$. Hence

$$\int \frac{6x^2-2}{x^3-x}dx = \int \frac{6x^2-2}{u} \frac{du}{(3x^2-1)} = \int \frac{2}{u} du = 2\int \frac{1}{u} du = 2(\ln u + c_1)$$
$$= 2\ln(x^3-x) + 2c_1 = 2\ln(x^3-x) + c$$

It should be noted that the above examples have been deliberately chosen so that the substitution rule is applicable. This is necessary because there are many product and quotient expressions which cannot be integrated by the substitution rule. As already noted, the methods of integrating such expressions will not be discussed in this book.

14-A PRACTICE PROBLEMS

14-1 Find the following:

(a) $\int -2x^{3/2}dx$ (b) $\int \frac{3}{t}dt$ (c) $\int (7-3x^{-2}+4x^3)dx$

(d) $\int \left(7x^6 - \frac{2}{x}\right)dx$ (e) $\int (8x+2)(2x^2+x)^{13}dx$

(f) $\int \frac{dx}{x-5}$ (g) $\int \frac{4x}{2x^2+7}dx$ (h) $\int \frac{4x^3+2}{(4x^4+8x)^9}dx$

In each case, check your answer by differentiation.

14-3 DEFINITE INTEGRALS

In Sec. 14-2, we noted that the indefinite integral of a function $f(x)$, denoted by $\int f(x)dx$, is a function of x (of form $F(x)+c$) with no definite numerical value. Now, in this section, we shall consider integrals, known as *definite integrals*, which have definite numerical values. To do this, note first that the indefinite integral, of a given continuous function $f(x)$, is

$$\int f(x)dx = F(x) + c \qquad (14\text{-}11)$$

If we now take a particular value of x, such as $x = a$ in the domain of $f(x)$, then substitution of $x = a$ into the right-hand side of (14-11) gives $F(a)+c$ (which is not a definite numerical value in the sense that the value of c is unknown). Similarly, if we take $x = b$ ($b > a$) in the domain of $f(x)$, then substitution of $x = b$ into the right-hand side of (14-11) gives $F(b)+c$. Finally, if we form the difference

$$[F(b)+c] - [F(a)+c] = F(b) - F(a) \qquad (14\text{-}12)$$

we obtain a definite numerical value which is independent of the arbitrary constant of integration c. This definite numerical value is called the *definite* integral of $f(x)$ from a to b, and is denoted by

$$\int_a^b f(x)dx \tag{14-13}$$

where a and b are referred to, respectively, as the *lower limit of integration* and the *upper limit of integration*.

The procedure for evaluating the definite integral of $f(x)$ from a to b can now be outlined as: (i) integrate $f(x)$ to obtain $F(x)$; (ii) evaluate $F(x)$ at $x = b$ to obtain $F(b)$; (iii) evaluate $F(x)$ at $x = a$ to obtain $F(a)$; and, finally, (iv) find the difference $F(b) - F(a) = \int_a^b f(x)dx$. This procedure can be stated symbolically as

$$\int_a^b f(x)dx = [F(x)]_a^b = F(b) - F(a) \tag{14-14}$$

where the symbol $[\ ]_a^b$, which may also be written as $]_a^b$ or $|_a^b$, is an instruction to perform steps (ii), (iii), and (iv).

As an example, let us evaluate $\int_2^3 f(x)dx = \int_2^3 4x^3 dx$. Since the indefinite integral is $F(x) + c = x^4 + c$, then

$$\int_2^3 f(x)dx = [F(x)]_2^3 = F(3) - F(2)$$

or

$$\int_2^3 4x^3 dx = [x^4]_2^3 = (3)^4 - (2)^4 = 81 - 16 = 65$$

Similarly, the value of the definite integral $\int_1^7 (2x+5)dx$ is

$$\int_1^7 (2x+5)dx = [x^2 + 5x]_1^7 = [(7)^2 + 5(7)] - [(1)^2 + 5(1)] = 78$$

The above examples indicate that the evaluation of definite integrals is relatively straightforward. However, care must be taken when using the substitution rule. For example, suppose we wish to evaluate $\int_1^3 2x(x^2+1)dx$. In this case, we can let $u = u(x) = x^2 + 1$ so that $du = u'(x)dx = 2xdx$ or $dx = du/2x$. But at this point note that the limits of integration, 1 and 3, which refer to values of the variable x; must now be stated in terms of the variable u. Thus, instead of $x = 1$ and $x = 3$, we must write $u = 2$ and $u = 10$ (since $u = x^2 + 1$). Therefore we have

$$\int_{x=1}^{x=3} 2x(x^2+1)dx = \int_{u=2}^{u=10} udu = \left[\frac{u^2}{2}\right]_2^{10} = \left[\frac{(10)^2}{2}\right] - \left[\frac{(2)^2}{2}\right] = 48$$

where $[u^2/2]_{u=2}^{u=10} = [(x^2+1)^2/2]_{x=1}^{x=3} = 48$.

Note, in the first example above, that

$$\int_2^3 4x^3 dx = 4\int_2^3 x^3 dx = 4\left[\frac{x^4}{4}\right]_2^3 = 4\left[\frac{3^4}{4} - \frac{2^4}{4}\right] = 65$$

In other words, the definite integral has (analogous to the indefinite integral) the property that

$$\int_a^b kf(x)dx = k\int_a^b f(x)dx \quad [k = \text{a constant}] \quad (14\text{-}15)$$

Also note, in the second example above, that

$$\int_1^7 (2x+5)dx = \int_1^7 2xdx + \int_1^7 5dx = [x^2]_1^7 + [5x]_1^7 = 48 + 30 = 78$$

In other words, the definite integral has (analogous to the indefinite integral) the property that

$$\int_a^b [f(x) + g(x)]dx = \int_a^b f(x)dx + \int_a^b g(x)dx \quad (14\text{-}16)$$

Finally, note that a definite integral has a value of zero when the two limits of integration are identical:

$$\int_a^a f(x)dx = F(a) - F(a) = 0 \quad (14\text{-}17)$$

14-B PRACTICE PROBLEMS

14-2 Evaluate the following:

(a) $\int_1^3 (x^2 - 2)dx$ (b) $\int_{-1}^2 (5x^4 - x^2)dx$ (c) $\int_1^4 \frac{1}{x}dx$

(d) $\int_0^2 \left(\frac{12x^2 - 12}{x^3 - 3x + 2}\right)dx$ (e) $\int_1^8 x^{1/3}dx$ (f) $\int_1^5 \left(\frac{1}{x} + 3x^2\right)dx$

Definite Integrals as Areas

Although it will not be proved here, a definite integral can be interpreted geometrically as a specific area under a given curve. Thus, in Fig. 14-1a, the shaded area *abcd* (which is bounded by the graph of the continuous function $y = f(x)$, the two vertical lines $x = a(=x_1)$ and $x = b(=x_3)$, and the x axis) is measured by the definite integral $\int_a^b f(x)dx$. In other words, the area under the continuous curve $y = f(x)$, between the points $x = a$ and $x = b$, is measured by $\int_a^b f(x)dx$, that is,

$$\int_a^b f(x)dx = \text{area } abcd \text{ in Fig. 14-1a} \quad (14\text{-}18)$$

In addition to the interpretation of a definite integral as an *area*, a definite integral can also be interpreted as a particular *sum*. To see this, we shall demonstrate that the shaded area *abcd* (which is equal to $\int_a^b f(x)dx$), in Fig. 14-1a, can be measured by a particular sum.

264 INTEGRATION AND EXPONENTIAL FUNCTIONS

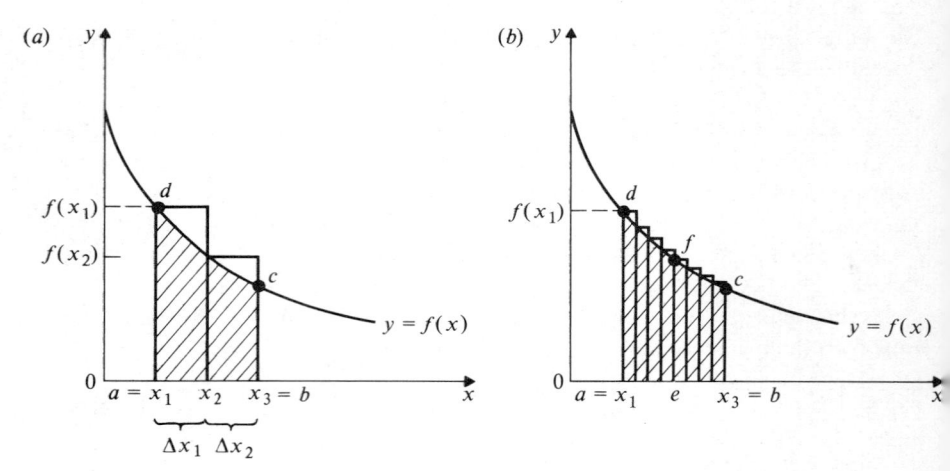

Figure 14-1

To measure the shaded area *abcd*, in Fig. 14-1a, as a particular sum, we proceed as follows: (i) divide the horizontal base (*ab*) of the required area into the two horizontal distances $x_2 - x_1 = \Delta x_1$ and $x_3 - x_2 = \Delta x_2$; (ii) treating Δx_1 as a horizontal base, erect the rectangle (shown in Fig. 14-1a) of height $f(x_1)$ and width Δx_1; (iii) similarly, treating Δx_2 as a horizontal base, erect the rectangle (shown in Fig. 14-1a) of height $f(x_2)$ and width Δx_2. The combined area of the two rectangles is therefore given by

$$f(x_1)\Delta x_1 + f(x_2)\Delta x_2 = \sum_{i=1}^{n} f(x_i)\Delta x_i \quad (n = 2) \quad (14\text{-}19)$$

which is clearly an *over*estimate of the true area *abcd*.

To improve upon our estimate of the true area note, in Fig. 14-1b, that if we erect narrower based (and therefore more numerous) rectangles, then the combined area of the narrower rectangles will represent less of an 'overestimate'. Thus, if we increase the number of rectangles to infinity, so that in (14-19) we have $n \to \infty$ and $\Delta x_i \to 0$, then the 'overestimate' will approach zero. In other words, the limiting value of the sum

$$\sum_{i=1}^{n} f(x_i)\Delta x_i$$

as n approaches infinity (and Δx_i approaches zero), will be a true measure of the area *abcd*, that is,

$$\lim_{n \to \infty} \sum_{i=1}^{n} f(x_i)\Delta x_i = \text{area } abcd \text{ in Fig. 14-1a} \quad (14\text{-}20)$$

Hence, combining (14-18) and (14-20), we have

$$\int_a^b f(x)dx = \lim_{n \to \infty} \sum_{i=1}^{n} f(x_i)\Delta x_i = \text{area } abcd \text{ in Fig. 14-1a} \quad (14\text{-}21)$$

Equation (14-21) indicates that a definite integral not only represents a particular area, but also represents a particular sum.

It should be noted, in Figs. 14-1a and 14-1b, that each rectangle has a *positive* width because we are moving from a to b ($b > a$). If, however, we are moving from b to a (and are therefore evaluating $\int_b^a f(x)dx$), each rectangle would have a *negative* width (for example, in Fig. 14-1a, $x_1 - x_2 = -\Delta x_1$). Consequently, in the latter situation, we would obtain a *negative area* (given by negative width times positive height of rectangles) which is equal in size to the negative of the area *abcd*. This means that the interchange of the limits of integration changes the sign of the definite integral, that is,

$$\int_b^a f(x)dx = -\int_a^b f(x)dx \qquad (14\text{-}22)$$

Also note, in Fig. 14-1b, that the shaded area *abcd* can be measured by the sum of the two areas *aefd* and *ebcf*. Since $aefd = \int_a^e f(x)dx$ and $ebcf = \int_e^b f(x)dx$, then we can state the following property of definite integrals:

$$\int_a^b f(x)dx = \int_a^e f(x)dx + \int_e^b f(x)dx \qquad (a < e < b) \qquad (14\text{-}23)$$

Finally, note that if we replace the upper limit of integration b by the variable x, then the integral becomes

$$\int_a^x f(x)dx = F(x) - F(a) \qquad (14\text{-}24)$$

Since the definite integral (14-24) is now a function of x (rather than a definite numerical value) it denotes a *variable* area under the curve of $f(x)$. However, since $-F(a)$ is a constant, we can let $c = -F(a)$ so that

$$\int_a^x f(x)dx = F(x) - F(a) = F(x) + c \qquad (14\text{-}25)$$

which is precisely the indefinite integral $\int f(x)dx$. Thus, in diagrammatic terms, the indefinite integral can be seen to represent a variable area under a curve. In contrast, the definite integral represents a particular area under a curve.

14-C PRACTICE PROBLEMS

14-3 Demonstrate that (14-22) and (14-23) are valid by checking that:

(a) $\displaystyle\int_1^3 3x^2 dx = -\int_3^1 3x^2 dx$

(b) $\displaystyle\int_0^3 (4x^3 - 21)dx = \int_0^1 (4x^3 - 21)dx + \int_1^2 (4x^3 - 21)dx + \int_2^3 (4x^3 - 21)dx$

It should be noted that while our discussion has been restricted to the integration of functions of one variable, it is also possible to integrate functions of more than one variable. The student who is interested in the integration of functions of several variables (known as *multiple integration*) should consult a more advanced text.

14-4 ECONOMIC APPLICATIONS OF INTEGRALS

One obvious application of the integral in economics is that of obtaining a total function from a given marginal function. For example, if the differentiation of a total cost function yields a marginal cost function, then the integration of the marginal cost function should enable us to get back to the total cost function. Similarly, the integration of a marginal revenue function should enable us to get back to the total revenue function. This application of the integral will be made clear by the following examples.

Marginal and Total Cost

If the marginal cost (MC) function of a firm is given by $C'(Q) = Q^2 - 4Q + 6$, and if the fixed cost is 2, then the total cost function $C(Q)$ may be found by integrating $C'(Q)$ with respect to Q. Thus,

$$C(Q) = \int C'(Q)dQ = \int (Q^2 - 4Q + 6)dQ = \tfrac{1}{3}Q^3 - 2Q^2 + 6Q + c \quad (14\text{-}26)$$

where c is the arbitrary constant of integration. Note, however, that (14-26) does not give us the exact form of $C(Q)$ since c is unknown. This raises the question: can the information that fixed cost is 2 be used as an initial condition to definitize c? Fortunately, the answer is yes. When $Q = 0$, total cost consists solely of fixed cost so that $C(0) = 2$. Since $C(0) = c$ in (14-26), then $c = 2$. Therefore, the exact form of the total cost function is

$$C(Q) = \tfrac{1}{3}Q^3 - 2Q^2 + 6Q + 2$$

Note that if we are now asked to find the increase in total cost, resulting from the firm increasing its output from 2 units to 4 units, we simply find the difference $C(4) - C(2) = \tfrac{46}{3} - \tfrac{26}{3} = \tfrac{20}{3}$. Alternatively, this increase in total cost could have been found by evaluating the definite integral of the marginal cost function from $Q = 2$ to $Q = 4$:

$$\int_2^4 (Q^2 - 4Q + 6)dQ = [\tfrac{1}{3}Q^3 - 2Q^2 + 6Q]_2^4 = \tfrac{40}{3} - \tfrac{20}{3} = \tfrac{20}{3}$$

Figure 14-2 provides a diagrammatic explanation of the above two ways of finding the increase in total cost. In particular, it should be noted that whereas the increase in $C(Q)$ in Fig. 14-2a appears as the vertical distance between points A and B (corresponding to the difference

(b)

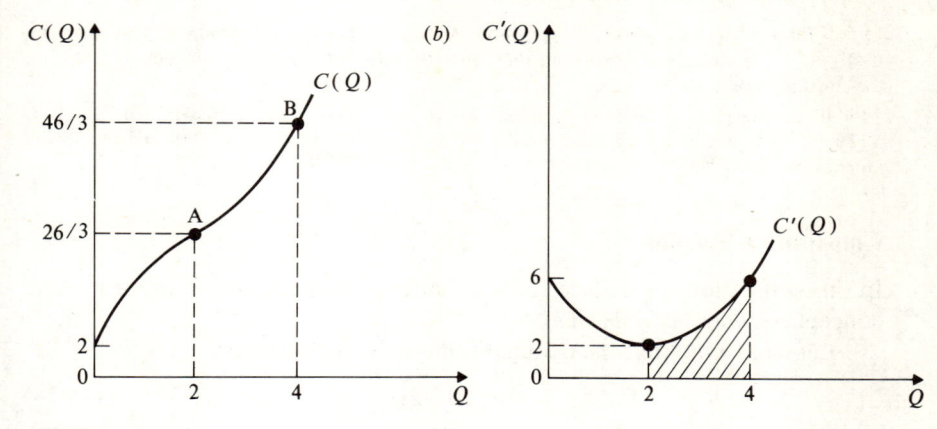

Figure 14-2

$C(4) - C(2)$), this increase is represented in Fig. 14-2b by the shaded area under the $C'(Q)$ curve (corresponding to $\int_2^4 C'(Q)dQ = \int_2^4 (Q^2 - 4Q + 6)dQ$).

Marginal and Total Revenue

If the marginal revenue (MR) function of a firm is $R'(Q) = 20 - 2Q$, and if total revenue R is zero when output is zero, then the total revenue function $R(Q)$ may be found by integrating $R'(Q)$ with respect to Q. Thus,

$$R(Q) = \int R'(Q)dQ = \int (20 - 2Q)dQ = 20Q - Q^2 + c \qquad (14\text{-}27)$$

Since we are told that $R(0) = 0$, and $R(0) = c$ in (14-27), then the constant c has zero value. Hence the exact form of the total revenue function is

$$R(Q) = 20Q - Q^2$$

As a further example, suppose we are asked to find the decrease in a firm's total revenue as output sold is reduced from 10 units to 5 units, given that its marginal revenue function is $R'(Q) = 100 - 4Q$. In this case, we evaluate the definite integral of $R'(Q)$ from $Q = 10$ to $Q = 5$:

$$\int_{10}^{5} (100 - 4Q)dQ = [100Q - 2Q^2]_{10}^{5} = 450 - 800 = -350$$

Thus, the decrease in total revenue is 350.

14-D PRACTICE PROBLEMS

14-4 Given $C'(Q) = 3Q^2 - 18Q + 30$, what is the decrease in total cost $C(Q)$ as output produced is reduced from 12 units to 3 units?

14-5 If the marginal propensity to consume (MPC) is a function of income (Y), as given by $C'(Y) = \frac{3}{2}Y^{-1/2}$, and if aggregate consumption expenditure (C) is 70 when income is zero, find the consumption function $C(Y)$.

14-6 If the marginal propensity to save (MPS) is a function of income (Y), as given by $S'(Y) = 1 - \frac{3}{2}Y^{-1/2}$, and if aggregate savings (S) is zero when income is 100, find the saving function $S(Y)$.

Consumer's Surplus

In this subsection we shall see how definite integration can be applied to the concept of *consumer's surplus*.

Let us assume that the demand function of a consumer is

$$P = 20 - 2Q_d \tag{14-28}$$

which is graphed in Fig. 14-3a. Given this demand function, the consumer will purchase 5 units, when the market price per unit is 10, for a total expenditure of $(10)(5) = 50$. Note, in this situation, that whereas the consumer has paid a uniform price per unit of 10 for each of the 5 units he has purchased, he would have been willing to pay more than $P = 10$ for each of the units preceding the 5th unit (as evidenced by his demand function). In fact, since the consumer would be willing to pay the amount of expenditure represented by the area under the demand curve up to $Q_d = 5$ (which, in Fig. 14-3a, is the sum of the dotted and shaded areas), in order to purchase 5 units, then the difference between this amount and the amount he actually pays may be regarded as a *consumer's surplus* (which, in Fig. 14-3a, is measured by the dotted area).

To obtain a monetary measure of the consumer surplus in the above example, we simply evaluate the definite integral of the demand function

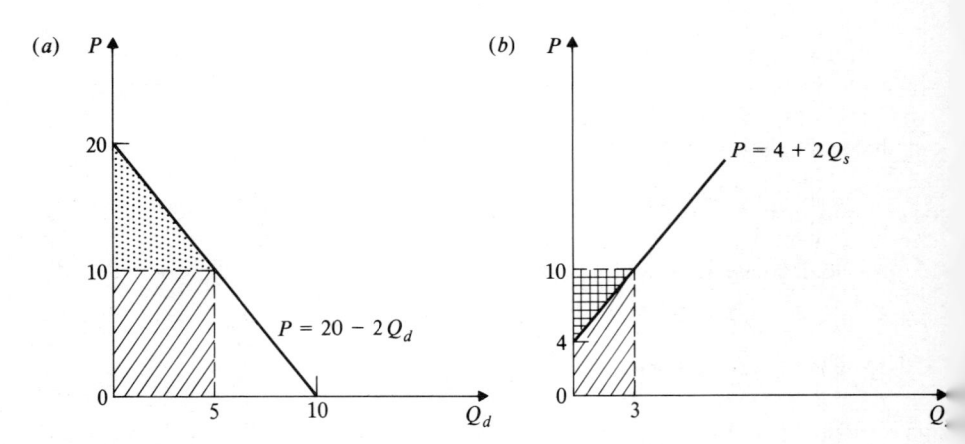

Figure 14-3

(14-28) from $Q_d = 0$ to $Q_d = 5$ and subtract the actual expenditure of 50, that is,

$$\text{Consumer's surplus} = \int_0^5 (20 - 2Q_d) dQ_d - 50$$
$$= [20Q_d - Q_d^2]_0^5 - 50 = 25$$

As a further example, suppose a consumer's demand function is $P = 32 - 2Q_d^2$, and the market price per unit is 14. In this case, $Q_d = 3$ (since $14 = 32 - 2Q_d^2 \Rightarrow Q_d = \pm 3$) and the consumer's actual expenditure is $(14)(3) = 42$. Hence,

$$\text{Consumer's surplus} = \int_0^3 (32 - 2Q_d^2) dQ_d - 42$$
$$= [32Q_d - \tfrac{2}{3}Q_d^3]_0^3 - 42 = 36$$

Producer's Surplus

The definite integral can be applied in an analogous manner to the concept of *producer's surplus*.

Let us assume that the supply function of a producer is

$$P = 4 + 2Q_s \tag{14-29}$$

which is graphed in Fig. 14-3b. Given this supply function, the producer will supply 3 units, when the market price per unit is 10, and receive total revenue of $(10)(3) = 30$. In this case, the producer receives the uniform price per unit of 10 for each of the 3 units he has supplied, even though he would have been willing to supply each of the units preceding the 3rd unit for less than $P = 10$ (as evidenced by his supply function). In fact, since the producer would be willing to supply 3 units for the revenue represented by the area under the supply curve up to $Q_s = 3$ (which, in Fig. 14-3b, is measured by the shaded area), then the additional revenue he receives (measured, in Fig. 14-3b, by the crossed area) may be regarded as a *producer's surplus*.

To obtain a monetary measure of the producer surplus in the above example, we simply evaluate the definite integral of the supply function (14-29) from $Q_s = 0$ to $Q_s = 3$ and subtract this value from the actual revenue of 30, that is,

$$\text{Producer's surplus} = 30 - \int_0^3 (4 + 2Q_s) dQ_s$$
$$= 30 - [4Q_s + Q_s^2]_0^3 = 9$$

As a further example, suppose a producer's supply function is $P = 2Q_s + 3Q_s^2$, and the market price per unit is 16. In this case, $Q_s = 2$ (since $16 = 2Q_s + 3Q_s^2 \Rightarrow Q_s = 2$ or $-8/3$ via the quadratic formula) and the producer's actual revenue is $(16)(2) = 32$. Hence,

$$\text{Producer's surplus} = 32 - \int_0^2 (2Q_s + 3Q_s^2) dQ_s$$
$$= 32 - [Q_s^2 + Q_s^3]_0^2 = 20$$

14-E PRACTICE PROBLEMS

14-7 If a consumer's demand function is $P = (16 - Q_d)^{1/2}$, and if the market price per unit is 2, what is the consumer's surplus?

14-8 If a producer's supply function is $P = (Q_s + 1)^2$, and if the market price per unit is 9, what is the producer's surplus?

14-5 EXPONENTIAL FUNCTIONS

In earlier chapters we encountered power functions, such as $y = x^2$, that are composed of a variable base (such as the variable x) and a constant exponent (such as the number 2). Now, in this section, we shall briefly consider *exponential functions*, such as $y = 2^x$, that are composed of a constant base and a variable exponent.

Since an *exponential function* is a function whose independent variable appears in the role of an exponent, then an exponential function may be represented in general by

$$y = f(x) = a^x \qquad (a > 0, a \neq 1; \therefore y > 0) \qquad (14\text{-}30)$$

where y and x are, respectively, the dependent and independent variables, and a is the constant base of the exponent.

Note, in (14-30), that the base a is restricted in value to being a positive number not equal to 1. The reasons for this restriction are: (i) by not permitting $a < 0$, we avoid the problem of finding the square root of a negative number when $x = \frac{1}{2}$, and (ii) by not permitting $a = 1$, we exclude the case $y = 1^x = 1$, which is a constant function rather than an exponential function.

While, in (14-30), the base a may be any positive real number other than 1, there is one base which is more convenient than others for mathematical analysis. This preferred base (which we have already encountered in our discussion of natural logarithms in Chapter 2) is the irrational number $e \simeq 2.71828$, where

$$e \equiv \lim_{m \to \infty} \left(1 + \frac{1}{m}\right)^m \simeq 2.71828 \qquad (14\text{-}31)$$

When the base e is used in an exponential function, it is referred to as a

14-5 EXPONENTIAL FUNCTIONS

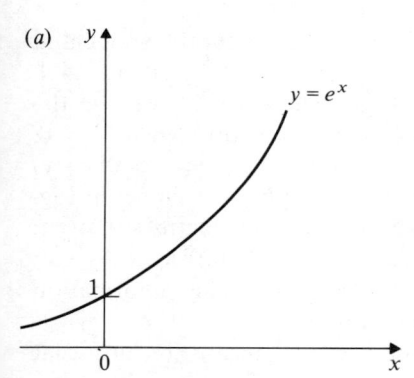

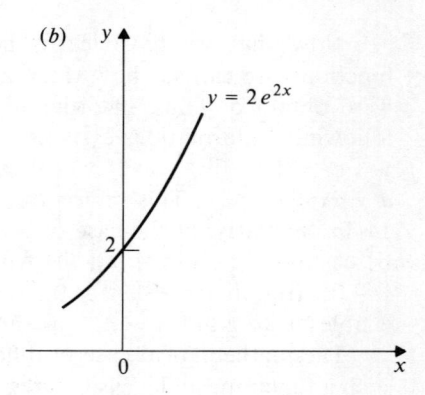

(a) graph of $y = e^x$

(b) graph of $y = 2e^{2x}$

Figure 14-4

natural exponential function. Thus, instead of (14-30), we may write

$$y = f(x) = e^x \qquad (14\text{-}32)$$

which is graphed in Fig. 14-4a.

A more general form of the natural exponential function is

$$y = Ae^{rx} \qquad (14\text{-}33)$$

where A and r are constants. A numerical example of (14-33) is graphed in Fig. 14-4b. Note, as a matter of notation, that (14-32) and (14-33) can also be written, respectively, as

$$y = \exp(x) \quad \text{and} \quad y = A \exp(rx)$$

where exp is an abbreviation for exponential and simply indicates that e is to have the parenthetical expression as its exponent.

We can now demonstrate why the seemingly unusual base of $e \simeq 2.71828$ is so convenient in mathematical analysis. To do this, note that the function $y = e^x$ possesses the property of being its own derivative! Thus we have the *exponential-function rule* of differentiation:

$$\frac{d}{dx}[e^x] = e^x \qquad (14\text{-}34)$$

which greatly eases the work of differentiation. For example, if $y = Ae^x$, where A is a constant, then application of the product rule of differentiation (to the product of A and e^x) gives $dy/dx = Ae^x$. In the more complicated case of $y = Ae^{rx}$, we simply let $u = u(x) = rx$, so that $y = Ae^u$, and apply the chain rule to obtain

$$\frac{dy}{dx} = \frac{dy}{du}\frac{du}{dx} = Ae^u(r) = rAe^{rx}$$

Now that we have learnt how to differentiate natural exponential functions, we can see how the graphs of $y = e^x$ and $y = 2e^{2x}$, in Fig. 14-4, were obtained. Thus, in order to sketch the graph of $y = e^x$, we use the following information: (i) as $x \to +\infty$, $y \to +\infty$; (ii) when $x = 0$, $y = e^0 = 1$; (iii) as $x \to -\infty$, $y \to 0$; (iv) $dy/dx = e^x > 0$; (v) $d^2y/dx^2 = e^x > 0$. This information enables us to graph e^x as shown in Fig. 14-4a. Similarly, in the case of $y = 2e^{2x}$, we use the following information: (i) as $x \to +\infty$, $y \to +\infty$; (ii) when $x = 0$, $y = 2e^0 = 2$; (iii) as $x \to -\infty$, $y \to 0$; (iv) $dy/dx = 4e^{2x} > 0$; (v) $d^2y/dx^2 = 8e^{2x} > 0$. This information enables us to graph $y = 2e^{2x}$ as shown in Fig. 14-4b.

The mathematical ease of differentiating $f(x) = e^x$ means, in turn, that such a function can be easily integrated. Thus,

$$\frac{d}{dx}[e^x] = e^x \Rightarrow \int e^x dx = e^x + c \qquad (14\text{-}35)$$

which is known as the *exponential rule* of integration. In the more complicated case of an exponential function such as $f(x) = 8e^{2x}$, the substitution rule of integration can be used. Thus, if we let $u = u(x) = 2x$, so that $du = u'(x)dx = 2dx$ or $dx = du/2$, then

$$\int 8e^{2x} dx = \int 8e^u \frac{du}{2} = 4 \int e^u du = 4(e^u + c_1) = 4e^u + c = 4e^{2x} + c$$

14-F PRACTICE PROBLEMS

14-9 Sketch the graph of the following exponential functions for $x \geq 0$:
 (a) $y = 20 - 15e^{-2x}$ (b) $y = 6e^{3x} - 4$ (c) $y = 24e^{-2x}$

14-10 Find dy/dx for each of the following exponential functions:
 (a) $y = e^{3x^2 + 2x - 6}$ (b) $y = xe^x$ (c) $y = e^{1-x}$ (d) $y = e^x/(x^2 - 2x)$
 (e) $y = \frac{3}{2}e^{x^{2/3} + 5}$ (f) $y = 4x^2 e^{3x^2 - 2}$

14-11 Find the following:
 (a) $\int 7e^x dx$ (b) $\int (3x^2 - e^x) dx$ (c) $\int 6e^{5-3x} dx$
 (d) $\int (8x^3 + 12x^2) e^{x^4 + 2x^3} dx$

14-12 Evaluate the following:
 (a) $\int_1^3 e^{-x} dx$ (b) $\int_0^7 (e^x + e^{5x}) dx$ (c) $\int_2^1 4x^3 e^{x^4} dx$

14-6 ECONOMIC APPLICATIONS OF THE EXPONENTIAL FUNCTION

In this section we shall briefly consider some economic applications of the exponential function and, in addition, provide an economic interpretation of the number e.

Compound Interest

If the rate of interest is 6 per cent per year, and if an individual lends £100 at this interest rate, then at the end of one year he will get back the initial £100 plus this initial sum multiplied by the rate of interest, that is, he will receive an amount

$$£100 + £100 \times 6\% = £100(1 + \tfrac{6}{100}) = £106$$

In general, if the interest rate is i per cent per year, and if the initial sum lent is V_0, then the amount (denoted by V_1) that the lender will receive at the end of one year is

$$V_1 = V_0(1+i)$$

For example, when $V_0 = £100$ and $i = 7$ per cent, the value of V_1 is $£100(1 + \tfrac{7}{100}) = £107$.

Let us suppose that V_1 is now lent for a further year, at the same rate of interest, so that the lender will receive the amount

$$V_2 = V_1(1+i)$$

at the end of this further year. Or, since $V_1 = V_0(1+i)$,

$$V_2 = V_0(1+i)(1+i) = V_0(1+i)^2$$

If the sum V_2 is now lent for yet a further year, at the same rate of interest, the lender will receive the amount

$$V_3 = V_2(1+i) = V_0(1+i)^2(1+i) = V_0(1+i)^3$$

at the end of this further year. In other words, the initial sum of V_0 has grown in value firstly to $V_0(1+i)$ after one year, then to $V_0(1+i)^2$ after two years, and finally to $V_0(1+i)^3$ after three years. Consequently, if V_0 is lent for t years, at the interest rate of i per cent per year, it will grow in value to the amount

$$V_t = V_0(1+i)^t \tag{14-36}$$

Note, in the above analysis, that interest is assumed to be compounded *once a year*. Now we must examine what happens if interest is compounded more frequently. For example, if interest is compounded *twice a year*, and if the interest rate is 6 per cent per year, then an individual who lends £100 will receive £103 at the end of six months. In other words, he receives $6/2 = 3$ per cent interest at the end of six months. The amount £103 is then lent for the second six months at $6/2 = 3$ per cent interest, so that at the end of one year the lender receives $£103(1 + \tfrac{3}{100}) = £106.09$ (which, as we would expect, is greater than the amount received when interest is compounded once a year). Therefore, if the interest rate is i per cent per year, and if interest is compounded twice a year, then a sum V_0 will have grown in value after six months to the amount

$$V_{1/2} = V_0\left(1 + \frac{i}{2}\right)$$

If $V_{1/2}$ is lent for the second six months, at an interest rate of i per cent per year, it will grow in value to

$$V_1 = V_{1/2}\left(1 + \frac{i}{2}\right) = V_0\left(1 + \frac{i}{2}\right)\left(1 + \frac{i}{2}\right) = V_0\left(1 + \frac{i}{2}\right)^2$$

If we now assume that interest is compounded *three times a year*, then (by analogous reasoning) V_0 would grow in value to $V_1 = V_0(1 + (i/3))^3$ at the end of one year. Similarly, if interest is compounded *four times a year*, V_0 will grow in value to $V_1 = V_0(1 + (i/4))^4$ at the end of one year. Thus, in general, if interest is compounded n times a year, V_0 will grow in value to

$$V_1 = V_0\left(1 + \frac{i}{n}\right)^n$$

at the end of one year.

Since V_0 grows to V_1 in one year, then if V_1 is lent for a further year, with interest being compounded n times a year, it will grow in value to

$$V_2 = V_1\left(1 + \frac{i}{n}\right)^n = V_0\left(1 + \frac{i}{n}\right)^n\left(1 + \frac{i}{n}\right)^n = V_0\left(1 + \frac{i}{n}\right)^{2n}$$

Similarly, if V_2 is lent for yet a further year, with interest being compounded n times a year, it will grow in value to

$$V_3 = V_2\left(1 + \frac{i}{n}\right)^n = V_0\left(1 + \frac{i}{n}\right)^{3n}$$

Consequently, with interest being compounded n times a year, V_0 will grow in value to

$$V_t = V_0\left(1 + \frac{i}{n}\right)^{tn} \tag{14-37}$$

after t years.

It should be noted that the formula (14-37) can be used to find the value of V_0 after some fraction of a year. For example, if interest is being compounded 12 times a year, we can let t take on, respectively, the (discontinuous or discrete) values of $\frac{1}{12}$, $\frac{2}{12}$, and $\frac{7}{12}$, in order to find the value to which V_0 has grown after 1, 2, and 7 months.

The formula (14-37) can now be transformed as follows:

$$V_t = V_0\left[\left(1 + \frac{i}{n}\right)^{n/i}\right]^{it}$$
$$= V_0\left[\left(1 + \frac{1}{m}\right)^m\right]^{it} \quad \text{where } m \equiv n/i \tag{14-38}$$

Note, in (14-38), that as the frequency of compounding n is increased, the variable $m \equiv n/i$ will also increase. Hence, as $n \to \infty$, $m \to \infty$ also, and (14-38) tends to

$$V_t = V_0 e^{it} \quad \text{[via (14-31)]} \tag{14-39}$$

Consequently, in this limiting case where interest is compounded *continuously* during the year (so that n tends to infinity), V_0 will grow in value to $V_0 e^{it}$ at the end of t years.

Note, in (14-39), that since interest is being compounded *continuously* during the year, then t can take on (continuous) values such as 0.731 or 0.892 in order to find the value to which V_0 has grown after 0.731 or 0.892 of a year. Also, note in (14-39) that if $V_0 = £1$, $i = 100$ per cent, and $t = 1$ year, we obtain $V_1 = £e \simeq £2.71828$. This means that the number e can be interpreted economically as the value to which £1 will grow in one year if interest at the rate of 100 per cent per year is compounded *continuously*.

14-G PRACTICE PROBLEMS

14-13 (*a*) If interest is compounded once a year, at a rate of 9 per cent per year, what is the value to which £90 will grow after 11 years?

(*b*) If interest is compounded 365 times a year, at a rate of 5 per cent per year, what is the value to which £100 will grow after 2 years?

14-14 Obtain an exponential expression for the following values:

(*a*) £100, compounded continuously at an interest rate of 6 per cent per year for 8 years

(*b*) £350, compounded continuously at an interest rate of 10 per cent per year for 3 years.

Discounting

In the foregoing discussion of compound interest, we were concerned with calculating a *future value* V_t (composed of the initial sum plus interest) from a given initial value or *present value* V_0 (the initial sum). If we now reverse the compound-interest problem, we are then faced with the *discounting* problem of calculating the present value V_0 of a given sum V_t which will be received t years from now.

To illustrate the concept of discounting, let us return to the discontinuous or discrete case which was summarized by the formula (14-36). Thus, as shown in (14-36), when interest is compounded once a year at a rate of i per cent per year, V_0 will grow into the future value of $V_t = V_0(1+i)^t$ after t years. Consequently, if we solve this equation for V_0, we obtain the (discrete) discounting formula:

$$V_0 = \frac{V_t}{(1+i)^t} = V_t(1+i)^{-t} \tag{14-40}$$

which states that an unknown present value V_0 can be calculated from a given future value V_t, plus given values of i (now called the rate of discount) and t.

In the continuous case, which was summarized by the formula (14-39), we noted that V_0 will grow into the future value $V_t = V_0 e^{it}$ after t years of continuous compounding at an interest rate of i per cent per year. Consequently, if we solve this equation for V_0 we obtain the (continuous) discounting formula:

$$V_0 = \frac{V_t}{e^{it}} = V_t e^{-it} \qquad (14\text{-}41)$$

which states that an unknown present value V_0 can be calculated from a given future value V_t, plus given values for the rate of discount i and the number of years t.

14-H PRACTICE PROBLEMS

14-15 If the sum £540.8 is to be received in 2 years' time, what is the present value of this sum if it is discounted annually at a rate of 4 per cent per year?

14-16 If the sum £271 828 is to be received in 10 years' time, what is the present value of this sum if it is discounted continuously at a rate of 10 per cent per year?

Constant Proportional Rates of Growth

In our discussion of compound interest, we learnt that the natural exponential function can be used to describe the growth of a sum of money over time. Now, in this subsection, we shall see that the natural exponential function can also be used to describe the growth of many other variables (such as population, labour force, output, investment, and national income) in economics. For example, the (exponential) growth of the labour force of a country may be written as

$$L_t = L_0 e^{rt} \qquad (14\text{-}42)$$

where L_t is the labour force at time t, L_0 is the given present (or base period) labour force, t is time, and the constant r is known as the *constant proportional rate of growth*.

To explain the interpretation of r, in (14-42), as the constant proportional rate of growth, let us note that the rate of change of L_t with respect to time t is given by the derivative

$$dL_t/dt = rL_0 e^{rt} = rL_t \quad [\text{where } L_0 \text{ is a given constant}]$$

Since the *proportional rate of growth* (known also as the percentage or relative rate of growth) of L_t is defined as

14-6 ECONOMIC APPLICATIONS OF THE EXPONENTIAL FUNCTION

$$\frac{dL_t/dt}{L_t} = \frac{1}{L_t}\frac{dL_t}{dt}$$

then, for any given point of time, the proportional rate of growth of L_t is

$$\frac{1}{L_t}\frac{dL_t}{dt} = \frac{rL_t}{L_t} = r \tag{14-43}$$

Thus, (14-43) indicates that L_t grows at the constant proportional growth rate r.

It is important to note that the proportional rate of growth $(dL_t/dt)/L_t$ is a rate of growth at a specific *instant* of time t. This follows from the fact that since dL_t/dt and L_t are functions of time t, then their ratio must have reference to a specific point of time. Thus whereas, in the particular case of the function (14-42), the proportional rate of growth is constant (and equal to r) at each instant of time, in other cases the proportional rate of growth may assume different values at each point of time.

An alternative method of demonstrating that r, in (14-42), is the constant proportional rate of growth is to take the (natural) logarithm of (14-42), which is given by

$$\ln L_t = \ln L_0 + rt \ln e = \ln L_0 + rt$$

and differentiate with respect to time t, to obtain (via the chain rule)

$$\frac{d \ln L_t}{dt} = \frac{d \ln L_t}{dL_t}\frac{dL_t}{dt} = \frac{1}{L_t}\frac{dL_t}{dt} = r \tag{14-44}$$

Since the derivative $(d \ln L_t/dt)$ is clearly a function of time t, then it should also be clear that the proportional rate of growth $(dL_t/dt)/L_t$ refers to a specific point of time.

As a further example, the continuous depreciation (or *negative* growth) in value of a stock of machinery may be written as

$$K_t = K_0 e^{-rt} \tag{14-45}$$

where K_t is the value of the stock of machinery at time t, K_0 is the given initial value of the stock of machinery, t is time, and $-r$ is the constant proportional rate of depreciation (since $d \ln K_t/dt \equiv (dK_t/dt)/K_t = -r$).

14-I PRACTICE PROBLEMS

14-17 If the labour force of a country is 20 million in 1975, and if the labour force is expected to grow exponentially at 2 per cent per year over the next 50 years, find the projected labour force in year 2025.

14-18 If a stock of machinery is assumed to depreciate continuously in value at a rate of minus 7 per cent per year, find (approximately) how many years it will take for the stock of machinery to be halved in value (assuming $\ln 2 = 0.6931$).

14-7 ADDITIONAL PROBLEMS

14-19 If the marginal cost function of a firm is given by $C'(Q) = 3Q^2 - 18Q + 33$, and if total cost C is 55 when output is 3, find the total cost function $C(Q)$.

14-20 If the marginal revenue function of a firm is given by $R'(Q) = 65(3+Q)^{-2}$, what is the increase in total revenue when output sold rises from 2 units to 10 units?

14-21 If a country's marginal propensity to import is a function of income (Y), as given by $M'(Y) = 0.13$, and if imports M are 26 when income is zero, find the import function $M(Y)$.

14-22 If the marginal propensity to consume is a function of income (Y), as given by $C'(Y) = 4800(2+Y)^{-3}$, and if aggregate consumption expenditure C is 400 when income is zero, find the consumption function $C(Y)$.

14-23 By definition the rate of net investment (I) is identical to the rate of capital formation $K'(t) \equiv dK/dt$, where K is capital stock and t is time. Given this definition, and assuming that the rate of net investment is given by the function $I(t) = 10t^{1/5}$, find the amount of capital formation during the time period between $t = 0$ and $t = 32$.

14-24 The market demand and supply functions for a particular good are, respectively, $P = 75(1+Q)^{-2}$ and $P = 2+Q^2/16$. If the market price per unit is 3, calculate the corresponding consumers' surplus and producers' surplus. Also, provide a graphical illustration of your result.

14-25 If the labour force of a country is growing continuously at a rate of 4 per cent per year, find (approximately) how many years it will take for the labour force to double (assuming $\ln 2 = 0.6931$).

14-26 If a stock of machinery, which has been depreciating continuously in value at a rate of minus 10 per cent per year for 10 years, is valued at £100 000, what was the initial value of the stock of machinery?

14-27 If the sum £148 510 is to be received in 10 years' time, what is the present value of this sum if it is discounted continuously at a rate of 5 per cent per year (assuming $e^5 = 148.51$)?

14-28 Demonstrate how the discrete compound-interest formula $V_t = V_0(1+i)^t$ may be transformed into the exponential form $V_t = V_0 e^{wt}$.

14-29 If the marginal cost function of a firm is given by $C'(Q) = 7.5e^{0.15Q}$, and if fixed cost is 80, find the total cost function $C(Q)$.

14-30 If the marginal propensity to consume is a function of income, as given by $C'(Y) = 125e^{-0.5Y}$, and if aggregate consumption expenditure is 50 when income is zero, find the consumption function $C(Y)$.

REFERENCES FOR FURTHER READING

The student who has successfully mastered *An Introduction to Mathematical Methods in Economics* is now in a position to proceed to both a more rigorous and a more extensive analysis of mathematical methods in economics. As a first step, the student is strongly encouraged to proceed to

Chiang, A. C., *Fundamental Methods of Mathematical Economics*, 2nd edition, McGraw-Hill, 1974.

Other books which the student should find helpful are:

Henderson, J. M. and R. E. Quandt, *Microeconomic Theory: A Mathematical Approach*, 3rd edition, McGraw-Hill, 1980.
Burrows, P. and T. Hitiris, *Macroeconomic Theory: A Mathematical Introduction*, Wiley, 1974.
Silberberg, E. *The Structure of Economics: A Mathematical Analysis*, McGraw-Hill, 1978.

ANSWERS TO PRACTICE PROBLEMS
(excluding graphical problems)

2-A **2-1** (b) and (c) are sets; (a) and (d) are not because no specific criteria for 'best' or 'rarest' are given
  2-2 (a) $\{x|x \geq 0\}$ (b) $\{x|-19 \leq x \leq 29\}$
  2-3 (a) false   (b) true   (c) false   (d) true   (e) true   (f) false   (g) true   (h) true
(i) true   (j) true
  2-4 $\emptyset, \{6\}, \{5\}, \{3\}, \{6,5\}, \{6,3\}, \{5,3\}, \{6,5,3\}$
2-B **2-5** (a) $A \times B = \{(a,c), (a,d), (b,c), (b,d)\}$
  (b) $B \times A = \{(c,a), (c,b), (d,a), (d,b)\}$
  2-6 Because $A \neq B$
  2-7 (a) is not a function because each x value is not associated with a unique y value
  2-8 (a) $\{y|-4 \leq y \leq 11\}$ (b) $\{y|-42 \leq y \leq 3\}$
  2-9 (a) $f(-2) = 5 - 2(-2) = 9; f(0) = 5 - 2(0) = 5; f(a) = 5 - 2(a) = 5 - 2a$
  (b) $f(-2) = \frac{14}{5}; f(0) = -10; f(a) = (2a-10)/(3a+1)$
  (c) $f(-2) = -2; f(0) = 0; f(a) = a(a+3)$
  2-10 (a) $y = -4; x = \frac{4}{3}$ (b) $y = 3; x = \frac{1}{3}$
2-C **2-13** (i) (a) $Q_d = 100$ (b) $Q_d = 285$
  (ii) (a) $\{P|P \geq 8\frac{1}{3}\}$ (b) $\{P|P \geq 95\}$
Thus, in Prob. 2-12, the restricted domains are (a) $\{P|0 \leq P \leq 8\frac{1}{3}\}$ (b) $\{P|0 \leq P \leq 95\}$
2-D **2-14** (a) $1/\sqrt[9]{x^7}$ (b) $\sqrt[3]{(2x+5y)^2}$ (c) $\sqrt[3]{x} - \sqrt[4]{y}$ (d) $\sqrt[5]{(xy)^3}$ (e) $1/\sqrt[4]{(y^2+x^{-2})}$
  2-15 (a) $2xy^{-1/3}$ (b) $(x-16)^{-1/4}$ (c) $-10x^{2/5}y$ (d) $(2x/y)^{1/3}$ (e) $9^{1/9}x^{1/9}y^{1/3}$
  2-16 (a) $x^{9/2}$ (b) $(3xy)^4$ (c) $x^3 + x$ (d) 1   (e) $3m^4n$
2-E **2-17** (a) true   (b) true   (c) false   (d) false
  2-18 (a) true   (b) true   (c) true   (d) true   (e) false   (f) true
  2-19 (a) By Rule 1: $5x + 6 - x - 6 > x - 2 - x - 6 \Rightarrow 4x > -8$. By Rule 2: $\frac{1}{4}(4x) > \frac{1}{4}(-8) \Rightarrow x > -2$.
  (b) By Rule 1: $9x^3 - 4x - 3x^3 + 4x > 3x^3 + 2x - 3x^3 + 4x \Rightarrow 6x^3 > 6x$. By Rule 2: $(1/6x)(6x^3) > (1/6x)(6x) \Rightarrow x^2 > 1$.

ANSWERS TO PRACTICE PROBLEMS **281**

2-20 (a) true (b) true
2-F 2-21 (a) -3 (b) 0 (c) -5 (d) 5 (e) 7 (f) 0 (g) -5 (h) 1 (i) 1 (j) 2 (k) $\frac{1}{3}$ (l) 6
2-22 (a) $2 = 32^{1/5}$ (b) $256 = 4^4$ (c) $81 = (\frac{1}{3})^{-4}$ (d) $t = t^1$ (e) $x^0 = e^0 = 1$
2-23 (a) $\log_{10}(0.0001)^{-17} = -17\log_{10}10^{-4} = -17(-4) = 68$
   (b) $1/(\log_{125}5) = \log_5 125 = 3$
   (c) $(\log_2 e)(\log_e 128) = \log_2 128 = 7$
   (d) $\ln 19e^{1/3} = \ln 19 + \ln e^{1/3} = \ln 19 + \frac{1}{3}\ln e = \ln 19 + \frac{1}{3}$
   (e) $\log_{10}(A/B) = \log_{10} A - \log_{10} B$
   (f) $\ln xyze^{-9} = \ln x + \ln y + \ln z - 9\ln e = \ln x + \ln y + \ln z - 9$
   (g) $\ln(e/w)^3 = 3\ln(e/w) = 3[\ln e - \ln w] = 3 - 3\ln w$
   (h) $2\log_{10} 100t = 2[\log_{10} 100 + \log_{10} t] = 4 + 2\log_{10} t$
2-24 (a) $\log_{10} 16 = \log_{10} 4^2 = 2\log_{10} 4 = 2(0.6021) = 1.2042$
   (b) $\log_{10}(\frac{1}{64}) = \log_{10} 4^{-3} = -3\log_{10} 4 = -3(0.6021) = -1.8063$
2-25 (a) true
   (b) false: $\log_{10}(6+3) = \log_{10} 9$; $\log_{10} 6 + \log_{10} 3 = \log_{10}(6 \times 3) = \log_{10} 18$
   (c) false: $\ln\frac{1}{2} + \ln\frac{1}{2} = \ln(\frac{1}{2} \times \frac{1}{2}) = \ln\frac{1}{4}$
   (d) true
3-B 3-5 (a) $(\bar{P}, \bar{Q}) = (7\frac{1}{2}, 4\frac{1}{2})$ (b) $(\bar{P}, \bar{Q}) = (\frac{17}{3}, \frac{10}{3})$
3-C 3-7 (a) $(\bar{P}, \bar{Q}) = (7\frac{7}{10}, 4\frac{1}{10})$ (b) $(\bar{P}, \bar{Q}) = (5\frac{53}{54}, 3\frac{5}{18})$
3-8 (a) price increase $(=\frac{1}{5}) < t (=\frac{1}{3})$ (b) price increase $(=\frac{17}{54}) < t (=\frac{1}{3})$
3-D 3-10 (a) $\bar{Y} = 240; \bar{C} = 190$ (b) $\bar{Y} = 300; \bar{C} = 207; \bar{T} = 70$
3-E 3-12 (a) $(\bar{P}, \bar{Q}) = (2, 3)$ (b) $(\bar{P}, \bar{Q}) = (2, 1)$

4-A 4-1 (a) $A = \begin{bmatrix} 1 & -1 & 0 \\ 1 & 0 & 7 \\ 0 & 1 & -5 \end{bmatrix} \quad x = \begin{bmatrix} Q_d \\ Q_s \\ P \end{bmatrix} \quad b = \begin{bmatrix} 0 \\ 20 \\ -4 \end{bmatrix}$

(b) $A = \begin{bmatrix} 1 & -1 & 0 \\ 1 & 0 & b \\ 0 & 1 & -d \end{bmatrix} \quad x = \begin{bmatrix} Q_d \\ Q_s \\ P \end{bmatrix} \quad b = \begin{bmatrix} 0 \\ a \\ -c \end{bmatrix}$

4-2 $A = \begin{bmatrix} 1 & -1 \\ -\beta & 1 \end{bmatrix} \quad x = \begin{bmatrix} Y \\ C \end{bmatrix} \quad b = \begin{bmatrix} I \\ \alpha \end{bmatrix}$

4-B 4-3 (a) $\begin{bmatrix} 5 & -3 \\ 1 & -2 \end{bmatrix}$ (b) $\begin{bmatrix} 1 & 5 \\ -1 & -2 \end{bmatrix}$ (c) $\begin{bmatrix} 5 & -3 \\ 1 & -2 \end{bmatrix}$ (d) $\begin{bmatrix} -2 & -6 \\ 2 & -1 \end{bmatrix}$

(e) $\begin{bmatrix} 7 & 3 \\ -1 & -1 \end{bmatrix}$ (f) $\begin{bmatrix} 6 & -12 \\ 3 & 0 \end{bmatrix}$ (g) $\begin{bmatrix} -6 & -2 \\ 0 & 4 \end{bmatrix}$ (h) $\begin{bmatrix} 0 & -14 \\ 3 & 4 \end{bmatrix}$

4-4 (a) Answers 4-3a and 4-3b show that $A + B = B + A$

(b) $\begin{bmatrix} 5 & -3 \\ 1 & -2 \end{bmatrix} + \begin{bmatrix} 5 & 7 \\ -2 & -1 \end{bmatrix} = \begin{bmatrix} 10 & 4 \\ -1 & -3 \end{bmatrix} = \begin{bmatrix} 3 & 1 \\ 0 & -2 \end{bmatrix} + \begin{bmatrix} 7 & 3 \\ -1 & -1 \end{bmatrix}$
$\quad (A+B) \quad + \quad C \quad = \quad D \quad = \quad A \quad + \quad (B+C)$

4-5 (a) $\begin{bmatrix} 5 \\ -5 \end{bmatrix}$ (b) $[5 \quad -5]$ (c) $\begin{bmatrix} 1 \\ 7 \end{bmatrix}$ (d) $[-1 \quad -7]$ (e) $\begin{bmatrix} 18 \\ -14 \end{bmatrix}$ (f) $[-5 \quad -5]$

4-C 4-10 (a) $\underset{(2\times 3)}{A} \quad \underset{(3\times 2)}{B} = \underset{(2\times 2)}{D}$ (b) $\underset{(3\times 2)}{B} \quad \underset{(2\times 3)}{A} = \underset{(3\times 3)}{E}$ (c), (d) and (e) not defined

(f) $\underset{(7\times 3)}{C} \quad \underset{(3\times 2)}{B} = \underset{(7\times 2)}{F}$

4-11 (a), (b) not defined (c) $\underset{(3\times 1)}{v} \quad \underset{(1\times 5)}{u'} = \underset{(3\times 5)}{P}$ (d) $\underset{(5\times 1)}{u} \quad \underset{(1\times 3)}{v'} = \underset{(5\times 3)}{Q}$

(e) $\underset{(3\times 1)}{v} \quad \underset{(1\times 3)}{v'} = \underset{(3\times 3)}{R}$ (f) $\underset{(1\times 5)}{u'} \quad \underset{(5\times 1)}{u} = \underset{(1\times 1)}{S}$

4-12 (a) $yb' = \begin{bmatrix} 2y_1 & y_1 & -3y_1 \\ 2y_2 & y_2 & -3y_2 \\ 2y_3 & y_3 & -3y_3 \end{bmatrix}$ (b) $bz' = \begin{bmatrix} 2z_1 & 2z_2 \\ z_1 & z_2 \\ -3z_1 & -3z_2 \end{bmatrix}$
$\quad\quad\quad\quad\quad\quad\quad\quad (3 \times 3) \quad\quad\quad\quad\quad\quad\quad\quad\quad\quad\quad\quad (3 \times 2)$

(c) $b'b = [14]$ (d) $bb' = \begin{bmatrix} 4 & 2 & -6 \\ 2 & 1 & -3 \\ -6 & -3 & 9 \end{bmatrix}$ (e), (f) not defined
$\quad\quad\quad (1 \times 1)$

4-13 (a) $AB = \begin{bmatrix} 15 & 0 & -6 \\ 7 & -2 & -5 \\ 7 & 8 & 6 \end{bmatrix}$ (b) $BA = \begin{bmatrix} 17 & -8 \\ 12 & 2 \end{bmatrix}$
$\quad\quad\quad\quad\quad\quad (3 \times 3) \quad\quad\quad\quad\quad\quad\quad\quad (2 \times 2)$

(c) $Bx = \begin{bmatrix} 5r + 0s - 2t \\ 3r + 2s + t \end{bmatrix}$ (d) $b'A = [-7 \quad 31]$
$\quad\quad\quad (2 \times 1) \quad\quad\quad\quad\quad\quad\quad\quad (1 \times 2)$

(e) $xb' = \begin{bmatrix} 2r & -3r & 7r \\ 2s & -3s & 7s \\ 2t & -3t & 7t \end{bmatrix}$ (f) $b'x = [2r - 3s + 7t]$ (g), (h) not defined
$\quad\quad\quad\quad (3 \times 3) \quad\quad\quad\quad\quad\quad\quad\quad (1 \times 1)$

4-14 (a) $AB = \begin{bmatrix} -4 & -1 \\ 6 & 3 \end{bmatrix} \neq BA = \begin{bmatrix} 0 & 3 \\ 2 & -1 \end{bmatrix}$ (b) $A(B+E) = \begin{bmatrix} -3 & 11 \\ 9 & -12 \end{bmatrix} = AB + AE$

(c) $(B+E)A = \begin{bmatrix} 3 & 3 \\ 3 & -18 \end{bmatrix} = BA + EA$ (d) $(AD)C = \begin{bmatrix} -14 & -10 \\ 24 & 24 \end{bmatrix} = A(DC)$

(e) $-3(A+E) = \begin{bmatrix} -12 & 0 \\ -3 & 6 \end{bmatrix} = -3A - 3E$ (f) $5B = \begin{bmatrix} 0 & 5 \\ 10 & 5 \end{bmatrix} = 2B + 3B$

4-15 $Ax = \begin{bmatrix} 1 & -1 & 0 \\ 1 & 0 & -a_1 \\ 0 & 1 & -b_1 \end{bmatrix} \begin{bmatrix} Q_d \\ Q_s \\ P \end{bmatrix} = \begin{bmatrix} 1Q_d - 1Q_s + 0P \\ 1Q_d + 0Q_s - a_1P \\ 0Q_d + 1Q_s - b_1P \end{bmatrix} = \begin{bmatrix} 0 \\ a_0 \\ b_0 \end{bmatrix} = b$
$\quad\quad\quad (3 \times 3) \quad\quad\quad\quad (3 \times 1) \quad\quad\quad\quad (3 \times 1) \quad\quad\quad\quad (3 \times 1)$

Since $Ax = b$, the definition of matrix equality implies that
$\begin{bmatrix} 1Q_d - 1Q_s + 0P \\ 1Q_d + 0Q_s - a_1P \\ 0Q_d + 1Q_s - b_1P \end{bmatrix} = \begin{bmatrix} 0 \\ a_0 \\ b_0 \end{bmatrix}$ is equivalent to $\begin{aligned} 1Q_d - 1Q_s + 0P &= 0 \\ 1Q_d + 0Q_s - a_1P &= a_0 \\ 0Q_d + 1Q_s - b_1P &= b_0 \end{aligned}$ as in (4-9)

4-D 4-16 (a) $I_3A = A$ (b) $AI_2 = A$ (c) $b'I_2 = b'$ (d) $I_2z = z$ (e) $I_3AI_2 = A$

4-17 (a) $A + 0 = A$ (b) $0 + b' = b'$ (c) $z - 0 = z$ (d) $\underset{(3\times 3)}{0} A = \underset{(3\times 2)}{0}$ (e) $\underset{(2\times 3)}{0} A = \underset{(2\times 2)}{0}$

4-E 4-18 (a) $(A+B)' = \begin{bmatrix} 7 & -1 \\ 7 & 7 \end{bmatrix}' = \begin{bmatrix} 7 & 7 \\ -1 & 7 \end{bmatrix} = \begin{bmatrix} 2 & 3 \\ 1 & 0 \end{bmatrix} + \begin{bmatrix} 5 & 4 \\ -2 & 7 \end{bmatrix} = A' + B'$

(b) $(AB)' = \begin{bmatrix} 14 & 3 \\ 15 & -6 \end{bmatrix}' = \begin{bmatrix} 14 & 15 \\ 3 & -6 \end{bmatrix} = \begin{bmatrix} 5 & 4 \\ -2 & 7 \end{bmatrix} \begin{bmatrix} 2 & 3 \\ 1 & 0 \end{bmatrix} = B'A'$

(c) Let $AB = D$.
Thus $(ABC)' \equiv (DC)' = C'D' \equiv C'(AB)' = C'(B'A') = C'B'A' = \begin{bmatrix} 6 & -12 \\ 59 & 54 \end{bmatrix}$

4-19 (a) $AB = \begin{bmatrix} 2 & 2 \\ 1 & 4 \end{bmatrix} \begin{bmatrix} \frac{2}{3} & -\frac{1}{3} \\ -\frac{1}{6} & \frac{1}{3} \end{bmatrix} = \begin{bmatrix} 1 & 0 \\ 0 & 1 \end{bmatrix}$

(b) $CD = \begin{bmatrix} 3 & 2 \\ 3 & 1 \end{bmatrix} \begin{bmatrix} -\frac{1}{3} & \frac{2}{3} \\ 1 & -1 \end{bmatrix} = \begin{bmatrix} 1 & 0 \\ 0 & 1 \end{bmatrix}$

ANSWERS TO PRACTICE PROBLEMS **283**

4-20 (a) $B^{-1}A^{-1} = \begin{bmatrix} 0 & 1 \\ \frac{1}{2} & -\frac{9}{2} \end{bmatrix} \begin{bmatrix} -\frac{1}{5} & \frac{4}{5} \\ \frac{2}{5} & -\frac{3}{5} \end{bmatrix} = \begin{bmatrix} \frac{2}{5} & -\frac{3}{5} \\ -\frac{19}{10} & \frac{31}{10} \end{bmatrix} = (AB)^{-1}$

(b) $(A^{-1})' = \begin{bmatrix} -\frac{1}{5} & \frac{4}{5} \\ \frac{2}{5} & -\frac{3}{5} \end{bmatrix}' = \begin{bmatrix} -\frac{1}{5} & \frac{2}{5} \\ \frac{4}{5} & -\frac{3}{5} \end{bmatrix} = (A')^{-1}$

4-21 (a) $1 + x + x^2$
(b) $b(x_5 + x_6 + x_7 + x_8 + x_9)$
(c) $a_2 x_2 + a_3 x_3 + \ldots + a_m x_m$
(d) $(x_0 + 0) + (x_1 + 1) + (x_2 + 2) + (x_3 + 3) = 6 + x_0 + x_1 + x_2 + x_3$

4-22 (a) $\sum_{k=1}^{2} a_{2k} b_{k1}$ (b) $\sum_{j=1}^{4} j a_j$ (c) $\sum_{i=1}^{3} x_i y^{-i}$ (d) $\sum_{j=1}^{n} a_{1j} x_j = b_1$ (e) $\sum_{i=3}^{5} b_i (x_{i-2} + 2i)$

4-F 4-23 (a) $-1 \begin{vmatrix} 1 & 5 \\ 1 & -2 \end{vmatrix} - 2 \begin{vmatrix} 3 & 5 \\ 2 & -2 \end{vmatrix} + 0 \begin{vmatrix} 3 & 1 \\ 2 & 1 \end{vmatrix} = 7 + 32 + 0 = 39$

(b) $a_1 \begin{vmatrix} b_2 & c_2 \\ b_3 & c_3 \end{vmatrix} - b_1 \begin{vmatrix} a_2 & c_2 \\ a_3 & c_3 \end{vmatrix} + c_1 \begin{vmatrix} a_2 & b_2 \\ a_3 & b_3 \end{vmatrix} = a_1(b_2 c_3 - b_3 c_2) - b_1(a_2 c_3 - a_3 c_2) + c_1(a_2 b_3 - a_3 b_2)$

(c) -24 (d) 0 (e) -138 (f) -22

4-24 (a) M_{15} (b) $-M_{23}$ (c) $-M_{41}$ (d) M_{66} (e) M_{11} (f) $(-1)^{i+j} M_{ij}$

4-25 (a) $C_{c_3} = M_{c_3} = \begin{vmatrix} a_1 & b_1 \\ a_2 & b_2 \end{vmatrix}$ (b) $C_{a_2} = -M_{a_2} = -\begin{vmatrix} b_1 & c_1 \\ b_3 & c_3 \end{vmatrix}$

4-26 Row 3 in (e) and column 2 in (f) are easiest for expansion

4-27 (a) $\sum_{i=1}^{4} a_{i2} C_{i2} = -2 \begin{vmatrix} 1 & 3 & 0 \\ -3 & 2 & 0 \\ 4 & 0 & 7 \end{vmatrix} = -154$

(b) $\sum_{j=1}^{4} a_{3j} C_{3j} = -3 \begin{vmatrix} 7 & 2 & 1 \\ 5 & -4 & 2 \\ 6 & 2 & 1 \end{vmatrix} = 24$

4-28 (a) $\sum_{j=1}^{5} a_{3j} C_{3j}$ (b) $\sum_{i=1}^{t} a_{i5} C_{i5}$

4-G 4-29 (a) $|A| = -34$ (b) $\sum_{i=1}^{3} a_{i2} C_{i1} = 0$ (as expected by Property III)

4-30 The matrix in (c) is nonsingular

4-31 When the system is written as $Ax = b$, then $|A| = 40 \ne 0$. Hence the equation system possesses a unique solution.

4-H 4-35 (a) $A^{-1} = \frac{1}{|A|} \operatorname{adj} A = \frac{1}{11} \begin{bmatrix} 2 & 1 \\ -3 & 4 \end{bmatrix}$ (b) $B^{-1} = -\frac{1}{6} \begin{bmatrix} 7 & 2 \\ 3 & 0 \end{bmatrix}$

(c) $C^{-1} = \frac{1}{18} \begin{bmatrix} 2 & 0 \\ 0 & 9 \end{bmatrix}$

4-36 (a) $A^{-1} = \frac{1}{45} \begin{bmatrix} -15 & 35 & -5 \\ 3 & -4 & 7 \\ 21 & -28 & 4 \end{bmatrix}$ (b) $B^{-1} = -\frac{1}{2} \begin{bmatrix} 2 & 2 & 0 \\ 0 & -1 & 0 \\ 6 & 6 & -2 \end{bmatrix}$

(c) $C^{-1} = \frac{1}{21} \begin{bmatrix} 3 & -6 & 2 \\ 0 & 21 & 0 \\ -3 & 6 & 5 \end{bmatrix}$

4-37 Writing the equation system as $Ax = b$, then

$$\bar{x} = A^{-1} b = \frac{1}{|A|} (\operatorname{adj} A) b = -\frac{1}{53} \begin{bmatrix} -15 & 6 & 19 \\ -4 & -9 & -2 \\ 10 & -4 & 5 \end{bmatrix} \begin{bmatrix} 8 \\ -4 \\ 2 \end{bmatrix} = \begin{bmatrix} 2 \\ 0 \\ -2 \end{bmatrix} = \begin{bmatrix} \bar{x}_1 \\ \bar{x}_2 \\ \bar{x}_3 \end{bmatrix}$$

4-I 4-40 (a) $|A| = -33$, $|A_1| = -11$, $|A_2| = -231$. Thus, $\bar{x}_1 = -11/-33 = \frac{1}{3}$; $\bar{x}_2 = -231/-33 = 7$.
(b) $|A| = -21$, $|A_1| = 3$, $|A_2| = -14$. Thus, $\bar{x}_1 = 3/-21 = -\frac{1}{7}$; $\bar{x}_2 = -14/-21 = \frac{2}{3}$.
(c) $|A| = 75$, $|A_1| = -150$, $|A_2| = 300$, $|A_3| = -25$. Thus, $\bar{x}_1 = -2$; $\bar{x}_2 = 4$; $\bar{x}_3 = \frac{1}{3}$.
(d) $|A| = -24$, $|A_1| = -72$, $|A_2| = 24$, $|A_3| = -24$. Thus, $\bar{x}_1 = 3$; $\bar{x}_2 = -1$; $\bar{x}_3 = 1$.

5-A 5-1 $|A| = -(d+b)$, $|A_1| = -(ad-bc)$, $|A_2| = -(ad-bc)$, $|A_3| = -(a+c)$. Thus, $\bar{Q}_d = \bar{Q}_s = \bar{Q} = (ad-bc)/(d+b)$ and $\bar{P} = (a+c)/(d+b)$.

5-2 (a) Writing the equation system as $Ax = b$, then

$$\bar{x} = A^{-1}b = \frac{1}{|A|}(\text{adj }A)b = \frac{1}{a_1-b_1}\begin{bmatrix} a_1 & -b_1 & a_1 \\ b_1 & -b_1 & a_1 \\ 1 & -1 & 1 \end{bmatrix}\begin{bmatrix} 0 \\ a_0 \\ b_0 \end{bmatrix} = -\frac{1}{(b_1-a_1)}\begin{bmatrix} -(a_0b_1-a_1b_0) \\ -(a_0b_1-a_1b_0) \\ -(a_0-b_0) \end{bmatrix}$$

Thus, $\bar{Q}_d = \bar{Q}_s = \bar{Q} = (a_0b_1 - a_1b_0)/(b_1-a_1)$ and $\bar{P} = (a_0-b_0)/(b_1-a_1)$.
(b) $|A| = d+f$, $|A_1| = ed-cf$, $|A_2| = ed-cf$, $|A_3| = c+e$. Thus, $\bar{Q}_d = \bar{Q}_s = \bar{Q} = (ed-cf)/(d+f)$ and $\bar{P} = (c+e)/(d+f)$.

5-B 5-3 $\bar{x} = A^{-1}b = \frac{1}{|A|}(\text{adj }A)b = \frac{1}{1-\beta(1-t)}\begin{bmatrix} 1 & 1 & -\beta \\ \beta(1-t) & 1 & -\beta \\ t & t & 1-\beta \end{bmatrix}\begin{bmatrix} I+G \\ \alpha \\ 0 \end{bmatrix}$

$= \frac{1}{1-\beta(1-t)}\begin{bmatrix} \alpha+I+G \\ \alpha+\beta(1-t)(I+G) \\ t(\alpha+I+G) \end{bmatrix}$

Thus,
$$\bar{Y} = (\alpha+I+G)/[1-\beta(1-t)]; \quad \bar{C} = [\alpha+\beta(1-t)(I+G)]/[1-\beta(1-t)]$$

and
$$\bar{T} = [t(\alpha+I+G)]/[1-\beta(1-t)]$$

5-4 $|A| = 1-\beta(1-\delta)$, $|A_Y| = \alpha-\beta\gamma+I+G$, $|A_C| = \alpha-\beta\gamma+\beta(1-\delta)(I+G)$, $|A_T| = \gamma-\beta\gamma+\delta(\alpha+I+G)$. Thus, $\bar{Y} = [\alpha-\beta\gamma+I+G]/[1-\beta(1-\delta)]$; $\bar{C} = [\alpha-\beta\gamma+\beta(1-\delta)(I+G)]/[1-\beta(1-\delta)]$ and $\bar{T} = [\gamma-\beta\gamma+\delta(\alpha+I+G)]/[1-\beta(1-\delta)]$. Note that while $\bar{T} > 0$, the numerators of $\bar{Y}$ and $\bar{C}$ must be positive to ensure $\bar{Y}, \bar{C} > 0$.

5-C 5-5 $|A| = \mu(1-\beta)+\lambda\delta$, $|A_Y| = \mu(\alpha+\gamma)+\delta(M_0-\sigma)$, $|A_r| = (1-\beta)(M_0-\sigma)-\lambda(\alpha+\gamma)$. Thus, $\bar{Y} = [\mu(\alpha+\gamma)+\delta(M_0-\sigma)]/[\mu(1-\beta)+\lambda\delta]$ and $\bar{r} = [(1-\beta)(M_0-\sigma)-\lambda(\alpha+\gamma)]/[\mu(1-\beta)+\lambda\delta]$. Note that the numerators of $\bar{Y}$ and $\bar{r}$ must be negative to ensure $\bar{Y}, \bar{r} > 0$.

5-D 5-7 $\begin{bmatrix} \bar{Y}_1 \\ \bar{Y}_2 \end{bmatrix} = (I-B)^{-1}e = 8\begin{bmatrix} \frac{3}{8} & \frac{1}{8} \\ \frac{1}{5} & \frac{2}{5} \end{bmatrix}\begin{bmatrix} 80 \\ 120 \end{bmatrix} = \begin{bmatrix} 360 \\ 512 \end{bmatrix}$

5-8 $\begin{bmatrix} \bar{Y}_1 \\ \bar{Y}_2 \end{bmatrix} = \begin{bmatrix} 760 \\ 1472 \end{bmatrix}$

5-E 5-9 $\begin{bmatrix} \bar{x}_1 \\ \bar{x}_2 \\ \bar{x}_3 \end{bmatrix} = (I-A)^{-1}d = \frac{120}{19}\begin{bmatrix} \frac{7}{20} & \frac{1}{12} & \frac{1}{6} \\ \frac{4}{25} & \frac{2}{5} & \frac{1}{6} \\ \frac{1}{20} & \frac{1}{8} & \frac{1}{4} \end{bmatrix}\begin{bmatrix} 10 \\ 8 \\ 4 \end{bmatrix} = \begin{bmatrix} 580/19 \\ 656/19 \\ 300/19 \end{bmatrix}$

5-10 $\begin{bmatrix} \bar{x}_1 \\ \bar{x}_2 \\ \bar{x}_3 \end{bmatrix} = \begin{bmatrix} 704/19 \\ 4052/95 \\ 372/19 \end{bmatrix}$

6-A 6-6 (a) $dy/dx = 2ax+b$ (b) $dy/dx = a_1+2a_2x+\ldots+na_nx^{n-1}$

6-7 (a) $60x^{13/2}-40x^9$ (b) $64x^7+120x^5+12x^2+10$ (c) $9x^2+1$
(d) $-60x^{-6}(1+2x^{-1})$ (e) $5acx^4+4bcx^3$ (f) $22+2x-9x^2$

6-8 (a) $(2x^4+8x^3)/(2x^2+4x)^2$ (b) $150x^{-3}/(3x^{-2}+1)^2$ (c) $[xf'(x)-f(x)]/x^2$

ANSWERS TO PRACTICE PROBLEMS **285**

(d) $\dfrac{d}{dx}\left[\dfrac{xf(x)}{g(x)}\right] = \dfrac{g(x)\dfrac{d}{dx}[xf(x)] - [xf(x)]g'(x)}{[g(x)]^2}$
(quotient rule)

$= \dfrac{g(x)[xf'(x) + f(x)(1)] - xf(x)g'(x)}{[g(x)]^2}$
(product rule)

6-B **6-12** $dy/dx = (dy/du)(du/dx) = (10u^4 - 8u^{-3})(-2) = 16(7-2x)^{-3} - 20(7-2x)^4$
6-13 (a) Let $u = 7x^7 - 2x^{1/2}$, so that $y = 4u^9$ where $u = 7x^7 - 2x^{1/2}$. Hence $dy/dx = (dy/du)(du/dx) = 36u^8(49x^6 - x^{-1/2}) = 36(7x^7 - 2x^{1/2})^8(49x^6 - x^{-1/2})$.
(b) Let $u = 3x^2 - 7x$.
Hence $dy/dx = (dy/du)(du/dx) = -5u^{-6}(6x - 7) = -5(3x^2 - 7x)^{-6}(6x - 7)$
(c) Let $u = 3x^3 - 2x$.
Hence $dy/dx = (dy/du)(du/dx) = -21u^6(9x^2 - 2) = -21(3x^3 - 2x)^6(9x^2 - 2)$
6-14 (a) Since $dy/dx = 19 + 3x^{-4} + x^4 > 0$ for all x, then $f(x)$ is monotonic and $dx/dy = 1/(dy/dx) = 1/(19 + 3x^{-4} + x^4)$
(b) Since $dy/dx = -8x^7 - 8x^3 < 0$ for $x > 0$, then $f(x)$ is monotonic for $x > 0$ and $dx/dy = 1/(dy/dx) = 1/(-8x^7 - 8x^3) = -1/8x^3(x^4 + 1)$ for $x > 0$.
6-C **6-17** (a) Let $u = x^2 - 3x + 2$, so that $y = \ln u$ with $u = x^2 - 3x + 2$. Hence $dy/dx = (1/u)(du/dx) = (2x - 3)/(x^2 - 3x + 2)$.
(b) $y = 6\ln t = \ln t^6$. Thus, if we let $u = t^6$, then $y = \ln u$ with $u = t^6$. Hence $dy/dt = (1/u)(du/dt) = 6/t$.
(c) Let $u = 7x^4 - 2x^2$. Hence $dy/dx = (1/u)(du/dx) = (28x^3 - 4x)/(7x^4 - 2x^2)$.
6-D **6-18** (a) $f'(x) = 24x^2; f''(x) = 48x; f'''(x) = 48$
(b) $f'(x) = 8(1 - 3x)^{-2}; f''(x) = 48(1 - 3x)^{-3}; f'''(x) = 432(1 - 3x)^{-4}$
(c) $f'(x) = a_1 + 2a_2 x + 3a_3 x^2 + \ldots + na_n x^{n-1}$;
$f''(x) = 2a_2 + 6a_3 x + \ldots + n(n-1)a_n x^{n-2}; f'''(x) = 6a_3 + \ldots + n(n-1)(n-2)a_n x^{n-3}$

7-B **7-5** (a) $E_d = -\dfrac{dQ_d}{dP}\dfrac{P}{Q_d} = -(-P)\dfrac{P}{Q_d} = P^2/Q_d$. When $P = 4$, $Q_d = 90$, so that $E_d = 16/90 = 8/45$.

(b) $E_d = -\dfrac{dQ_d}{dP}\dfrac{P}{Q_d} = -(-70P^{-6})\dfrac{P}{Q_d} = 70P^{-5}/14P^{-5} = 5$ for $P > 0$. Thus, when $P = 4$, $E_d = 5$.

7-6 (a) $E_s = \dfrac{dQ_s}{dP}\dfrac{P}{Q_s} = 5\dfrac{P}{Q_s}$. When $P = 3$, $Q_s = 13$, so that $E_s = 15/13$.

(b) $E_s = \dfrac{dQ_s}{dP}\dfrac{P}{Q_s} = (4 + 2P)\dfrac{P}{Q_s}$. When $P = 3$, $Q_s = 9$, so that $E_s = 30/9 = 10/3$.

7-7 (a) $R = PQ = 60Q - 3Q^2$
(b) $MR = dR/dQ = 60 - 6Q$
(c) noting that $dQ/dP = 1/(dP/dQ)$,
$E_d = -(dQ/dP)(P/Q) = (1/3)(P/Q) = (1/3)(45/5) = 3$
7-8 E_d is dimensionless
7-9 When $Q = 5$, $P = 45$, $MR = 30$, and $E_d = 3$. Thus (7-20) holds since $MR = P(1 - 1/E_d) = 45(1 - 1/3) = 30$.
8-A **8-6** (a) Max. at $x = 5$ with $f(5) = 89.5$
(b) Min. at $x = -5$ with $f(-5) = -8$
(c) Min. at $x = 6$ with $f(6) = -18$
(d) Max. at $x = 0$ with $f(0) = \frac{1}{9}$
(e) Min. at $x = 5$ with $f(5) = -\frac{16}{3}$. Max. at $x = 1$ with $f(1) = \frac{16}{3}$.
(f) Min. at $x = 0$ with $f(0) = 1$. Max. at $x = -\frac{1}{3}$ with $f(-\frac{1}{3}) = \frac{28}{27}$.
(g) Min. at $x = -4$ with $f(-4) = -\frac{1}{8}$

286 ANSWERS TO PRACTICE PROBLEMS

8-B 8-9 (a) Max. at $(2, \frac{35}{3})$; min. at $(4, \frac{31}{3})$; non-stationary inflection point at $(3, 11)$
(b) No max. or min.; non-stationary inflection point at $(4, \frac{26}{3})$
(c) Max. at $(-1, 5)$; min. at $(1, 1)$; non-stationary inflection point at $(0, 3)$
(d) Max. at $(1, 10)$; min. at $(3, 6)$; non-stationary inflection point at $(2, 8)$
(e) No max. or min.; stationary inflection point at $(2, 5)$
(f) Max. at $(-1, 11)$; min. at $(2, -16)$; non-stationary inflection point at $(\frac{1}{2}, -\frac{5}{2})$

8-10 (a) Non-stationary point of inflection when $x = -b/3a$
(b) Stationary point of inflection when $x = -b/3a$

8-11 (a) Max. at $(1, 24)$; min. at $(3, 20)$; non-stationary inflection point at $(2, 22)$
(b) Max. at $(0, 4)$; min. at $(2, 0)$; non-stationary inflection point at $(1, 2)$
(c) No max. or min.; stationary inflection point at $(-\frac{1}{3}, 0)$
(d) Max. at $(1, \frac{23}{3})$; min. at $(3, 5)$; non-stationary inflection point at $(2, \frac{19}{3})$

9-A 9-19 Given that maximum profit occurs when

$$MR = 67, \quad E_d = \frac{89}{22}, \quad \text{and} \quad \frac{dR}{dP} = -\frac{67}{2}$$

This information permits us to find the monopolist's output level. Since $R = P \cdot Q$ and $dR/dP = P(dQ/dP) + Q = Q(1 - E_d)$ then

$$\frac{dR}{dP} = -\frac{67}{2} = Q\left(1 - \frac{89}{22}\right) \quad \text{or} \quad Q = 11$$

To derive the monopolist's profit function we must first obtain the values of a and b as follows:

$$MR = \frac{dR}{dQ} = P + Q\frac{dP}{dQ} = P\left(1 - \frac{1}{E_d}\right) = P\left(1 - \frac{22}{89}\right) \quad \text{or} \quad P = 89$$

Also,

$$E_d = -\frac{dQ}{dP}\frac{P}{Q} = -\frac{dQ}{dP}\frac{89}{11} = \frac{89}{22} \quad \text{or} \quad \frac{dQ}{dP} = -\frac{1}{2}$$

Since $P = a - bQ$ and $dP/dQ = 1/(dQ/dP) = -b$, then $b = 2$. Substituting for P, b and Q in the AR function gives a:

$$P = a - bQ \quad \text{or} \quad 89 = a - 2(11)$$

which gives $a = 111$

$$\therefore P = 111 - 2Q \quad \text{and} \quad R = P \cdot Q = 111Q - 2Q^2$$

The profit function is therefore

$$\pi = R - C = 111Q - 2Q^2 - [\tfrac{1}{3}Q^3 - 7Q^2 + 100Q + 50]$$
$$= -\tfrac{1}{3}Q^3 + 5Q^2 + 11Q - 50$$
$$\pi'(Q) = -Q^2 + 10Q + 11 = 0 \quad \text{when} \quad Q = -1 \quad \text{or} \quad Q = 11$$
$$\pi''(Q) = -2Q + 10 < 0 \quad \text{when} \quad Q = 11$$

Thus $Q = 11$ is the monopolist's profit-maximizing output level.

9-20 The first step is to find the monopolist's output and price after a tax levy, of t per unit output, has been imposed. Profit after tax is

$$\pi = R - C^T = aQ - bQ^2 - [\alpha Q^2 + \beta Q + \gamma + tQ]$$
$$= -(\alpha + b)Q^2 + [a - (\beta + t)]Q - \gamma$$
$$\pi'(Q) = -2(\alpha + b)Q + [a - (\beta + t)] = 0$$

when

$$\bar{Q} = \frac{[a - (\beta + t)]}{2(\alpha + b)}$$
$$\pi''(Q) = -2(\alpha + b) < 0 \quad \therefore \pi \text{ maximum at } \bar{Q}$$

To find the change in $\bar{Q}$ resulting from an infinitesimal change in t we find $d\bar{Q}/dt$:

$$\frac{d\bar{Q}}{dt} = -\frac{1}{2(\alpha + b)} < 0$$

Thus an increase in t will reduce the monopolist's output by $1/2(\alpha+b)$. Since

$$\left|\frac{d\bar{Q}}{dt}\right| = \left|-\frac{1}{2(\alpha+b)}\right| < \tfrac{1}{2}$$

this demonstrates that the decrease in monopoly output is less than half the increase in t. The change in $\bar{P}$ resulting from an infinitesimal change in t is found likewise:

$$\bar{P} = a - b\bar{Q} = a - b\frac{[a-(\beta+t)]}{2(\alpha+b)} = \frac{2a\alpha + ab + b\beta + bt}{2(\alpha+b)}$$

$$\therefore \frac{d\bar{P}}{dt} = \frac{b}{2(\alpha+b)} > 0 \quad \text{with} \quad \frac{b}{2(\alpha+b)} < \tfrac{1}{2}$$

Thus an increase in t will increase the monopolist's price by less than half the increase in t.

To find the tax rate which maximizes tax revenue:

$$T = t\bar{Q} = \frac{t[a-(\beta+t)]}{2(\alpha+b)} = \frac{(a-\beta)t - t^2}{2(\alpha+b)}$$

$$T'(t) = \frac{(a-\beta) - 2t}{2(\alpha+b)} = 0 \quad \text{when} \quad \bar{t} = \frac{(a-\beta)}{2}$$

$$T''(t) = -\frac{1}{(\alpha+b)} < 0$$

Therefore maximum tax revenue when $t = \bar{t} = (a-\beta)/2$.

9-21 The consumer's expenditure cannot exceed his food budget M. Hence, if he spends all M on x and y, his budget constraint is

$$p_x x + p_y y = M \quad \text{or} \quad y = \frac{M - p_x x}{p_y}$$

This constraint must be taken into account in maximizing U. This is done by substituting this y value into the utility function, to give U as a function of x alone:

$$U = A x^\alpha y^\beta = A x^\alpha \left(\frac{M - p_x x}{p_y}\right)^\beta = \frac{A}{p_y^\beta} x^\alpha (M - p_x x)^\beta$$

or $U = C x^\alpha (M - p_x x)^\beta$ where $C = A/p_y^\beta$ is a constant.
To find maximum U:

$$U'(x) = \beta C x^\alpha (M - p_x x)^{\beta-1}(-p_x) + (M - p_x x)^\beta \alpha C x^{\alpha-1} = 0$$
$$\text{(product and chain rule)}$$

Dividing through by $C x^{\alpha-1}(M - p_x x)^{\beta-1}$ gives

$$\beta x(-p_x) + (M - p_x x)\alpha = 0 \quad \text{or} \quad \alpha M = \alpha p_x x + \beta p_x x = (\alpha + \beta)p_x x$$

whence

$$x = \bar{x} = \frac{\alpha M}{(\alpha+\beta)p_x}$$

Since $U''(\bar{x})$ is assumed negative, then U is maximized when $x = \bar{x}$. The corresponding value of y is

$$\bar{y} = \frac{M - p_x \bar{x}}{p_y} = \frac{M - p_x\left(\frac{\alpha M}{(\alpha+\beta)p_x}\right)}{p_y} = \frac{M - \left(\frac{\alpha M}{(\alpha+\beta)}\right)}{p_y} = \frac{\beta M}{(\alpha+\beta)p_y}$$

To check answer we substitute $\bar{x}$ and $\bar{y}$ into the budget constraint:

$$p_x \bar{x} + p_y \bar{y} = p_x\left(\frac{\alpha M}{(\alpha+\beta)p_x}\right) + p_y\left(\frac{\beta M}{(\alpha+\beta)p_y}\right) = \frac{\alpha M + \beta M}{(\alpha+\beta)} = \frac{(\alpha+\beta)M}{(\alpha+\beta)} = M$$

Thus the budget constraint is met.

9-22 Since $H = W + L$ and $Y = rW$, we can substitute for L and Y in the utility function as follows:
$$U = aLY - bY^2 - cL^2$$
$$= a(H-W)rW - b(rW)^2 - c(H-W)^2$$

Thus we have utility as a function of W alone. To find maximum U:
$$U'(W) = a(H-W)r - rWa - 2br^2W + 2c(H-W) = 0$$
when
$$W = \bar{W} = \frac{(ar+2c)H}{2(ar+br^2+c)}$$

$U''(W) = -2(ar+br^2+c) < 0$ as required for a utility maximum. Thus the number of hours worked daily will be $\bar{W}$.

Note that if we know the values of a, b and c, the number of hours worked will depend on the wage rate r (obviously $H = 24$). The consumer's income is $r\bar{W}$, and his leisure time is $(H - \bar{W})$. The imposition of an income tax of rate t, $(0 < t < 1)$, will reduce the consumer's income from work by the amount tY:
$$Y - tY = (1-t)Y = (1-t)rW$$
If we let $(1-t)r = r'$, then our previous result will be obtained, except that we have r' instead of r. Thus
$$\bar{W} = \frac{(ar'+2c)H}{2[ar'+b(r')^2+c]} = \frac{[a(1-t)r+2c]H}{2[a(1-t)r+b(1-t)^2r^2+c]}$$

9-23 Ignoring fixed cost, the monopolist's profit function is
$$\pi = R - C = P \cdot Q - wL = h(Q) \cdot Q - w(L) \cdot L \quad \text{or} \quad \pi(L) = h[g(L)]g(L) - w(L) \cdot L$$

The first-order condition for a profit maximum is
$$\pi'(L) = P\frac{dQ}{dL} + Q\frac{dP}{dL} - w - L\frac{dw}{dL} = 0$$
$$= P\frac{dQ}{dL} + Q\frac{dP}{dQ}\frac{dQ}{dL} - w - L\frac{dw}{dL} = 0$$
or
$$h[g(L)]g'(L) + g(L)\frac{d[h(Q)]}{dQ}g'(L) - w(L) - Lw'(L) = 0$$
whence
$$\left[P + Q\frac{dP}{dQ}\right]\frac{dQ}{dL} = \left[w + L\frac{dw}{dL}\right]$$

Since $R = P \cdot Q$ then
$$MR = \frac{dR}{dQ} = P + Q\frac{dP}{dQ}$$

This permits us to rewrite the left-hand side of the above expression as
$$\left[P + Q\frac{dP}{dQ}\right]\frac{dQ}{dL} = MR \cdot MP = MRP$$

where MP and MRP represent the marginal product and marginal revenue product of labour, respectively. Also, since $\theta = (dL/dw)(w/L)$, the right-hand side becomes
$$\left[w + L\frac{dw}{dL}\right] = w + \frac{w}{\theta} = w\left(1 + \frac{1}{\theta}\right)$$

Therefore the relation between marginal revenue product, wage, and the elasticity of labour supply is

$$MRP = w\left(1 + \frac{1}{\theta}\right)$$

Since $MR = P(1 - 1/E_d)$, where E_d is the price elasticity of demand, the relation can also be written as

$$P\left(1 - \frac{1}{E_d}\right)MP = w\left(1 + \frac{1}{\theta}\right)$$

9-24 (i) (a) $\pi = R - C = 24Q - 2Q^2 - [Q^2 + 5] = 24Q - 3Q^2 - 5$. To find maximum profit:
$\pi'(Q) = 24 - 6Q = 0$ when $Q = 4$
$\pi''(Q) = -6 < 0$ as required for a profit maximum

Thus the profit-maximizing output level is $Q = 4$. The values of profit, price and total revenue at $Q = 4$ are $\pi(4) = 43$, $P(4) = 24 - 2(4) = 16$, and $R(4) = 64$, respectively.

(b) Imposition of the lump-sum tax of 30 will increase total cost by 30, so that the profit function becomes

$$\pi = 24Q - 3Q^2 - 35$$

The lump-sum tax will not affect output, price or revenue (check that this is so by repeating (i) (a) for $\pi = 24Q - 3Q^2 - 35$). However, profit will be reduced by the amount of the tax—in this case from 43 to 13.

(ii) (a) $R = 24Q - 2Q^2$. To find maximum revenue:
$R'(Q) = 24 - 4Q = 0$ when $Q = 6$
$R''(Q) = -4 < 0$ as required for a revenue maximum

Thus the revenue-maximizing output level is $Q = 6$. The values of profit, price and total revenue at $Q = 6$ are $\pi(6) = 31$, $P(6) = 12$, and $R(6) = 72$, respectively. Since $\pi(6) = 31$, the 'minimum' profit constraint of $\pi \geq 10$ does not prevent attainment of the revenue-maximizing output level.

(b) Imposition of the lump-sum tax of 30 would reduce profit, at the revenue-maximizing output level of $Q = 6$, to 1. Hence the profit constraint of $\pi \geq 10$ will prevent attainment of the revenue-maximizing output level. If, however, we set $\pi = 10$, and solve $\pi(Q)$ for Q, we can find the output levels which are just compatible with $\pi = 10$. Thus

$$\pi = 10 \quad \text{or} \quad 24Q - 3Q^2 - 35 = 10 \quad \text{(note that the tax is included)}$$

i.e.

$$-Q^2 + 8Q - 15 = 0$$

Solving for Q we obtain the two roots $Q = 3$ or $Q = 5$. Since $R(3) = 54$ and $R(5) = 70$, the highest revenue which can be achieved, subject to $\pi \geq 10$, is thus $R(5) = 70$ at output level $Q = 5$. The corresponding values of profit and price are $\pi(5) = 10$ and $P(5) = 14$, respectively. Thus, in contrast to the profit-maximizing case, imposition of the lump-sum tax affects the revenue-maximizer's price and output. [Check how a lump-sum tax of 20, instead of 30, would alter the answer to (ii) (b).]

9-25 (a) $\pi = R - C = 9Q - [Q^3 - 9Q^2 + 33Q + 10] = -Q^3 + 9Q^2 - 24Q - 10$. To find maximum profit:
$\pi'(Q) = -3Q^2 + 18Q - 24 = 0$ when $Q = 2$ or $Q = 4$
$\pi''(Q) = -6Q + 18 < 0$ when $Q = 4$

Thus the profit-maximizing output level is $Q = 4$. The corresponding value of profit at this output level is $\pi(4) = -26$.

(b) The firm will not produce at all since the fixed costs of $C(0) = 10$ are less than the loss of 26.

(c) Such a perfectly competitive firm will only produce when the profit-maximizing output level exceeds the output level for which AVC is a minimum. Hence we first find minimum AVC:

$$TVC = Q^3 - 9Q^2 + 33Q$$
$$AVC = Q^2 - 9Q + 33$$
$$\frac{d(AVC)}{dQ} = 2Q - 9 = 0 \quad \text{when} \quad Q = \tfrac{9}{2}$$
$$\frac{d^2(AVC)}{dQ^2} = 2 > 0 \quad \text{as required for an } AVC \text{ minimum}$$

Thus the firm will only produce if $Q > \tfrac{9}{2}$. Note that when $Q = \tfrac{9}{2}$, the value of AVC is $12\tfrac{3}{4}$. Hence the price must exceed $12\tfrac{3}{4}$ before the firm will produce.

10-A 10-7 (a) $\partial y/\partial x_1 = -6x_1^{-3} + 6x_2^2$; $\partial y/\partial x_2 = 12x_1 x_2 + 21x_2^2$
(b) $\partial y/\partial x_1 = 4x_2$; $\partial y/\partial x_2 = 4x_1 - 2x_2 x_3$
(c) $\partial y/\partial x_1 = (x_1 x_2 + 3x_2^2)(0) + (x_2^3 - 2)(x_2) = x_2^4 - 2x_2$;
$\partial y/\partial x_2 = (x_1 x_2 + 3x_2^2)(3x_2^2) + (x_2^3 - 2)(x_1 + 6x_2)$
(d) $\partial y/\partial x_1 = [(x_1^2 + 2x_2^2)(9x_1^2) - (3x_1^3 - 2x_2)(2x_1)]/(x_1^2 + 2x_2^2)^2$;
$\partial y/\partial x_2 = [(x_1^2 + 2x_2^2)(-2) - (3x_1^3 - 2x_2)(4x_2)]/(x_1^2 + 2x_2^2)^2$
(e) $y = u^{-5}$, where $u = x_1^2 x_2 + x_1^3 x_3^2 + x_2^2 x_3$, gives
$\partial y/\partial x_1 = (dy/du)(\partial u/\partial x_1) = -5u^{-6}(2x_1 x_2 + 3x_1^2 x_3^2)$
$\quad = -5(x_1^2 x_2 + x_1^3 x_3^2 + x_2^2 x_3)^{-6}(2x_1 x_2 + 3x_1^2 x_3^2)$
$\partial y/\partial x_2 = (dy/du)(\partial u/\partial x_2) = -5u^{-6}(x_1^2 + 2x_2 x_3)$
$\quad = -5(x_1^2 x_2 + x_1^3 x_3^2 + x_2^2 x_3)^{-6}(x_1^2 + 2x_2 x_3)$
(f) $y = \ln u$, where $u = 2x_1 x_2^2 - 3x_1^3 x_2 + 10$, gives
$\partial y/\partial x_1 = (dy/du)(\partial u/\partial x_1) = (1/u)(\partial u/\partial x_1)$
$\quad = [1/(2x_1 x_2^2 - 3x_1^3 x_2 + 10)](2x_2^2 - 9x_1^2 x_2)$
$\partial y/\partial x_2 = (dy/du)(\partial u/\partial x_2) = (1/u)(\partial u/\partial x_2)$
$\quad = [1/(2x_1 x_2^2 - 3x_1^3 x_2 + 10)](4x_1 x_2 - 3x_1^3)$

10-8 (a) $f_x = 4x - 7y^2$; $f_y = -14xy$
(b) $f_x = 2/x$; $f_y = 3/y$
(c) $f_x = 3(w - y^2)$; $f_y = (3x + w^2)(-2y)$
(d) $f_x = -22(x^2 y^3)^{-12}(2xy^3)$; $f_y = -22(x^2 y^3)^{-12}(3x^2 y^2)$

10-9 $f_x = f_x(x,y) = 4xy - y^3$. Thus, $f_x(2,1) = 7$. Since $f_x = 7 > 0$, then z changes in the same direction as x, for infinitesimal changes in x from the point $(x,y) = (2,1)$. The magnitude of the rate of change of z is 7 units per unit change in x.

10-B 10-12 (a) $f_x = -3x^{-4}y + 8y^3 x - 2$ and $f_y = x^{-3} + 12y^2 x^2$. Hence, $f_{xx} = 12x^{-5}y + 8y^3$, $f_{yy} = 24yx^2$, and $f_{xy} = f_{yx} = -3x^{-4} + 24y^2 x$.
(b) $f_x = x^{-1/2}y^3 - 9x^2 y^5$ and $f_y = 6x^{1/2}y^2 - 15x^3 y^4$. Hence, $f_{xx} = -\tfrac{1}{2}x^{-3/2}y^3 - 18xy^5$, $f_{yy} = 12x^{1/2}y - 60x^3 y^3$, and $f_{xy} = f_{yx} = 3x^{-1/2}y^2 - 45x^2 y^4$.

10-13 (a) $f_1 = 9x_1^8 x_3 + x_2$, $f_2 = -2x_2^3 + x_1$, and $f_3 = x_1^9 - 4x_2 x_3$. Hence, $f_{11} = 72x_1^7 x_3$, $f_{22} = 0$, $f_{33} = -4x_2$, $f_{12} = f_{21} = 1$, $f_{13} = f_{31} = 9x_1^8$, and $f_{23} = f_{32} = -4x_3$.
(b) $f_1 = 5x_1^4 x_3$, $f_2 = 3x_2^2 x_3^3$, and $f_3 = 2x_3 x_2^3 + x_1^5$. Hence, $f_{11} = 20x_1^3 x_3$, $f_{22} = 6x_2 x_3^2$, $f_{33} = 2x_2^3$, $f_{12} = f_{21} = 0$, $f_{13} = f_{31} = 5x_1^4$, and $f_{23} = f_{32} = 6x_3 x_2^2$.

10-C 10-14 (a) $dy = (9x^2 - 14x)dx$
(b) $dy = [(x^2 + 2x)(3x^2) + (x^3 - 3)(2x + 2)]dx$
(c) $dy = [15x^2(x^3 - 4)^4]dx$

10-15 (a) $dz = f_x dx + f_y dy = (3x^2 y^2 - 14yx)dx + (2x^3 y - 7x^2)dy$
(b) $dz = f_1 dx_1 + f_2 dx_2 = (4x_1 x_2^3 + 3x_1^2 x_2)dx_1 + (6x_1^2 x_2^2 + x_1^3 + 2x_2)dx_2$

10-D 10-16 $\dfrac{dz}{dy} = f_x \dfrac{dx}{dy} + f_y = (4y + 2x)(3) + 4x = 42y + 50$

10-17 $\dfrac{dz}{dw} = f_x \dfrac{dx}{dw} + f_y \dfrac{dy}{dw} = 2x(2) - 2y(2w) = 8w - 4w^3 + 12$

10-18 $\dfrac{dz}{du}\bigg|_{v \text{ constant}} = \dfrac{\partial z}{\partial x}\dfrac{\partial x}{\partial u} + \dfrac{\partial z}{\partial y}\dfrac{\partial y}{\partial u} = (7y-4x)(2) + (7x)(2u) = 42u^2 - 16u + 38v - 42uv$

$\dfrac{dz}{dv}\bigg|_{u \text{ constant}} = \dfrac{\partial z}{\partial x}\dfrac{\partial x}{\partial v} + \dfrac{\partial z}{\partial y}\dfrac{\partial y}{\partial v} = (7y-4x)(-3) + (7x)(1) = 38u - 78v - 21u^2$

10-E 10-19 (a) $dy/dx = -F_x/F_y = -(4x - y^3 + 3x^2y)/(-3y^2x + x^3)$
(b) $dy/dx = -F_x/F_y = -(y + 2y^5x - 30yx^2)/(x + 5y^4x^2 - 10x^3)$

10-20 $\partial y/\partial w = -F_w/F_y = -(5w^4x^2)/(2x^4 - 7z^3y^6 - 9y^2)$
$\partial y/\partial z = -F_z/F_y = -(-3z^2y^7)/(2x^4 - 7z^3y^6 - 9y^2)$

11-A 11-1 $\partial \bar{P}/\partial c = 1/(d+b) > 0;\ \partial \bar{P}/\partial d = -(a+c)/(d+b)^2 < 0;\ \partial \bar{Q}/\partial c = -b/(d+b) < 0;$
$\partial \bar{Q}/\partial d = b(a+c)/(d+b)^2 > 0$

11-2 $\partial \bar{Y}/\partial \alpha = 1/[1 - \beta(1-t)] > 0$ measures the change in equilibrium income resulting from an infinitesimal change in autonomous (non-income induced) consumption.

$\partial \bar{Y}/\partial \beta = (\alpha + I + G)(1-t)/[1 - \beta(1-t)]^2 = (1-t)\bar{Y}/[1 - \beta(1-t)] > 0$

measures the change in equilibrium income resulting from an infinitesimal change in the marginal propensity to consume out of disposable income $(Y - T)$.

11-B 11-3 (a) $E_{11} = -\dfrac{\partial Q_1}{\partial P_1}\dfrac{P_1}{Q_1} = 2\dfrac{P_1}{Q_1} = 2\dfrac{(4)}{10} = \dfrac{4}{5};$

$E_{12} = \dfrac{\partial Q_1}{\partial P_2}\dfrac{P_2}{Q_1} = -\dfrac{1}{8}\dfrac{P_2}{Q_1} = -\dfrac{1}{8}\dfrac{(32)}{10} = -\dfrac{2}{5};$

$E_{1Y} = \dfrac{\partial Q_1}{\partial Y}\dfrac{Y}{Q_1} = \dfrac{1}{5}\dfrac{Y}{Q_1} = \dfrac{1}{5}\dfrac{(100)}{10} = 2.$

Since $E_{12} < 0$, goods 1 and 2 are complements.

(b) $E_{11} = -\dfrac{\partial Q_1}{\partial P_1}\dfrac{P_1}{Q_1} = \left(\dfrac{1}{200}P_1^{-3/2}P_2^{1/5}Y^{3/2}\right)\dfrac{P_1}{Q_1} = \dfrac{1}{2}$

$E_{12} = \dfrac{\partial Q_1}{\partial P_2}\dfrac{P_2}{Q_1} = \left(\dfrac{1}{500}P_1^{-1/2}P_2^{-4/5}Y^{3/2}\right)\dfrac{P_2}{Q_1} = \dfrac{1}{5}.$

Since $E_{12} > 0$, goods 1 and 2 are substitutes.

$E_{1Y} = \dfrac{\partial Q_1}{\partial Y}\dfrac{Y}{Q_1} = \left(\dfrac{3}{200}P_1^{-1/2}P_2^{1/5}Y^{1/2}\right)\dfrac{Y}{Q_1} = \dfrac{3}{2}$

11-4 $\partial Q_1/\partial P_1 = (-\partial F/\partial P_1)/(\partial F/\partial Q_1) = -10Q_1/(10P_1 + 5)$. Thus
$E_{11} = -(\partial Q_1/\partial P_1)(P_1/Q_1) = 10P_1/(10P_1 + 5) = 4/5$
$\partial Q_1/\partial P_2 = (-\partial F/\partial P_2)/(\partial F/\partial Q_1) = 2/(10P_1 + 5)$

Thus
$E_{12} = (\partial Q_1/\partial P_2)(P_2/Q_1) = 2P_2/(10P_1Q_1 + 5Q_1) = 1/50$
$\partial Q_1/\partial Y = (-\partial F/\partial Y)/(\partial F/\partial Q_1) = 4/(10P_1 + 5)$

Thus, $E_{1Y} = (\partial Q_1/\partial Y)(Y/Q_1) = 4Y/(10P_1Q_1 + 5Q_1) = 2/5$. Since $E_{12} > 0$, goods 1 and 2 are substitutes.

11-5 (a) $E_{AA} = \dfrac{\partial Q_A}{\partial P_A}\dfrac{P_A}{Q_A}$ (b) $E_{AS} = \dfrac{\partial Q_A}{\partial S}\dfrac{S}{Q_A}$

11-C 11-6 Since $\ln Q_s = \ln \delta + \sigma \ln P$, then

$$E_s = \dfrac{d(\ln Q_s)}{d(\ln P)} = \dfrac{dQ_s/Q_s}{dP/P} = \dfrac{dQ_s}{dP}\dfrac{P}{Q_s} = \sigma$$

11-7 Since $\ln Q_1 = \ln \tfrac{1}{200} - \tfrac{3}{8}\ln P_1 - \tfrac{2}{5}\ln P_2 + \tfrac{5}{2}\ln Y$, then

$E_{11} = -\dfrac{\partial(\ln Q_1)}{\partial(\ln P_1)} = \tfrac{3}{8},\ \ E_{12} = \dfrac{\partial(\ln Q_1)}{\partial(\ln P_2)} = -\tfrac{2}{5}$, and $E_{1Y} = \dfrac{\partial(\ln Q_1)}{\partial(\ln Y)} = \tfrac{5}{2}$

11-D 11-8 (1') $MP_L = f_L = \tfrac{400}{3}K^{1/2}L^{-1/3} = \tfrac{2}{3}\dfrac{Q}{L};\ MP_K = f_K = 100K^{-1/2}L^{2/3} = \tfrac{1}{2}\dfrac{Q}{K}$

$(2')$ $f_{LL} = -\frac{400}{9}K^{1/2}L^{-4/3} = -\frac{2}{9}\frac{Q}{L^2}$; $f_{KK} = -50K^{-3/2}L^{2/3} = -\frac{1}{4}\frac{Q}{K^2}$

$(3')$ $f_{KL} = \frac{200}{3}K^{-1/2}L^{-1/3} = \frac{1}{3}\frac{Q}{KL} = f_{LK}$

$(4')$ $E_{QL} = (\partial Q/\partial L)(L/Q) = \frac{2}{3}$; $E_{QK} = (\partial Q/\partial K)(K/Q) = \frac{1}{2}$

11-9 $200(\lambda K)^{1/2}(\lambda L)^{2/3} = \lambda^{1/2+2/3}(200K^{1/2}L^{2/3}) = \lambda^{7/6}Q$. Thus, if $\lambda = 2$, then doubling of both inputs leads to an increase in output of $2^{7/6}Q$. Since $2^{7/6}Q > 2Q$, then the twofold increase in both inputs has led to a more than twofold increase in output. Hence, output is subject to increasing returns to scale (or the production function is homogeneous of degree more than one).

12-A 12-6 (a) Stat. value at $\bar{z} = f(\bar{x}, \bar{y}) = f(1, 1) = 5$
(b) Stat. value at $\bar{z} = f(\bar{x}, \bar{y}) = f(4, 3) = 10$
(c) Stat. value at $\bar{z} = f(\bar{x}, \bar{y}) = f(1, 3) = 11$
(d) Stat. value at $\bar{z} = f(\bar{x}, \bar{y}) = f(3, 2) = -20$
(e) Stat. values at $z = f(x, y) = f(0, 0) = 0$ and $z = f(x, y) = f(-2, -1) = \frac{16}{3}$
(f) Stat. values at $z = f(x, y) = f(0, 0) = -8$ and $z = f(x, y) = f(-6, 6) = -44$

12-B 12-13 (i) $\bar{Q}_1 = 5$; $\bar{Q}_2 = 9$; $\bar{\pi} = 300$ (ii) $\bar{Q}_1 = 4$; $\bar{Q}_2 = 7$; $\bar{\pi} = 368$
12-14 $\bar{Q}_1 = 3$; $\bar{Q}_2 = 4$; $\bar{P}_1 = 31$; $\bar{P}_2 = 36$; $\bar{\pi} = 140$
12-15 $\bar{Q}_1 = \frac{5}{2}$; $\bar{Q}_2 = 15$; $\bar{P}_1 = \frac{105}{2}$; $\bar{P}_2 = \frac{135}{2}$; $\bar{\pi} = 790$
12-16 $\bar{Q}_1 = 8$; $\bar{Q}_2 = 2$; $\bar{P}_1 = 36$; $\bar{P}_2 = 16$; $\bar{\pi} = 196$; $E_{d1} = \frac{3}{2}$; $E_{d2} = 4$
12-17 $\bar{Q} = \bar{Q}_1 + \bar{Q}_2 = 2 + 3 = 5$; $\bar{\pi} = 170$; $\bar{P} = 44$
12-18 $\bar{K} = 16$; $\bar{L} = 64$; $\bar{Q} = 128$; $\bar{\pi} = 128$

13-A 13-4 (a) $L = x^2 - xy + \frac{3}{2}y^2 + \lambda(3 - x - 2y)$. Since $L_\lambda = 3 - x - 2y = 0$, $L_x = 2x - y - \lambda = 0$ and $L_y = -x + 3y - 2\lambda = 0$, then $(\bar{x}, \bar{y}, \bar{\lambda}) = (1, 1, 1)$ and $\bar{L} = \bar{z} = \frac{3}{2}$.
(b) $(\bar{x}, \bar{y}, \bar{\lambda}) = (-3, 13, 25)$; $\bar{z} = 50$
(c) $(\bar{x}, \bar{y}, \bar{\lambda}) = (18, 30, -3)$; $\bar{z} = 0$
(d) $(\bar{x}, \bar{y}, \bar{\lambda}) = (18, -9, 18)$; $\bar{z} = 70$

13-B 13-9 (a) $(\bar{x}, \bar{y}) = (16, 8)$ (b) $\bar{U} = 32$ (c) $\bar{\lambda} = 1$
13-10 (a) $(\bar{x}, \bar{y}) = (3, 1)$ (b) $\bar{U} = 81$ (c) $\bar{\lambda} = 9$
13-11 (a) $(\bar{x}, \bar{y}) = (6, 2)$ (b) $\bar{U} = 6\ln 6 + 7\ln 2 = 12.14$ (c) $\bar{\lambda} = \frac{1}{2}$
13-12 (a) $(\bar{x}, \bar{y}) = (4, 8)$ (b) $\bar{U} = 4$ (c) $\bar{\lambda} = \frac{1}{12}$
13-13 $\bar{x} = \alpha M/(\alpha + \beta)p_x$; $\bar{y} = \beta M/(\alpha + \beta)p_y$. These expressions constitute the *demand functions* for x and y, respectively. Note that these demand functions give quantity demanded as a function of M and own price only.
13-14 (a) $(\bar{K}, \bar{L}) = (16, 16)$ (b) $\bar{C} = 96$ (c) $\bar{\lambda} = 2$
13-15 (a) $(\bar{K}, \bar{L}) = (8, 64)$ (b) $\bar{C} = 192$ (c) $\bar{\lambda} = 6$
13-16 (a) $(\bar{K}, \bar{L}) = (36, 4)$ (b) $\bar{C} = 54$ (c) $\bar{\lambda} = \frac{3}{2}$
13-17 (a) $(\bar{K}, \bar{L}) = (3, 3)$ (b) $\bar{C} = 9$ (c) $\bar{\lambda} = 3$

14-A 14-1 (a) $\int -2x^{3/2}dx = -2\int x^{3/2}dx = -2(\frac{2}{5}x^{5/2} + c_1) = -\frac{4}{5}x^{5/2} + c$

(b) $\int \frac{3}{t}dt = 3\int \frac{1}{t}dt = 3(\ln t + c_1) = 3\ln t + c$

(c) $\int (7 - 3x^{-2} + 4x^3)dx = 7\int dx - 3\int x^{-2}dx + 4\int x^3 dx = 7x + 3x^{-1} + x^4 + c$

(d) $7\int x^6 dx - 2\int \frac{1}{x}dx = x^7 - 2\ln x + c$

(e) Let $u = u(x) = 2x^2 + x$, so that $du = u'(x)dx = (4x + 1)dx$ or $dx = du/(4x + 1)$. Thus

$$\int (8x + 2)u^{13}\frac{du}{(4x + 1)} = \int 2u^{13}du = 2\int u^{13}du = 2\frac{u^{14}}{14} + c = \frac{1}{7}(2x^2 + x)^{14} + c$$

(f) Let $u = u(x) = x - 5$, so that $du = u'(x)dx = 1dx$ or $dx = du$. Thus

$$\int \frac{du}{u} = \int \frac{1}{u}du = \ln u + c = \ln(x - 5) + c$$

(g) Let $u = u(x) = 2x^2 + 7$, so that $du = u'(x)dx = 4xdx$ or $dx = du/4x$. Thus

$$\int \frac{4x}{u} \frac{du}{4x} = \int \frac{1}{u} du = \ln u + c = \ln(2x^2 + 7) + c$$

(h) Let $u = u(x) = 4x^4 + 8x$, so that $du = u'(x)dx = (16x^3 + 8)dx$ or $dx = du/(16x^3 + 8)$. Thus

$$\int \frac{4x^3 + 2}{u^9} \frac{du}{(16x^3 + 8)} = \int \frac{1}{4u^9} du = \tfrac{1}{4} \int u^{-9} du = -\tfrac{1}{32} u^{-8} + c = -\tfrac{1}{32}(4x^4 + 8x)^{-8} + c$$

14-B 14-2 (a) $\int_1^3 (x^2 - 2)dx = \left[\frac{x^3}{3} - 2x\right]_1^3 = \left[\frac{(3)^3}{3} - 2(3)\right] - \left[\frac{(1)^3}{3} - 2(1)\right] = \frac{14}{3}$

(b) $\int_{-1}^2 (5x^4 - x^2)dx = \left[x^5 - \frac{x^3}{3}\right]_{-1}^2 = [32 - \tfrac{8}{3}] - [-1 + \tfrac{1}{3}] = 30$

(c) $\int_1^4 \frac{1}{x} dx = [\ln x]_1^4 = [\ln 4] - [\ln 1] = \ln 4$

(d) Let $u = u(x) = x^3 - 3x + 2$, so that $du = u'(x)dx = (3x^2 - 3)dx$ or $dx = du/(3x^2 - 3)$. Thus, since $u = 2$ when $x = 0$ and $u = 4$ when $x = 2$, we have

$$\int_0^2 \left(\frac{12x^2 - 12}{x^3 - 3x + 2}\right) dx = \int_2^4 \frac{4}{u} du = 4 \int_2^4 \frac{1}{u} du = 4[\ln u]_2^4$$
$$= 4[\ln 4 - \ln 2] = 4 \ln 2 = \ln 16$$

(e) $\int_1^8 x^{1/3} dx = [\tfrac{3}{4} x^{4/3}]_1^8 = [\tfrac{3}{4}(8)^{4/3} - \tfrac{3}{4}(1)^{4/3}] = 12 - \tfrac{3}{4} = \tfrac{45}{4}$

(f) $\int_1^5 \left(\frac{1}{x} + 3x^2\right) dx = [\ln x + x^3]_1^5 = [\ln 5 + 5^3] - [\ln 1 + 1^3] = \ln 5 + 124$

14-C 14-3 (a) $\int_1^3 3x^2 dx = [x^3]_1^3 = 26$ and $\int_3^1 3x^2 dx = [x^3]_3^1 = -26$. Thus,

$$\int_1^3 3x^2 dx = -\int_3^1 3x^2 dx$$

(b) $\int_0^3 (4x^3 - 21)dx = \int_0^1 (4x^3 - 21)dx + \int_1^2 (4x^3 - 21)dx + \int_2^3 (4x^3 - 21)dx$ since $[x^4 - 21x]_0^3 = [x^4 - 21x]_0^1 + [x^4 - 21x]_1^2 + [x^4 - 21x]_2^3$ or $18 = -20 - 6 + 44$

14-D 14-4 $\int_{12}^3 (3Q^2 - 18Q + 30)dQ = [Q^3 - 9Q^2 + 30Q]_{12}^3 = 36 - 792 = -756$. Thus, the decrease in total cost is 756.

14-5 Since $MPC = dC/dY \equiv C'(Y)$, then $C(Y)$ can be found by integrating $C'(Y)$:

$$C(Y) = \int \tfrac{3}{2} Y^{-1/2} dY = 3Y^{1/2} + c$$

Since we are told that $C(0) = 70$, and $C(0) = c$ in the above integral, then $C(Y) = 70 + 3Y^{1/2}$.

14-6 Since $MPS = dS/dY \equiv S'(Y)$, then $S(Y)$ can be found by integrating $S'(Y)$:

$$S(Y) = \int (1 - \tfrac{3}{2} Y^{-1/2}) dY = Y - 3Y^{1/2} + c$$

Since we are told that $S(100) = 0$, then substitution of this information into the above integral gives $S(100) = 100 - 3(100)^{1/2} + c = 0$ or $c = -70$. Hence, $S(Y) = -70 + Y - 3Y^{1/2}$.

14-E 14-7 When $P = 2$, $Q_d = 12$ (since $2 = (16 - Q_d)^{1/2}$ or $4 = 16 - Q_d \Rightarrow Q_d = 12$) and the consumer's actual expenditure is $(2)(12) = 24$. Hence,

$$\text{Consumer's surplus} = \int_0^{12} (16 - Q_d)^{1/2} dQ_d - 24$$
$$= \int_{16}^4 -u^{1/2} du - 24 \quad \text{(where } u = 16 - Q_d \Rightarrow dQ_d = -du\text{)}$$
$$= [-\tfrac{2}{3} u^{3/2}]_{16}^4 - 24 = \tfrac{40}{3}$$

14-8 When $P = 9$, $Q_s = 2$ (since $9 = (Q_s+1)^2$ or $9^{1/2} = Q_s+1 \Rightarrow Q_s = 2$ or -4) and the producer's actual revenue is $(9)(2) = 18$. Hence,

$$\text{Producer's surplus} = 18 - \int_0^2 (Q_s+1)^2 dQ_s$$

$$= 18 - \int_1^3 u^2 du \quad (\text{where } u = Q_s+1)$$

$$= 18 - \left[\frac{u^3}{3}\right]_1^3 = \frac{28}{3}$$

14-F 14-10 (a) Let $u = u(x) = 3x^2+2x-6$. Thus,

$$\frac{dy}{dx} = \frac{dy}{du}\frac{du}{dx} = e^u \frac{du}{dx} = e^u(6x+2) = (6x+2)e^{3x^2+2x-6}$$

(b) $dy/dx = xe^x + e^x(1) = e^x(x+1)$ via product rule

(c) Let $u = u(x) = 1-x$. Thus,

$$\frac{dy}{dx} = \frac{dy}{du}\frac{du}{dx} = e^u \frac{du}{dx} = e^u(-1) = -e^{1-x}$$

(d) $dy/dx = [(x^2-2x)e^x - e^x(2x-2)]/(x^2-2x)^2$ via quotient rule

(e) Let $u = u(x) = x^{2/3}+5$. Thus,

$$\frac{dy}{dx} = \frac{dy}{du}\frac{du}{dx} = \frac{3}{2}e^u \frac{du}{dx} = \frac{3}{2}e^u(\frac{2}{3}x^{-1/3}) = x^{-1/3}e^{x^{2/3}+5}$$

(f) $dy/dx = [4x^2(6x\, e^{3x^2-2}) + e^{3x^2-2}(8x)]$ via product rule

14-11 (a) $7\int e^x dx = 7e^x + c$

(b) $3\int x^2 dx - \int e^x dx = x^3 - e^x + c$

(c) Let $u = u(x) = 5-3x$, so that $du = u'(x)dx = -3dx$ or $dx = -du/3$. Hence

$$\int 6e^{5-3x}dx = \int 6e^u \frac{du}{-3} = -2\int e^u du = -2e^u + c = -2e^{5-3x} + c$$

(d) Let $u = u(x) = x^4 + 2x^3$, so that $du = u'(x)dx = (4x^3+6x^2)dx$ or $dx = du/(4x^3+6x^2)$. Hence,

$$\int (8x^3+12x^2)e^{x^4+2x^3}dx = \int (8x^3+12x^2)e^u \frac{du}{(4x^3+6x^2)} = \int 2e^u du = 2e^u + c = 2e^{x^4+2x^3} + c$$

14-12 (a) $[-e^{-x}]_1^3 = -e^{-3} + e^{-1}$

(b) $[e^x + \frac{1}{5}e^{5x}]_0^7 = (e^7 + \frac{1}{5}e^{35}) - (1+\frac{1}{5}) = e^7(1+\frac{1}{5}e^{28}) - \frac{6}{5}$

(c) $[e^{x^2}]_1^2 = e - e^{16} = e(1-e^{15})$

14-G 14-13 (a) Using (14-36), $V_{11} = £90(1 + \frac{9}{100})^{11}$

(b) Using (14-37), $V_2 = £100(1 + \frac{5/100}{365})^{2(365)} = £100(1 + \frac{1}{7300})^{730}$

14-14 Using (14-39), (a) $£100e^{0.06(8)} = £100e^{0.48}$ (b) $£350e^{0.3}$

14-H 14-15 Using (14-40), $V_0 = £540.8(1.04)^{-2} = £540.8/1.0816 = £500$

14-16 Using (14-41), $V_0 = £271828e^{-0.1(10)} = £271828/e \simeq £271828/2.71828 \simeq £100{,}000$

14-I 14-17 Using (14-42), $L_t = 20e^{0.02(50)} = 20e^1 \simeq 20(2.71828) \simeq 54.3656$. Therefore, the labour force in year 2025 is 54.3656 million.

14-18 Using (14-45), let $K_t/K_0 = 1/2$, and $-r = -0.07$, so that $1 = 2e^{-0.07t}$. Taking logs: $\ln 1 = \ln 2 - 0.07t \ln e$ or $-\ln 2 = -0.07t$. Hence,

$$t = \frac{\ln 2}{0.07} = \frac{0.6931}{0.07} \simeq 10$$

Therefore, the stock of machinery will be halved in value after 10 years.

INDEX

Abscissa, 14
Absolute extrema (*see* Extrema)
Absolute value, 30
Accounting price, 247
Adjoint, 86
Aggregate demand, 51
Aggregate output, 51
Alien cofactor (*see* Cofactor)
Antiderivative, 256
Area under a curve, 263–265
Argument, 18
Asymptote, 131
Average fixed cost, 181
Average product, 171
    function, 171
    and relation to marginal product, 174–175
Average revenue, 139
    function, 139
Average total cost, 177
    and relation to marginal cost, 180–183
Average variable cost, 181
    and relation to marginal cost, 181–183

Base:
    of exponential function, 270
    of logarithm, 31
Behavioural equation, 41
Boundary condition, 256

Budget constraint, 234
Budget line, 234

Cartesian coordinate plane, 15
Cartesian product, 15
Chain rule, 121–123
Chiang, A. C., 58, 156, 221, 242
Choice variable, 158
Cobb-Douglas production function, 33, 214–215
Coefficient, 25
Coefficient matrix, 64
Cofactor, 79
    alien, 82
Column vector (*see* Vector)
Common logarithm (*see* Logarithm)
Comparative-static analysis, 205
Comparative statics, 207
Complex numbers, 13
Composite function, 123
Composite-function rule, 123
Compound interest, 273–275
Conformability conditions, 66–69
Constant, 25
Constant function, 25
Constant-function rule, 118
Constant of integration, 256
Constant proportional rates of growth, 276–277

Constrained extrema (see Extrema)
Constraint, 234, 241
Consumer's surplus, 268–269
Consumption function, 50, 142
Continuous function, 115
Cost, minimization of, 250–253
Cost functions, 142, 177
    cubic, 178
Cost theory, 177–185
Cramer's rule, 89–91
Cross price elasticity of demand, 209
    and complements, 209, 211
    and substitutes, 209, 210
Cube root, 23
Cubic function, 26
Curve-sketching, 130–131, 133–135

Definite integral, 261–265
    as area under a curve, 263–265
Degree of polynomial, 26
Demand function, 21, 132
    derivative of, 132
    and price elasticity, 136–137
    sketching of, 133–135
Dependence:
    among columns, 84–85
    among equations, 54
    linear, 84–85
    among rows, 84–85
Dependent variable (see Variables)
Depreciation, 277
Derivative, 113–116
    and curve-sketching, 130–131
    as function, 113–115, 116
    partial, 192
    as rate of change, 115, 116
    as ratio of two differentials, 198
    second, 127
    and slope of curve, 114, 116
    total, 200
Descartes, R., 15
Determinant, 77
    Laplace expansion of, 78–81
    order of, 77
    properties of, 82–83
    vanishing, 82
Difference quotient, 37
Differentiability, 115
Differential(s), 198
    and elasticity, 212–213
    total, 199
Differentiation, 114

Differentiation (continued)
    partial, 191–196
    total, 199
Differentiation rules:
    chain rule, 121–123
    composite-function rule, 123
    constant-function rule, 118
    exponential-function rule, 271
    function-of-a-function rule, 123
    inverse-function rule, 123–125
    log-function rule, 126–127
    power-function rule, 117
    product rule, 119–120
    quotient rule, 120–121
    sum-difference rule, 118–119
Discounting, 275–276
Disjoint sets (see Sets)
Domain, 18

e, the number, 32, 270
    economic interpretation of, 275
Economic model, 8–9
Elasticity, 135–138
    cross price, 209–213
    and differentials, 212–213
    income, 210, 212
    of labour supply, 188, 289
    and logarithms, 212–213
    of output, 214
    partial, 209–213
    partial price, 209, 212
    point, 136
    price, 136–138
    and price discrimination, 225–227
    of substitution, 254
Elements, 10, 64
Elimination of variables, 43, 46–48
Empty set (see Sets)
Endogenous variable (see Variables)
Equalities, 28–29
Equation, 16
Equilibrium, 42
    general, 61
    partial, 42
    static, 42
Equilibrium condition, 42
Equilibrium price, 42
Equilibrium quantity, 42
Equilibrium values, 42
Excess demand, 42
Excise tax, 45
    in competitive market model, 45–49, 167–171

Excise tax (*continued*)
  in monopoly model, 164–167
Exogenous variable (*see* Variables)
Exponent, 22
Exponential function, 270–277
  and compound interest, 273–275
  derivative of, 271
  and growth, 276–277
  integration of, 272
  natural, 271
Extrema:
  absolute, 144
  constrained, 232
    conditions for, 241, 242
  of a function of one variable, 145–150
  of a function of two variables, 217–222
  subject to a constraint, 232–244
  global, 144
  local, 145
  relative, 145–150
  unconstrained, 217
    conditions for, 220
Extreme value, 144
Extremum, 144

Final demand, 103, 104
Finite set (*see* Sets)
First-order condition, 147, 218–221, 241
Fixed cost, 179, 181
  average, 181
  total, 181
Flow, 97
Fraction, 12
Function, 17–19
  continuous, 115
  explicit, 202
  general form of, 18
  graphical form of, 18–19
  implicit, 202
  specific form of, 18
Function-of-a-function rule, 123

General equilibrium (*see* Equilibrium)
Goods market, 97
Government-expenditure multiplier, 208
Graph:
  of a function (*see* Function)
  one-dimensional, 12
  two-dimensional, 14
  three-dimensional, 27

Homogeneous function, 215
  linearly, 215

Horizontal intercept (*see* Intercept)
Hypersurface, 28

Identity, 51
Identity matrix, 72
Image, 17
Imaginary numbers, 13
Implicit function, 202
Implicit-function rule, 202
Import function, 100, 142
Income elasticity of demand, 210, 212
Income-tax-rate multiplier, 208
Indefinite integral, 256–261
Independence (*see* Dependence)
Independent variable (*see* Variables)
Indices, 22–24
Indifference curve, 234
  curvature and slope of, 234, 245
Inequalities, 16, 29–30
Infinite set (*see* Sets)
Inflection points, 151–156
  criteria for, 154
  non-stationary, 151
  stationary, 151
Initial condition, 256
Input coefficient, 105
Input-output analysis, 103–106
  and government planning, 106
Integers, 11
Integral, 256
  definite, 261–265
  indefinite, 256–261
  sign, 256
Integrand, 256
Integration, 255
  constant of, 256
  of exponential function, 272
  limits of, 262
  multiple, 266
  rules of, 257–261
Intercept:
  horizontal, 19
  vertical, 19
Intersectoral demand, 103
Intersectoral flows, 103
Inverse-function rule, 123–125
Inverse matrix, 74
  calculation of, 85–89
Investment function, 97
Investment multiplier, 143, 208
Irrational numbers, 12
IS function, 99

Isocost, 251
Isoquant, 250
   curvature and slope of, 251

Labour:
   demand for, 185
   profit-maximizing input level of, 185–188
Lagrange multiplier, 239
   interpretation of, 246–249
Lagrange-multiplier method, 236–244
Lagrangian function, 239
Laplace expansion, 78–81
Law of diminishing marginal product, 141, 171, 178, 186
Law of diminishing marginal utility, 141
Limit, 113
   evaluation of, 114
Linear dependence, 84–85
Linear independence, 84–85
Linear function, 26
Linearly homogeneous function, 215
LM function, 99
Locus, 27
Logarithm, 31
   common, 31
   conversion formulae, 34
   and elasticity, 212–213
   natural, 32
   rules of, 33–34
Logarithmic function, 33, 126
   derivative of, 126–127
Log-function rule, 126–127

Mapping, 17
Marginal cost, 142, 177, 252, 266
   and relation to average total cost, 180
   and relation to average variable cost, 181
Marginal product, 141, 171, 213
   diminishing, 141, 171, 178, 186
   and relation to average product, 174–177
   value of the, 186, 229
Marginal propensity to consume, 50, 142
Marginal propensity to import, 142
Marginal propensity to save, 142
Marginal rate of substitution, 245
   diminishing, 245
Marginal rate of technical substitution, 251
   diminishing, 251

Marginal revenue, 139, 267
   and elasticity of demand, 139–141
   function, 140
Marginal revenue product, 141, 188
Marginal utility, 141
   diminishing, 141
   of money, 247
Market demand function, 39
Market models, 41–49, 55–58, 60–64, 93–95, 206–208
Market supply function, 40, 41
Matrix, 62–65
   addition, 66
   dimension of, 64
   equality, 65
   identity, 72
   inverse, 74
   inversion of, 85–89
   multiplication, 68–71
   nonsingular, 74, 83
   null, 72
   order of, 64
   scalar multiplication of, 67
   singular, 74, 83
   square, 64
   subtraction, 66
   symmetric, 73
   transpose of, 73
   zero, 72
Maxima (*see* Extrema)
Minima (*see* Extrema)
Minor, 78
Money, defined, 97
   marginal utility of, 247
Money market, 97
Monotonic function, 124
Multiplant monopoly, 227–228
Multiple integration, 266
Multiplier:
   government expenditure, 208
   income-tax-rate, 208
   investment, 143, 208
   Lagrange, 239
Multi-product firm, 222
   monopolistic, 224–225
   perfectly competitive, 222–224

National-income models, 49–53, 95–96, 208–209
Necessary condition, 74, 147, 151, 220
Nonsingular matrix, 74, 83
Nonsingularity, 83–85

Nonsingularity (*continued*)
   determinantal test of, 83
Null matrix, 72
Null set (*see* Sets)

Objective function, 157
One-to-one correspondence, 14
Opportunity cost, 247
Ordered pairs, 13
Ordered set, 14, 64
Ordinate, 14
Own price elasticity of demand, 209, 212

Parameter, 25
Partial derivative, 192
   cross, 196
   as function, 194
   mixed, 196
   second, 196–197
   second-order, 196–197
Partial differentiation, 191–196
   and comparative-static analysis, 205–209
   techniques of, 193–196
Partial elasticities, 209–213
Partial equilibrium (*see* Equilibrium)
Point elasticity of demand, 136
Polynomial functions, 24–26
Power-function rule, 117
Present value, 275
Price discrimination, 225–227
Price elasticity of demand, 136–138
   and marginal revenue, 139–141
Price elasticity of supply, 137–138
Principal diagonal, 72
Producer's surplus, 269–270
Product rule, 119–120
Production function, 141, 171
   analysis of, 213–216
   Cobb-Douglas, 33, 214–215
   and homogeneity, 215
   and returns to scale, 215
Production theory, 171–177
Profit, 157
Profit constraint, 162
Profit maximization, 157–162
   and input decisions, 229–230
   and multiplant monopolist, 227–228
   and multi-product firm, 222–225
   and price discrimination, 225–227
Proportional rate of growth, 276

Quadratic equation, 56, 57
   roots of, 56
Quadratic formula, 57
Quadratic function, 26
Quotient rule, 120–121

Range, 18
Rate of change, 115
   instantaneous, 115–116
Rate of depreciation, 277
Rate of growth, 276–277
Rational numbers, 12
Real numbers, 11–13
Rectangular array, 63
Rectangular coordinate plane, 14
Relative extrema, 145–150
   criteria for, 147
Relation, 16
Restraint, 241
Returns to scale:
   constant, 215
   decreasing and increasing, 215
   and homogeneous function, 215
Revenue, 139
   average, 139
   function, 139
   marginal, 139
   maximization of, 162–164
   total, 139
Roots (*see* Quadratic equation)
Row vector (*see* Vector)

Sales maximization, 162–164
Saving function, 59, 142
Scalar, 67
Scalar multiplication, 67
Second derivative, 127
Second-order condition, 147, 220, 242
Set(s), 10
   disjoint, 11
   empty, 10
   equality of, 11
   finite, 10
   infinite, 10
   members of, 10
   null, 10
Shadow price, 247
Side relation, 241
Simultaneous-equation system, 42
   linear, 60
   solution of, 43, 75–76, 88–91
Singular matrix, 74, 83
Slope, 36

Square matrix, 64
Square root, 23
Standard forms, 260
Static equilibrium (*see* Equilibrium)
Stationary value, 146
Stock, 97
Subset, 10
Subsidiary condition, 241
Sufficient condition, 74, 147, 154, 220
Sum-difference rule, 118–119
Summand, 76
Summation index, 76
Summation sign, 76
Supply function, 40–41
   derivative of, 133
   sketching of, 134–135
   and unit elasticity, 138
Surface, 27, 218
Symmetric matrix, 73

Tangent line, 111
Tax:
   in competitive market model, 167–171
   excise, 45
   income, 52
   in monopoly model, 164–167
Total cost, 142, 181, 266
Total cost function, 142, 177
   cubic, 178
Total derivative, 200
Total differential, 199
Total differentiation, 199

Total fixed cost, 181
Total product function, 171
   cubic, 171
Total revenue, 139, 267
Total utility, 141
Total variable cost, 181
Transformation, 17
Transitivity, 29, 30
Transpose matrix, 73–74

Unconstrained extrema (*see* Extrema)
Utility, 141
   function, 141
   marginal, 141
   maximization of, 233–241, 244–250
   total, 141

Value:
   of function, 18
   of marginal product, 186
Variables, 18
   dependent and independent, 18
   endogenous and exogenous, 20
Vertical intercept (*see* Intercept)
Vector, 64
   addition, 66
   multiplication, 69–71
   subtraction, 67

Young's theorem, 197

Zero, the number, 11, 13
Zero matrix, 72